UQ HOLDER!

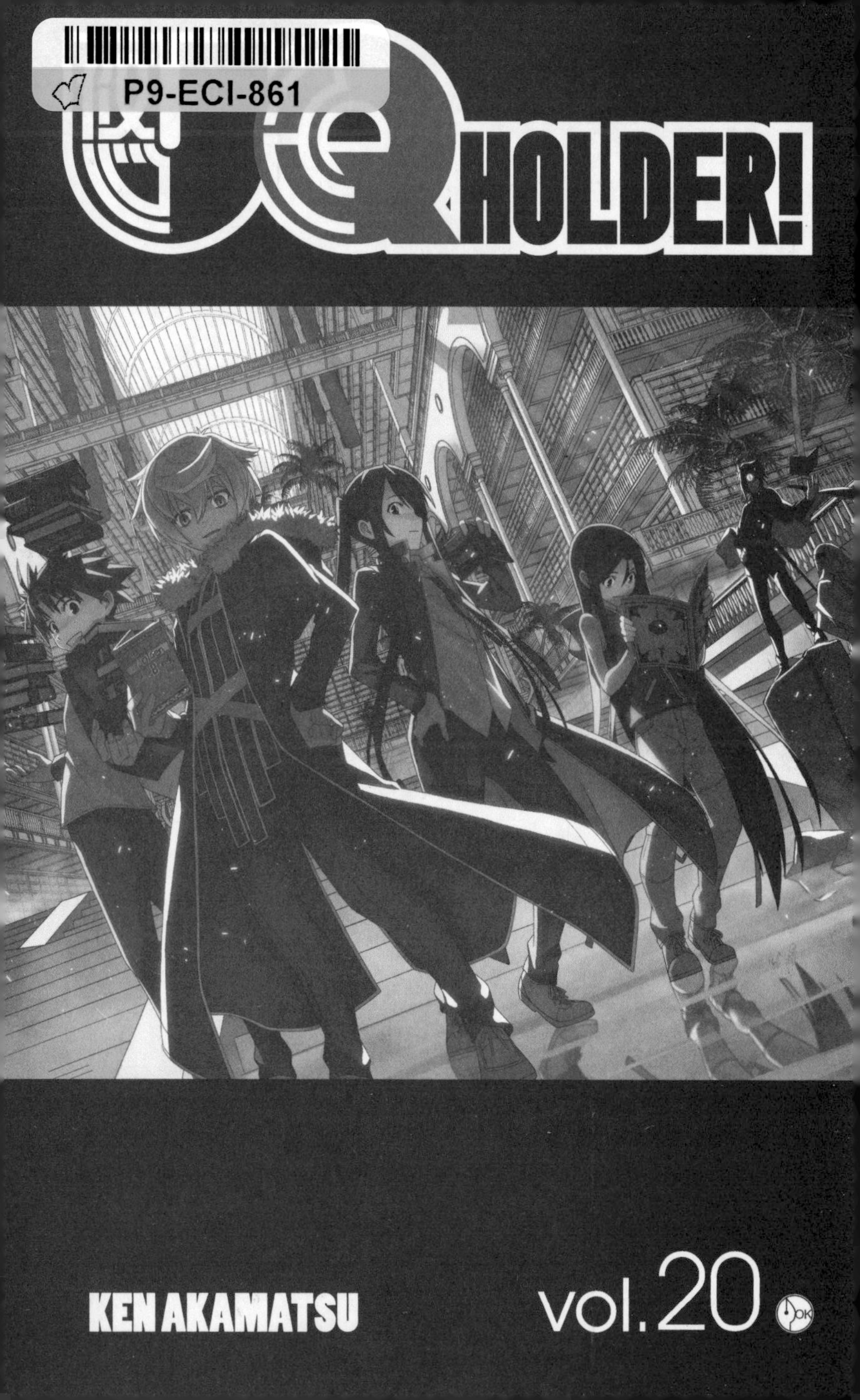

KEN AKAMATSU

vol. 20

CHARACTERS

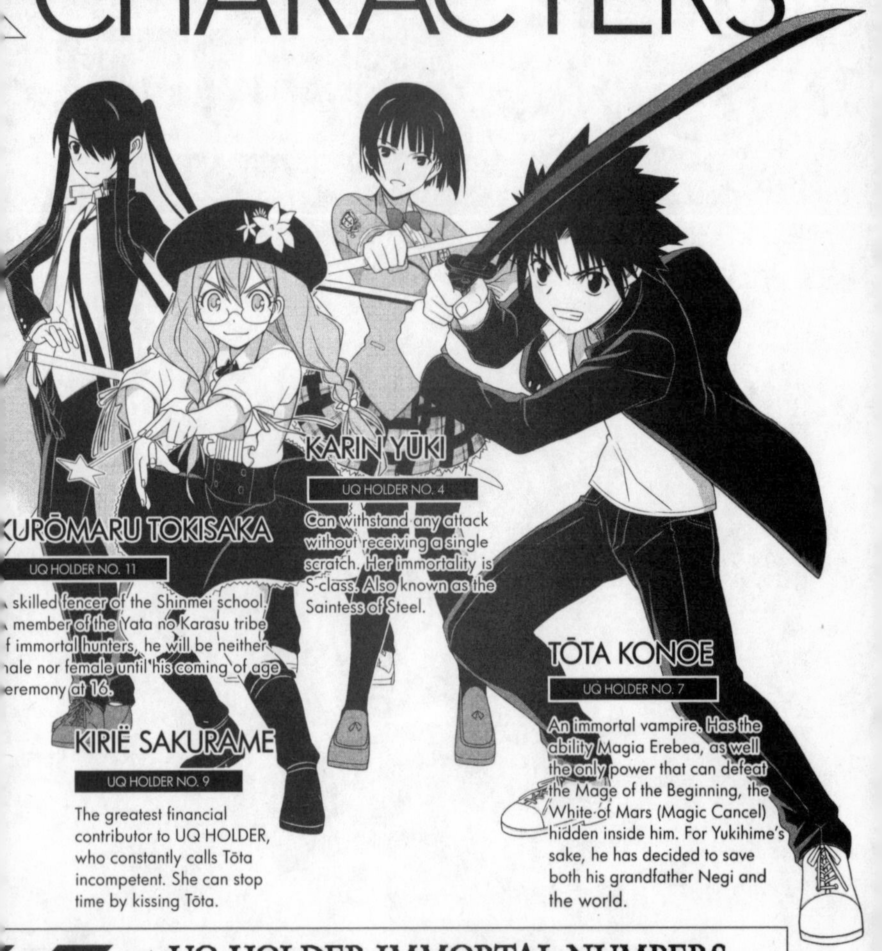

KARIN YŪKI

UQ HOLDER NO. 4

Can withstand any attack without receiving a single scratch. Her immortality is S-class. Also known as the Saintess of Steel.

TŌTA KONOE

UQ HOLDER NO. 7

An immortal vampire. Has the ability Magia Erebea, as well the only power that can defeat the Mage of the Beginning, the White of Mars (Magic Cancel) hidden inside him. For Yukihime's sake, he has decided to save both his grandfather Negi and the world.

KURŌMARU TOKISAKA

UQ HOLDER NO. 11

skilled fencer of the Shinmei school. member of the Yata no Karasu tribe f immortal hunters, he will be neither nale nor female until his coming of age eremony at 16.

KIRIË SAKURAME

UQ HOLDER NO. 9

The greatest financial contributor to UQ HOLDER, who constantly calls Tōta incompetent. She can stop time by kissing Tōta.

UQ HOLDER IMMORTAL NUMBERS

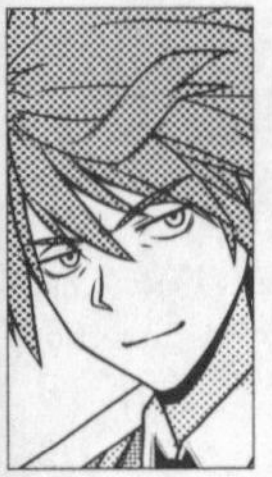

JINBEI SHISHIDO

UQ HOLDER NO. 2

UQ HOLDER's oldest member. Became an immortal in the middle ages, when he ate mermaid flesh in the Muromachi Period. Has the "Switcheroo" skill that switches the locations of physical objects.

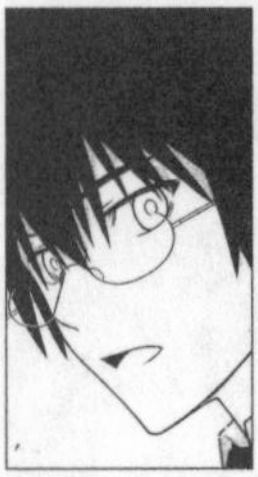

GENGORŌ MAKABE

UQ HOLDER NO. 6

Manages the business side of UQ HOLDER's hideout and inn. He has a skill known as "Multiple Lives," so when he dies, another Gengorō appears.

UQ HOLDER!...

Ken Akamatsu Presents

EVANGELINE (YUKIHIME)

The female leader of UQ HOLDER and a 700-year-old vampire. Her past self met Tōta in a rift in time-space, and that encounter gave hope to her bleak immortal existence.

FATE AVERRUNCUS

Negi's sworn friend. Currently UQ HOLDER's enemy.

SHINOBU YŪKI

A skilled mechanic. Her dream is to participate in the grand-race across the solar system!

MIZORE YUKIHIRO

Heir to the Yukihiro conglomerate. Intends to make Tōta her husband.

IKKŪ AMEYA

UQ HOLDER NO. 10

After falling into a coma at age 13 and lying in a hospital bed for 72 years, he became a full-body cyborg at age 85. He's very good with his hands. ♡

SANTA SASAKI

UQ HOLDER NO. 12

A revenant brought back to life through necromancy. He has multiple abilities, including flight, intangibility, possession, telekinesis, etc.

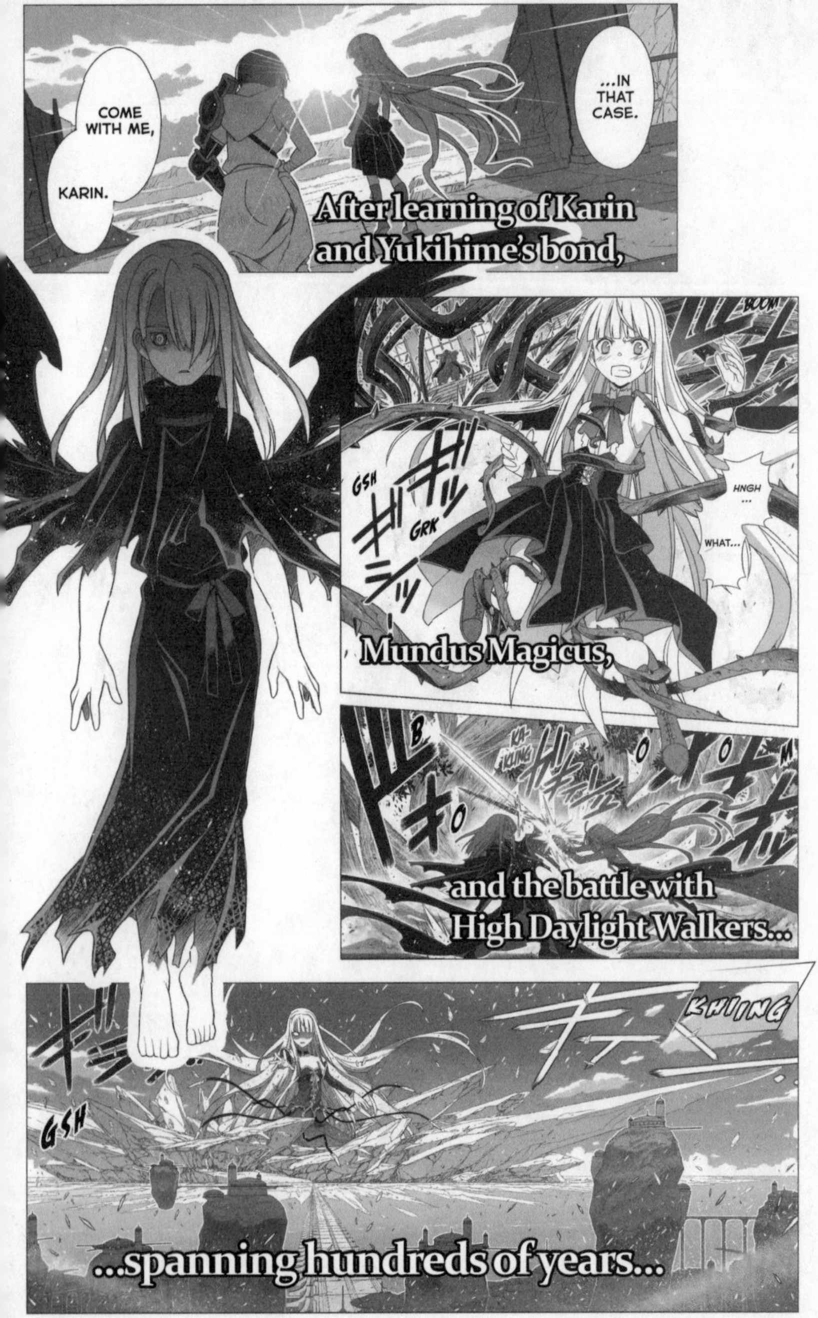
...IN THAT CASE.
COME WITH ME,
KARIN.
After learning of Karin and Yukihime's bond,
BOOM
GSH
GRK
HNGH...
WHAT...
Mundus Magicus,
KA-KLING
B O O M
and the battle with High Daylight Walkers...
KHIING
GSH
...spanning hundreds of years...

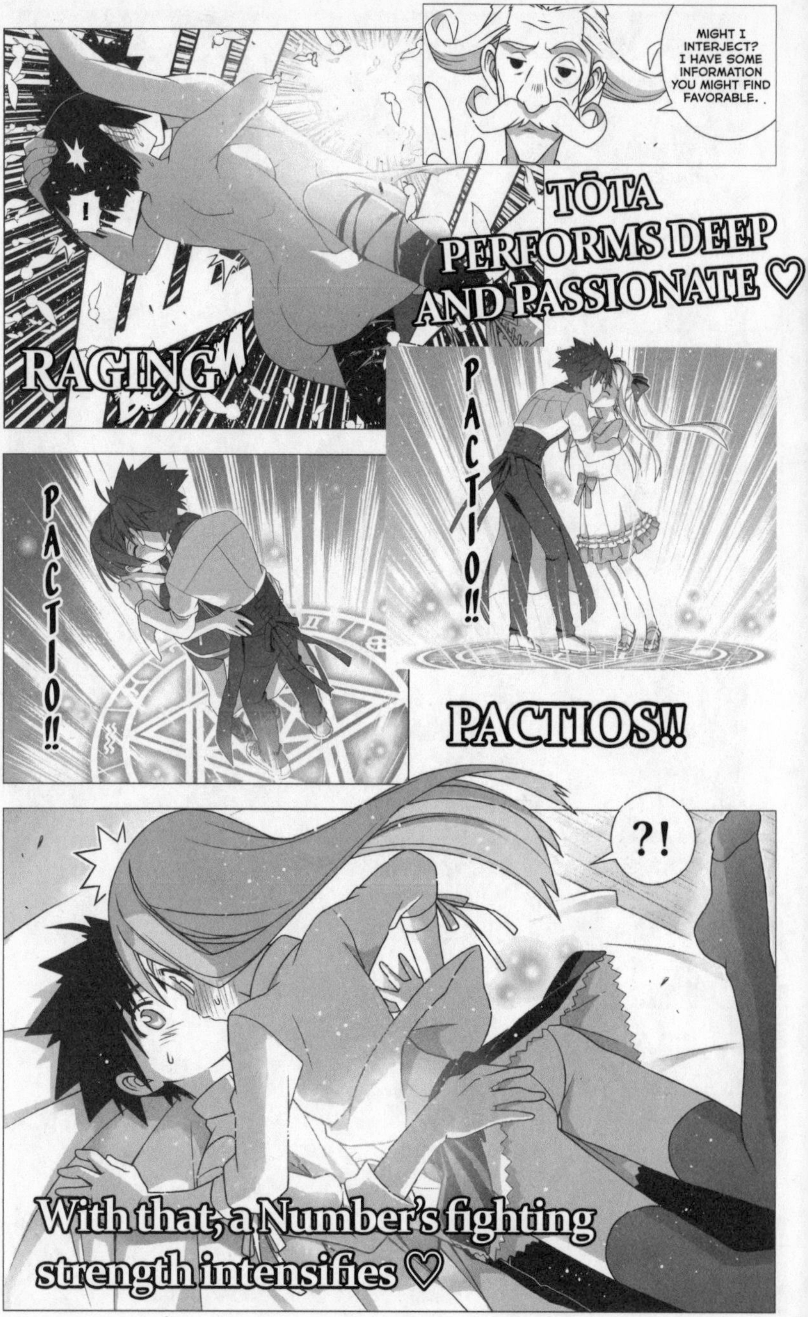
MIGHT I INTERJECT? I HAVE SOME INFORMATION YOU MIGHT FIND FAVORABLE.
TŌTA PERFORMS DEEP AND PASSIONATE ♡
PACTIO!!
!
RAGING
PACTIO!!
PACTIOS!!
?!
With that, a Number's fighting strength intensifies ♡

CONTENTS

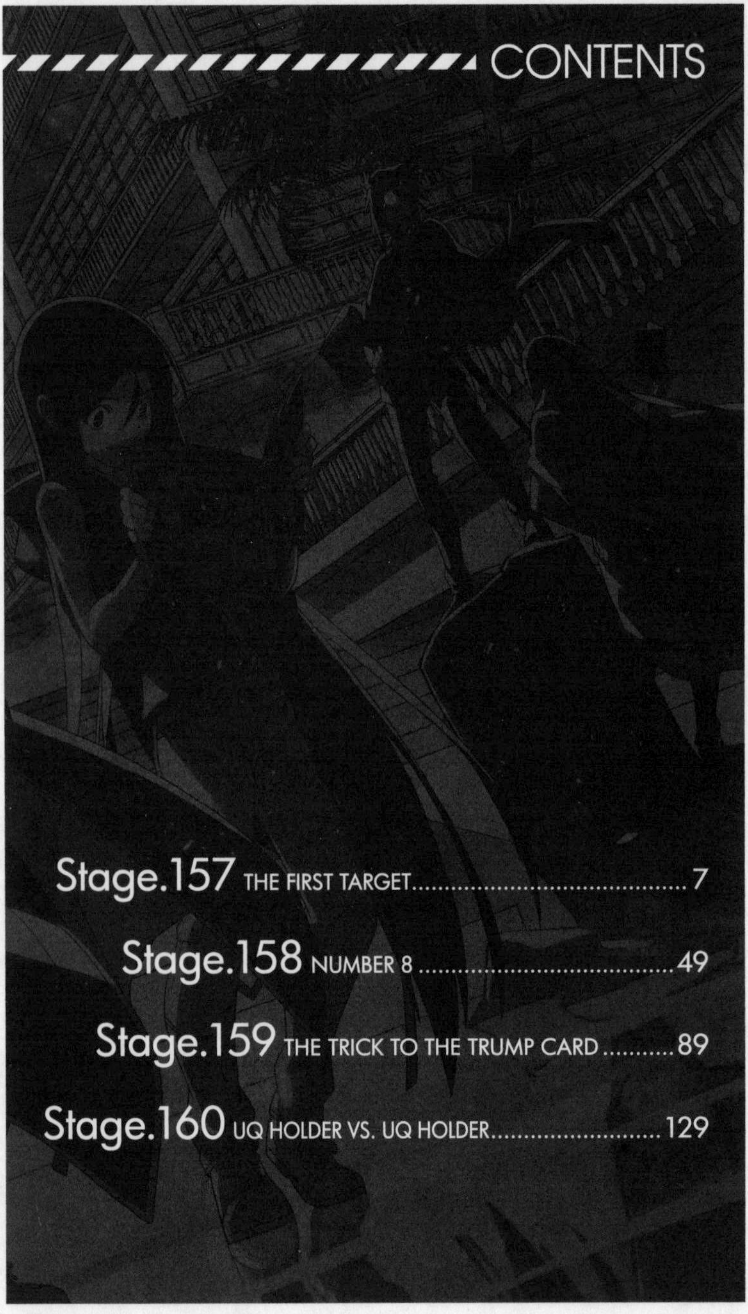

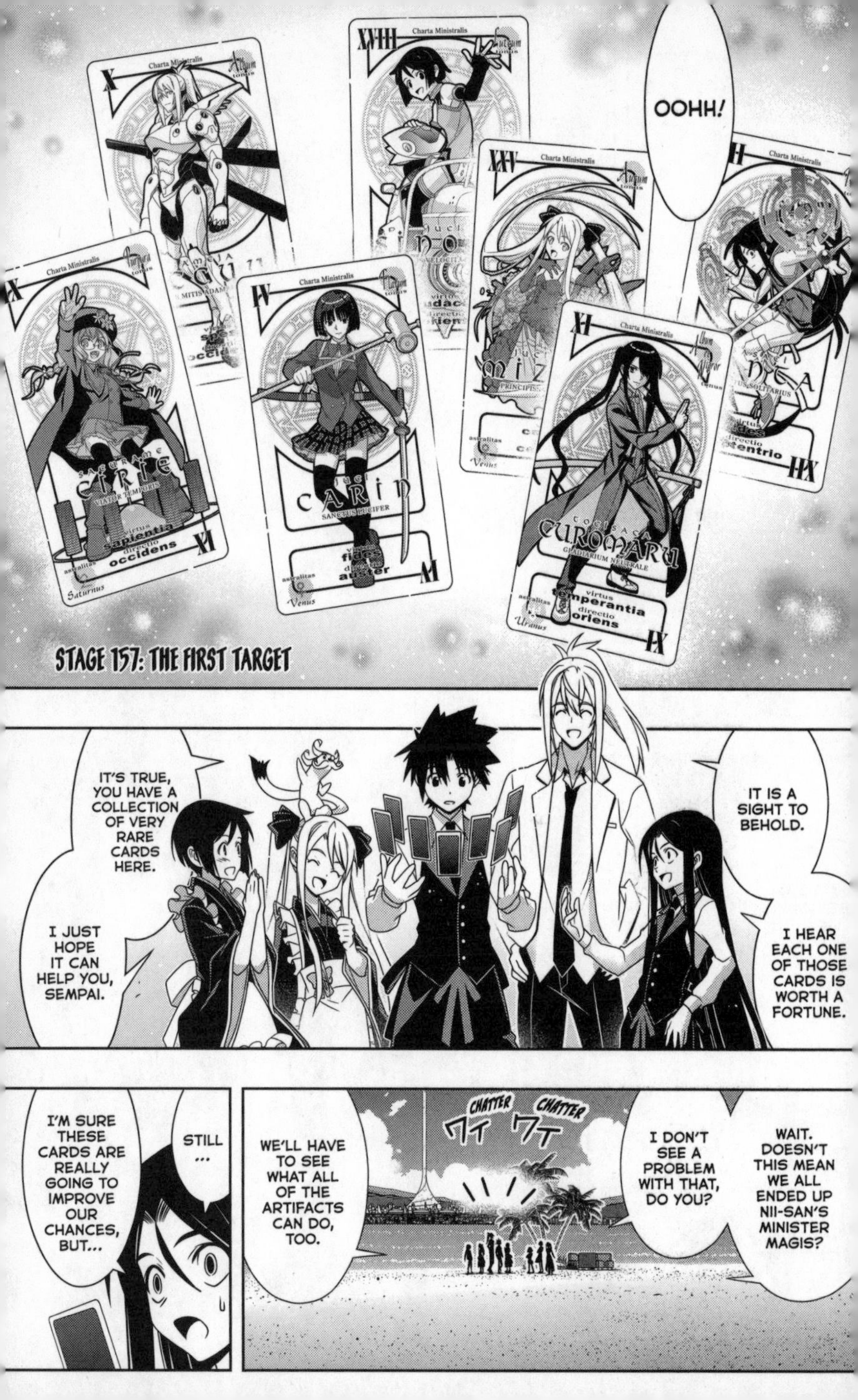
OOHH!
STAGE 157: THE FIRST TARGET
IT IS A SIGHT TO BEHOLD.
I HEAR EACH ONE OF THOSE CARDS IS WORTH A FORTUNE.
IT'S TRUE, YOU HAVE A COLLECTION OF VERY RARE CARDS HERE.
I JUST HOPE IT CAN HELP YOU, SEMPAI.
WAIT. DOESN'T THIS MEAN WE ALL ENDED UP NII-SAN'S MINISTER MAGIS?
I DON'T SEE A PROBLEM WITH THAT, DO YOU?
CHATTER CHATTER
WE'LL HAVE TO SEE WHAT ALL OF THE ARTIFACTS CAN DO, TOO.
STILL...
I'M SURE THESE CARDS ARE REALLY GOING TO IMPROVE OUR CHANCES, BUT...

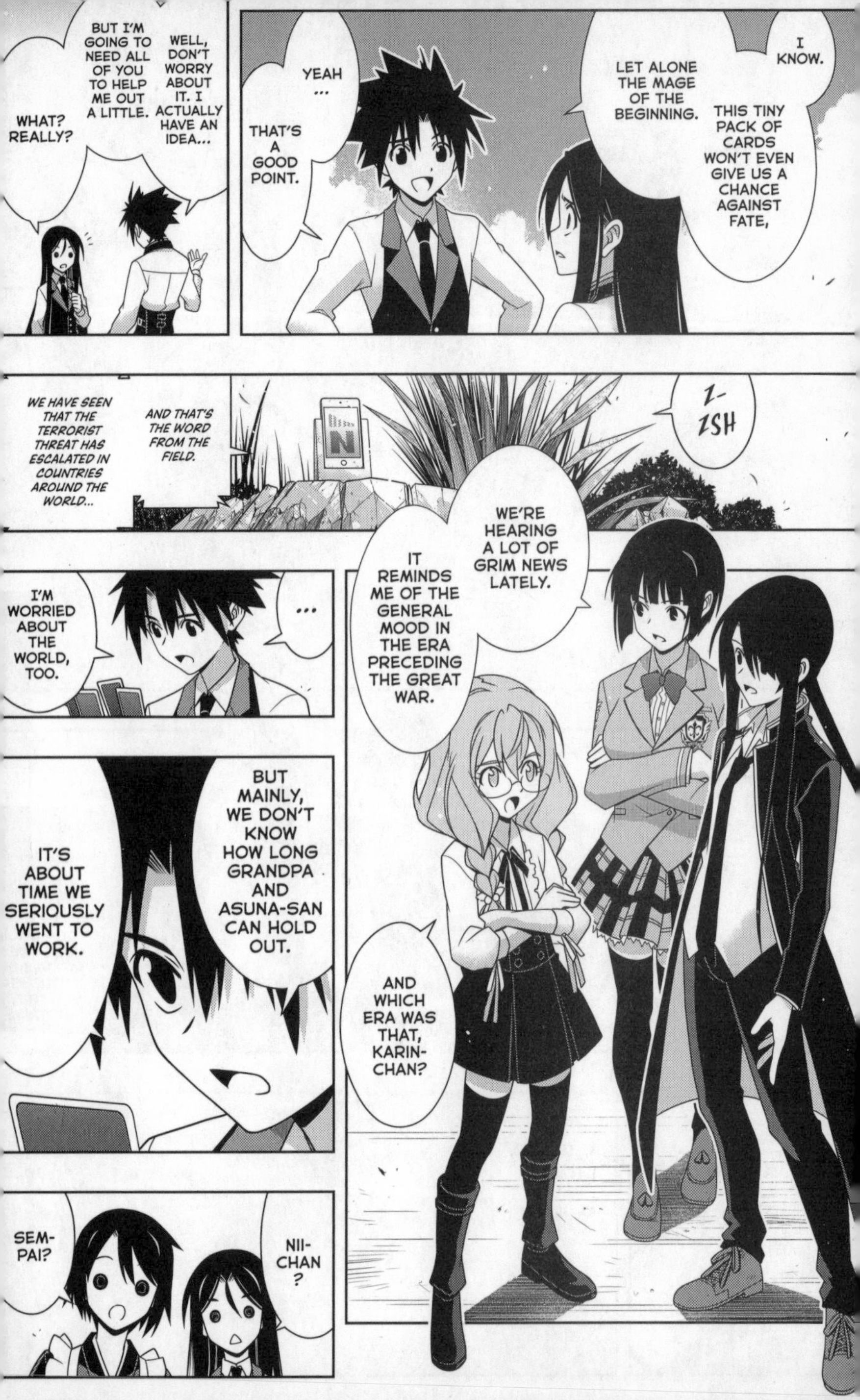
I KNOW.
THIS TINY PACK OF CARDS WON'T EVEN GIVE US A CHANCE AGAINST FATE,
LET ALONE THE MAGE OF THE BEGINNING.
YEAH ...
THAT'S A GOOD POINT.
WELL, DON'T WORRY ABOUT IT. I ACTUALLY HAVE AN IDEA...
BUT I'M GOING TO NEED ALL OF YOU TO HELP ME OUT A LITTLE.
WHAT? REALLY?
Z-ZSH
WE HAVE SEEN THAT THE TERRORIST THREAT HAS ESCALATED IN COUNTRIES AROUND THE WORLD...
AND THAT'S THE WORD FROM THE FIELD.
WE'RE HEARING A LOT OF GRIM NEWS LATELY.
IT REMINDS ME OF THE GENERAL MOOD IN THE ERA PRECEDING THE GREAT WAR.
AND WHICH ERA WAS THAT, KARIN-CHAN?
...
I'M WORRIED ABOUT THE WORLD, TOO.
BUT MAINLY, WE DON'T KNOW HOW LONG GRANDPA AND ASUNA-SAN CAN HOLD OUT.
IT'S ABOUT TIME WE SERIOUSLY WENT TO WORK.
NII-CHAN?
SEM-PAI?

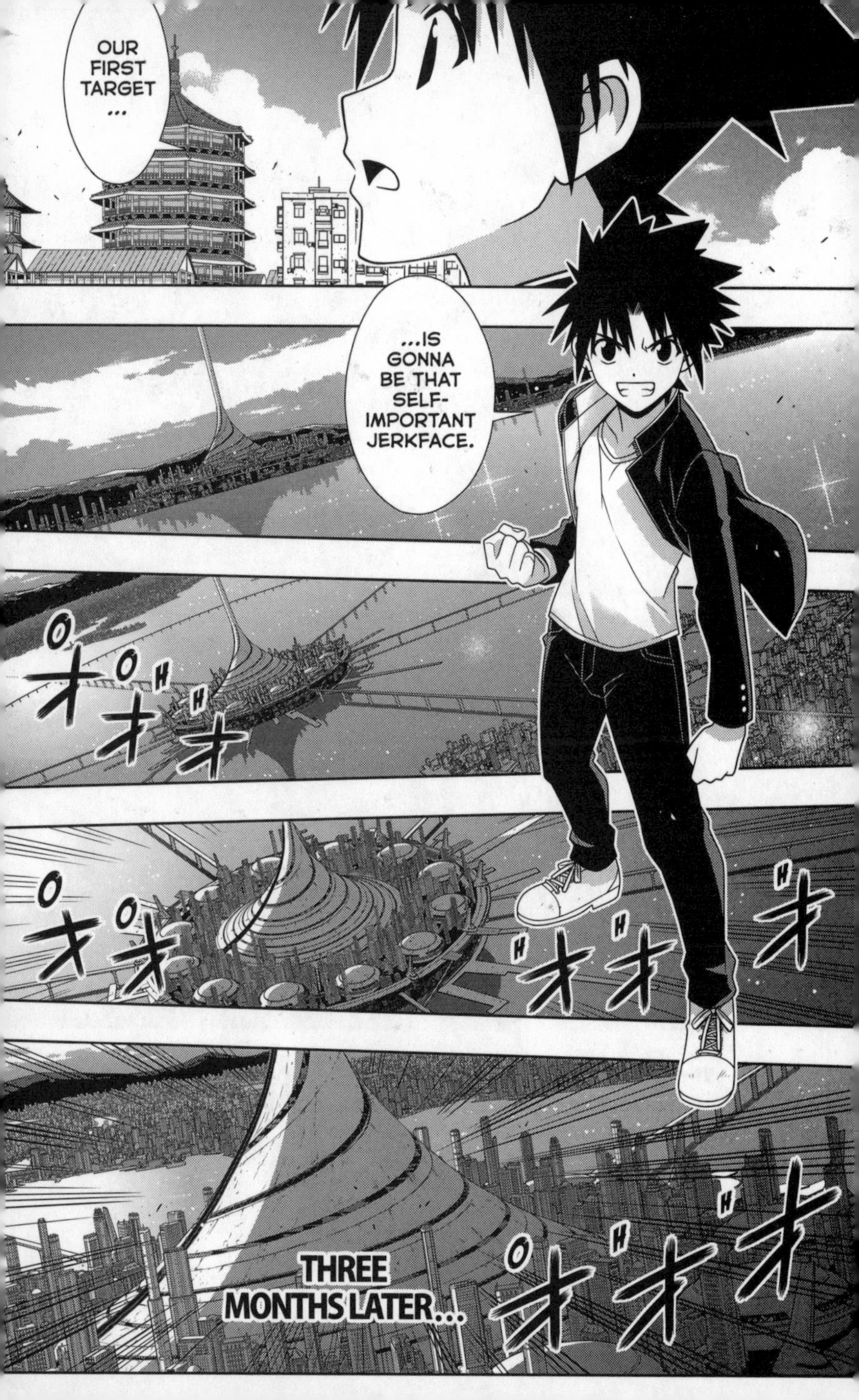
OUR FIRST TARGET ...
...IS GONNA BE THAT SELF-IMPORTANT JERKFACE.
OOHH
オオオ
OOHH
オオオ
HHH
オオオ
OHH
オオオ
THREE MONTHS LATER...

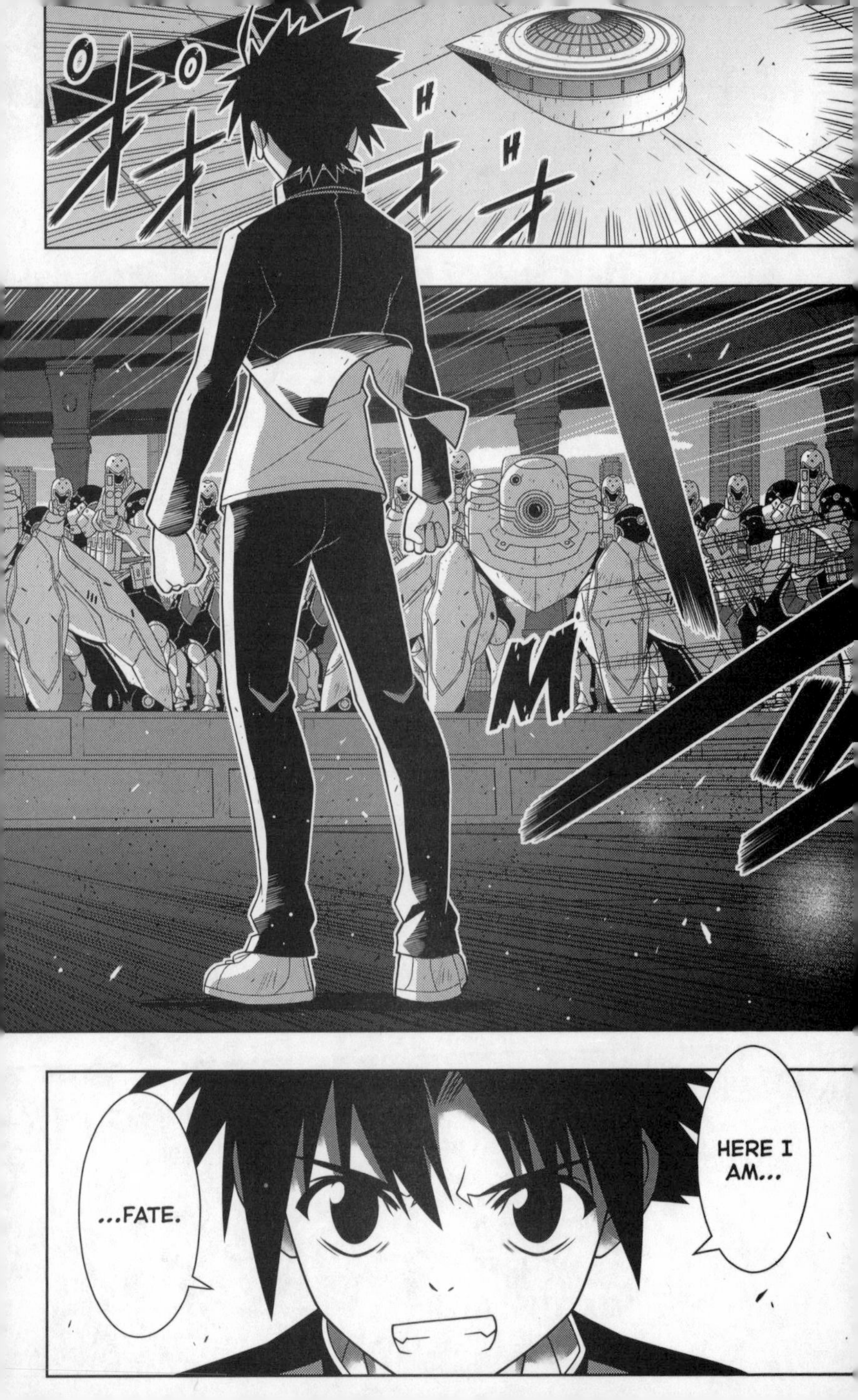
HERE I AM...
...FATE.

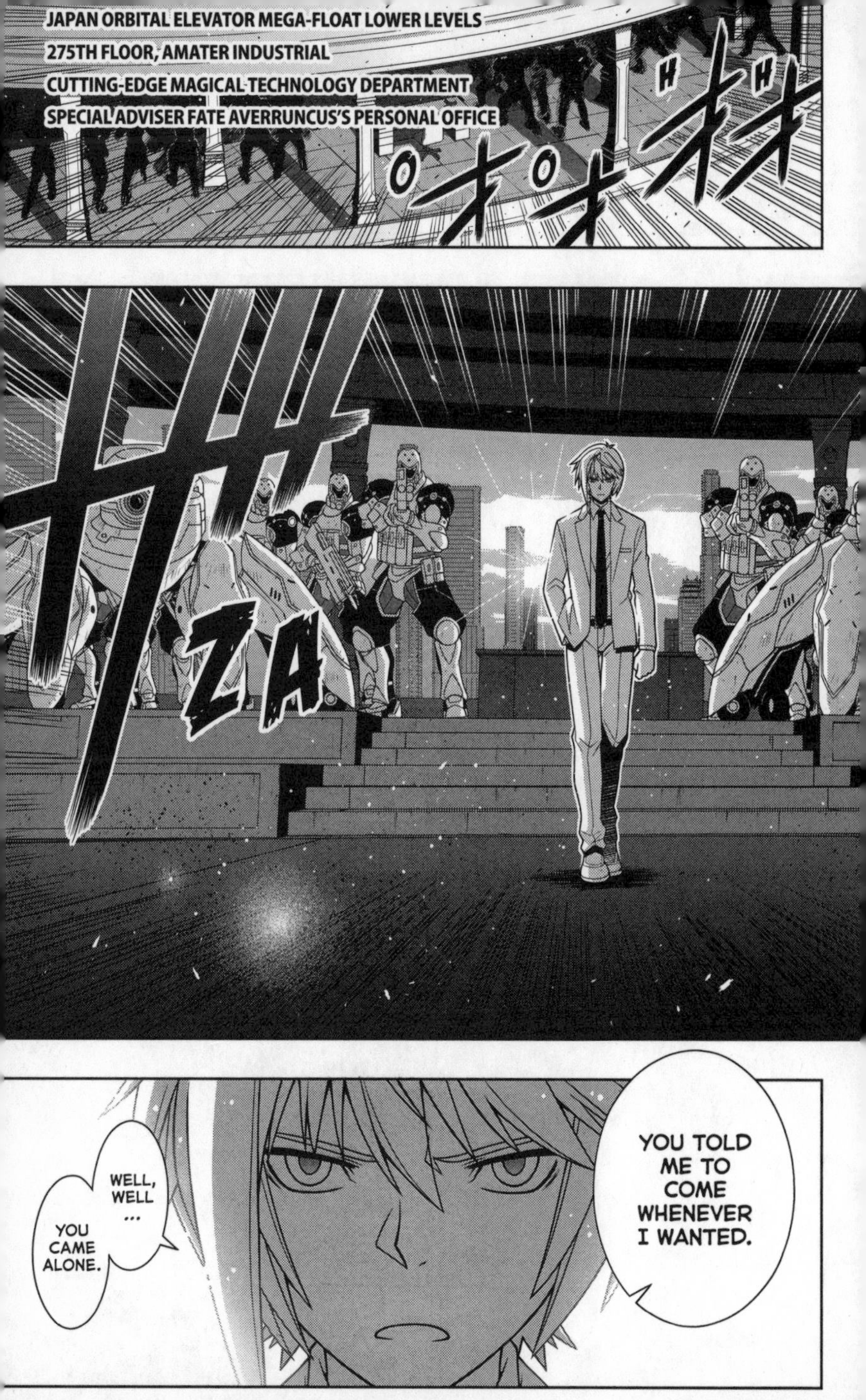
JAPAN ORBITAL ELEVATOR MEGA-FLOAT LOWER LEVELS
275TH FLOOR, AMATER INDUSTRIAL
CUTTING-EDGE MAGICAL-TECHNOLOGY DEPARTMENT
SPECIAL ADVISER FATE AVERRUNCUS'S PERSONAL OFFICE
OH OH
ZA
YOU TOLD ME TO COME WHENEVER I WANTED.
WELL, WELL... YOU CAME ALONE.

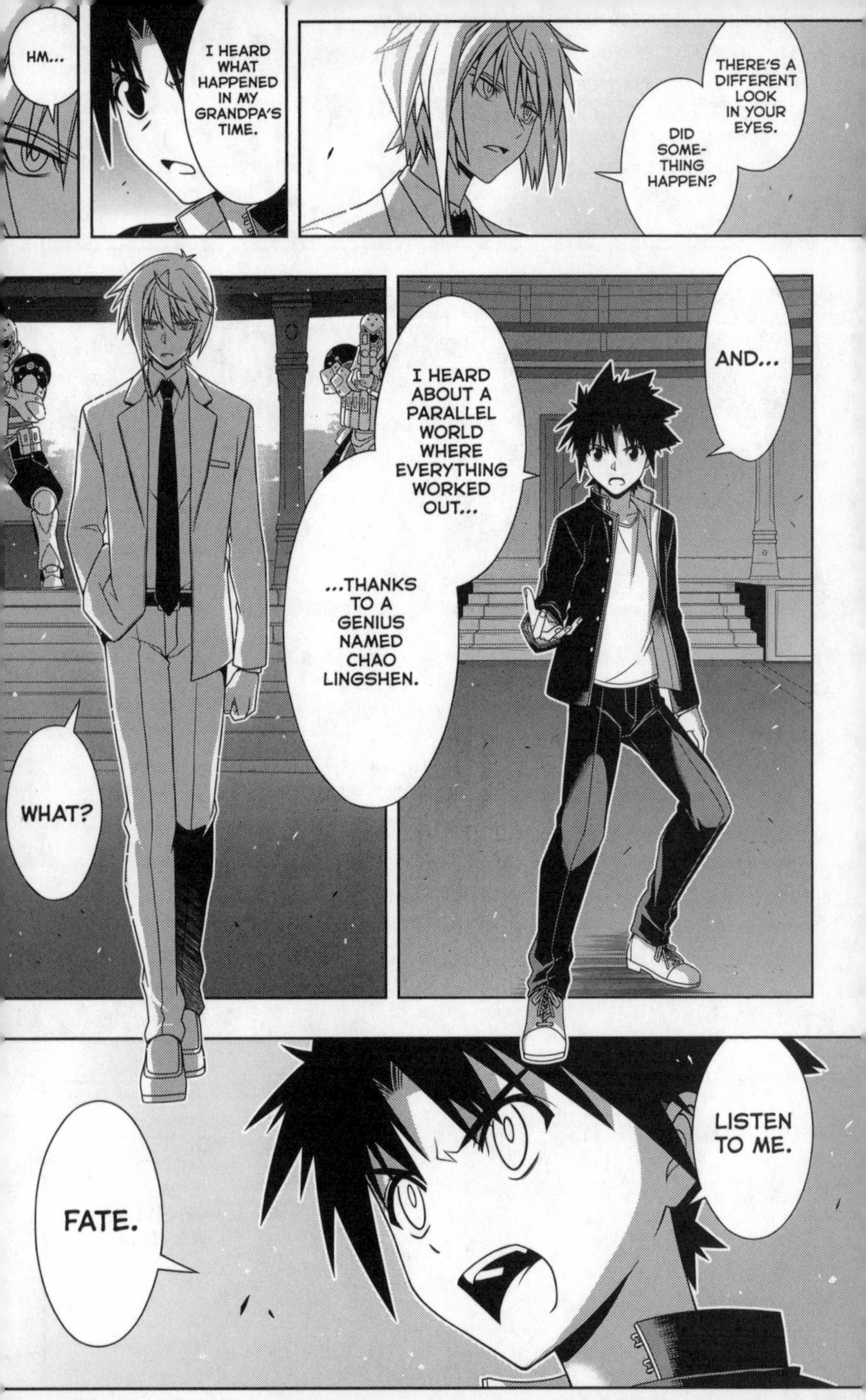
THERE'S A DIFFERENT LOOK IN YOUR EYES.
DID SOME-THING HAPPEN?
I HEARD WHAT HAPPENED IN MY GRANDPA'S TIME.
HM...
AND...
I HEARD ABOUT A PARALLEL WORLD WHERE EVERYTHING WORKED OUT...
...THANKS TO A GENIUS NAMED CHAO LINGSHEN.
WHAT?
LISTEN TO ME.
FATE.

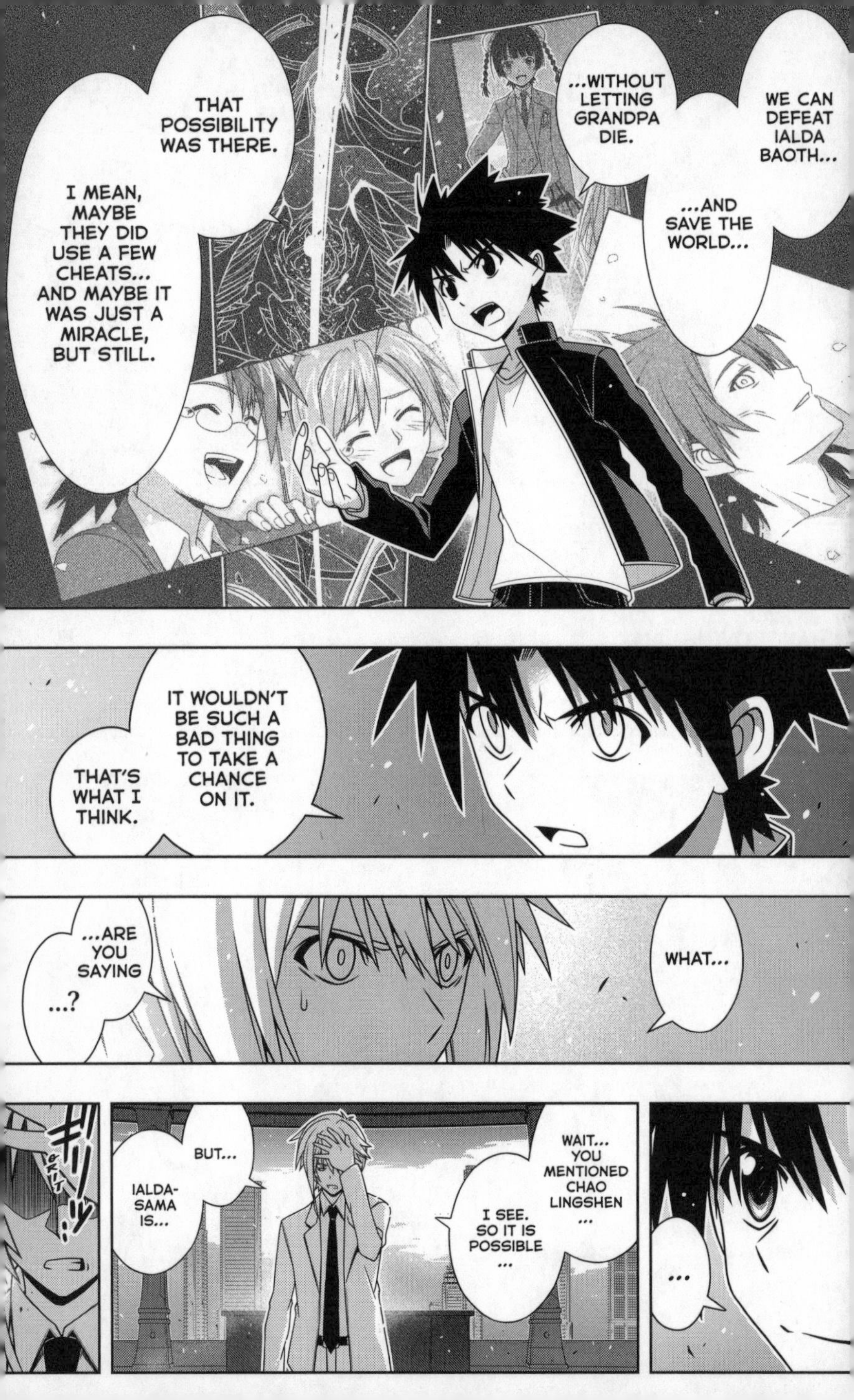
WE CAN DEFEAT IALDA BAOTH...
...WITHOUT LETTING GRANDPA DIE.
...AND SAVE THE WORLD...
THAT POSSIBILITY WAS THERE.
I MEAN, MAYBE THEY DID USE A FEW CHEATS... AND MAYBE IT WAS JUST A MIRACLE, BUT STILL.
IT WOULDN'T BE SUCH A BAD THING TO TAKE A CHANCE ON IT.
THAT'S WHAT I THINK.
WHAT...
...ARE YOU SAYING ...?
...
WAIT... YOU MENTIONED CHAO LINGSHEN ...
I SEE. SO IT IS POSSIBLE ...
BUT...
IALDA-SAMA IS...
ギリッ
GRIT

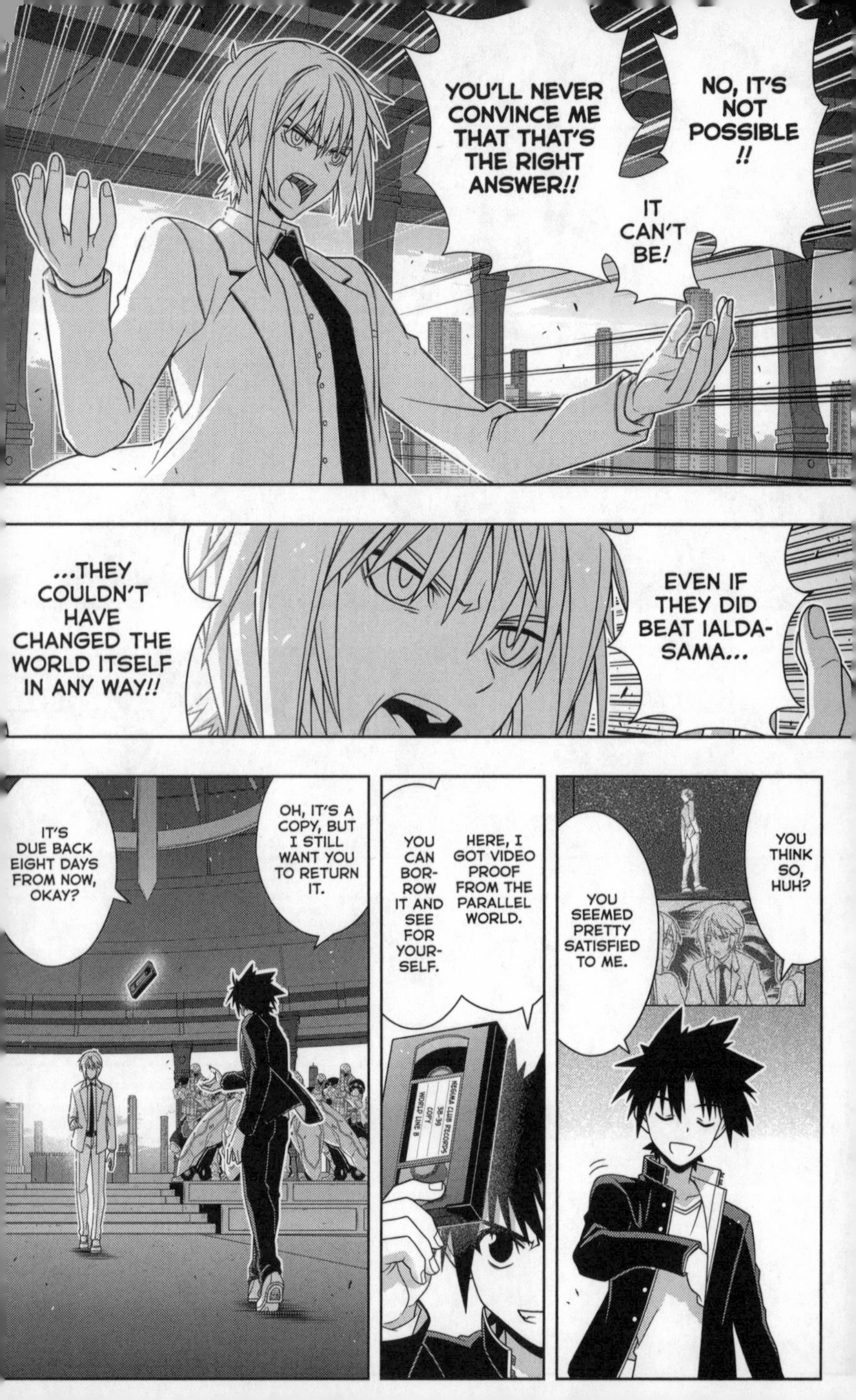
NO, IT'S NOT POSSIBLE!!
IT CAN'T BE!
YOU'LL NEVER CONVINCE ME THAT THAT'S THE RIGHT ANSWER!!
EVEN IF THEY DID BEAT IALDA-SAMA...
...THEY COULDN'T HAVE CHANGED THE WORLD ITSELF IN ANY WAY!!
YOU THINK SO, HUH?
YOU SEEMED PRETTY SATISFIED TO ME.
HERE, I GOT VIDEO PROOF FROM THE PARALLEL WORLD.
YOU CAN BOR-ROW IT AND SEE FOR YOUR-SELF.
NEGIMA CLUB RECORDS
38-39
COPY
WORLD LINE B
OH, IT'S A COPY, BUT I STILL WANT YOU TO RETURN IT.
IT'S DUE BACK EIGHT DAYS FROM NOW, OKAY?

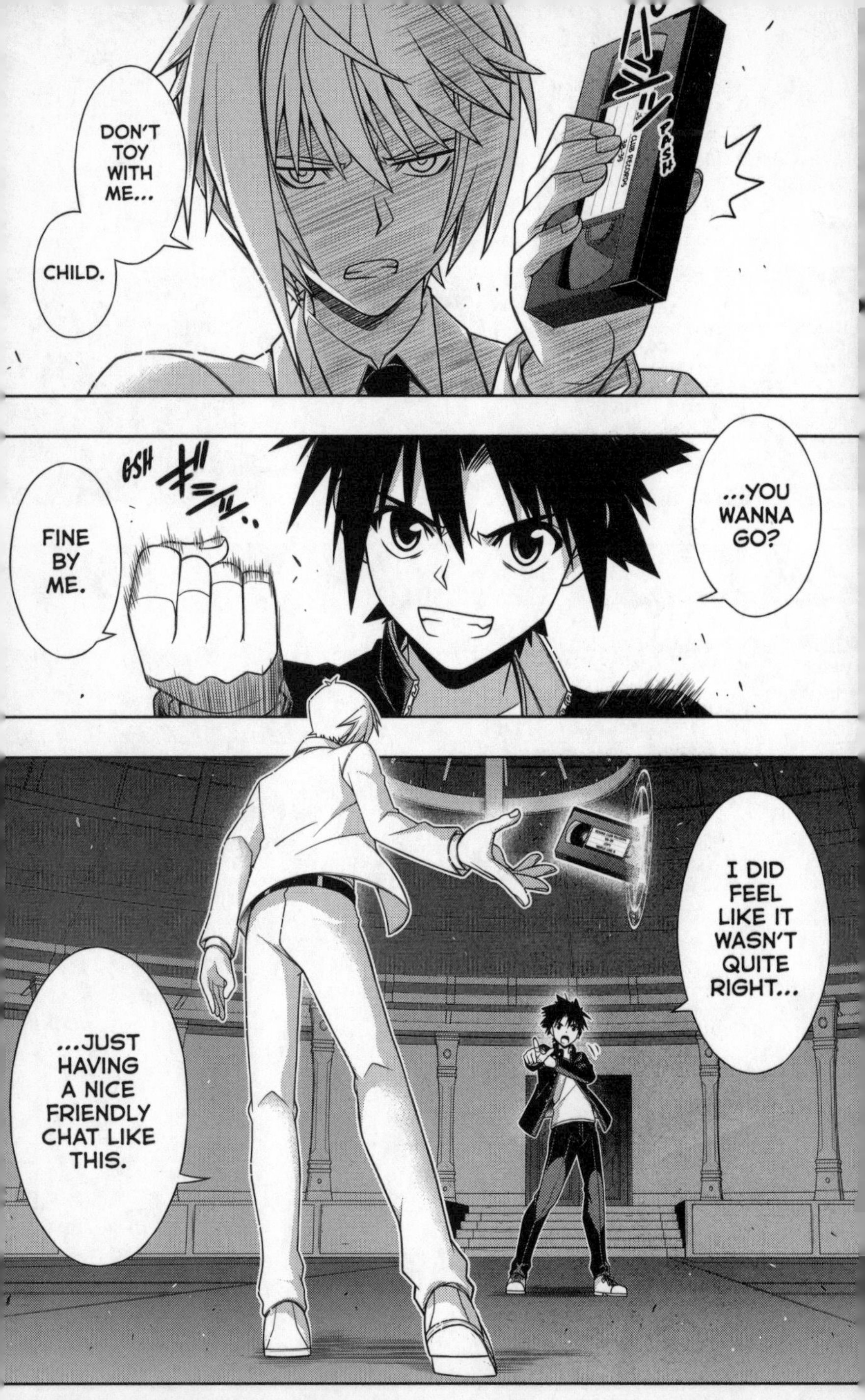
FASH
DON'T TOY WITH ME...
CHILD.
...YOU WANNA GO?
GSH
FINE BY ME.
I DID FEEL LIKE IT WASN'T QUITE RIGHT...
...JUST HAVING A NICE FRIENDLY CHAT LIKE THIS.

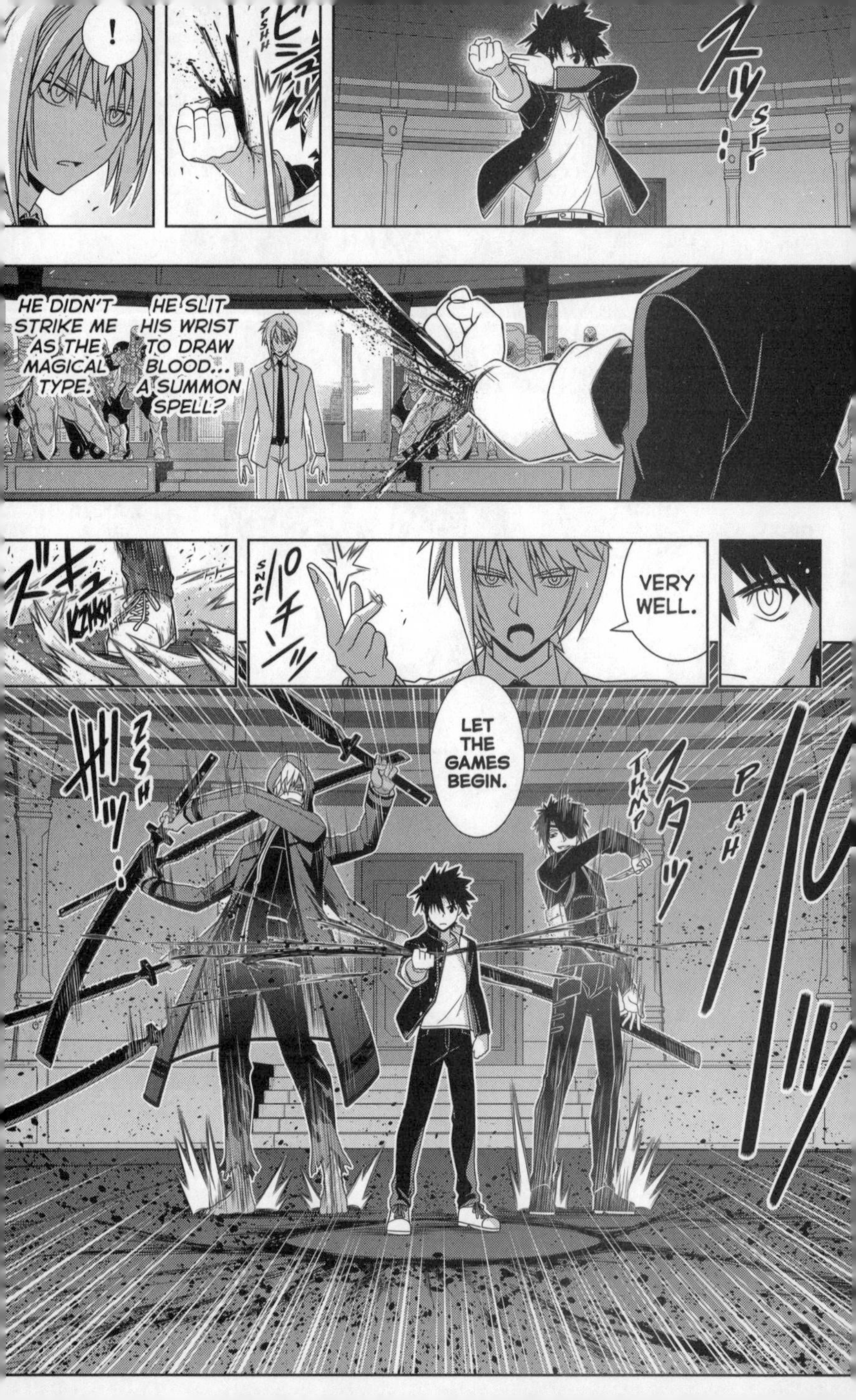
SFF
PSHH
!
HE SLIT HIS WRIST TO DRAW BLOOD... A SUMMON SPELL?
HE DIDN'T STRIKE ME AS THE MAGICAL TYPE.
VERY WELL.
SNAP
KZHSH
PAH
THMP
LET THE GAMES BEGIN.
ZSH

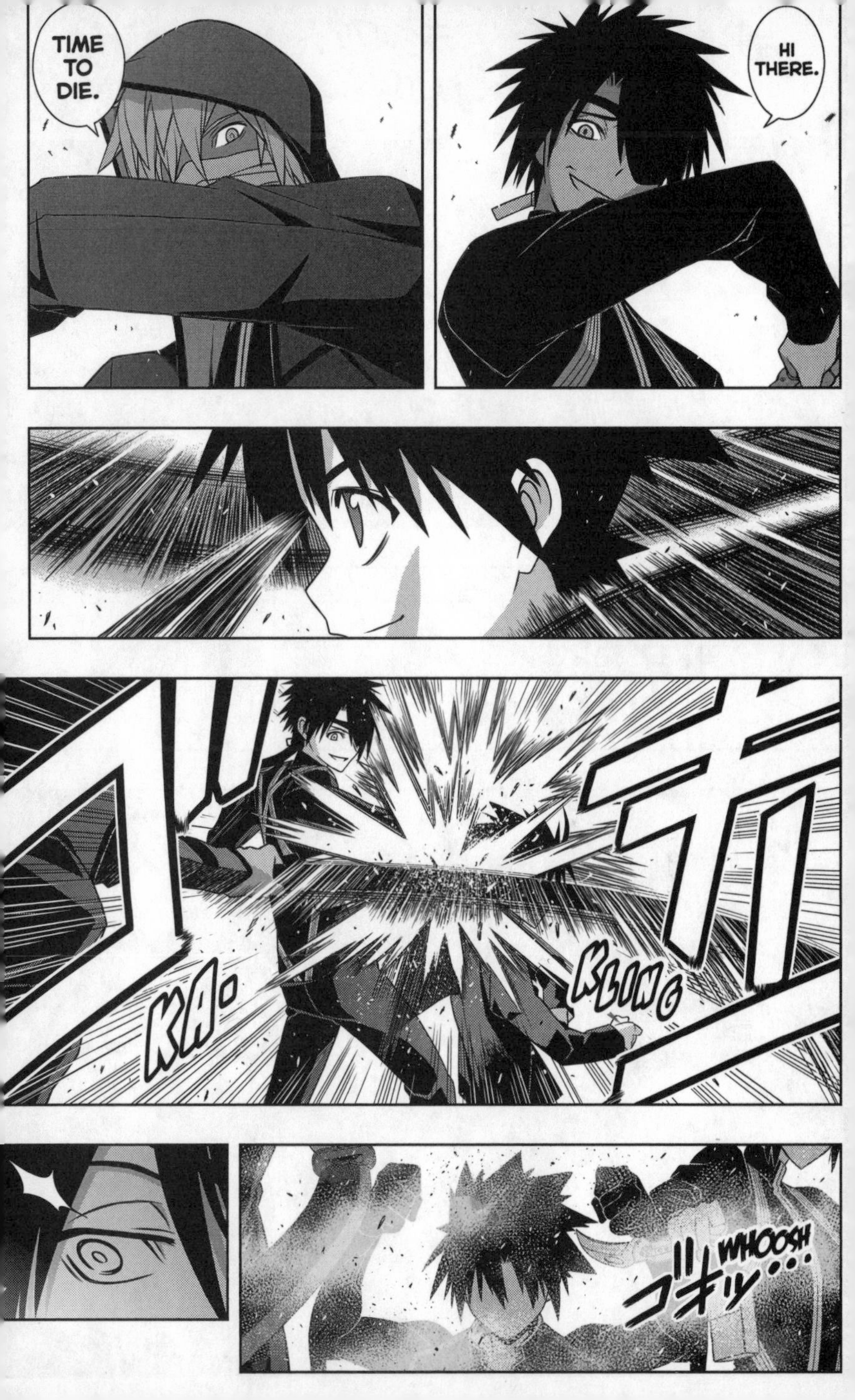
HI THERE.
TIME TO DIE.
KLING
KA-
WHOOSH!
ゴオッ

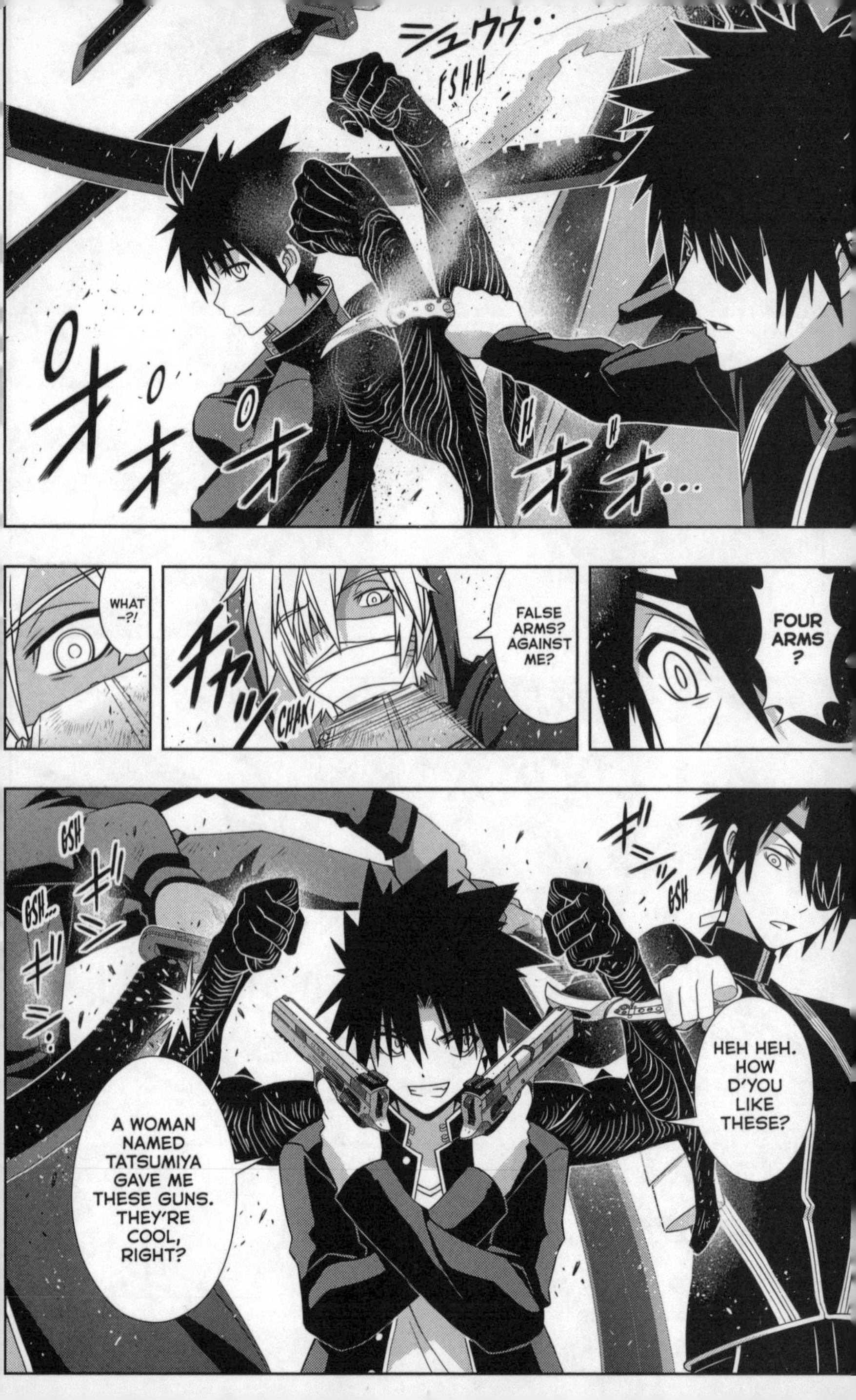
シュウウ・・
FSHH
オオオオ…
FOUR ARMS?
FALSE ARMS? AGAINST ME?
チャッ
CHAK
WHAT—?!
ギシッ
GSH
HEH HEH. HOW D'YOU LIKE THESE?
GSH
GSH...
A WOMAN NAMED TATSUMIYA GAVE ME THESE GUNS. THEY'RE COOL, RIGHT?

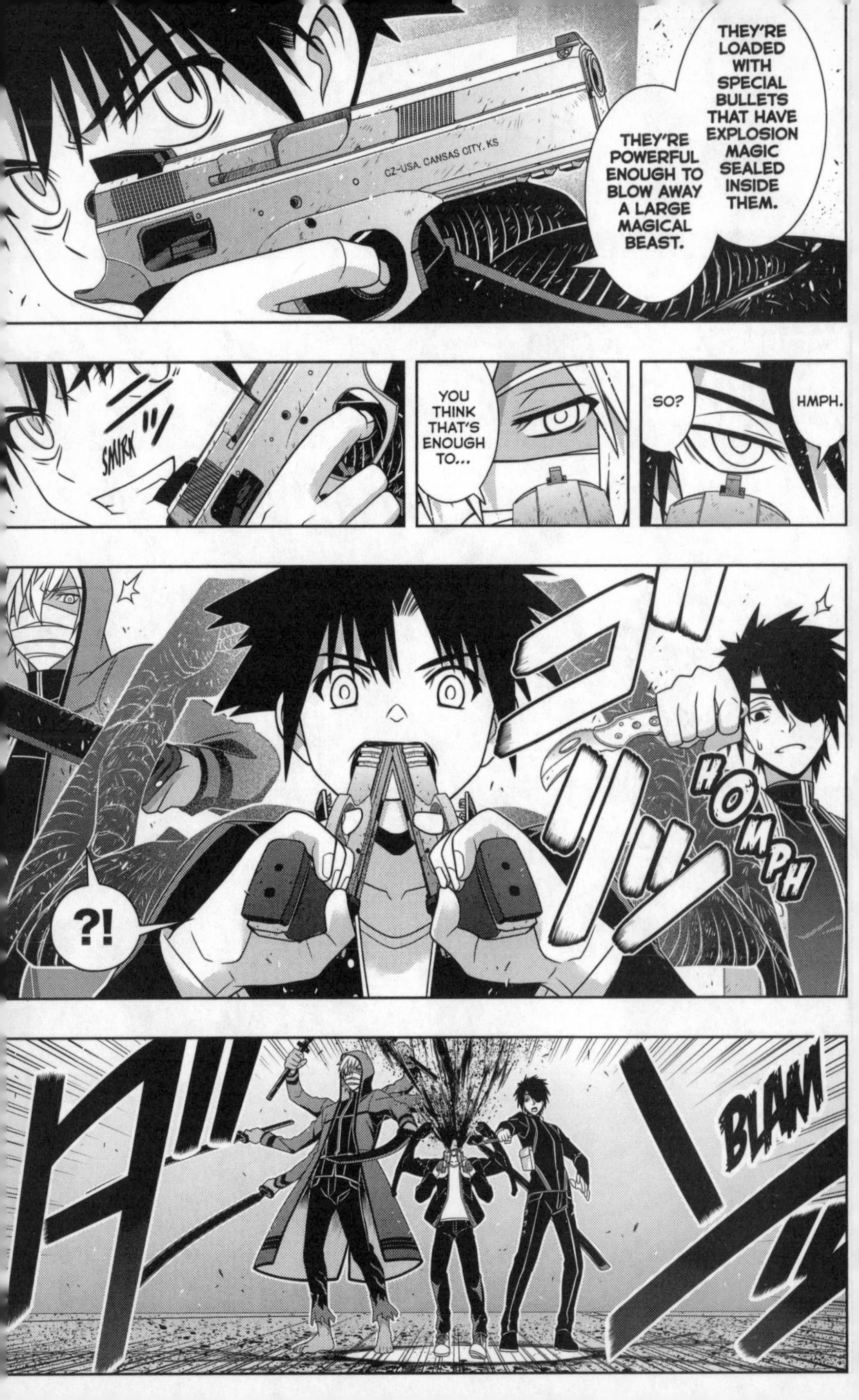
CZ-USA. CANSAS CITY. KS
THEY'RE LOADED WITH SPECIAL BULLETS THAT HAVE EXPLOSION MAGIC SEALED INSIDE THEM.
THEY'RE POWERFUL ENOUGH TO BLOW AWAY A LARGE MAGICAL BEAST.
HMPH.
SO?
YOU THINK THAT'S ENOUGH TO...
SMIRK
HOMPH
?!
BLAM

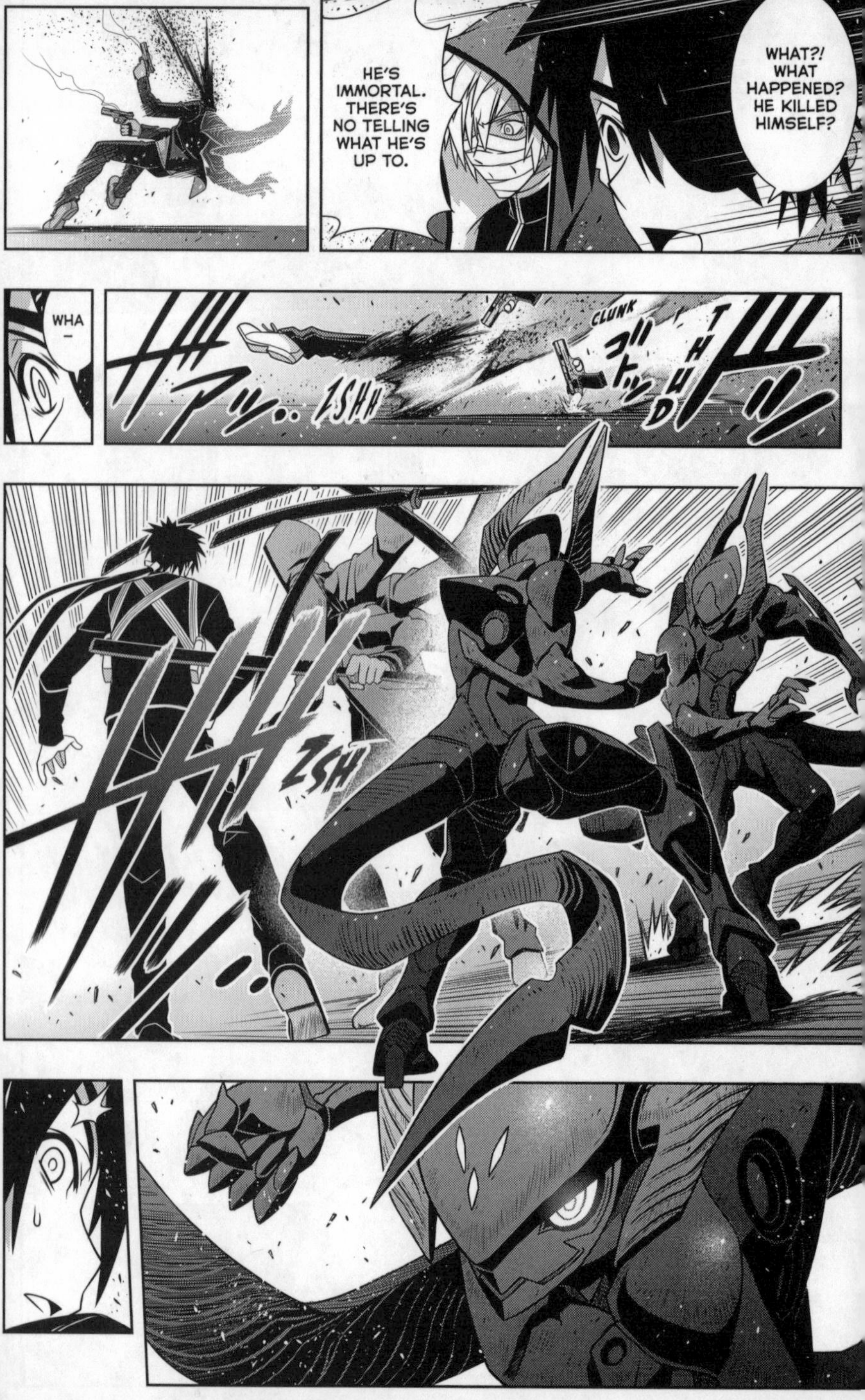
WHAT?! WHAT HAPPENED? HE KILLED HIMSELF?
HE'S IMMORTAL. THERE'S NO TELLING WHAT HE'S UP TO.
THUD
CLUNK
ZSHH
WHA —
ZSH

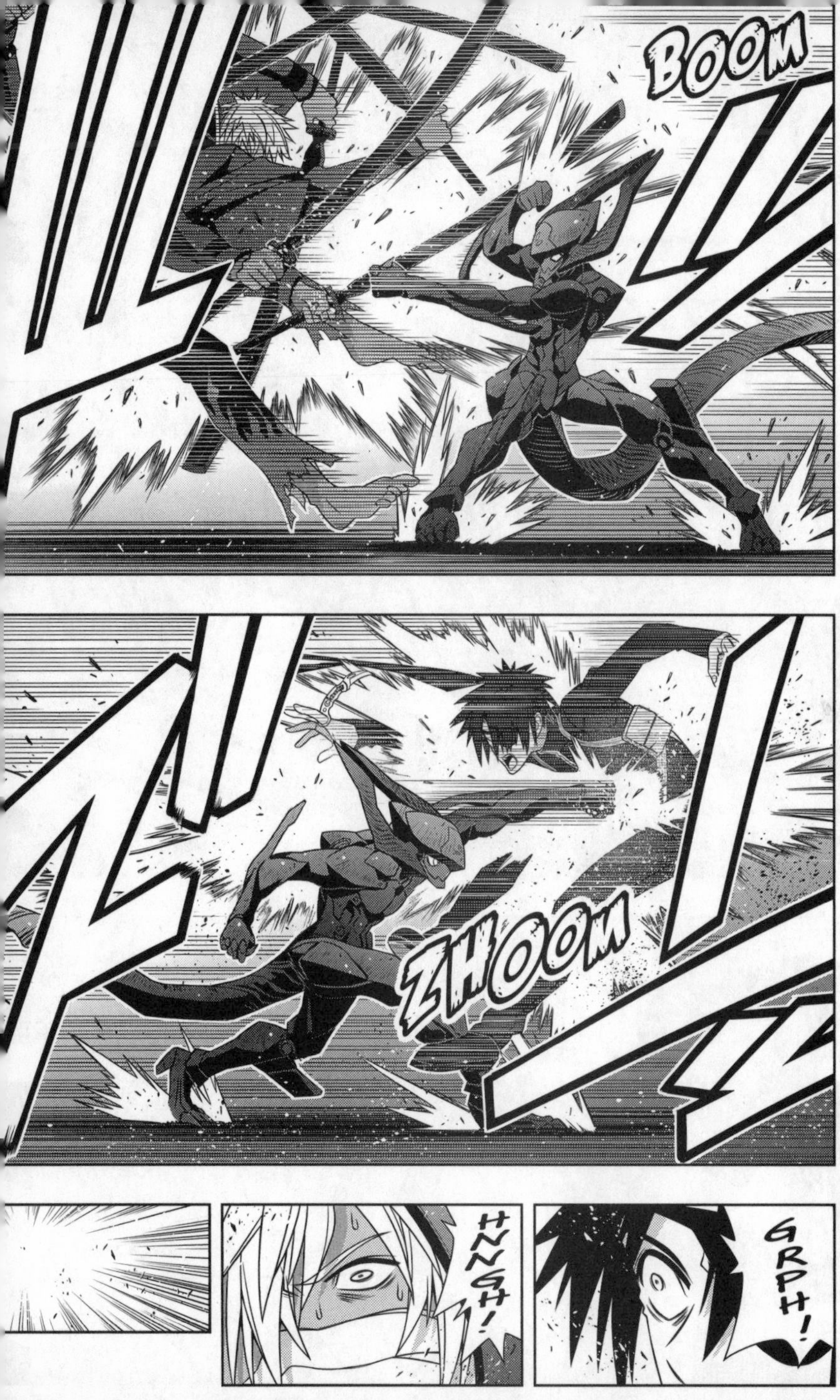
BOOM
ZHOOM
GRPH!
HNNGH!

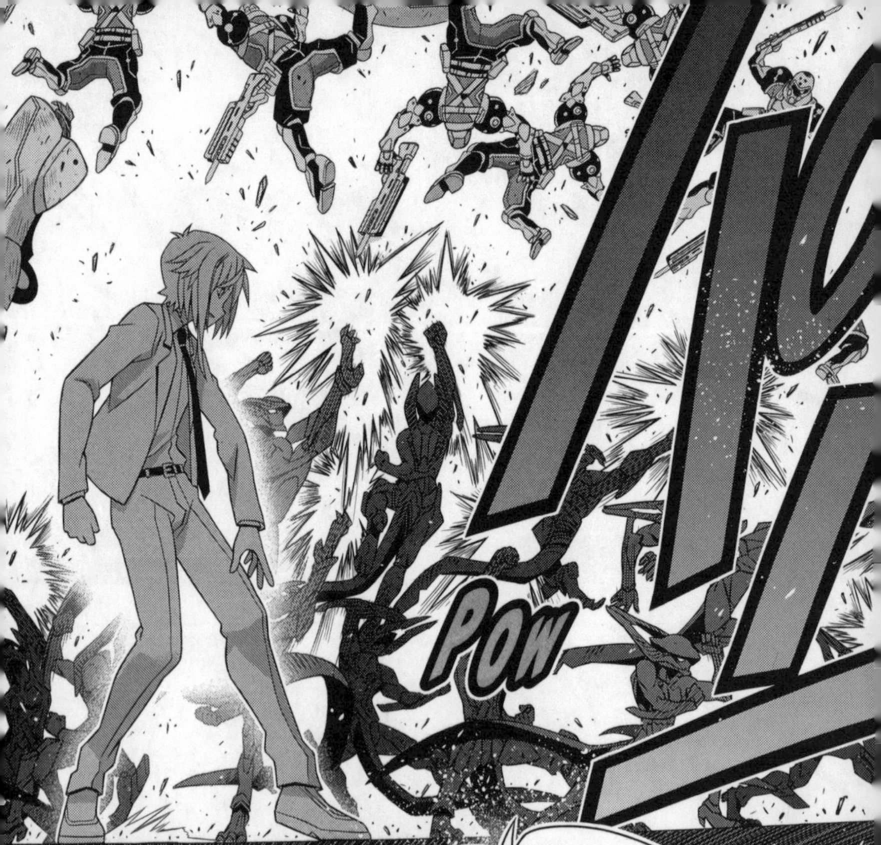
POW

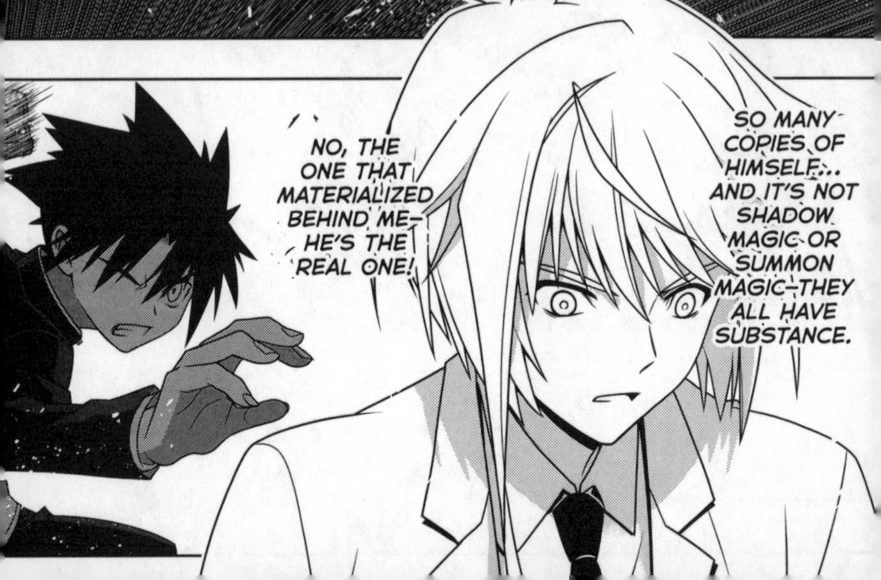
SO MANY COPIES OF HIMSELF... AND IT'S NOT SHADOW MAGIC OR SUMMON MAGIC—THEY ALL HAVE SUBSTANCE.
NO, THE ONE THAT MATERIALIZED BEHIND ME— HE'S THE REAL ONE!

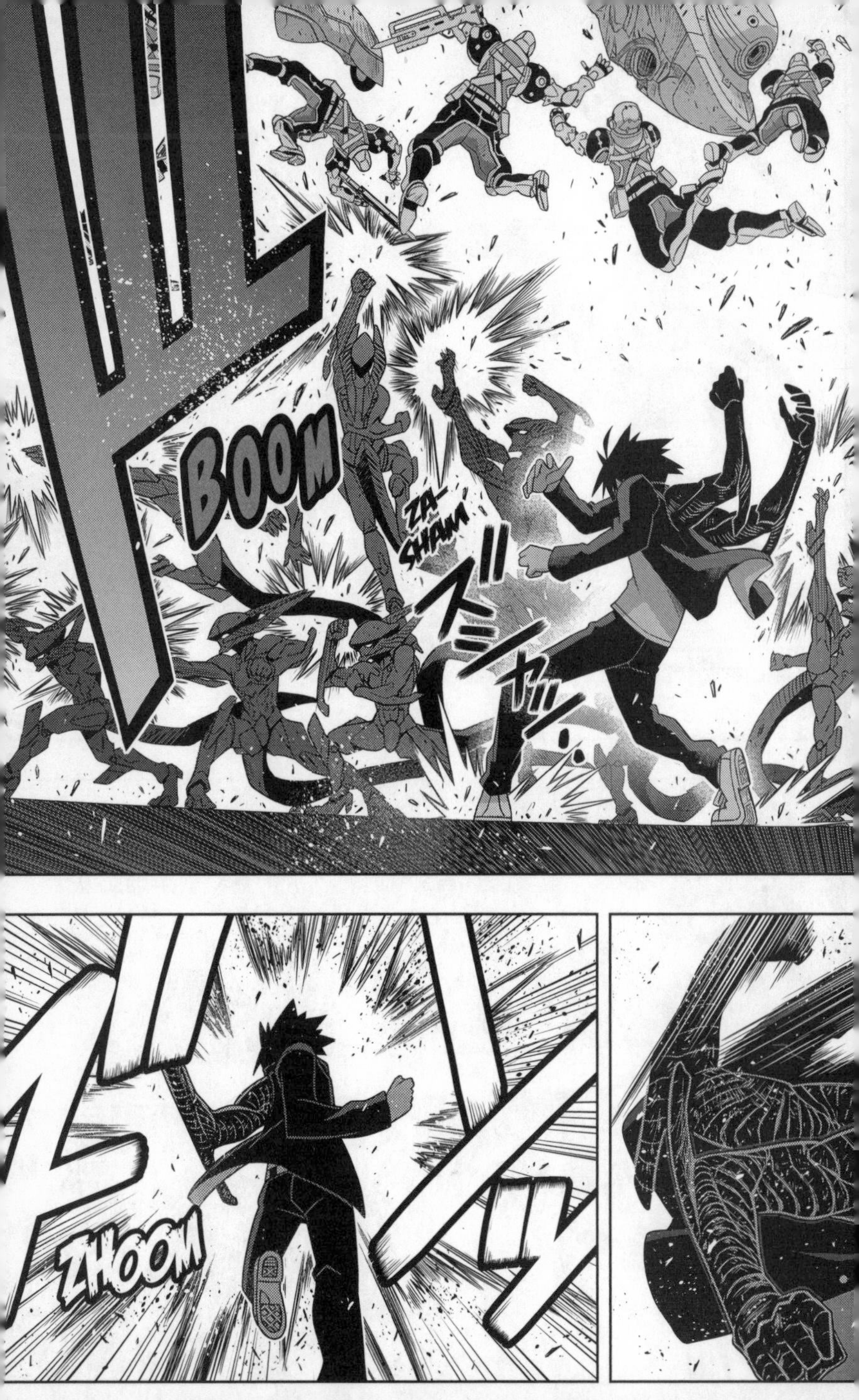
ZA-SHAM
BOOM
ZHOOM

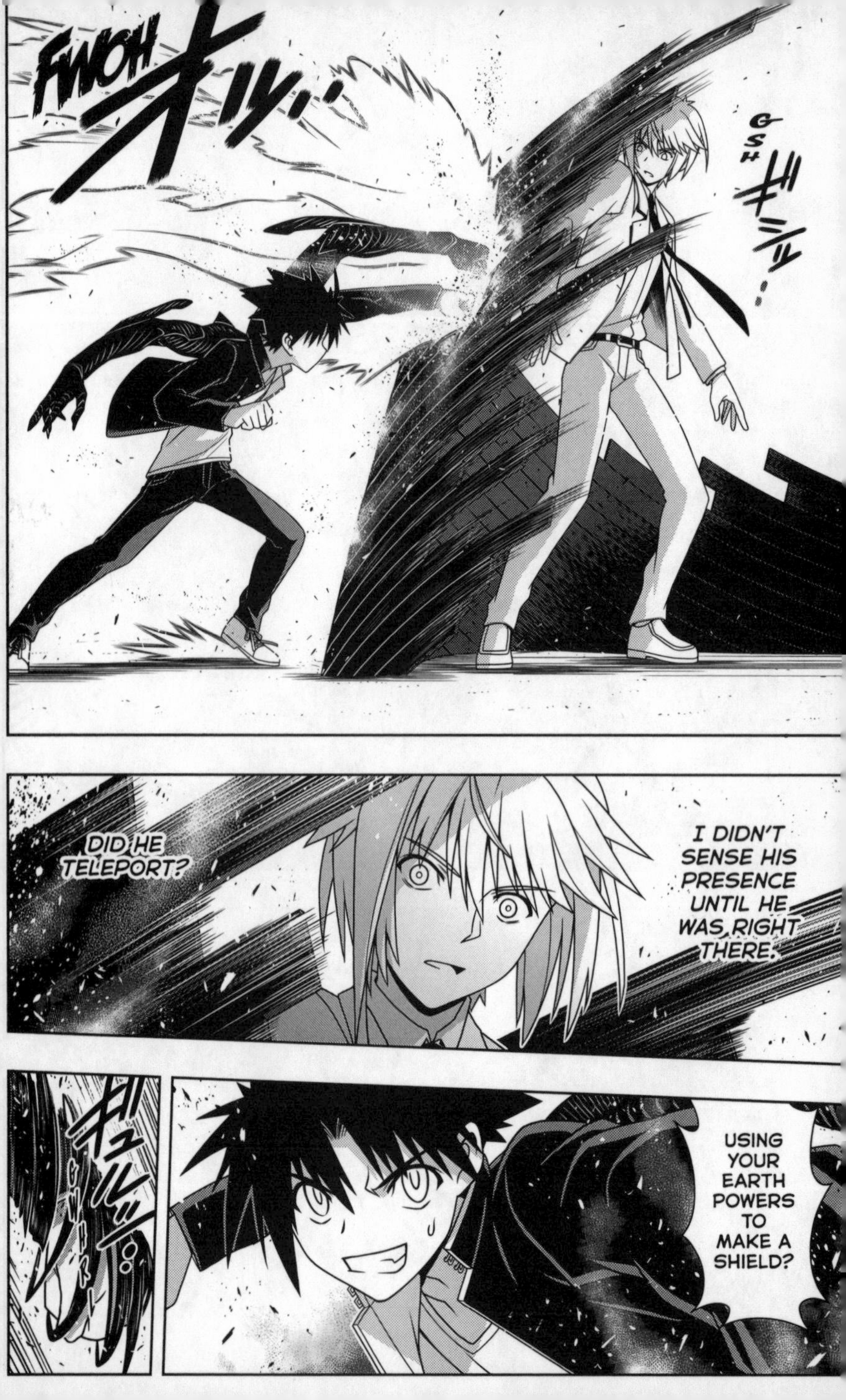
FWOH
GSH
I DIDN'T SENSE HIS PRESENCE UNTIL HE WAS RIGHT THERE.
DID HE TELEPORT?
USING YOUR EARTH POWERS TO MAKE A SHIELD?

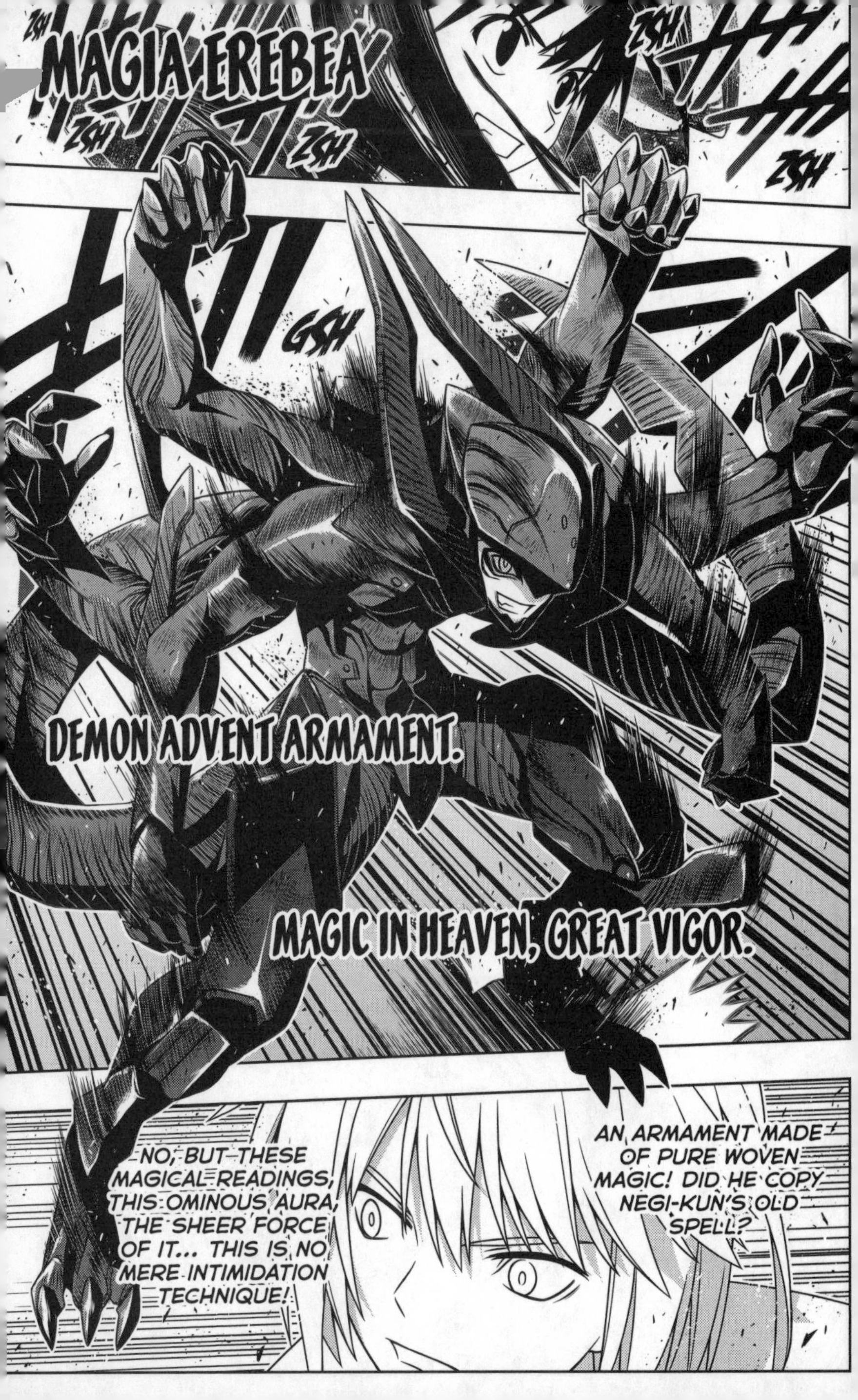

ZSH
ZSH
MAGIA EREBEA
ZSH
ZSH
ZSH
GSH
DEMON ADVENT ARMAMENT.
MAGIC IN HEAVEN, GREAT VIGOR.
AN ARMAMENT MADE OF PURE WOVEN MAGIC! DID HE COPY NEGI-KUN'S OLD SPELL?
NO, BUT THESE MAGICAL READINGS, THIS OMINOUS AURA, THE SHEER FORCE OF IT... THIS IS NO MERE INTIMIDATION TECHNIQUE!

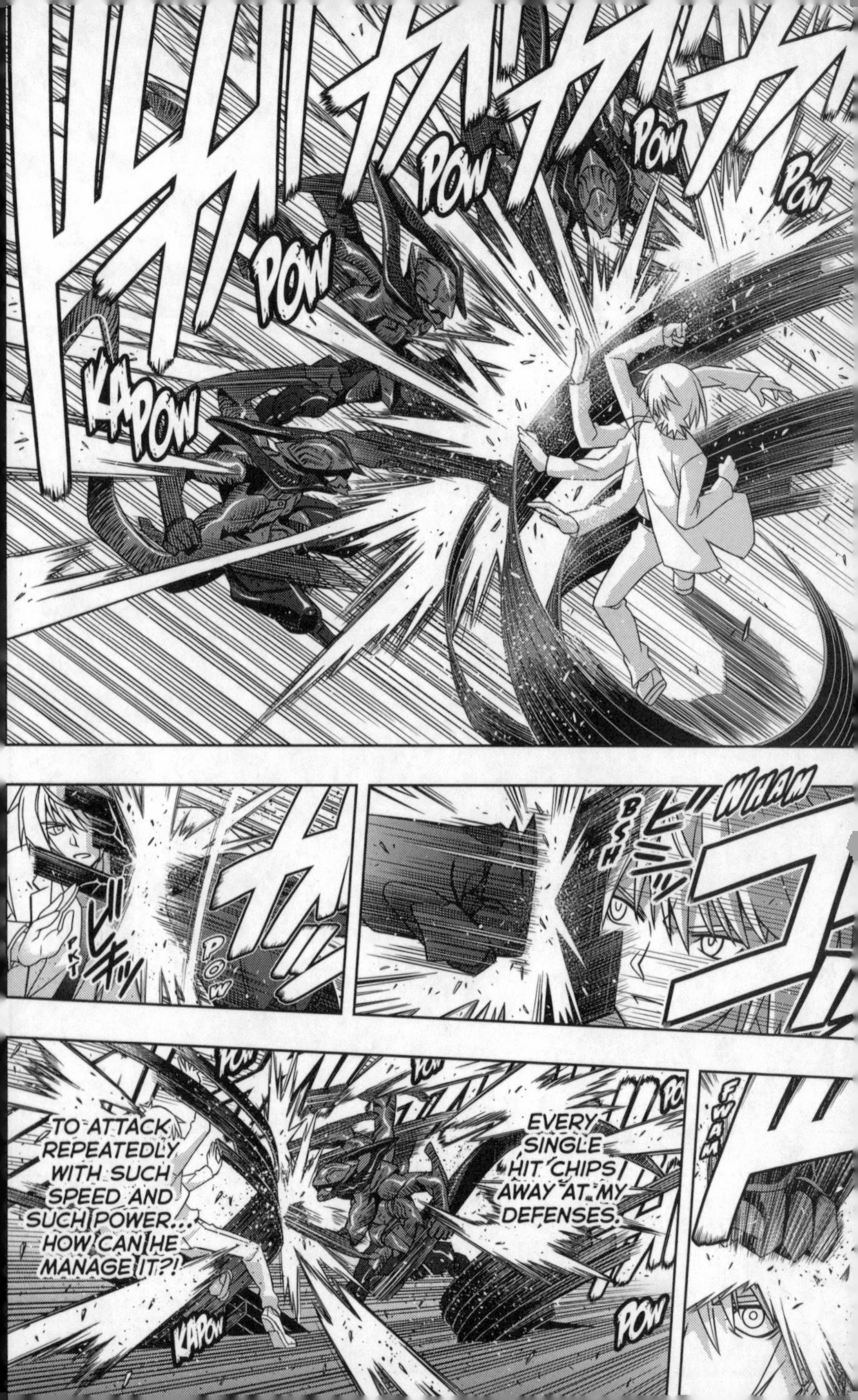
POW
POW
POW
POW
KAPOW
WHAM
BSH
POW
PKT
FWAM
POW
EVERY SINGLE HIT CHIPS AWAY AT MY DEFENSES.
TO ATTACK REPEATEDLY WITH SUCH SPEED AND SUCH POWER... HOW CAN HE MANAGE IT?!
POW
KAPOW

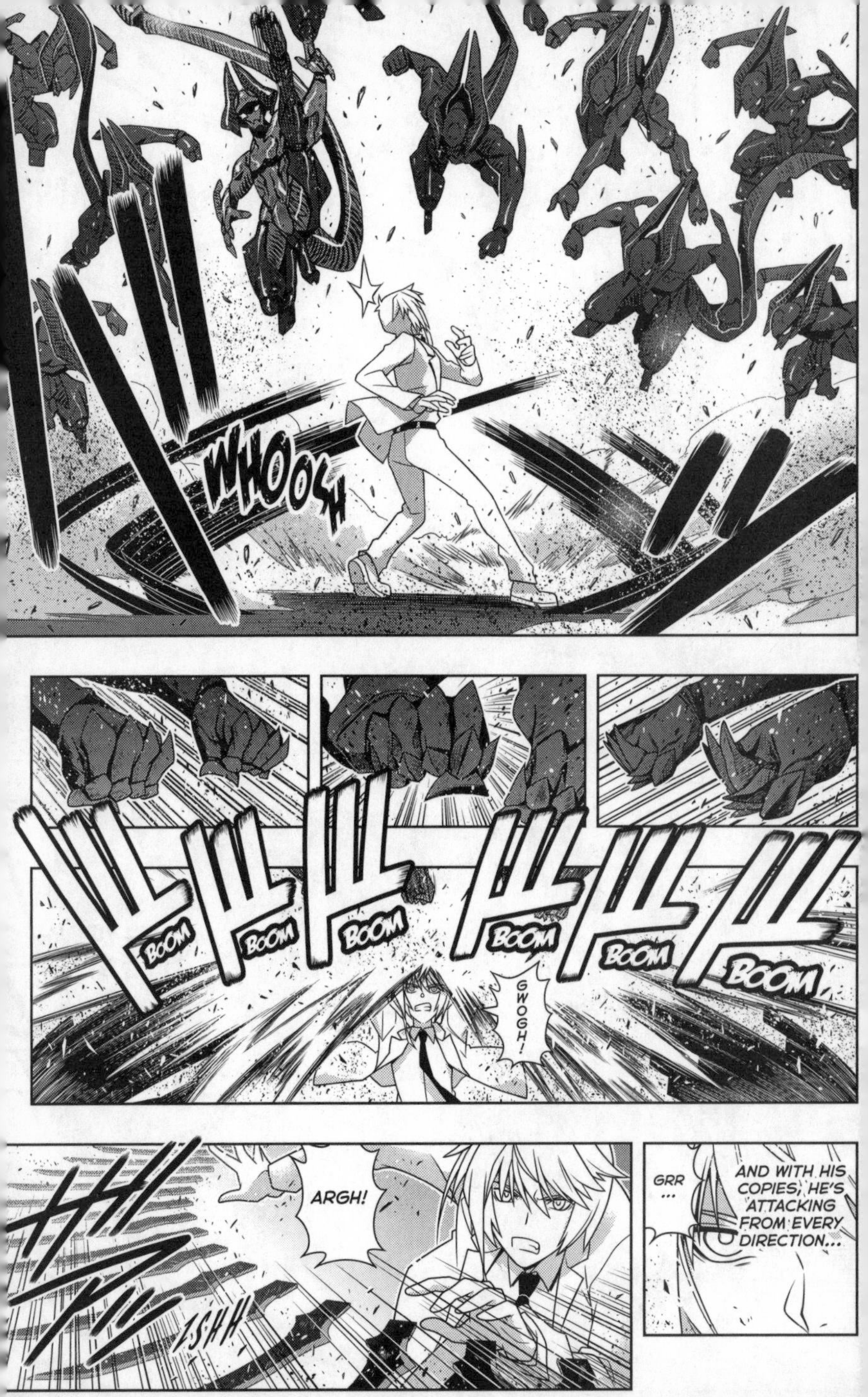
WHOOSH
BOOM
BOOM
BOOM
BOOM
BOOM
BOOM
GWOGH!
GRR...
AND WITH HIS COPIES, HE'S ATTACKING FROM EVERY DIRECTION...
ARGH!
ZSHH

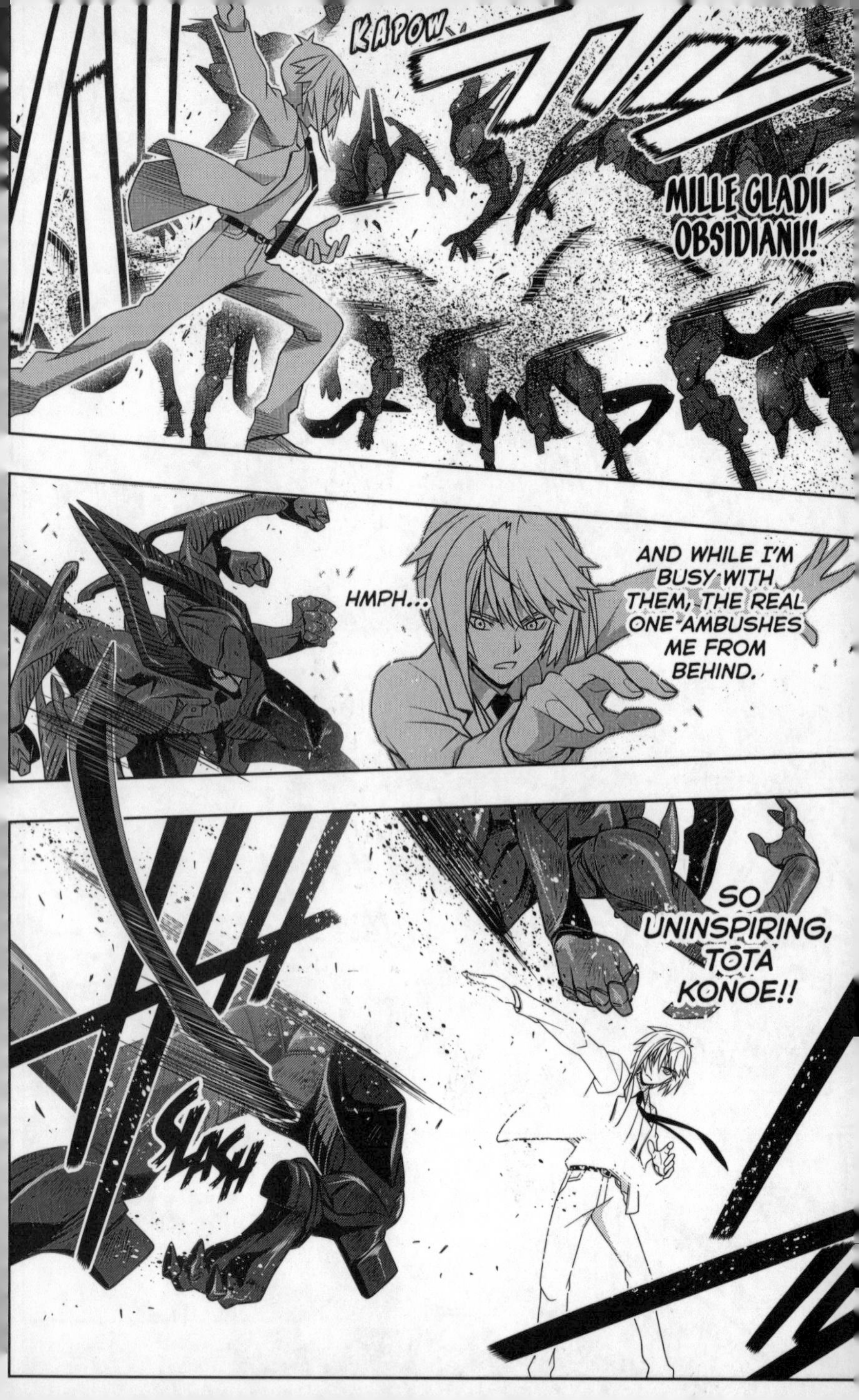
KAPOW
MILLE GLADII OBSIDIANI!!
AND WHILE I'M BUSY WITH THEM, THE REAL ONE AMBUSHES ME FROM BEHIND.
HMPH...
SO UNINSPIRING, TŌTA KONOE!!
SLASH

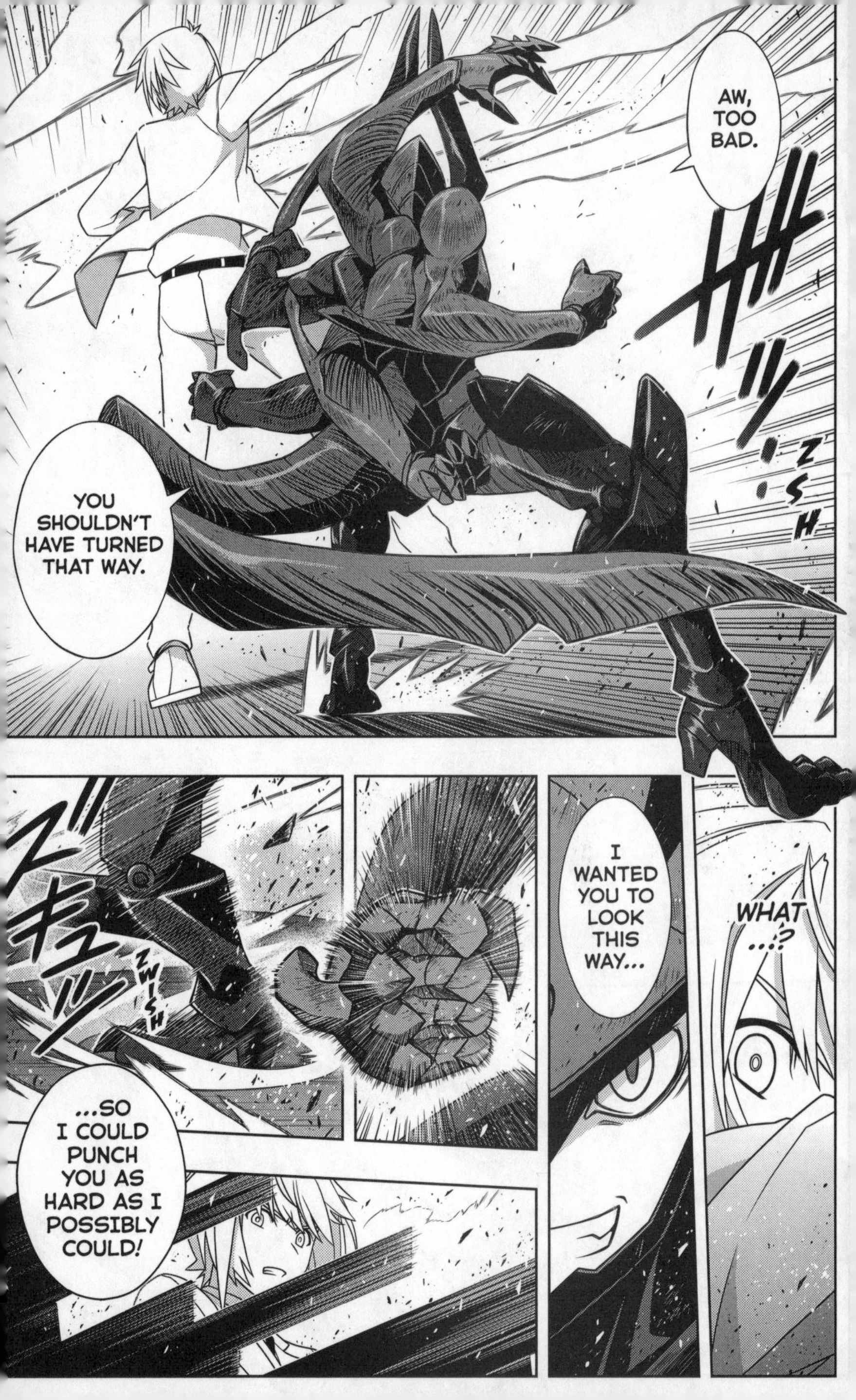
AW, TOO BAD.
ZSH
YOU SHOULDN'T HAVE TURNED THAT WAY.
WHAT ...!?
I WANTED YOU TO LOOK THIS WAY...
ZWISH
...SO I COULD PUNCH YOU AS HARD AS I POSSIBLY COULD!

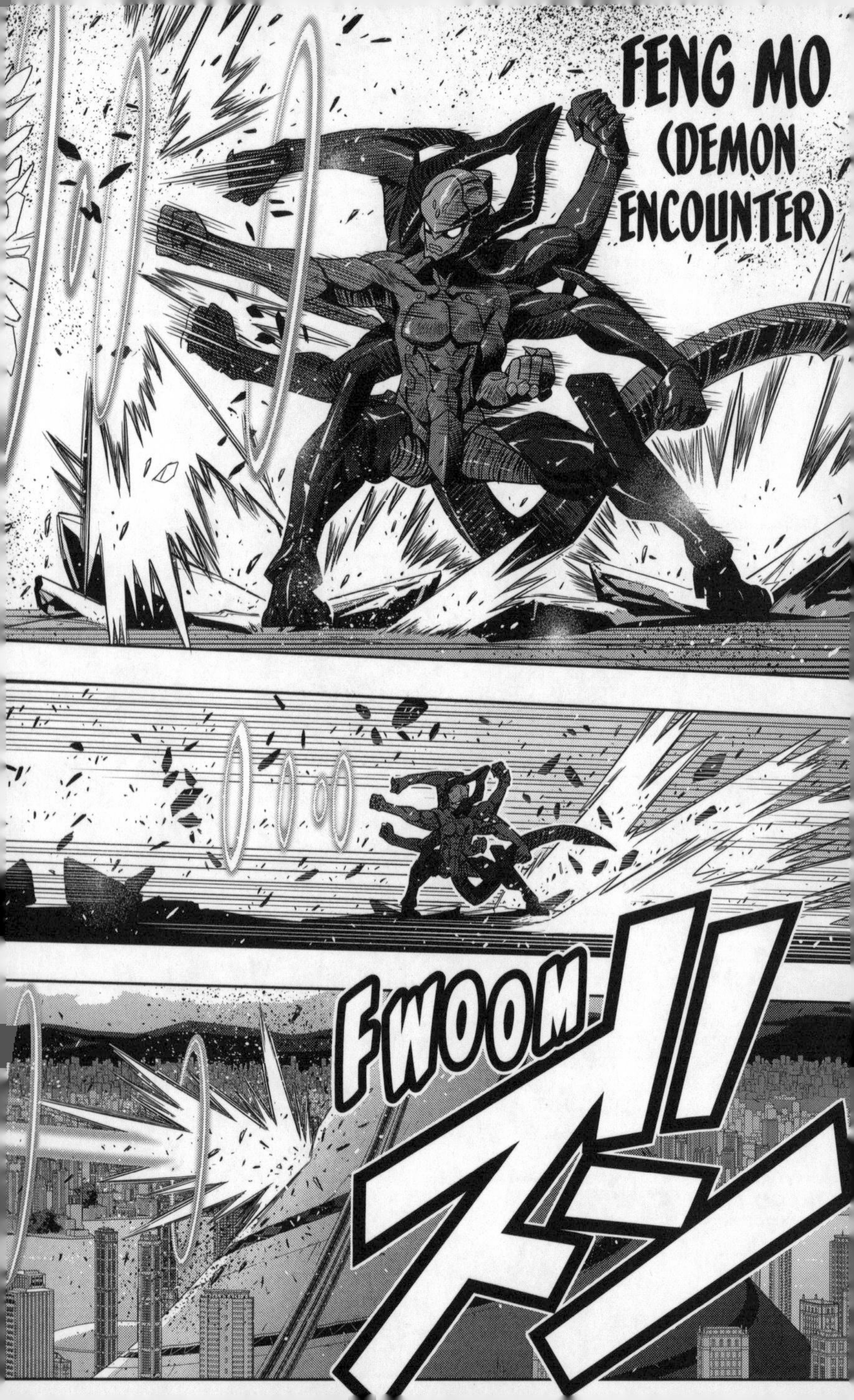
FENG MO
(DEMON ENCOUNTER)
FWOOM

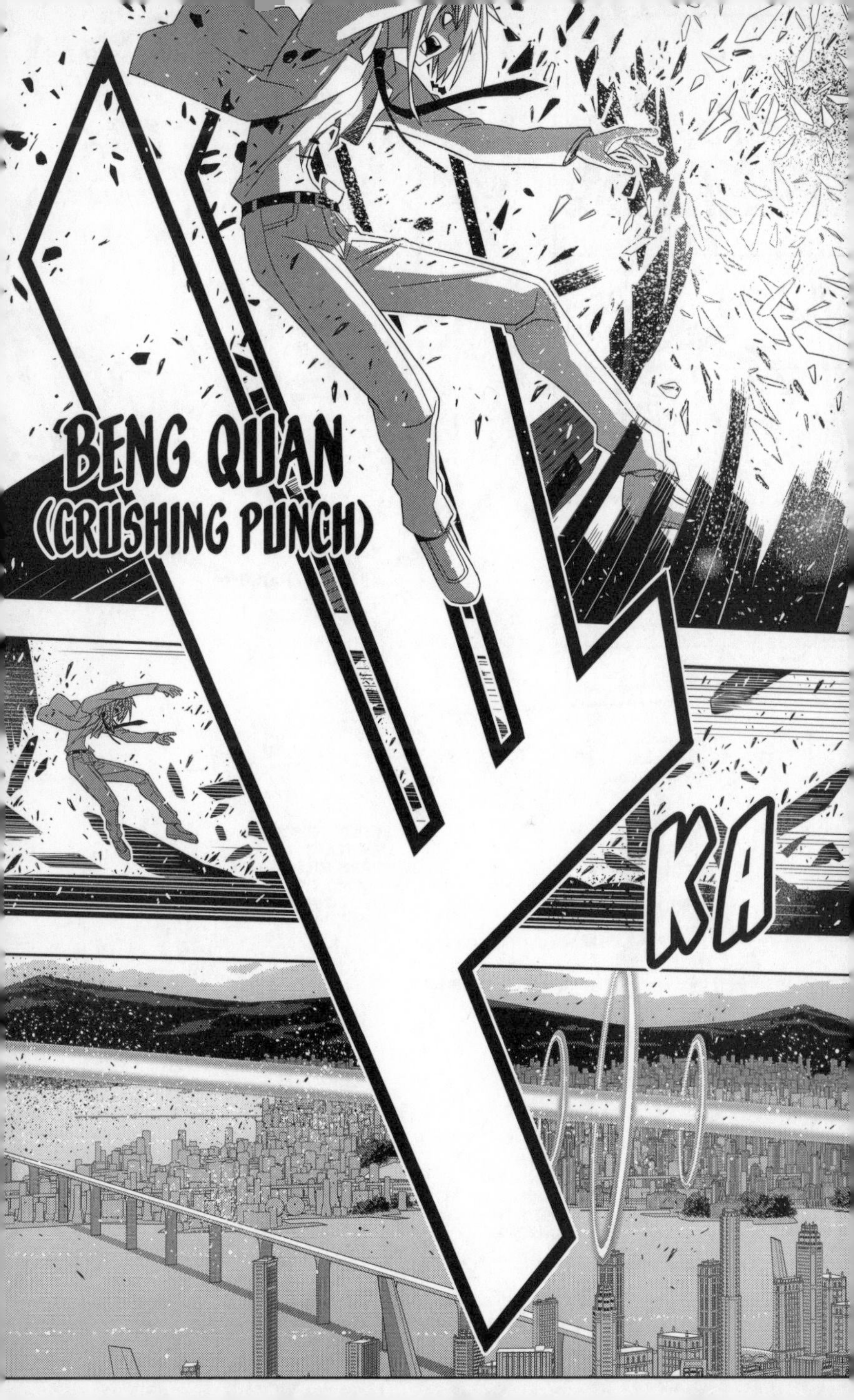
BENG QUAN
(CRUSHING PUNCH)
KA

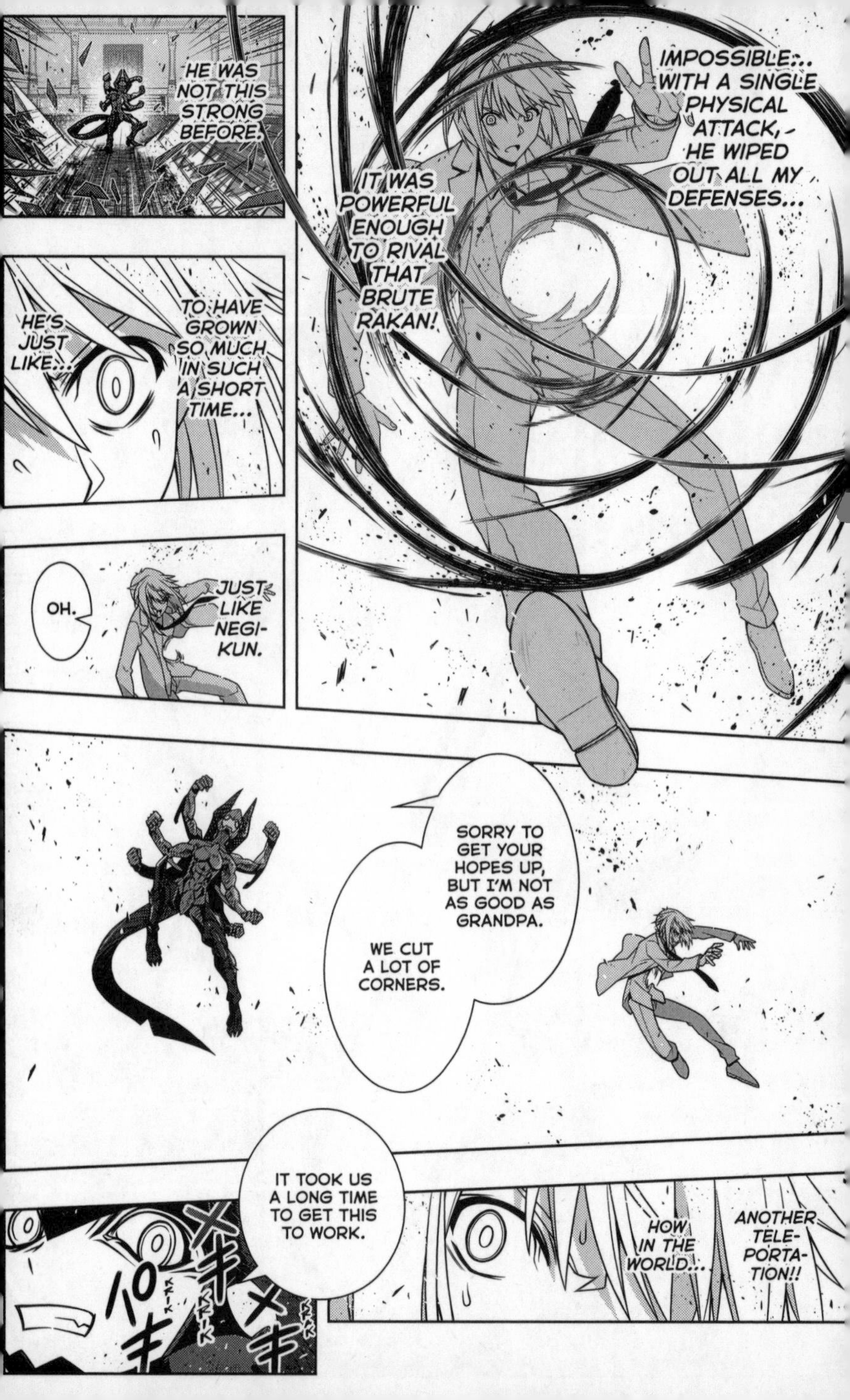
IMPOSSIBLE... WITH A SINGLE PHYSICAL ATTACK, HE WIPED OUT ALL MY DEFENSES...
IT WAS POWERFUL ENOUGH TO RIVAL THAT BRUTE RAKAN!
HE WAS NOT THIS STRONG BEFORE.
TO HAVE GROWN SO MUCH IN SUCH A SHORT TIME...
HE'S JUST LIKE...
JUST LIKE NEGI-KUN.
OH.
SORRY TO GET YOUR HOPES UP, BUT I'M NOT AS GOOD AS GRANDPA.
WE CUT A LOT OF CORNERS.
IT TOOK US A LONG TIME TO GET THIS TO WORK.
ANOTHER TELE-PORTATION!!
HOW IN THE WORLD...
メキ
KRIK
パキ
KRIK
メキ
KRAK

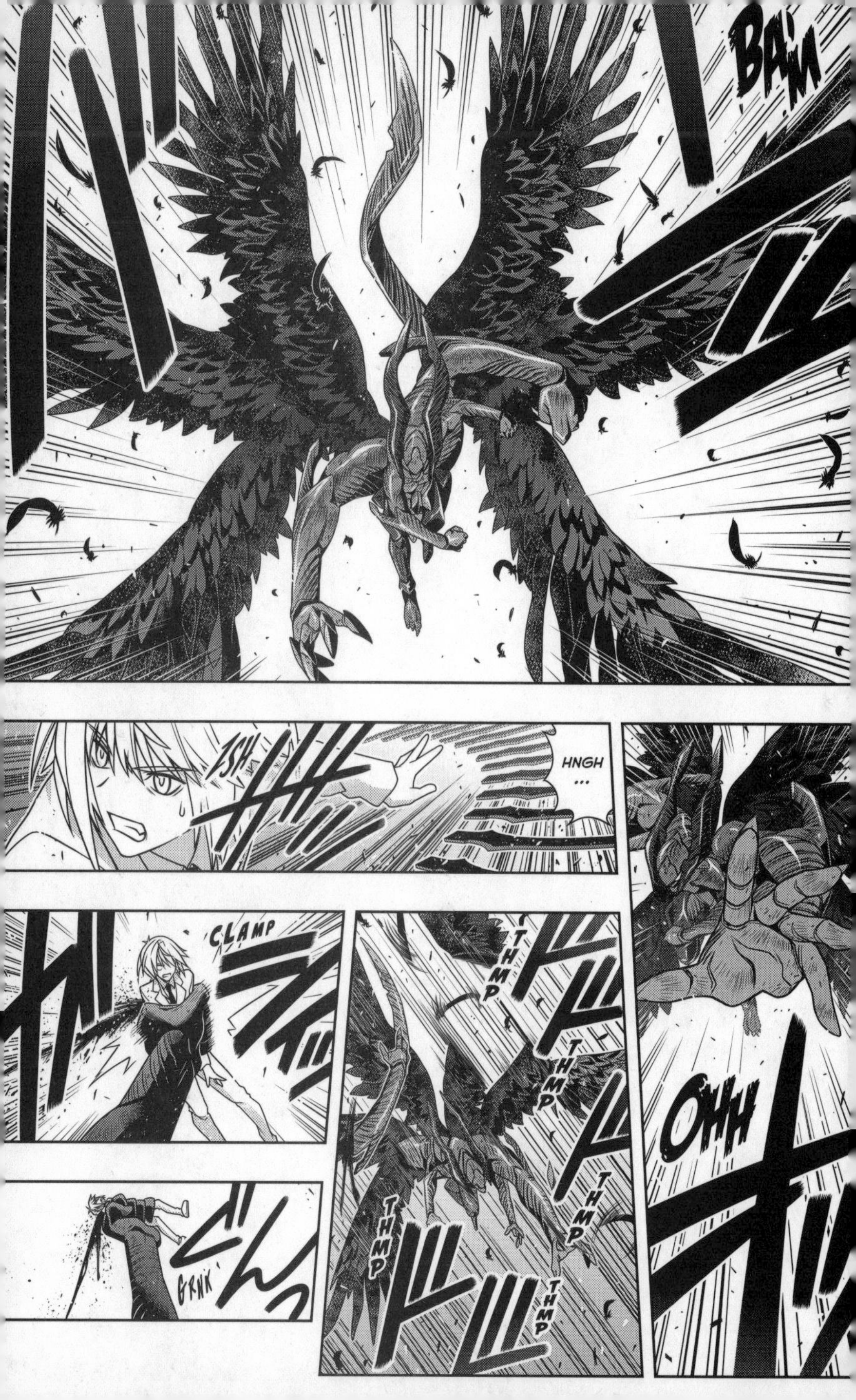
BAM
OHH
HNGH ...
TSH
THMP
THMP
THMP
THMP
CLAMP
GRNK

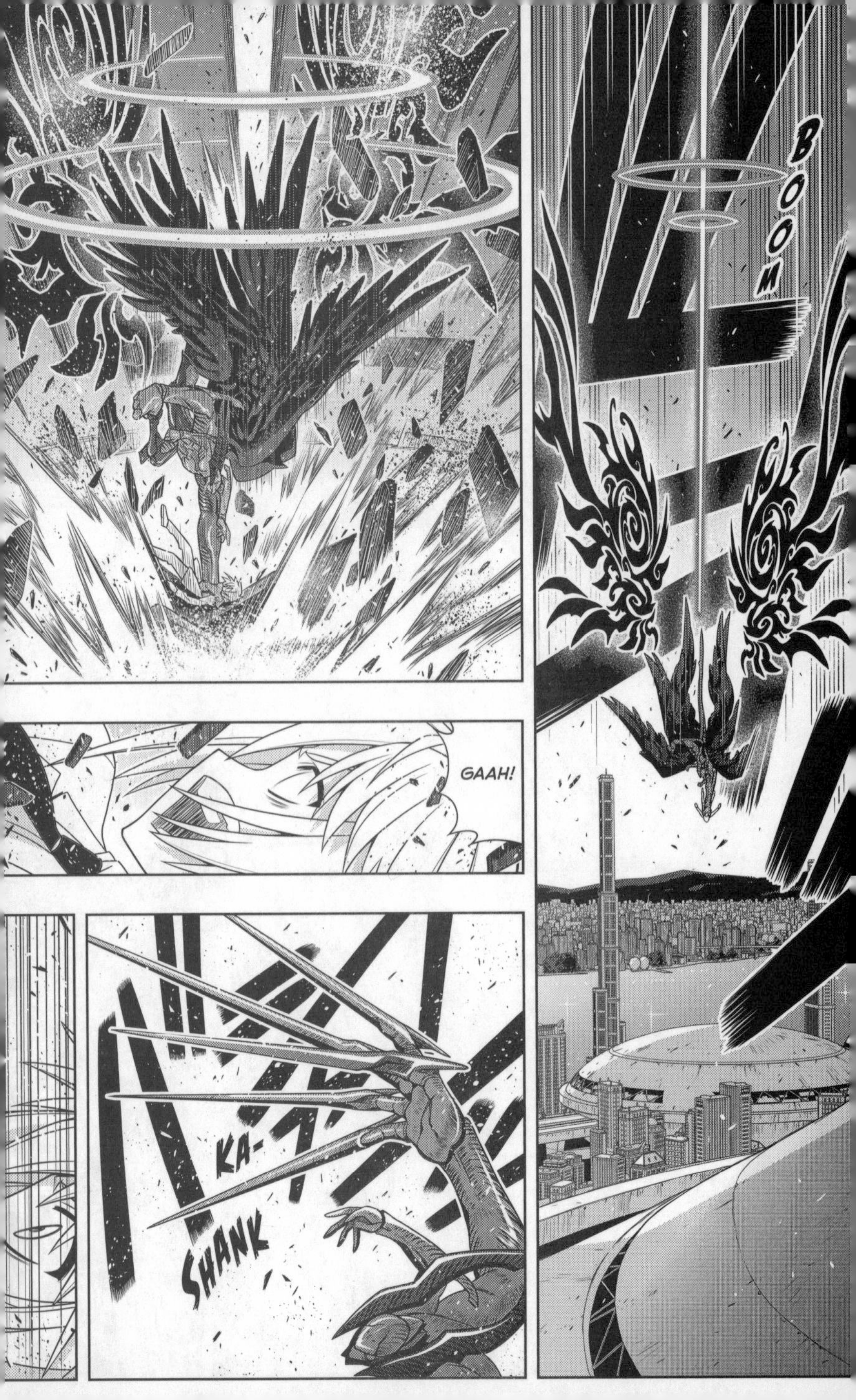
BOOOM
GAAH!
KA-SHANK

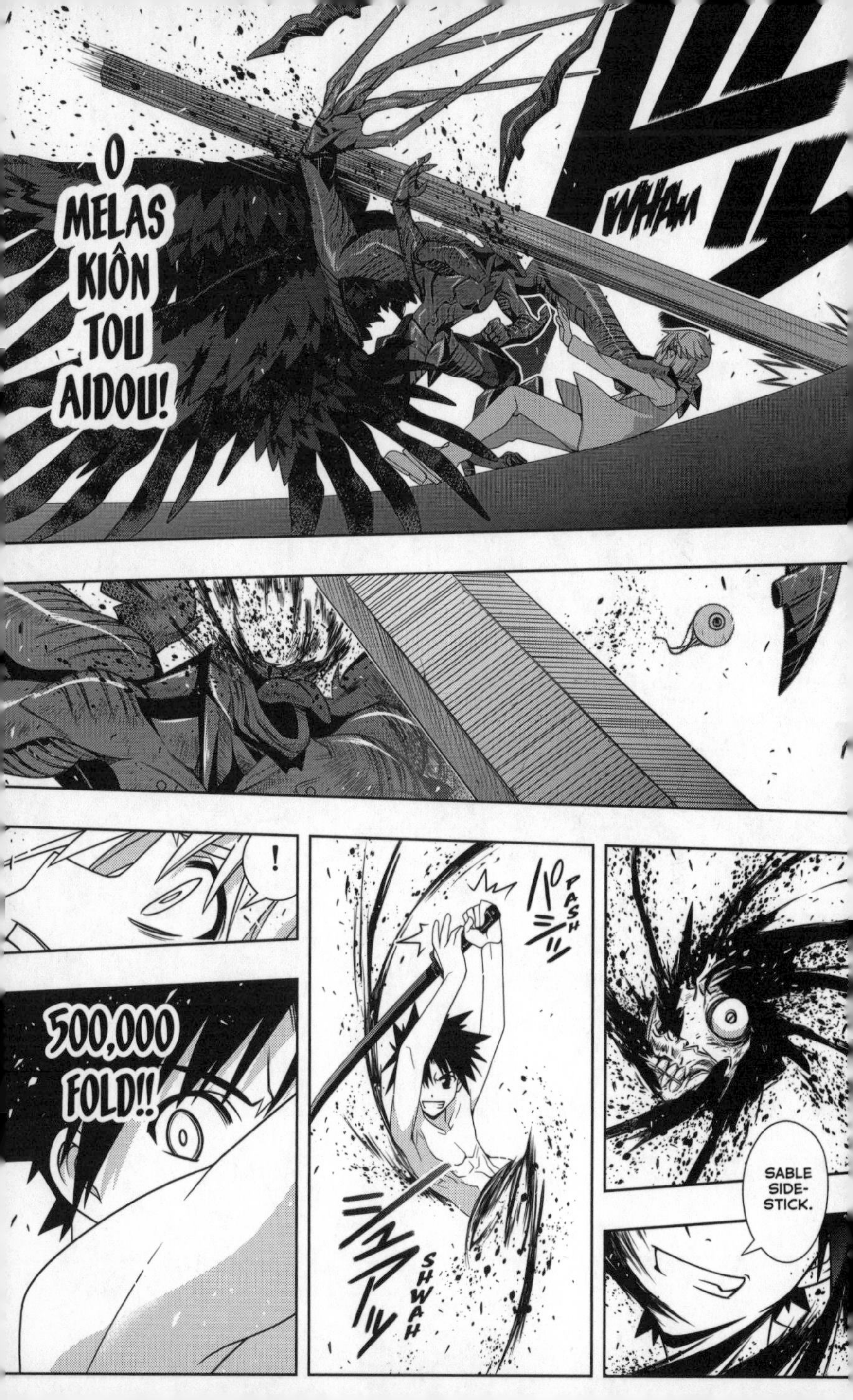
WHAM
O MELAS KIÔN TOU AIDOU!
SABLE SIDE-STICK.
PASH
SHWAH
!
500,000 FOLD!!

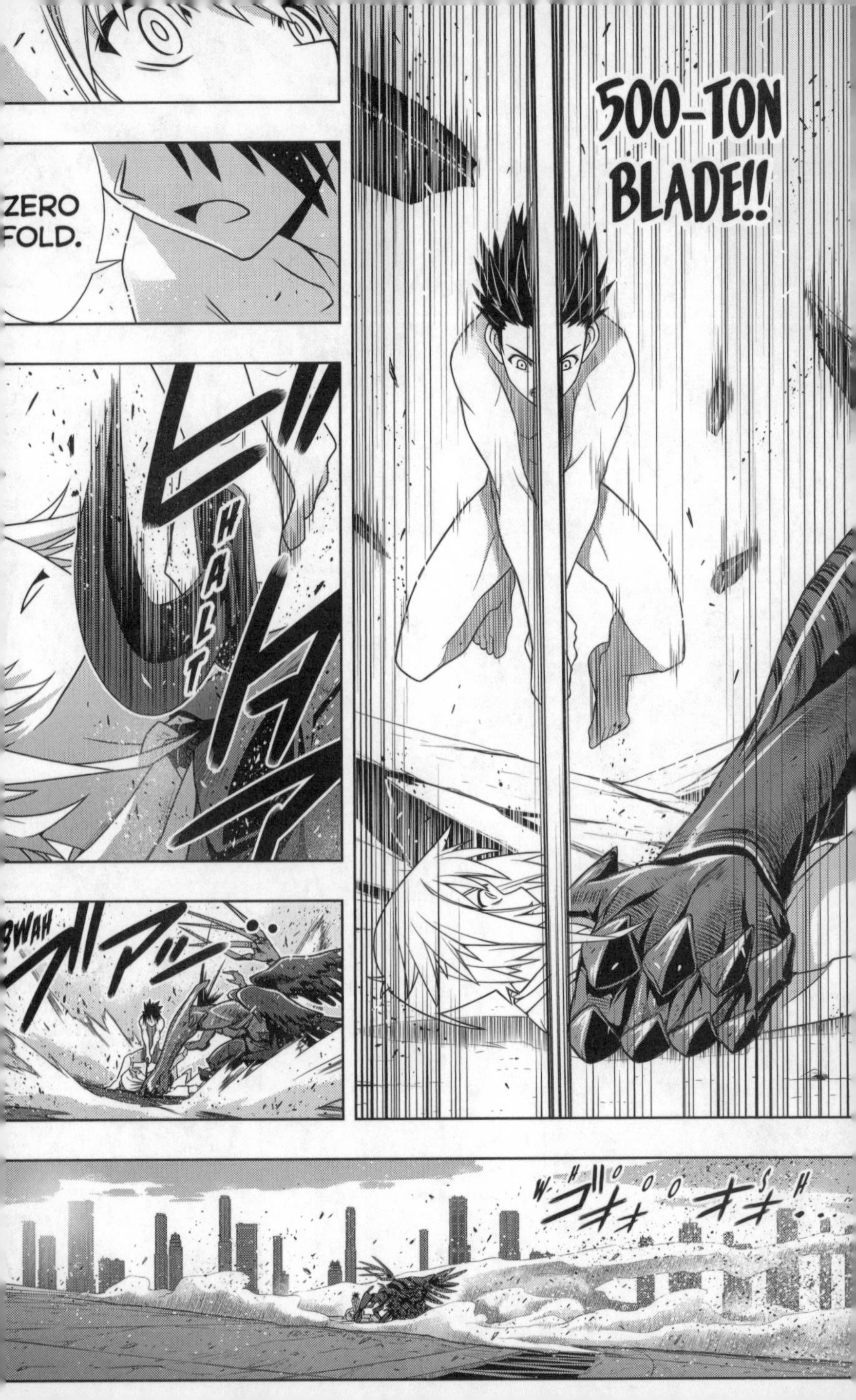
500-TON BLADE!!
ZERO FOLD.
HALT
BWAH
WHOOSH

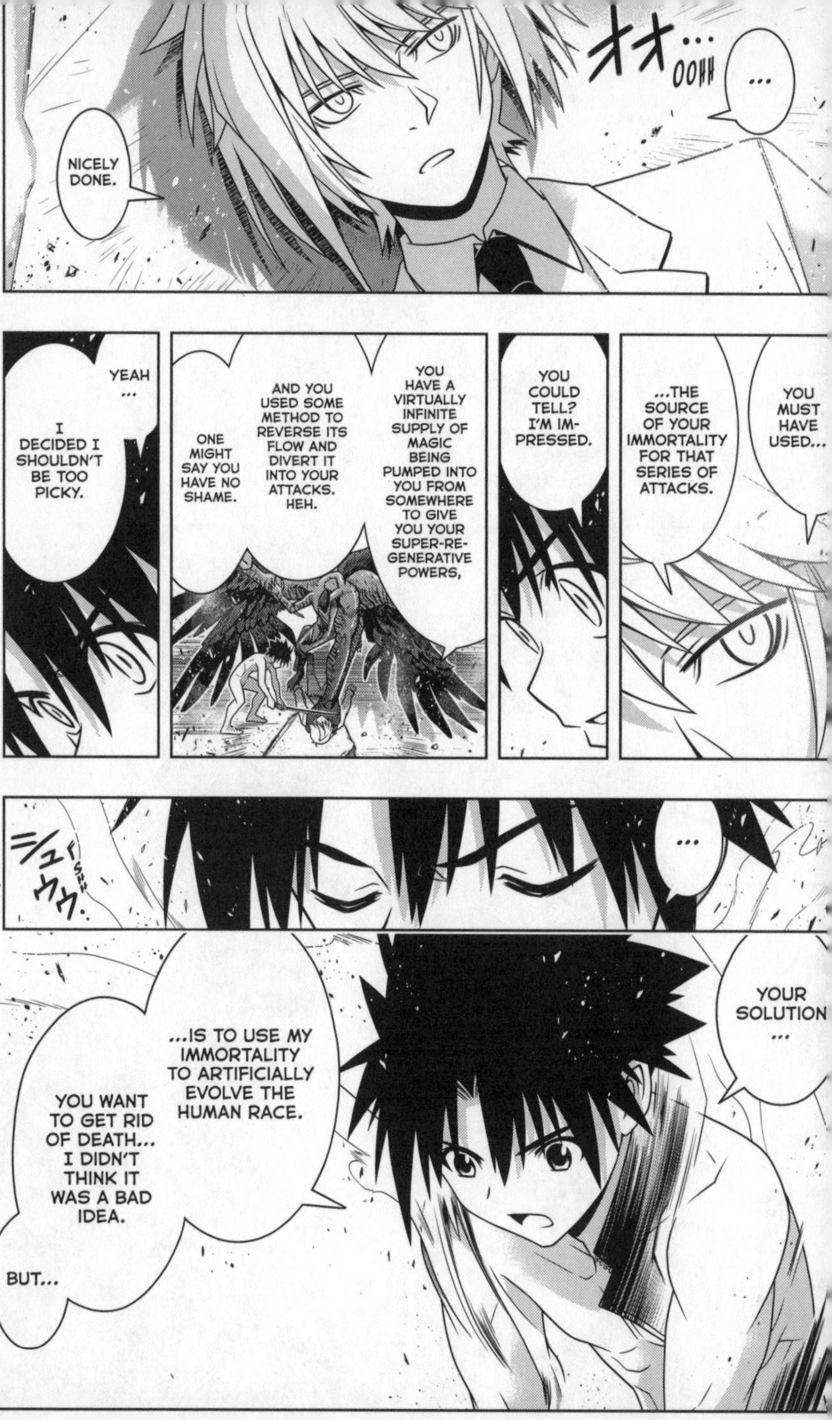
...
オオ…
OOHH
NICELY DONE.
YOU MUST HAVE USED...
...THE SOURCE OF YOUR IMMORTALITY FOR THAT SERIES OF ATTACKS.
YOU COULD TELL? I'M IM-PRESSED.
YOU HAVE A VIRTUALLY INFINITE SUPPLY OF MAGIC BEING PUMPED INTO YOU FROM SOMEWHERE TO GIVE YOU YOUR SUPER-RE-GENERATIVE POWERS,
AND YOU USED SOME METHOD TO REVERSE ITS FLOW AND DIVERT IT INTO YOUR ATTACKS. HEH.
ONE MIGHT SAY YOU HAVE NO SHAME.
YEAH ...
I DECIDED I SHOULDN'T BE TOO PICKY.
...
シュウウ
FSHH
YOUR SOLUTION ...
...IS TO USE MY IMMORTALITY TO ARTIFICIALLY EVOLVE THE HUMAN RACE.
YOU WANT TO GET RID OF DEATH... I DIDN'T THINK IT WAS A BAD IDEA.
BUT...

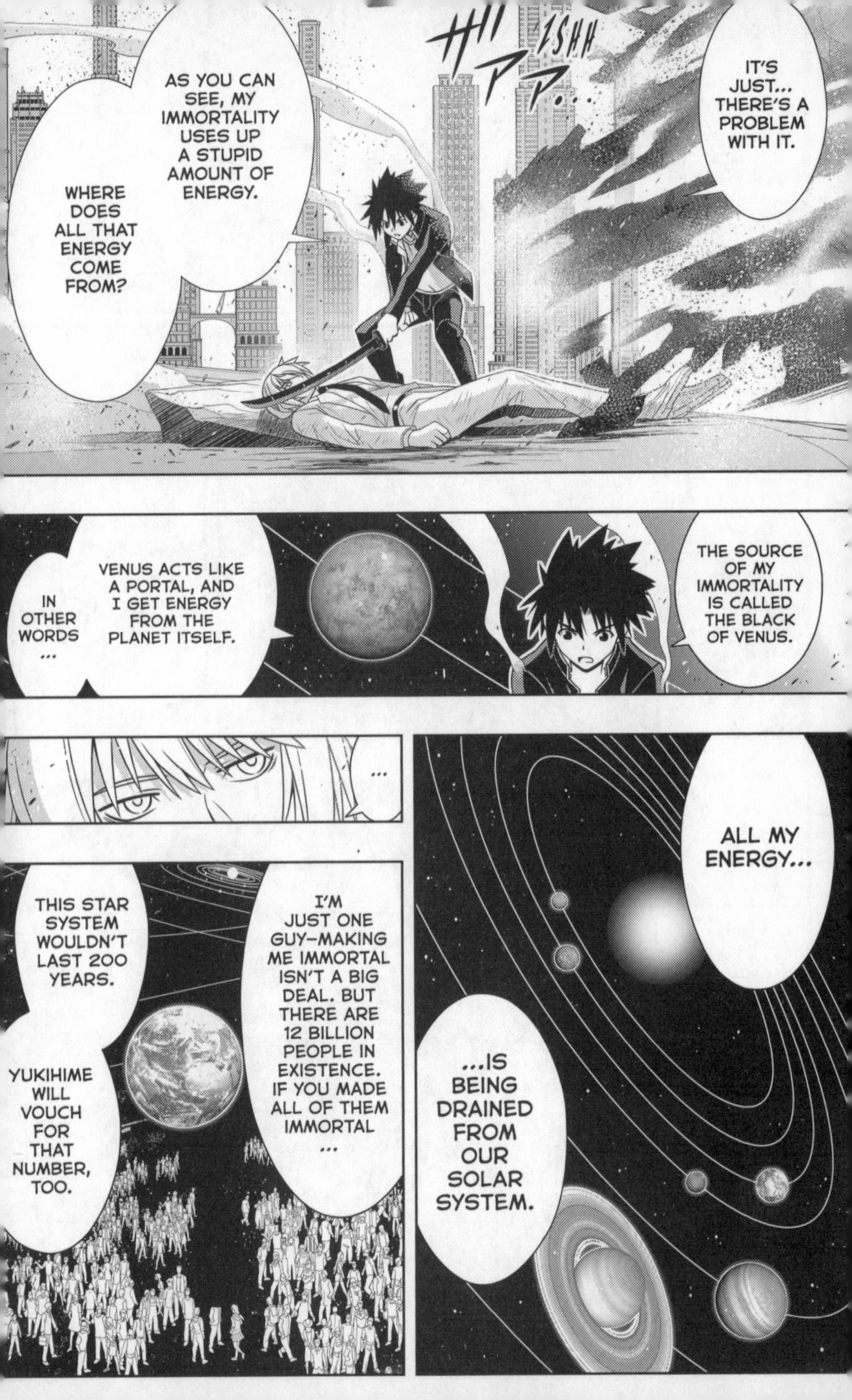
IT'S JUST... THERE'S A PROBLEM WITH IT.
AS YOU CAN SEE, MY IMMORTALITY USES UP A STUPID AMOUNT OF ENERGY.
WHERE DOES ALL THAT ENERGY COME FROM?
THE SOURCE OF MY IMMORTALITY IS CALLED THE BLACK OF VENUS.
VENUS ACTS LIKE A PORTAL, AND I GET ENERGY FROM THE PLANET ITSELF.
IN OTHER WORDS ...
ALL MY ENERGY...
...IS BEING DRAINED FROM OUR SOLAR SYSTEM.
...
I'M JUST ONE GUY—MAKING ME IMMORTAL ISN'T A BIG DEAL. BUT THERE ARE 12 BILLION PEOPLE IN EXISTENCE. IF YOU MADE ALL OF THEM IMMORTAL ...
THIS STAR SYSTEM WOULDN'T LAST 200 YEARS.
YUKIHIME WILL VOUCH FOR THAT NUMBER, TOO.

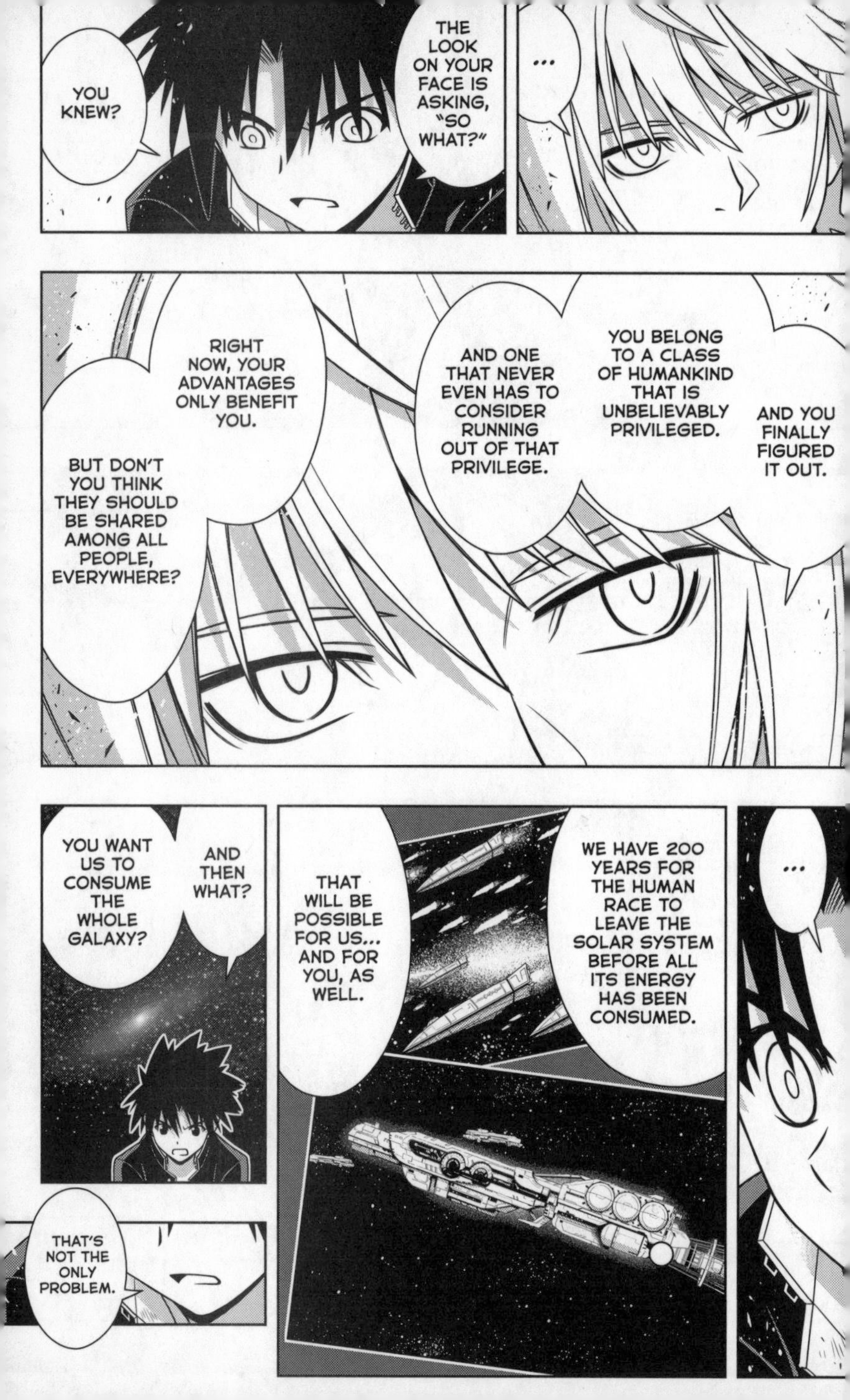
...
THE LOOK ON YOUR FACE IS ASKING, "SO WHAT?"
YOU KNEW?
AND YOU FINALLY FIGURED IT OUT.
YOU BELONG TO A CLASS OF HUMANKIND THAT IS UNBELIEVABLY PRIVILEGED.
AND ONE THAT NEVER EVEN HAS TO CONSIDER RUNNING OUT OF THAT PRIVILEGE.
RIGHT NOW, YOUR ADVANTAGES ONLY BENEFIT YOU.
BUT DON'T YOU THINK THEY SHOULD BE SHARED AMONG ALL PEOPLE, EVERYWHERE?
...
WE HAVE 200 YEARS FOR THE HUMAN RACE TO LEAVE THE SOLAR SYSTEM BEFORE ALL ITS ENERGY HAS BEEN CONSUMED.
THAT WILL BE POSSIBLE FOR US... AND FOR YOU, AS WELL.
AND THEN WHAT?
YOU WANT US TO CONSUME THE WHOLE GALAXY?
THAT'S NOT THE ONLY PROBLEM.

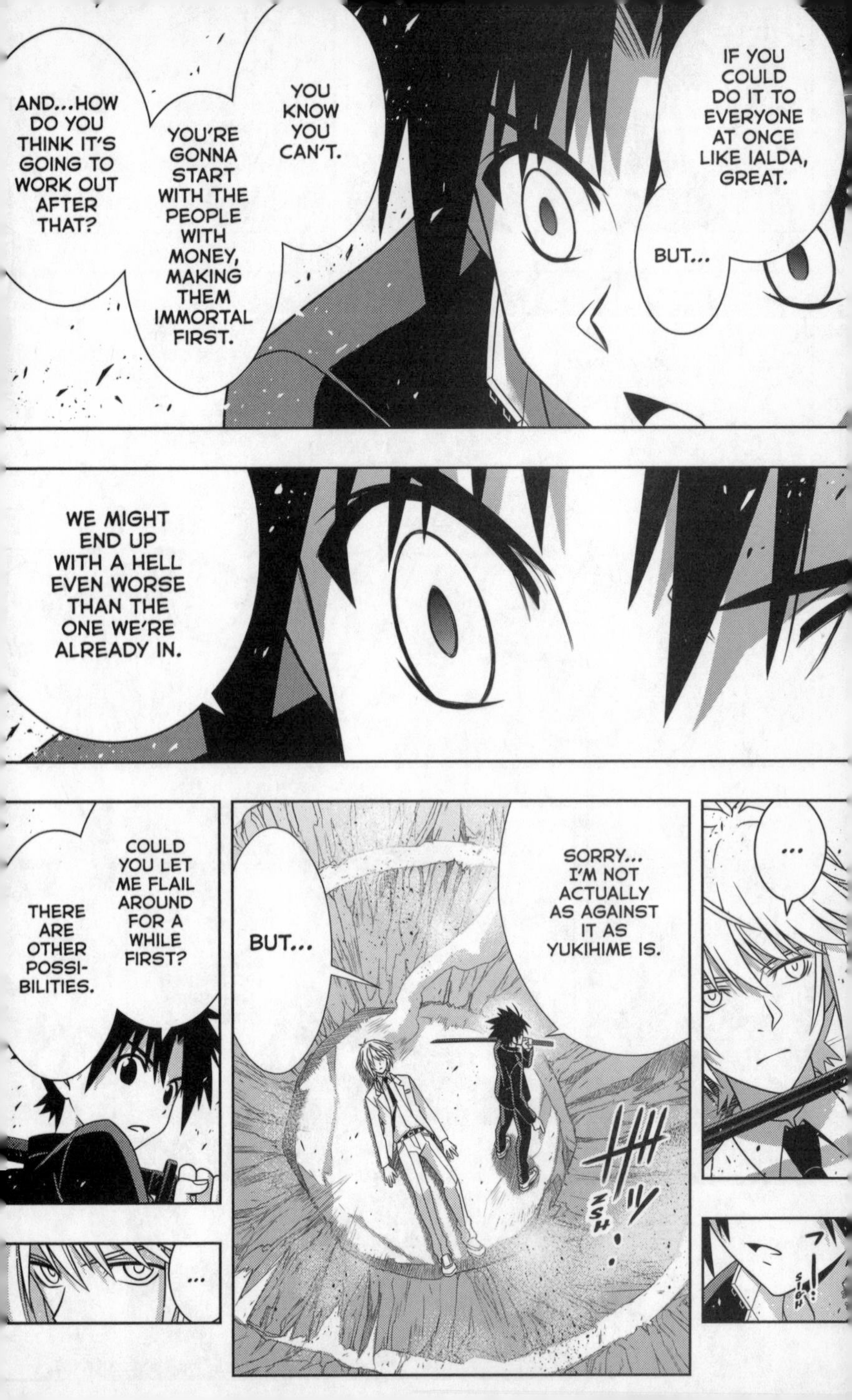
IF YOU COULD DO IT TO EVERYONE AT ONCE LIKE IALDA, GREAT.
BUT...
YOU KNOW YOU CAN'T.
YOU'RE GONNA START WITH THE PEOPLE WITH MONEY, MAKING THEM IMMORTAL FIRST.
AND...HOW DO YOU THINK IT'S GOING TO WORK OUT AFTER THAT?
WE MIGHT END UP WITH A HELL EVEN WORSE THAN THE ONE WE'RE ALREADY IN.
...
SIGH
SORRY... I'M NOT ACTUALLY AS AGAINST IT AS YUKIHIME IS.
BUT...
ZSH
COULD YOU LET ME FLAIL AROUND FOR A WHILE FIRST?
THERE ARE OTHER POSSIBILITIES.
...

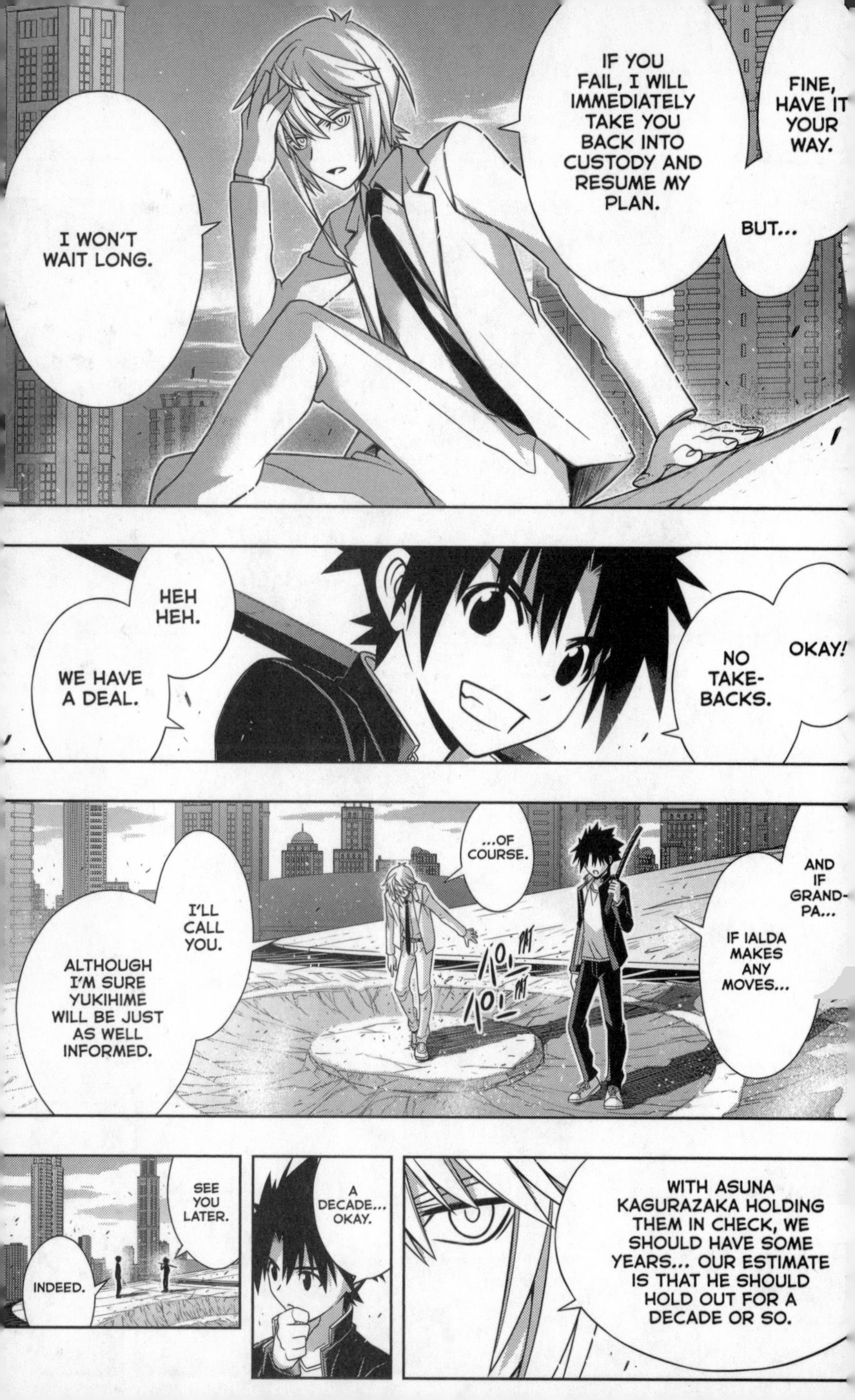
FINE, HAVE IT YOUR WAY.
BUT...
IF YOU FAIL, I WILL IMMEDIATELY TAKE YOU BACK INTO CUSTODY AND RESUME MY PLAN.
I WON'T WAIT LONG.
OKAY!
NO TAKE-BACKS.
HEH HEH.
WE HAVE A DEAL.
AND IF GRAND-PA...
IF IALDA MAKES ANY MOVES...
...OF COURSE.
PAT
PAT
I'LL CALL YOU.
ALTHOUGH I'M SURE YUKIHIME WILL BE JUST AS WELL INFORMED.
WITH ASUNA KAGURAZAKA HOLDING THEM IN CHECK, WE SHOULD HAVE SOME YEARS... OUR ESTIMATE IS THAT HE SHOULD HOLD OUT FOR A DECADE OR SO.
A DECADE... OKAY.
SEE YOU LATER.
INDEED.

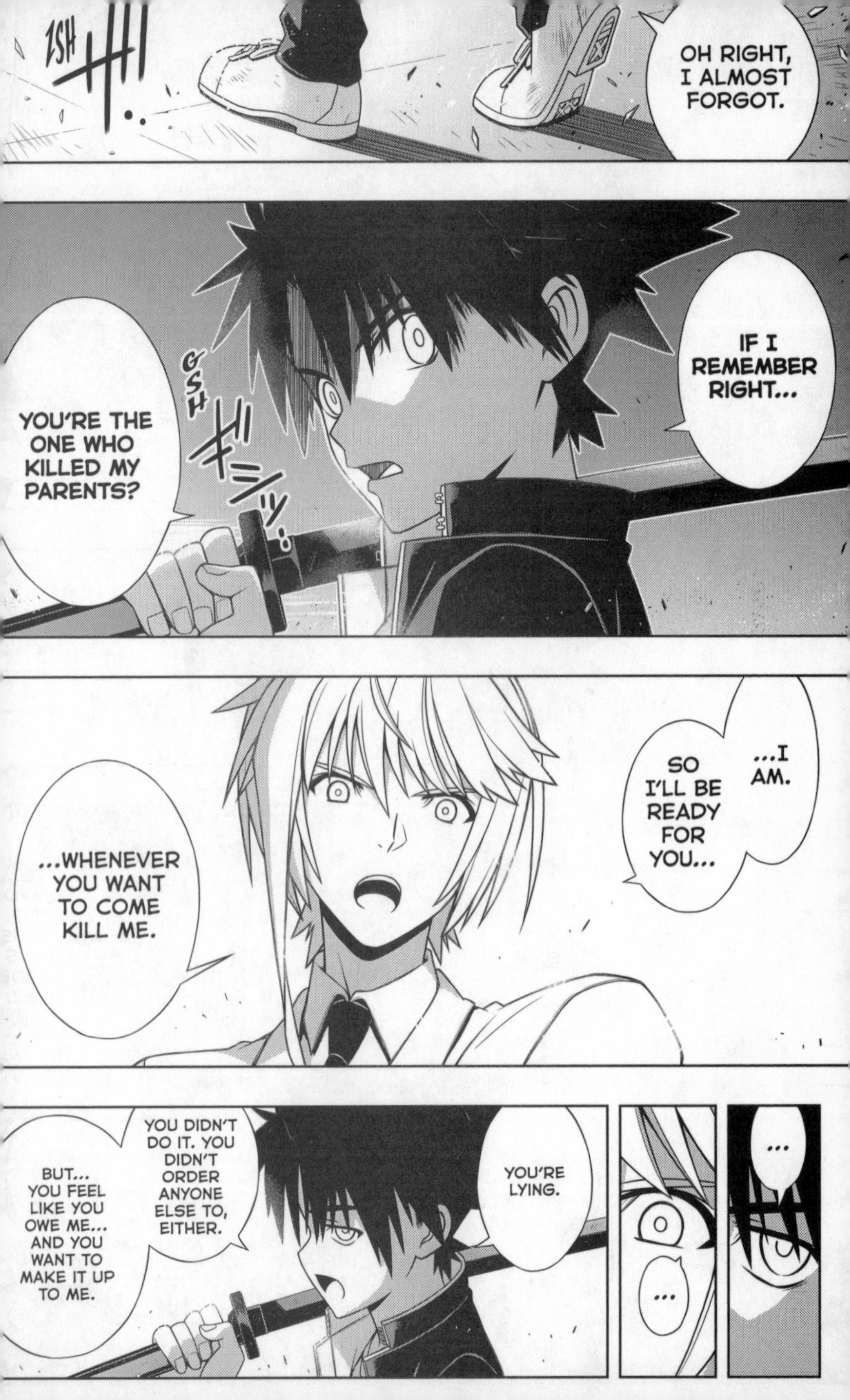
ZSH
OH RIGHT, I ALMOST FORGOT.
IF I REMEMBER RIGHT...
GSH
YOU'RE THE ONE WHO KILLED MY PARENTS?
...I AM.
SO I'LL BE READY FOR YOU...
...WHENEVER YOU WANT TO COME KILL ME.
...
...
YOU'RE LYING.
YOU DIDN'T DO IT. YOU DIDN'T ORDER ANYONE ELSE TO, EITHER.
BUT... YOU FEEL LIKE YOU OWE ME... AND YOU WANT TO MAKE IT UP TO ME.

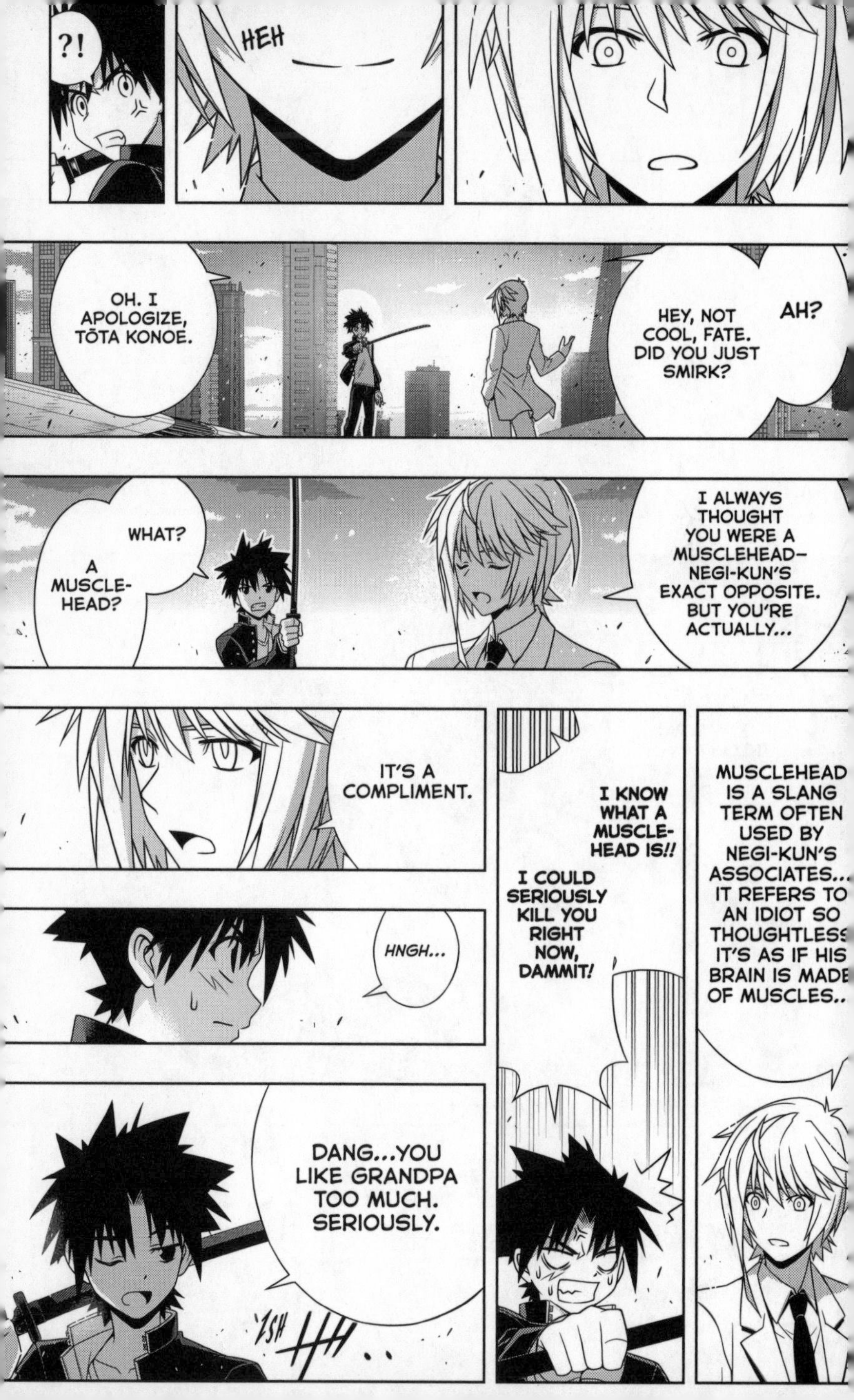
HEH
?!
AH?
HEY, NOT COOL, FATE. DID YOU JUST SMIRK?
OH. I APOLOGIZE, TŌTA KONOE.
I ALWAYS THOUGHT YOU WERE A MUSCLEHEAD— NEGI-KUN'S EXACT OPPOSITE. BUT YOU'RE ACTUALLY...
WHAT?
A MUSCLE-HEAD?
MUSCLEHEAD IS A SLANG TERM OFTEN USED BY NEGI-KUN'S ASSOCIATES... IT REFERS TO AN IDIOT SO THOUGHTLESS IT'S AS IF HIS BRAIN IS MADE OF MUSCLES...
I KNOW WHAT A MUSCLE-HEAD IS!!
I COULD SERIOUSLY KILL YOU RIGHT NOW, DAMMIT!
IT'S A COMPLIMENT.
HNGH...
DANG...YOU LIKE GRANDPA TOO MUCH. SERIOUSLY.
ZSH

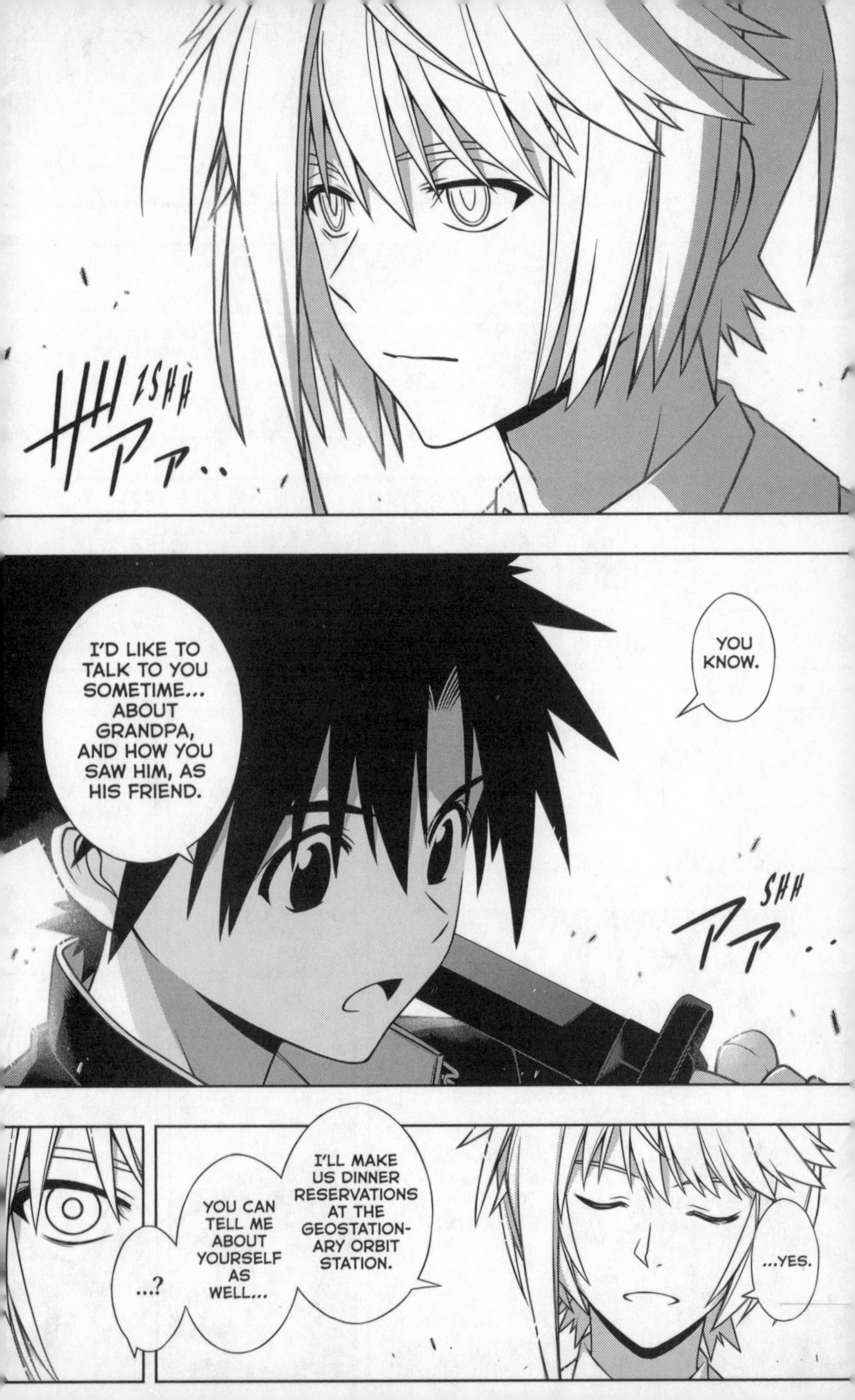
HHISHH
アア..
YOU KNOW.
I'D LIKE TO TALK TO YOU SOMETIME... ABOUT GRANDPA, AND HOW YOU SAW HIM, AS HIS FRIEND.
SHH
アア..
...YES.
I'LL MAKE US DINNER RESERVATIONS AT THE GEOSTATION-ARY ORBIT STATION.
YOU CAN TELL ME ABOUT YOURSELF AS WELL...
...?

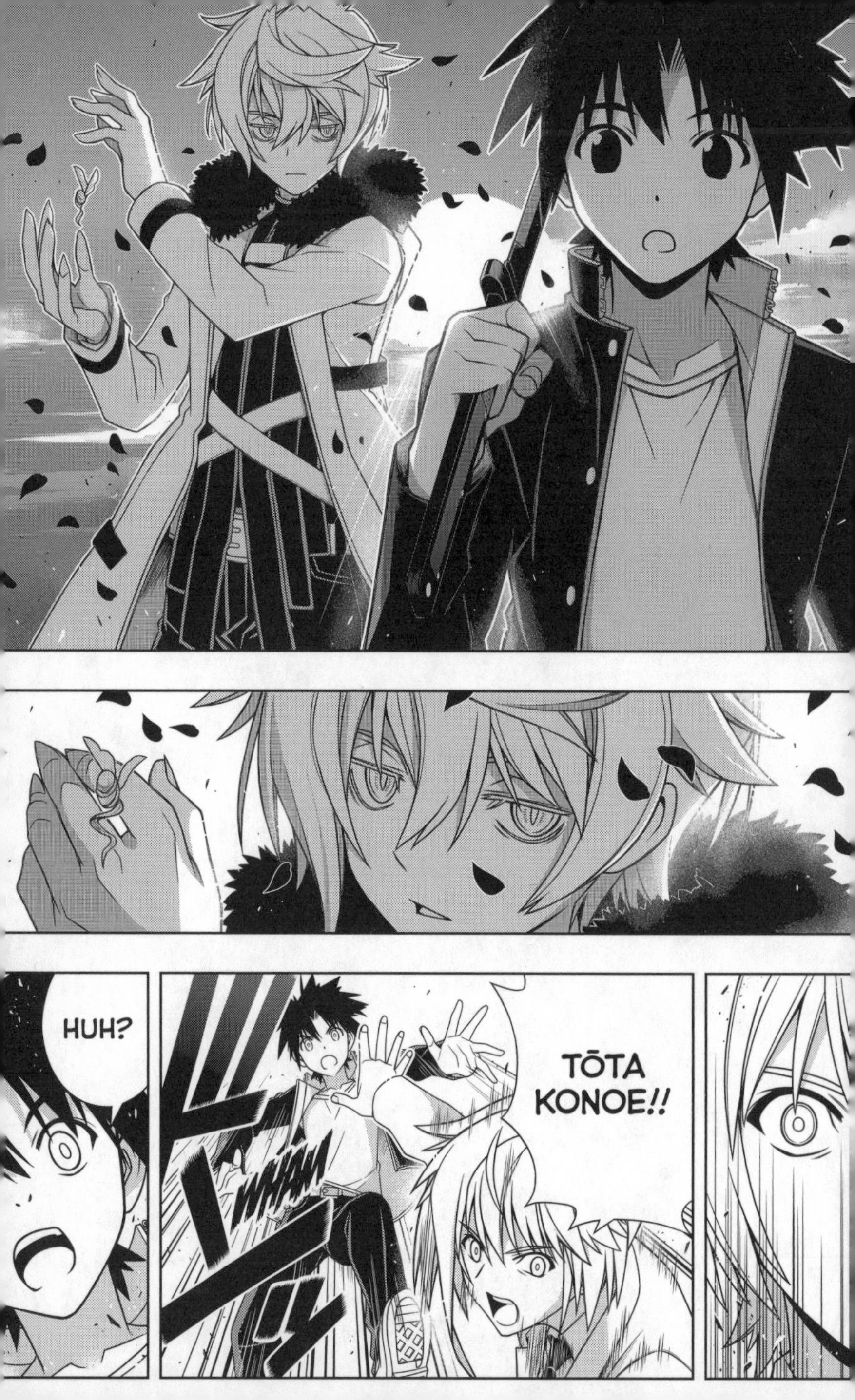
TŌTA KONOE!!
HUH?

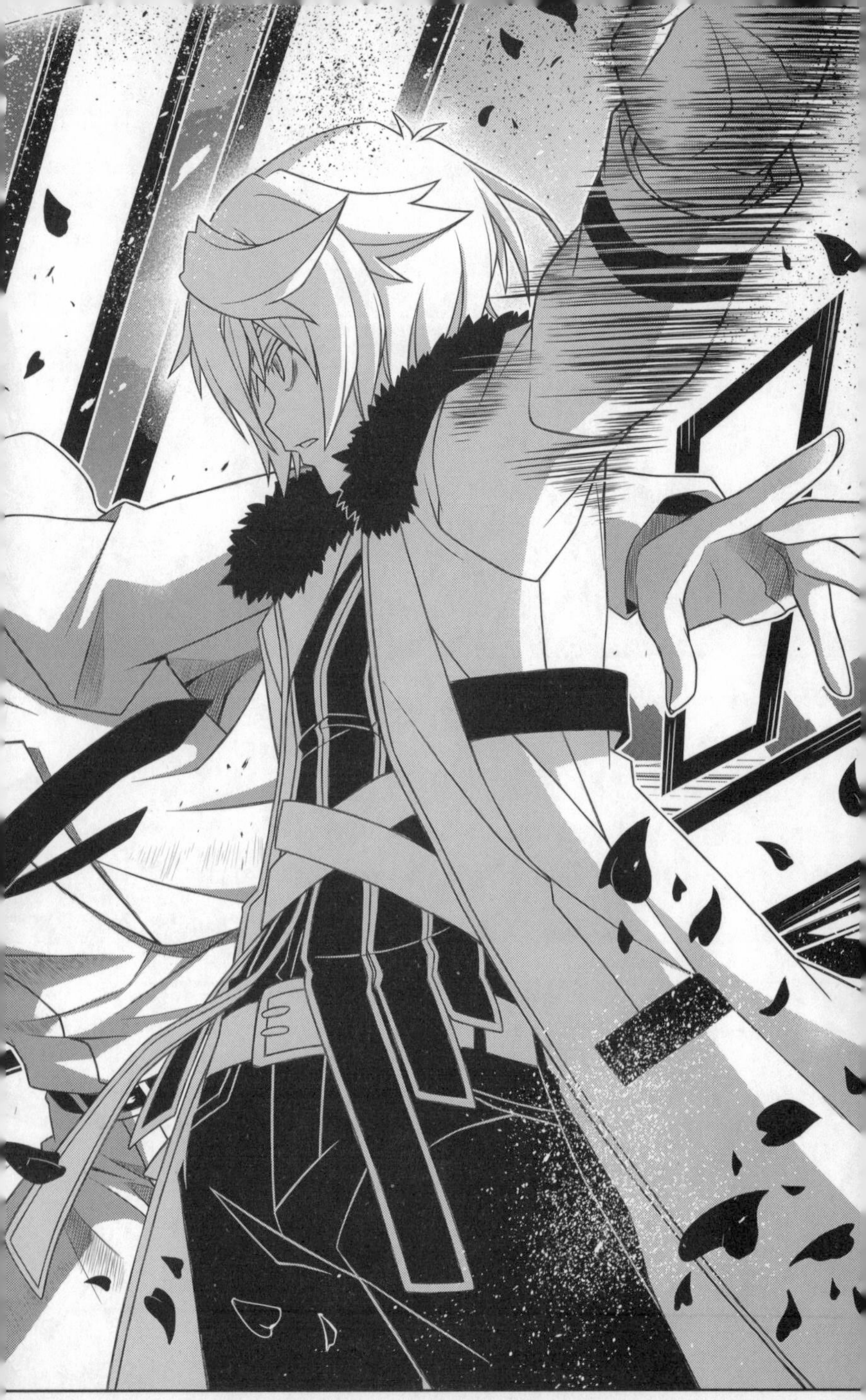

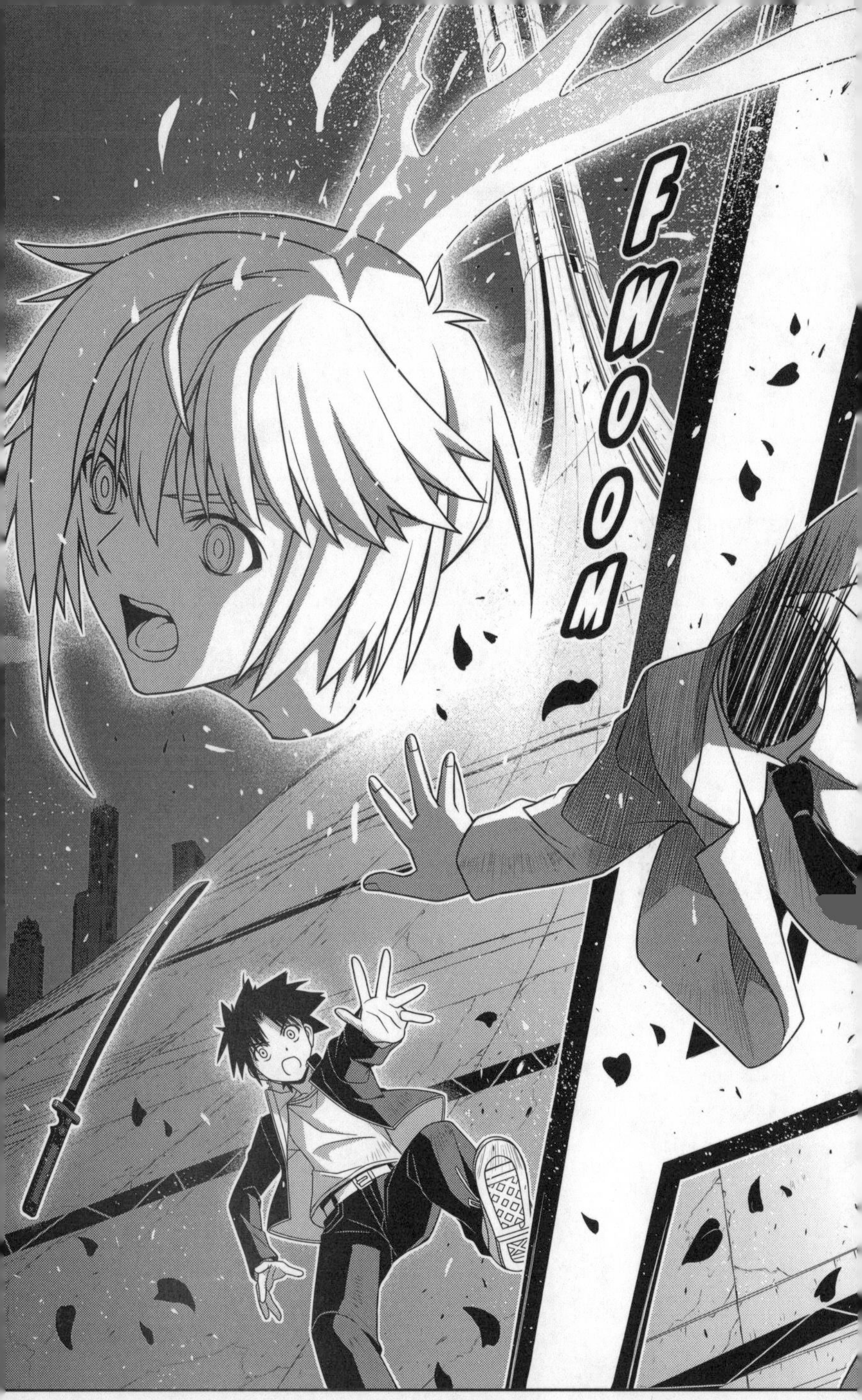
FWOOOM

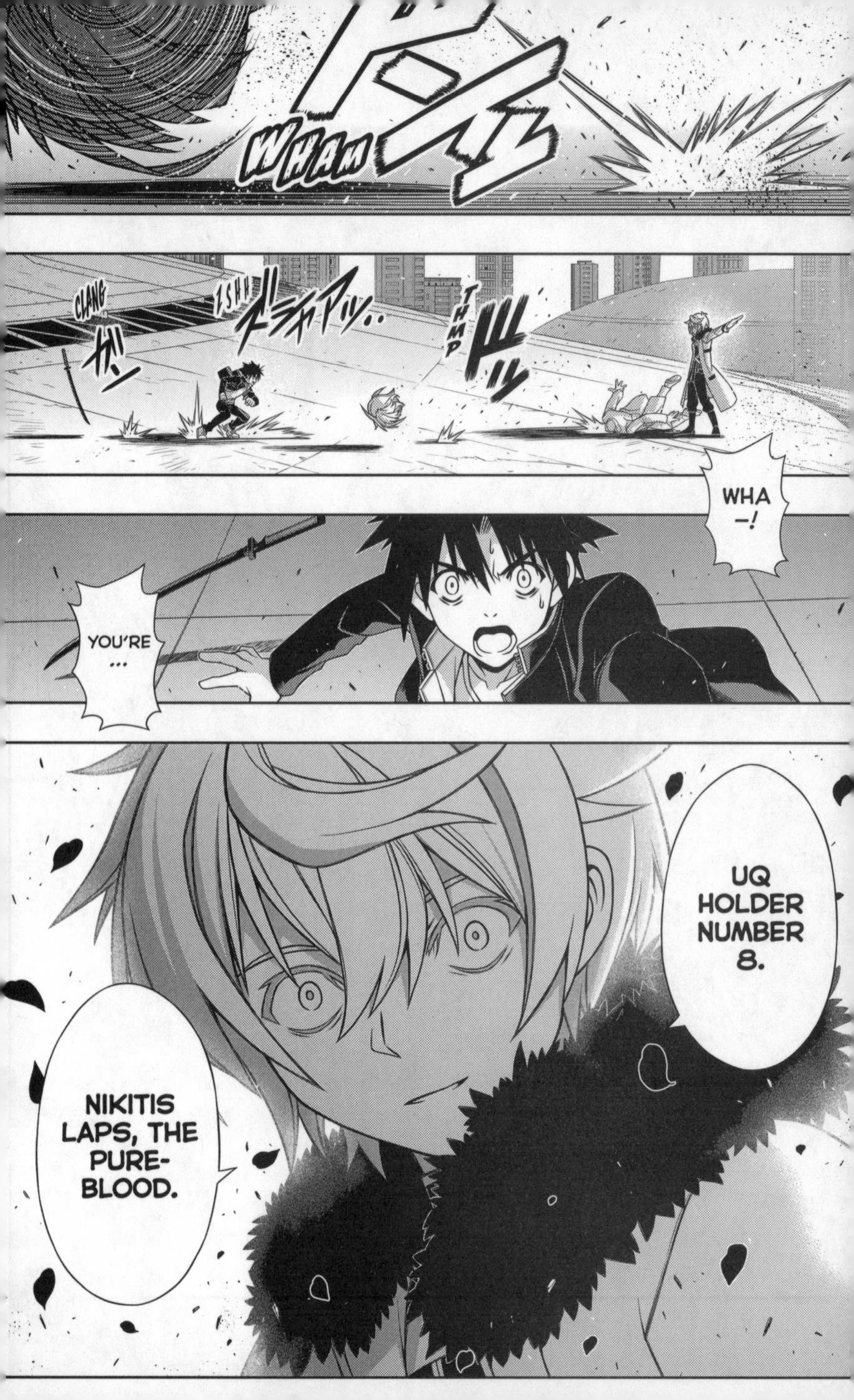
WHAM
THUMP
ZSHH
CLANG
WHA—!
YOU'RE ...
UQ HOLDER NUMBER 8.
NIKITIS LAPS, THE PURE-BLOOD.

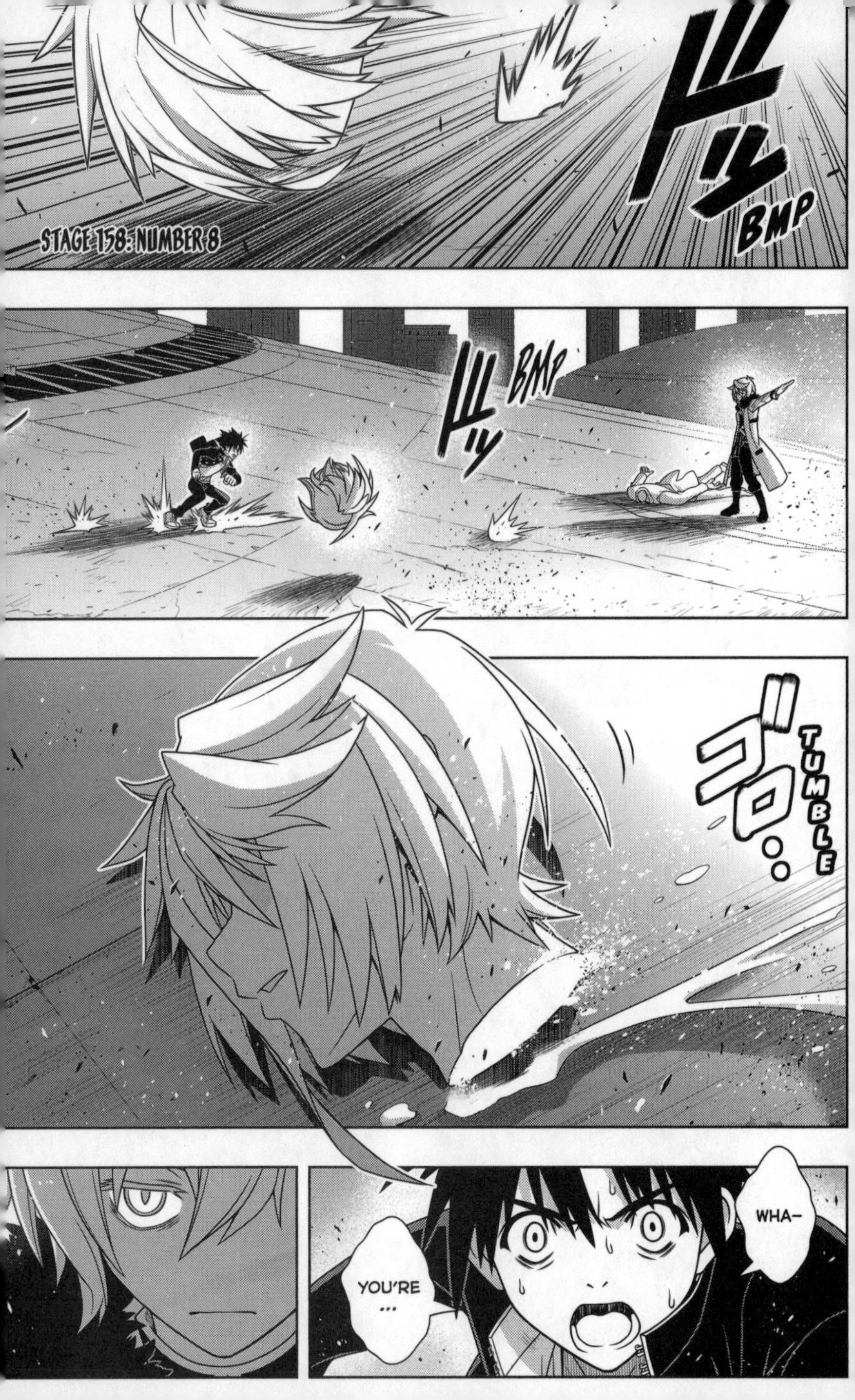
ドム
BMP
STAGE 158: NUMBER 8
ドッ
BMP
ゴロ‥
TUMBLE
WHA—
YOU'RE ...

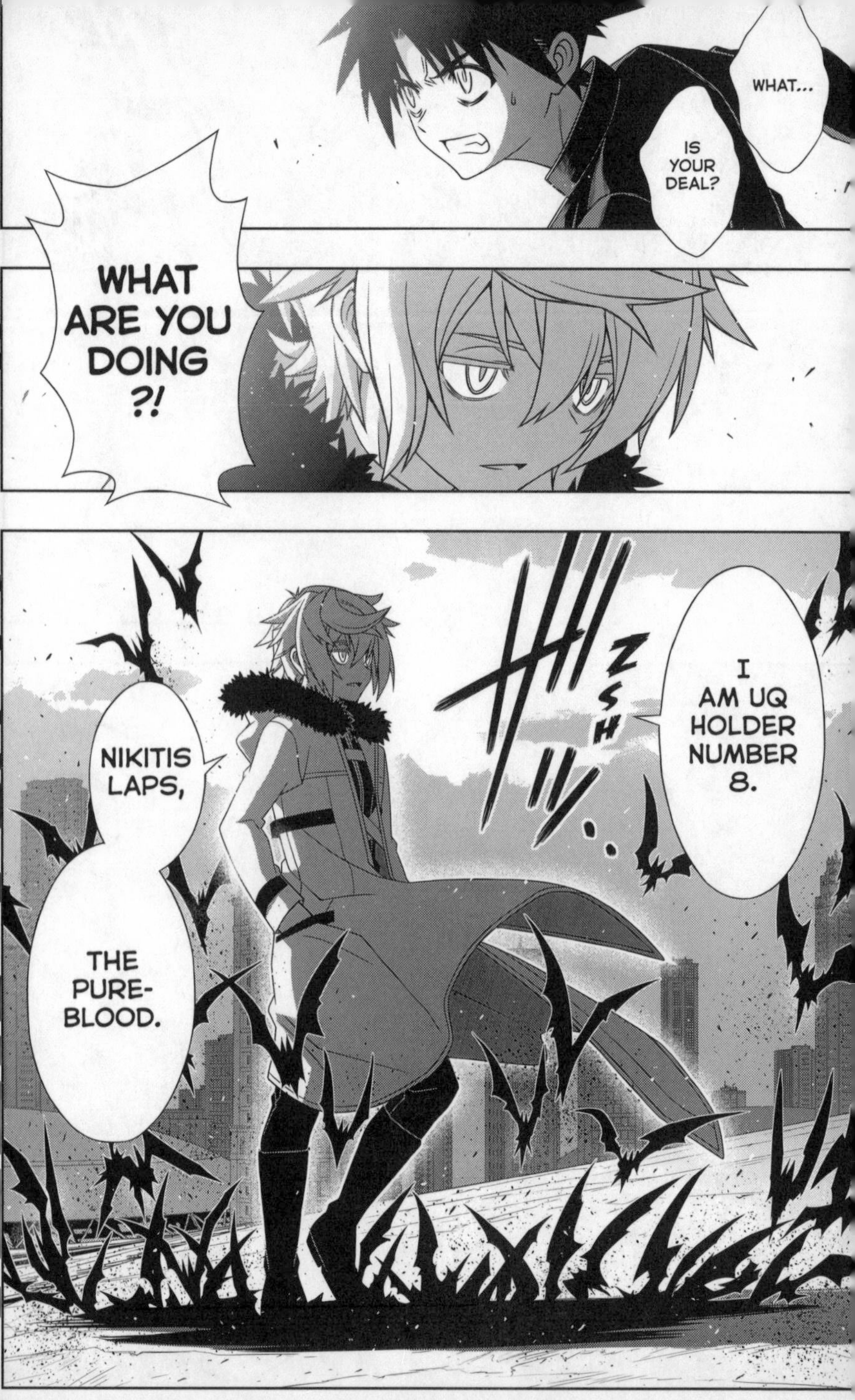
WHAT...
IS YOUR DEAL?
WHAT ARE YOU DOING?!
I AM UQ HOLDER NUMBER 8.
ZSHH
NIKITIS LAPS,
THE PURE-BLOOD.

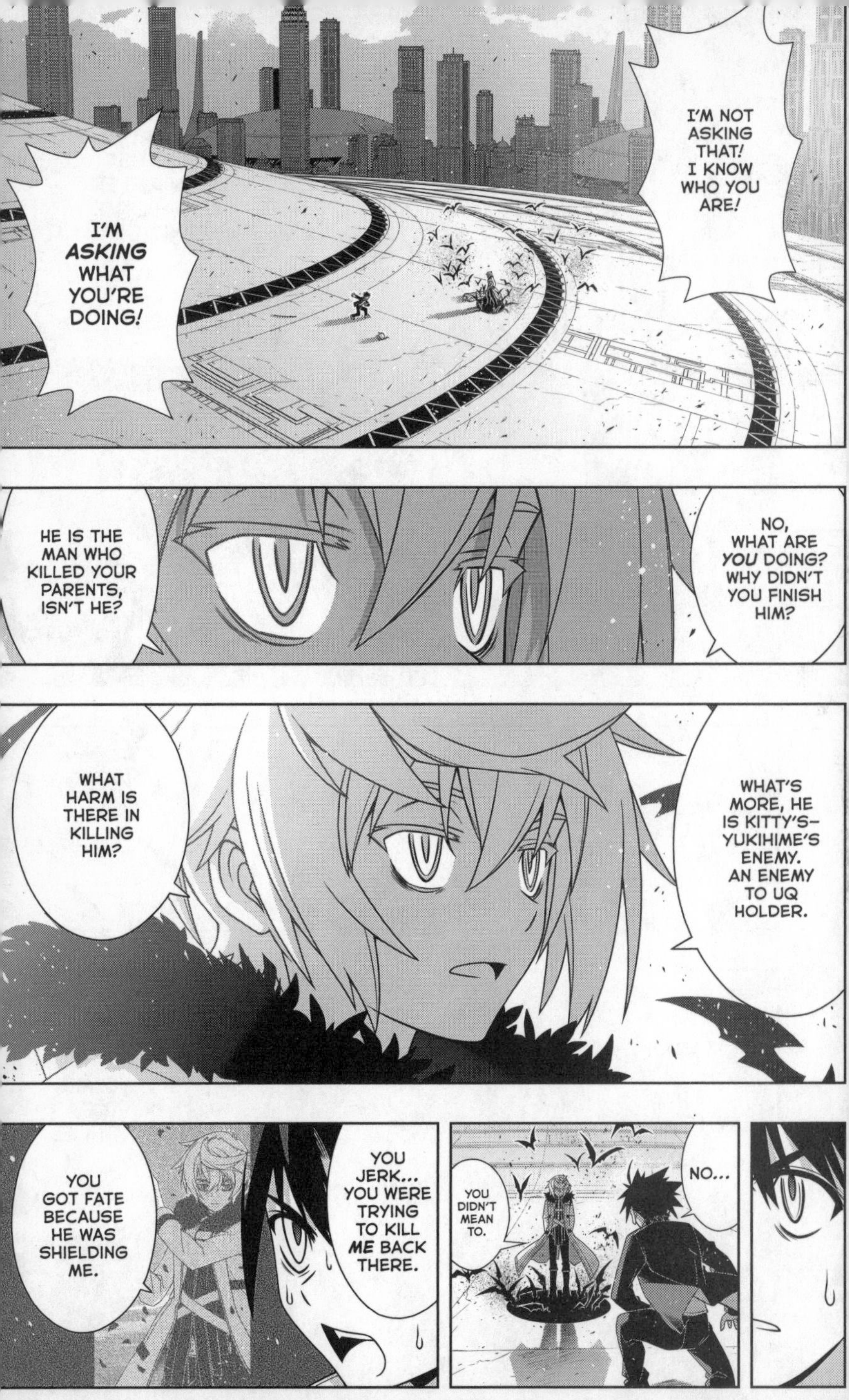
I'M NOT ASKING THAT! I KNOW WHO YOU ARE!
I'M *ASKING* WHAT YOU'RE DOING!
NO, WHAT ARE *YOU* DOING? WHY DIDN'T YOU FINISH HIM?
HE IS THE MAN WHO KILLED YOUR PARENTS, ISN'T HE?
WHAT'S MORE, HE IS KITTY'S— YUKIHIME'S ENEMY. AN ENEMY TO UQ HOLDER.
WHAT HARM IS THERE IN KILLING HIM?
NO...
YOU DIDN'T MEAN TO.
YOU JERK... YOU WERE TRYING TO KILL *ME* BACK THERE.
YOU GOT FATE BECAUSE HE WAS SHIELDING ME.

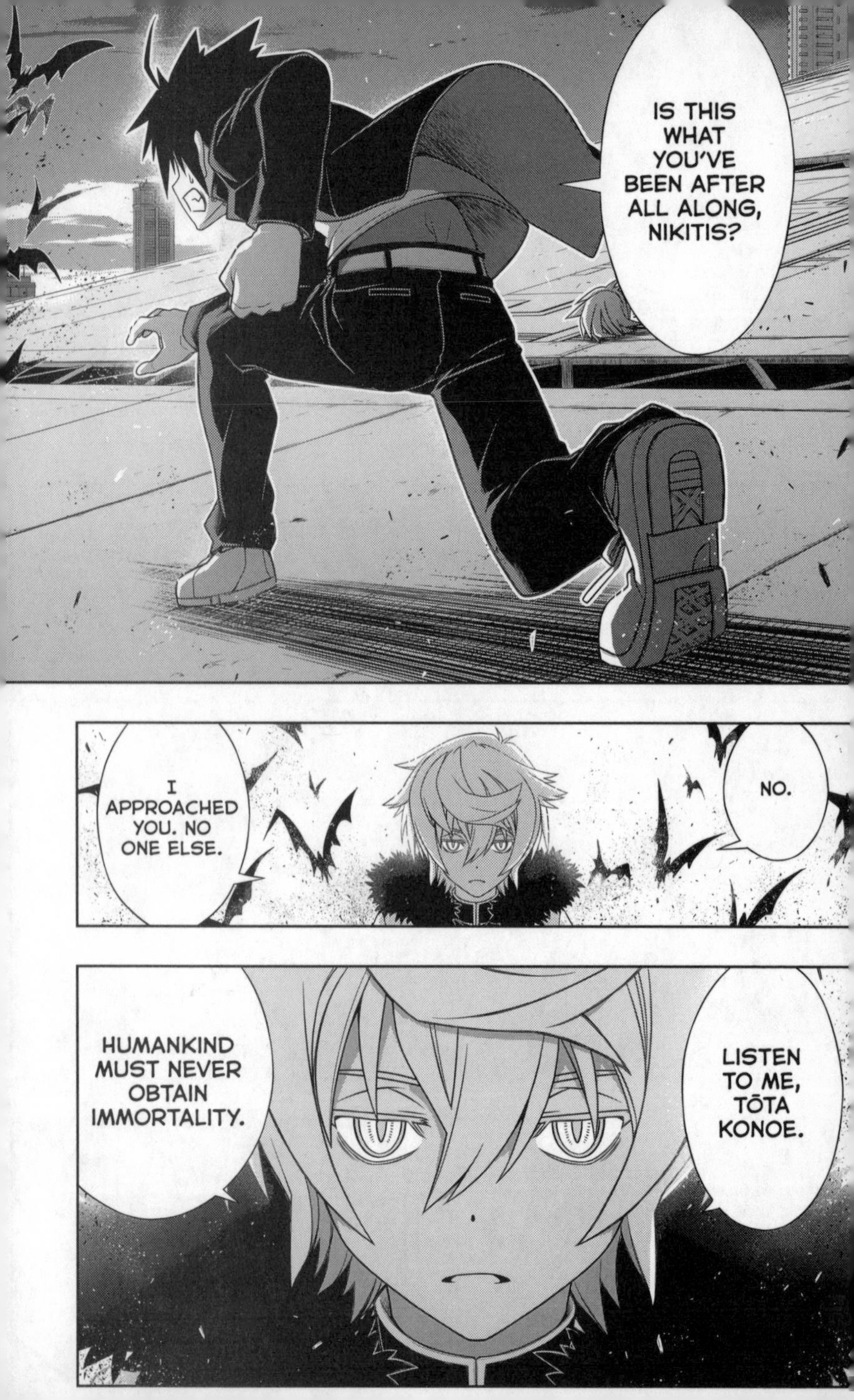
IS THIS WHAT YOU'VE BEEN AFTER ALL ALONG, NIKITIS?
NO.
I APPROACHED YOU. NO ONE ELSE.
LISTEN TO ME, TŌTA KONOE.
HUMANKIND MUST NEVER OBTAIN IMMORTALITY.

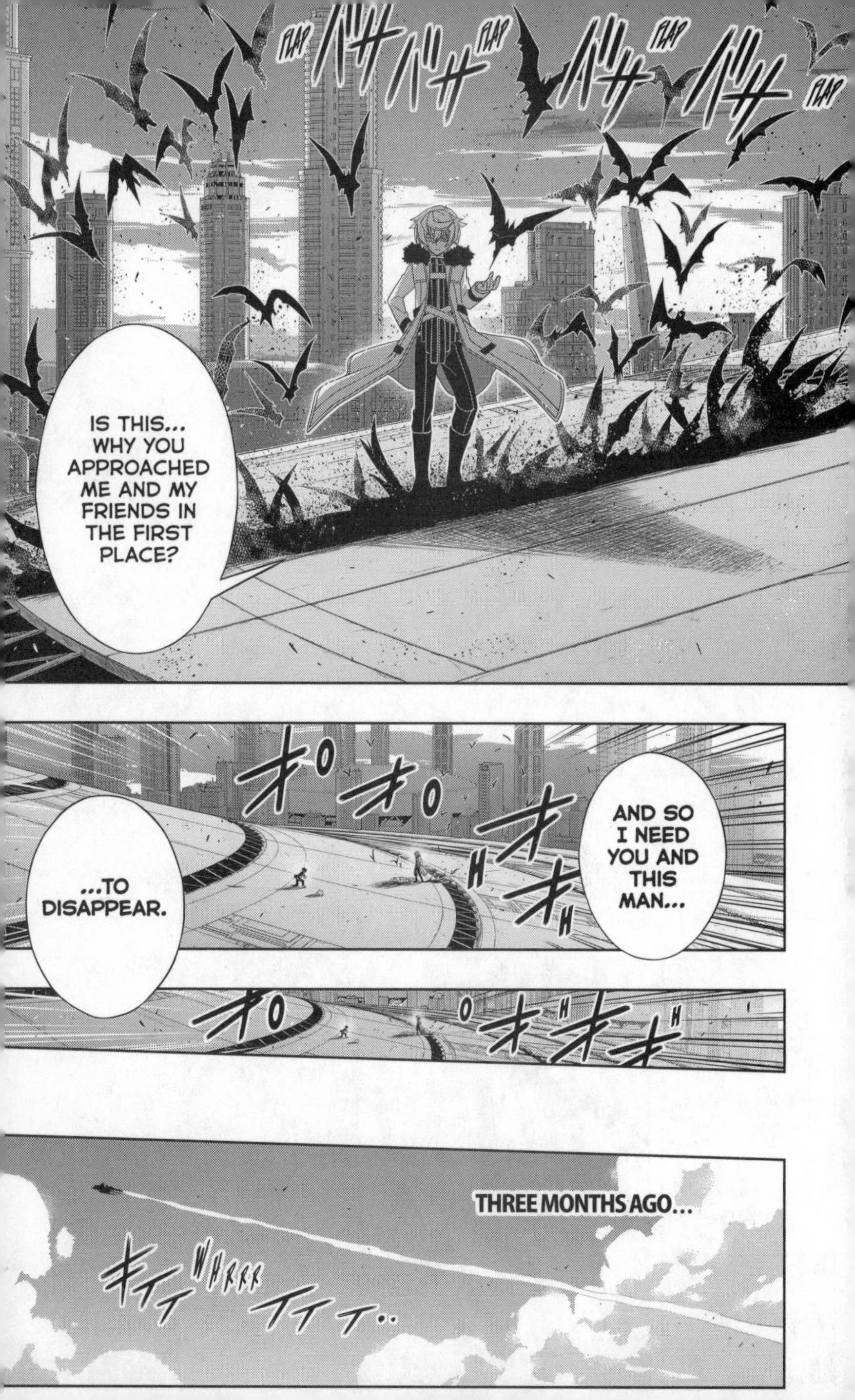
FLAP
FLAP
FLAP
FLAP
IS THIS... WHY YOU APPROACHED ME AND MY FRIENDS IN THE FIRST PLACE?
AND SO I NEED YOU AND THIS MAN...
...TO DISAPPEAR.
THREE MONTHS AGO...
WHRRR

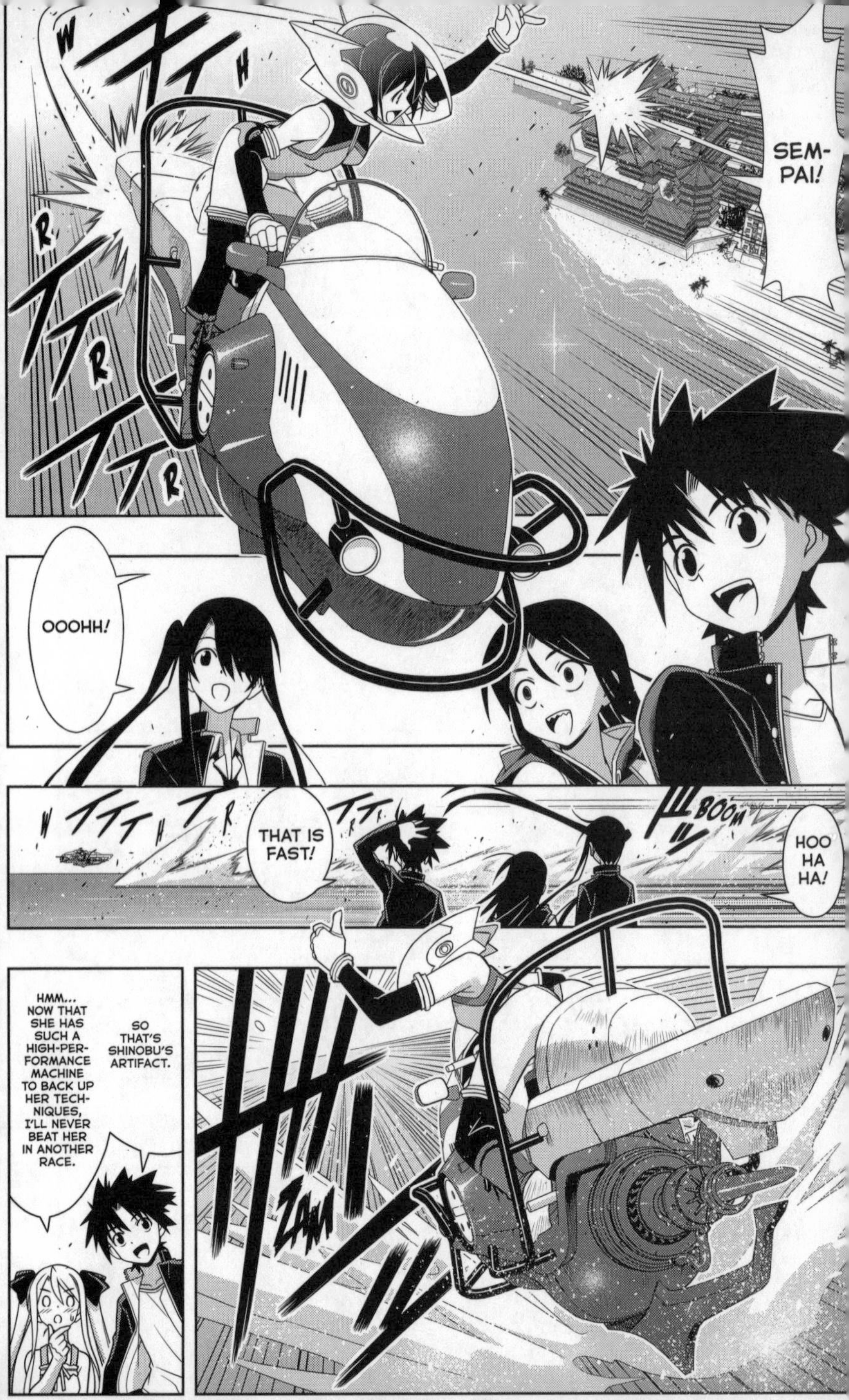
SEM-PAI!
WHRRR
OOOHH!
HOO HA HA!
BOOM
THAT IS FAST!
WHRRR
ZAM
SO THAT'S SHINOBU'S ARTIFACT.
HMM... NOW THAT SHE HAS SUCH A HIGH-PERFORMANCE MACHINE TO BACK UP HER TECHNIQUES, I'LL NEVER BEAT HER IN ANOTHER RACE.

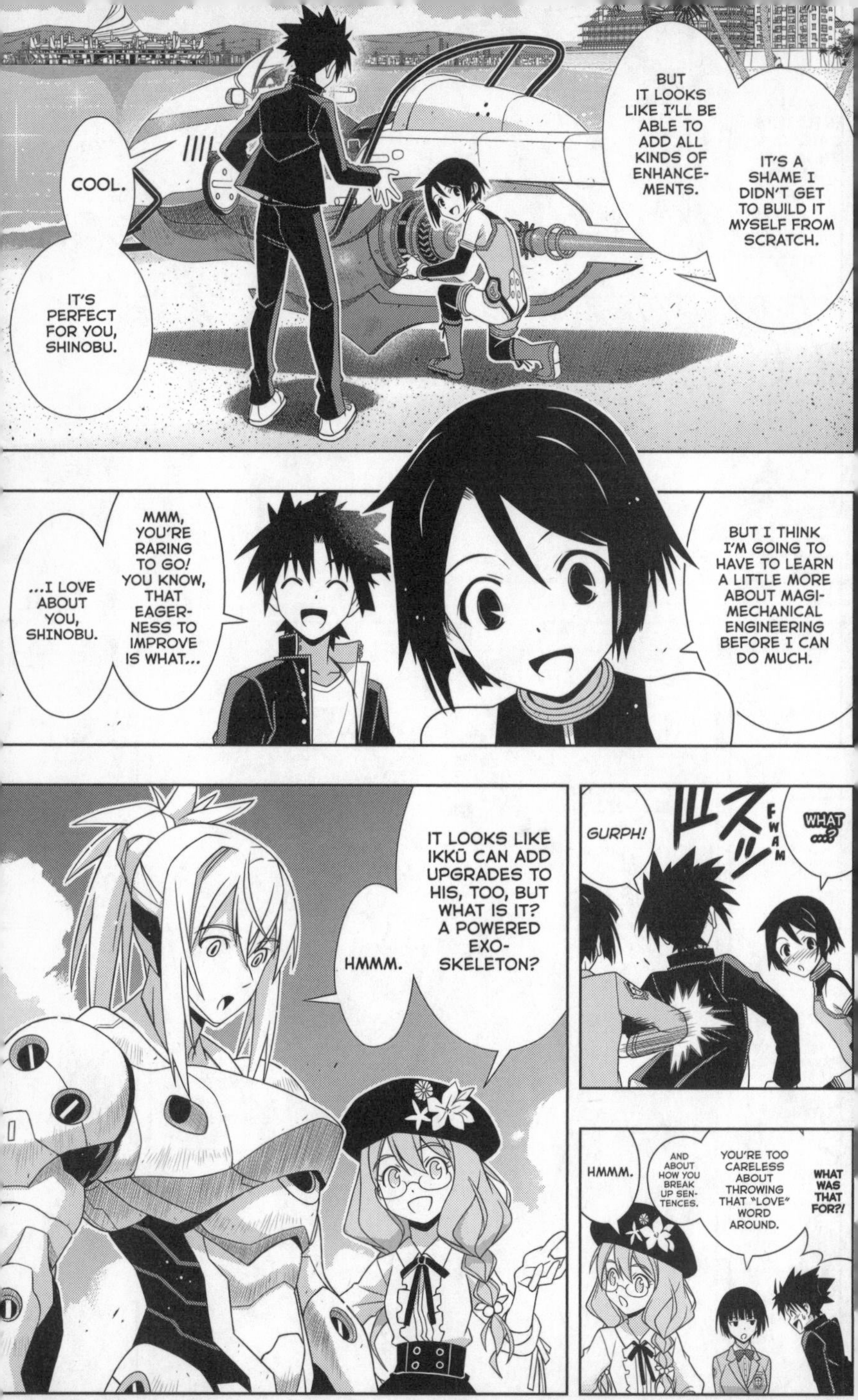
IT'S A SHAME I DIDN'T GET TO BUILD IT MYSELF FROM SCRATCH.
BUT IT LOOKS LIKE I'LL BE ABLE TO ADD ALL KINDS OF ENHANCE-MENTS.
COOL.
IT'S PERFECT FOR YOU, SHINOBU.
BUT I THINK I'M GOING TO HAVE TO LEARN A LITTLE MORE ABOUT MAGI-MECHANICAL ENGINEERING BEFORE I CAN DO MUCH.
MMM, YOU'RE RARING TO GO! YOU KNOW, THAT EAGER-NESS TO IMPROVE IS WHAT...
...I LOVE ABOUT YOU, SHINOBU.
WHAT ...?
FWAM
GURPH!
WHAT WAS THAT FOR?!
YOU'RE TOO CARELESS ABOUT THROWING THAT "LOVE" WORD AROUND.
AND ABOUT HOW YOU BREAK UP SEN-TENCES.
HMMM.
IT LOOKS LIKE IKKŪ CAN ADD UPGRADES TO HIS, TOO, BUT WHAT IS IT? A POWERED EXO-SKELETON?
HMMM.

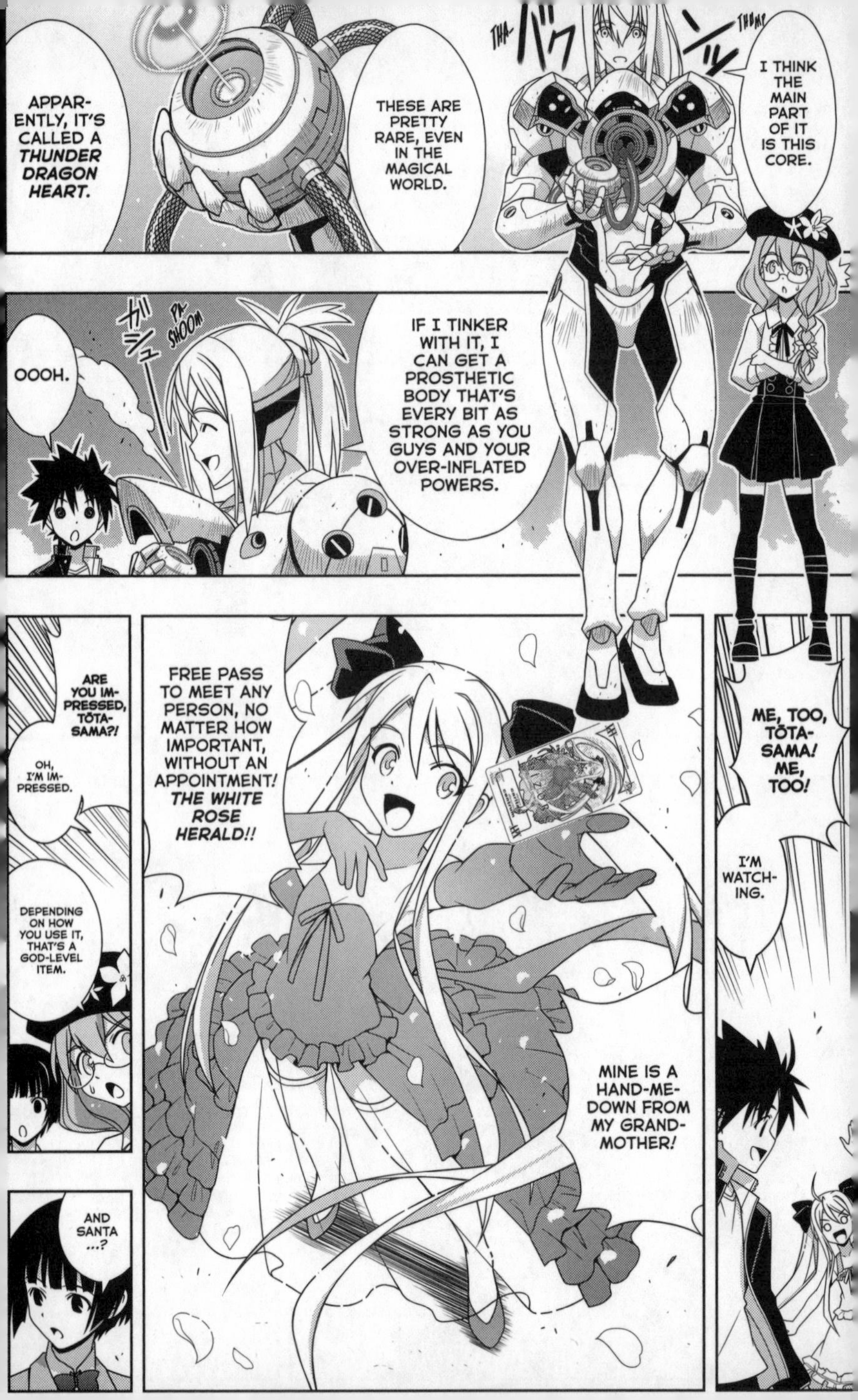
THA- バクンッ THUMP
I THINK THE MAIN PART OF IT IS THIS CORE.
THESE ARE PRETTY RARE, EVEN IN THE MAGICAL WORLD.
APPARENTLY, IT'S CALLED A *THUNDER DRAGON HEART.*
IF I TINKER WITH IT, I CAN GET A PROSTHETIC BODY THAT'S EVERY BIT AS STRONG AS YOU GUYS AND YOUR OVER-INFLATED POWERS.
ガシュ PA SHOOM
OOOH.
ME, TOO, TŌTA-SAMA! ME, TOO!
I'M WATCHING.
FREE PASS TO MEET ANY PERSON, NO MATTER HOW IMPORTANT, WITHOUT AN APPOINTMENT! *THE WHITE ROSE HERALD!!*
MINE IS A HAND-ME-DOWN FROM MY GRAND-MOTHER!
ARE YOU IM-PRESSED, TŌTA-SAMA?!
OH, I'M IM-PRESSED.
DEPENDING ON HOW YOU USE IT, THAT'S A GOD-LEVEL ITEM.
AND SANTA ...?

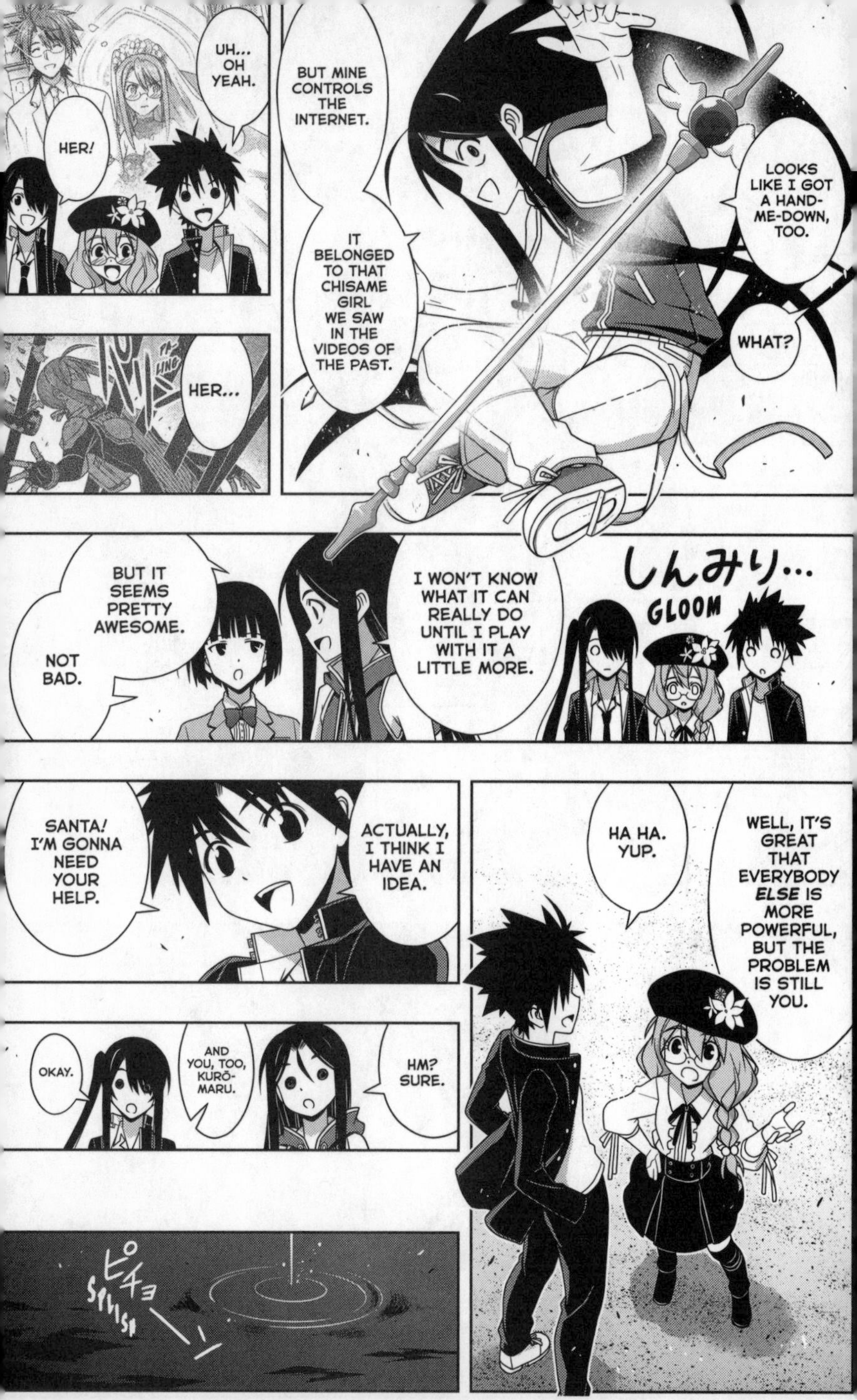

LOOKS LIKE I GOT A HAND-ME-DOWN, TOO.
WHAT?
BUT MINE CONTROLS THE INTERNET.
IT BELONGED TO THAT CHISAME GIRL WE SAW IN THE VIDEOS OF THE PAST.
UH... OH YEAH.
HER!
HER...
しんみり…
GLOOM
I WON'T KNOW WHAT IT CAN REALLY DO UNTIL I PLAY WITH IT A LITTLE MORE.
BUT IT SEEMS PRETTY AWESOME.
NOT BAD.
WELL, IT'S GREAT THAT EVERYBODY *ELSE* IS MORE POWERFUL, BUT THE PROBLEM IS STILL YOU.
HA HA. YUP.
ACTUALLY, I THINK I HAVE AN IDEA.
SANTA! I'M GONNA NEED YOUR HELP.
HM? SURE.
AND YOU, TOO, KURŌ-MARU.
OKAY.
ピチョ
SPLISH

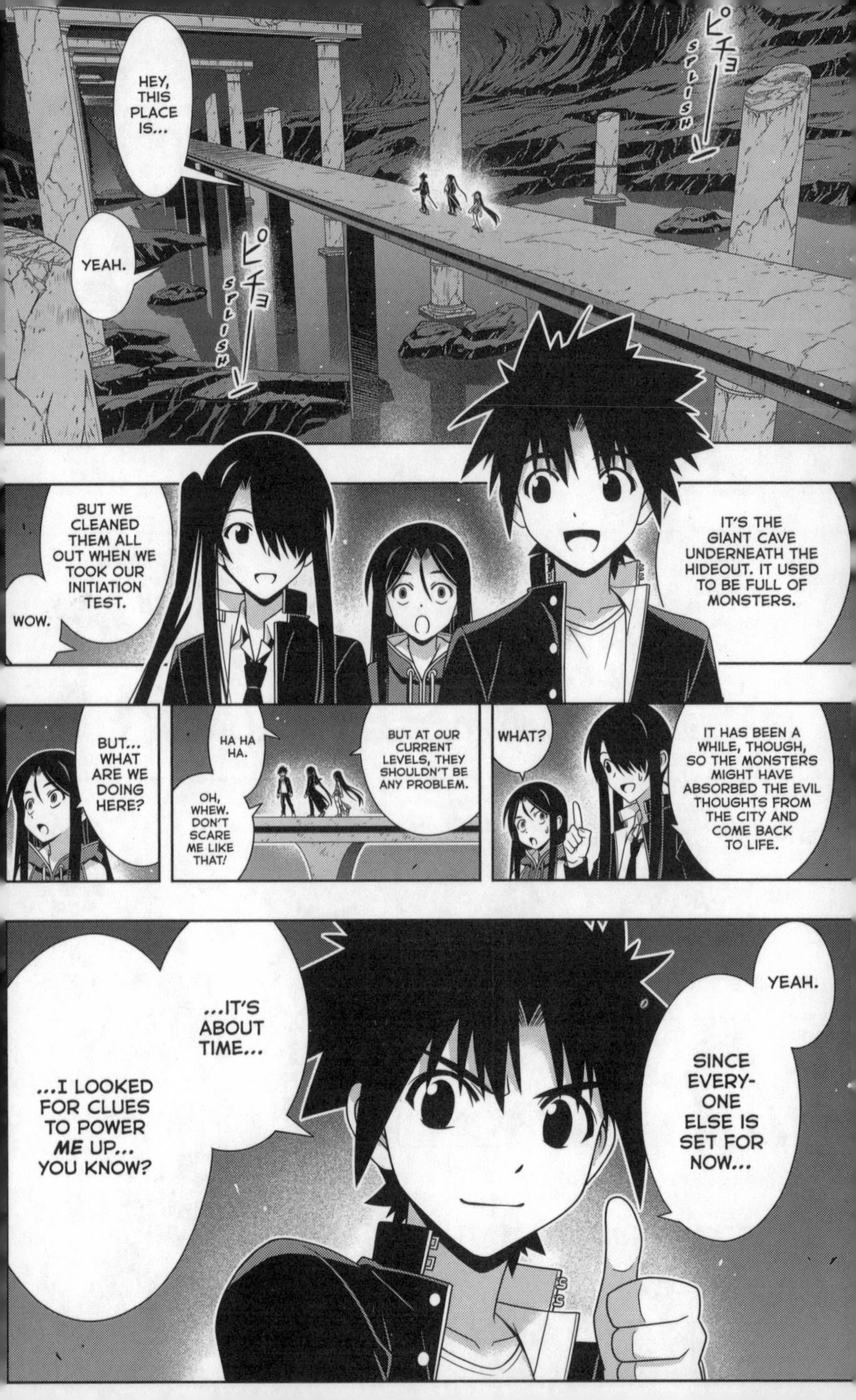
ピチョ SPLISH
HEY, THIS PLACE IS...
YEAH.
ピチョ SPLISH
IT'S THE GIANT CAVE UNDERNEATH THE HIDEOUT. IT USED TO BE FULL OF MONSTERS.
BUT WE CLEANED THEM ALL OUT WHEN WE TOOK OUR INITIATION TEST.
WOW.
IT HAS BEEN A WHILE, THOUGH, SO THE MONSTERS MIGHT HAVE ABSORBED THE EVIL THOUGHTS FROM THE CITY AND COME BACK TO LIFE.
WHAT?
BUT AT OUR CURRENT LEVELS, THEY SHOULDN'T BE ANY PROBLEM.
HA HA HA.
OH, WHEW. DON'T SCARE ME LIKE THAT!
BUT... WHAT ARE WE DOING HERE?
YEAH.
SINCE EVERY-ONE ELSE IS SET FOR NOW...
...IT'S ABOUT TIME...
...I LOOKED FOR CLUES TO POWER *ME* UP... YOU KNOW?

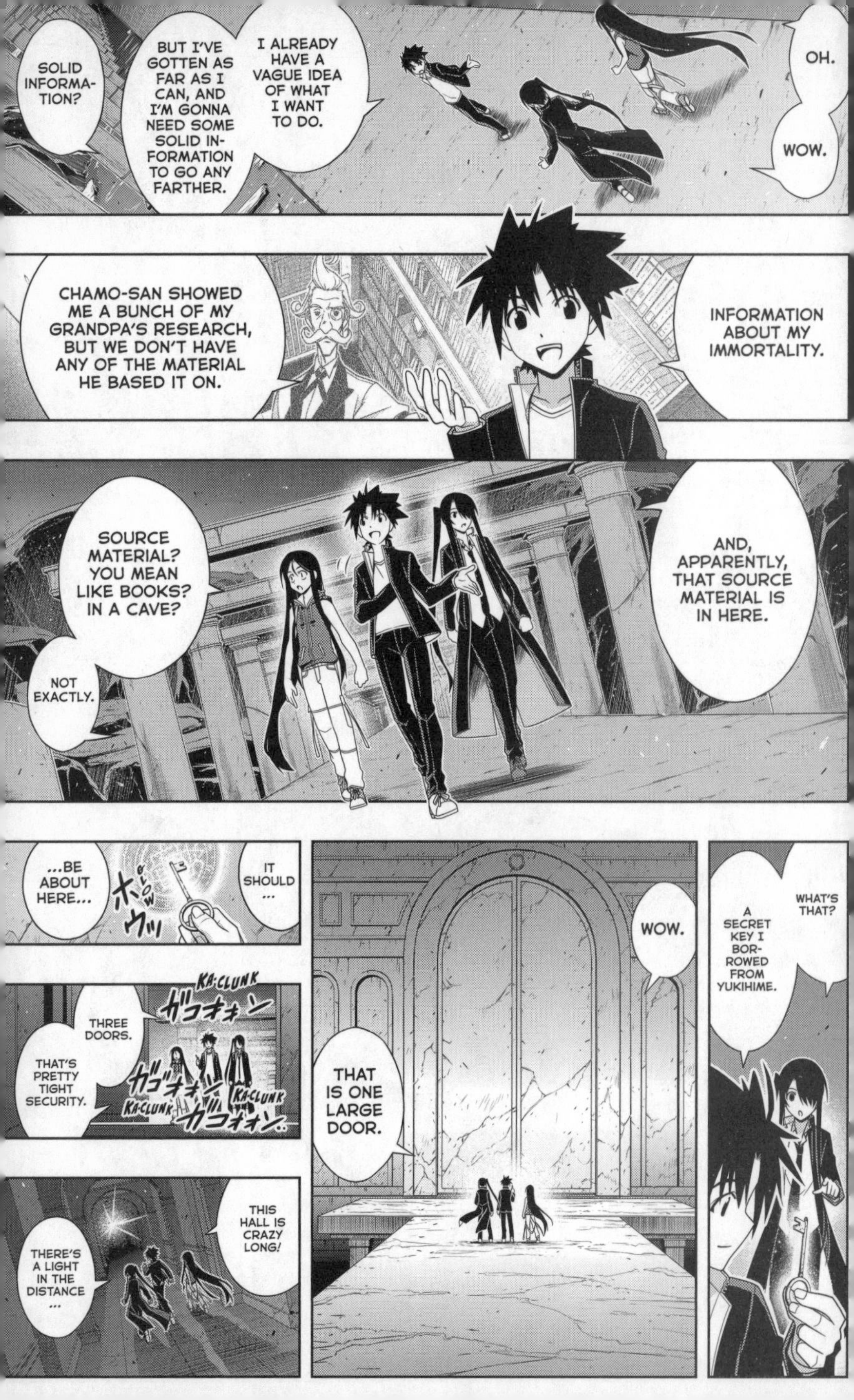
OH.
WOW.
I ALREADY HAVE A VAGUE IDEA OF WHAT I WANT TO DO.
BUT I'VE GOTTEN AS FAR AS I CAN, AND I'M GONNA NEED SOME SOLID INFORMATION TO GO ANY FARTHER.
SOLID INFORMATION?
INFORMATION ABOUT MY IMMORTALITY.
CHAMO-SAN SHOWED ME A BUNCH OF MY GRANDPA'S RESEARCH, BUT WE DON'T HAVE ANY OF THE MATERIAL HE BASED IT ON.
AND, APPARENTLY, THAT SOURCE MATERIAL IS IN HERE.
SOURCE MATERIAL? YOU MEAN LIKE BOOKS? IN A CAVE?
NOT EXACTLY.
WHAT'S THAT?
A SECRET KEY I BORROWED FROM YUKIHIME.
WOW.
THAT IS ONE LARGE DOOR.
IT SHOULD ...
...BE ABOUT HERE...
GLOW
KA-CLUNK
THREE DOORS.
THAT'S PRETTY TIGHT SECURITY.
KA-CLUNK
KA-CLUNK
THIS HALL IS CRAZY LONG!
THERE'S A LIGHT IN THE DISTANCE ...

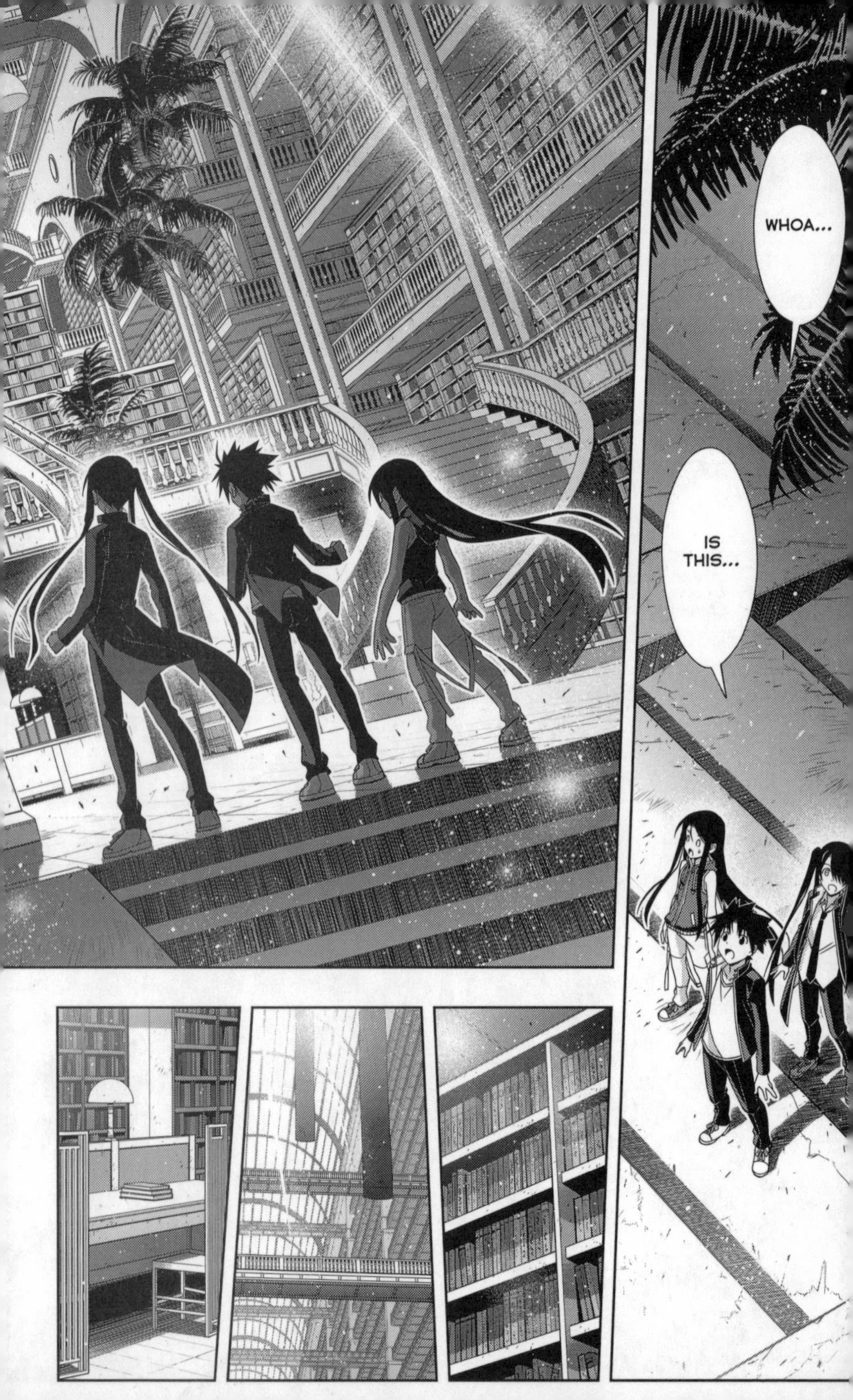
WHOA...
IS THIS...

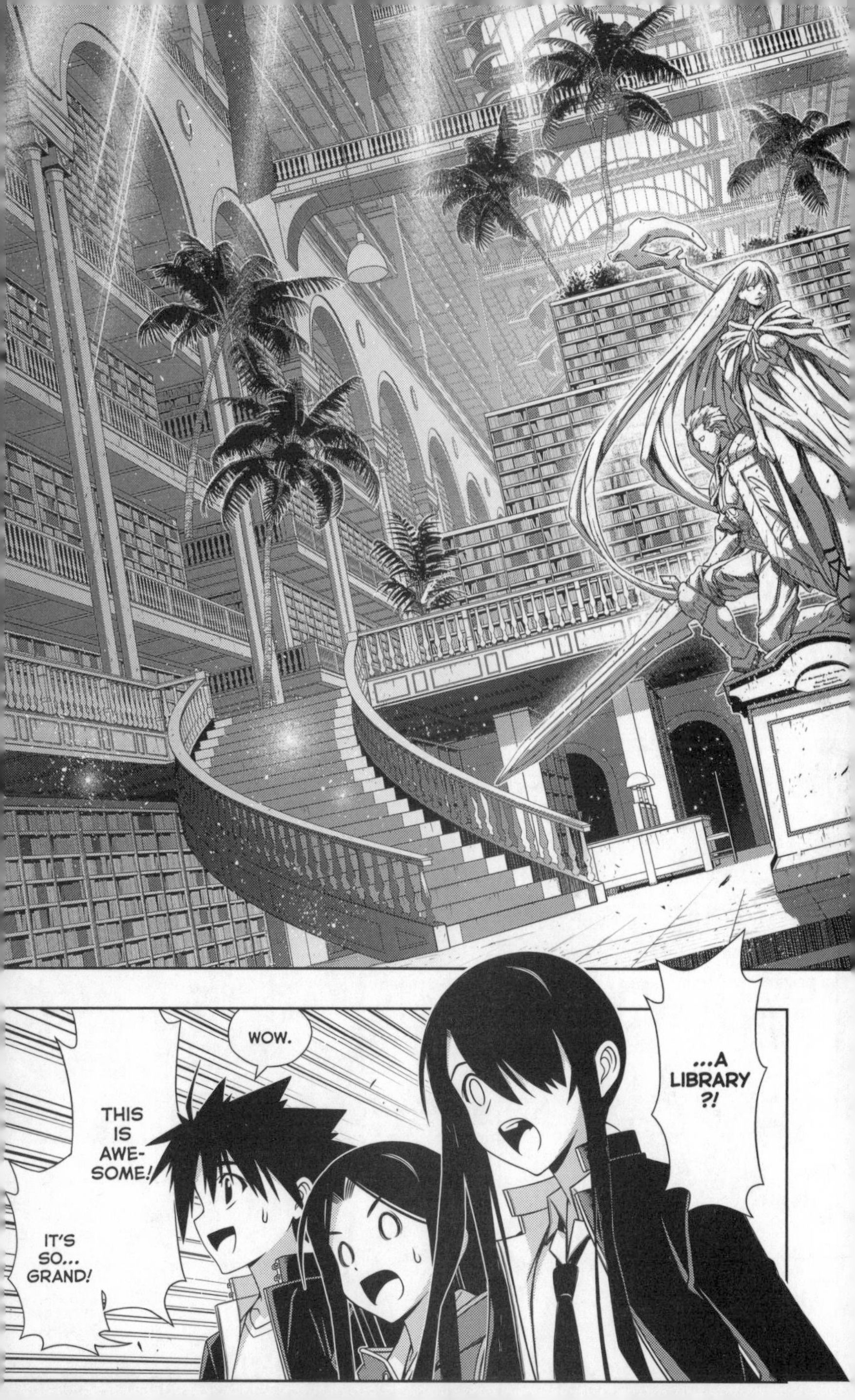
...A LIBRARY?!
WOW.
THIS IS AWESOME!
IT'S SO... GRAND!

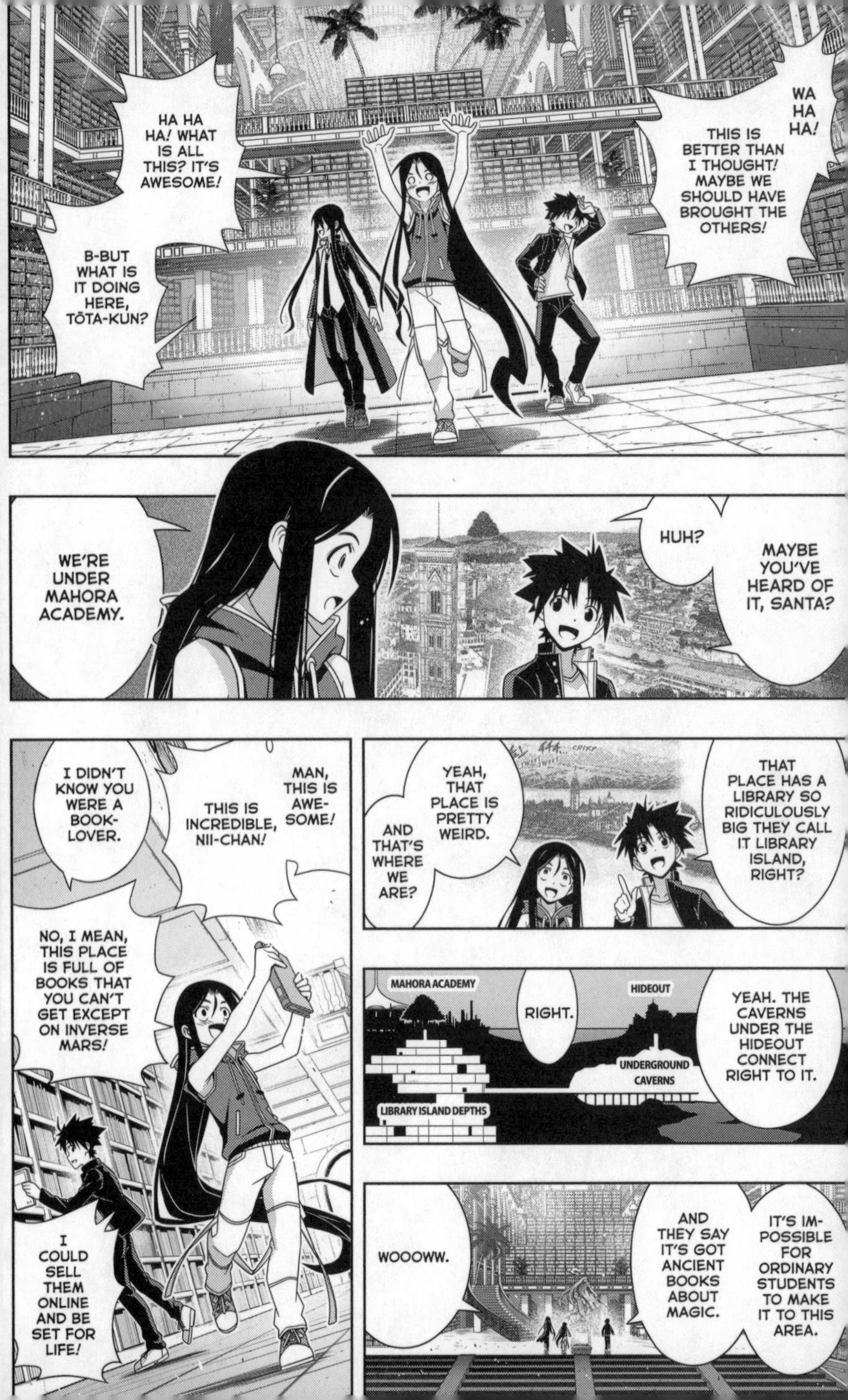
WA HA HA!
THIS IS BETTER THAN I THOUGHT! MAYBE WE SHOULD HAVE BROUGHT THE OTHERS!
HA HA HA! WHAT IS ALL THIS? IT'S AWESOME!
B-BUT WHAT IS IT DOING HERE, TŌTA-KUN?
MAYBE YOU'VE HEARD OF IT, SANTA?
HUH?
WE'RE UNDER MAHORA ACADEMY.
CHIRP
THAT PLACE HAS A LIBRARY SO RIDICULOUSLY BIG THEY CALL IT LIBRARY ISLAND, RIGHT?
YEAH, THAT PLACE IS PRETTY WEIRD.
AND THAT'S WHERE WE ARE?
YEAH. THE CAVERNS UNDER THE HIDEOUT CONNECT RIGHT TO IT.
HIDEOUT
UNDERGROUND CAVERNS
RIGHT.
MAHORA ACADEMY
LIBRARY ISLAND DEPTHS
IT'S IMPOSSIBLE FOR ORDINARY STUDENTS TO MAKE IT TO THIS AREA.
AND THEY SAY IT'S GOT ANCIENT BOOKS ABOUT MAGIC.
WOOOWW.
MAN, THIS IS AWESOME!
THIS IS INCREDIBLE, NII-CHAN!
I DIDN'T KNOW YOU WERE A BOOK-LOVER.
NO, I MEAN, THIS PLACE IS FULL OF BOOKS THAT YOU CAN'T GET EXCEPT ON INVERSE MARS!
I COULD SELL THEM ONLINE AND BE SET FOR LIFE!

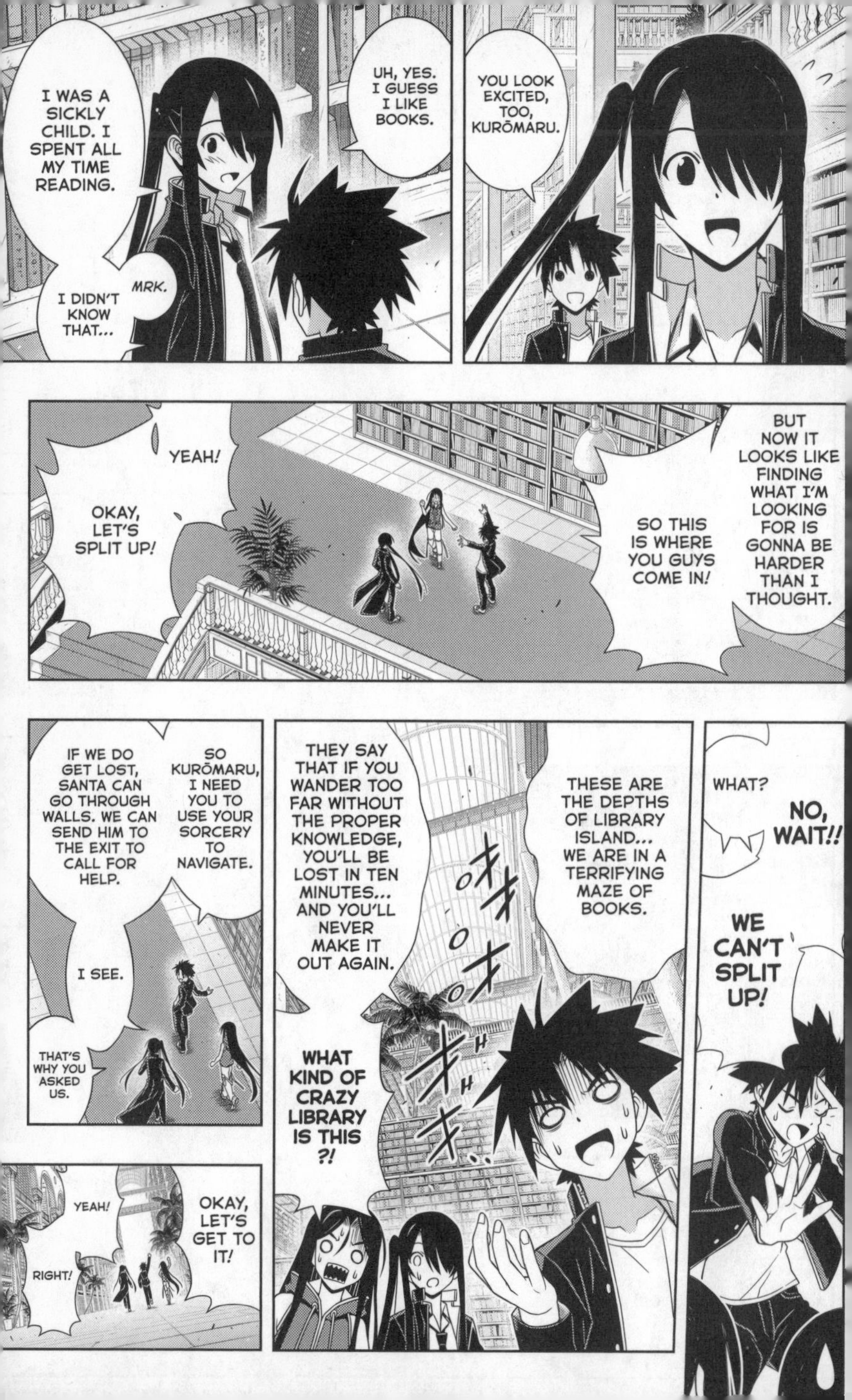

YOU LOOK EXCITED, TOO, KURŌMARU.
UH, YES. I GUESS I LIKE BOOKS.
I WAS A SICKLY CHILD. I SPENT ALL MY TIME READING.
MRK.
I DIDN'T KNOW THAT...
BUT NOW IT LOOKS LIKE FINDING WHAT I'M LOOKING FOR IS GONNA BE HARDER THAN I THOUGHT.
SO THIS IS WHERE YOU GUYS COME IN!
OKAY, LET'S SPLIT UP!
YEAH!
NO, WAIT!!
WHAT?
WE CAN'T SPLIT UP!
THESE ARE THE DEPTHS OF LIBRARY ISLAND... WE ARE IN A TERRIFYING MAZE OF BOOKS.
THEY SAY THAT IF YOU WANDER TOO FAR WITHOUT THE PROPER KNOWLEDGE, YOU'LL BE LOST IN TEN MINUTES... AND YOU'LL NEVER MAKE IT OUT AGAIN.
WHAT KIND OF CRAZY LIBRARY IS THIS?!
SO KURŌMARU, I NEED YOU TO USE YOUR SORCERY TO NAVIGATE.
IF WE DO GET LOST, SANTA CAN GO THROUGH WALLS. WE CAN SEND HIM TO THE EXIT TO CALL FOR HELP.
I SEE.
THAT'S WHY YOU ASKED US.
OKAY, LET'S GET TO IT!
YEAH!
RIGHT!

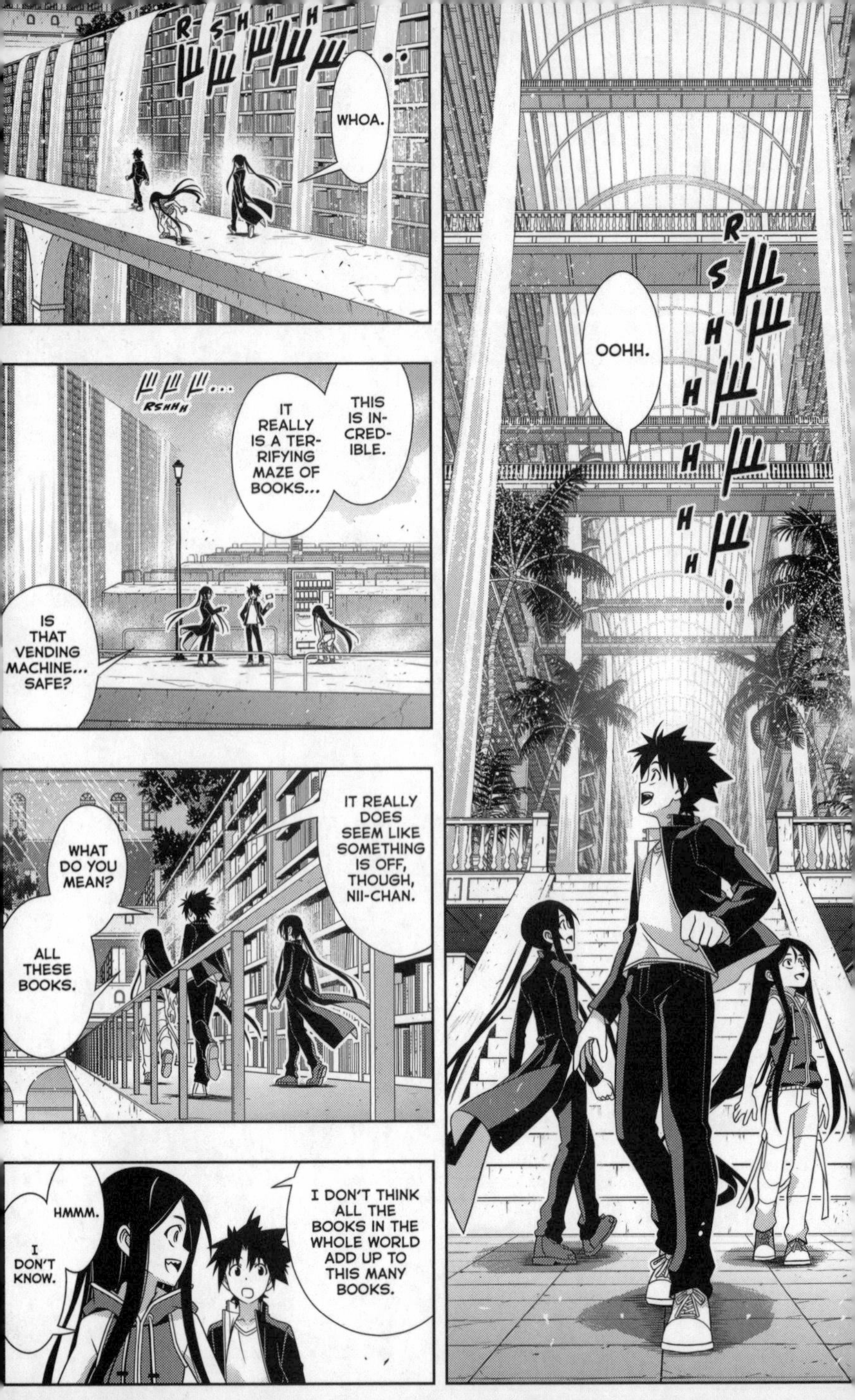
RSHHHHHH
OOHH.
RSHHH
WHOA.
RSHHH
THIS IS INCREDIBLE.
IT REALLY IS A TERRIFYING MAZE OF BOOKS...
IS THAT VENDING MACHINE... SAFE?
IT REALLY DOES SEEM LIKE SOMETHING IS OFF, THOUGH, NII-CHAN.
WHAT DO YOU MEAN?
ALL THESE BOOKS.
I DON'T THINK ALL THE BOOKS IN THE WHOLE WORLD ADD UP TO THIS MANY BOOKS.
HMMM.
I DON'T KNOW.

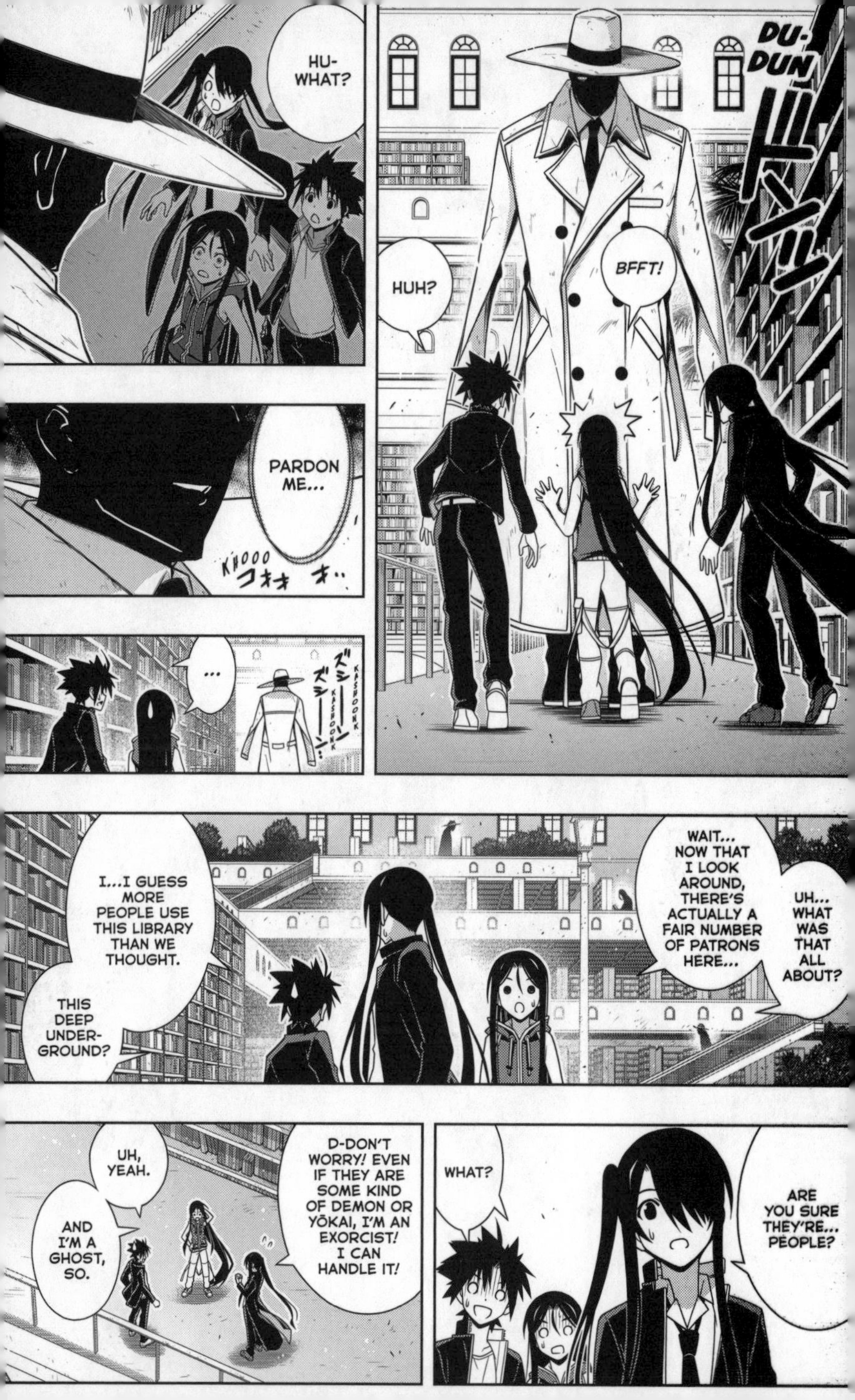
DU-DUN
BFFT!
HUH?
HU-WHAT?
PARDON ME...
KHOOO
...
KASHOONK KASHOONK
UH... WHAT WAS THAT ALL ABOUT?
WAIT... NOW THAT I LOOK AROUND, THERE'S ACTUALLY A FAIR NUMBER OF PATRONS HERE...
I...I GUESS MORE PEOPLE USE THIS LIBRARY THAN WE THOUGHT.
THIS DEEP UNDER-GROUND?
ARE YOU SURE THEY'RE... PEOPLE?
WHAT?
D-DON'T WORRY! EVEN IF THEY ARE SOME KIND OF DEMON OR YŌKAI, I'M AN EXORCIST! I CAN HANDLE IT!
UH, YEAH.
AND I'M A GHOST, SO.

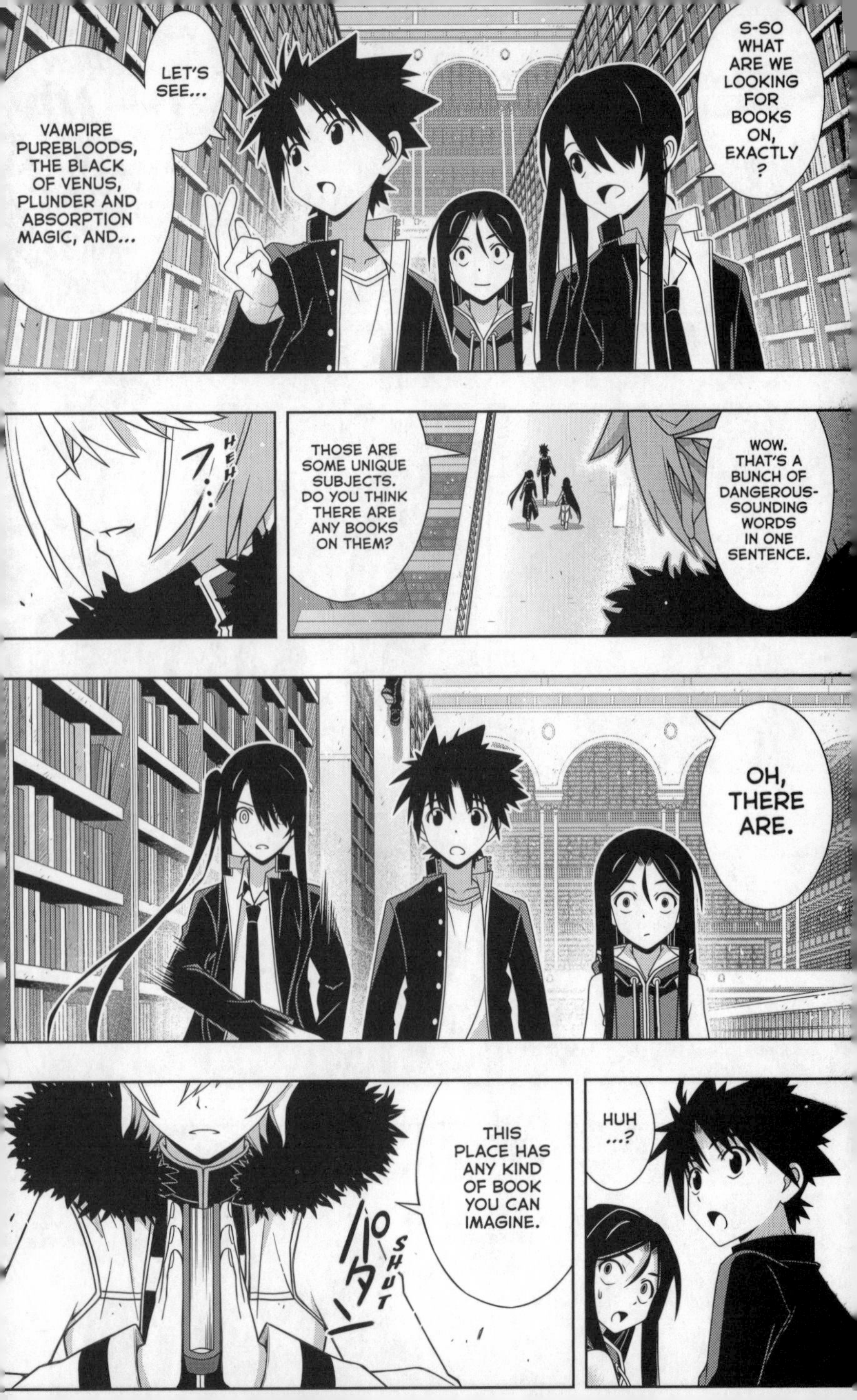
S-SO WHAT ARE WE LOOKING FOR BOOKS ON, EXACTLY?
LET'S SEE...
VAMPIRE PUREBLOODS, THE BLACK OF VENUS, PLUNDER AND ABSORPTION MAGIC, AND...
WOW. THAT'S A BUNCH OF DANGEROUS-SOUNDING WORDS IN ONE SENTENCE.
THOSE ARE SOME UNIQUE SUBJECTS. DO YOU THINK THERE ARE ANY BOOKS ON THEM?
HEH
OH, THERE ARE.
HUH ...?
THIS PLACE HAS ANY KIND OF BOOK YOU CAN IMAGINE.
SHUT

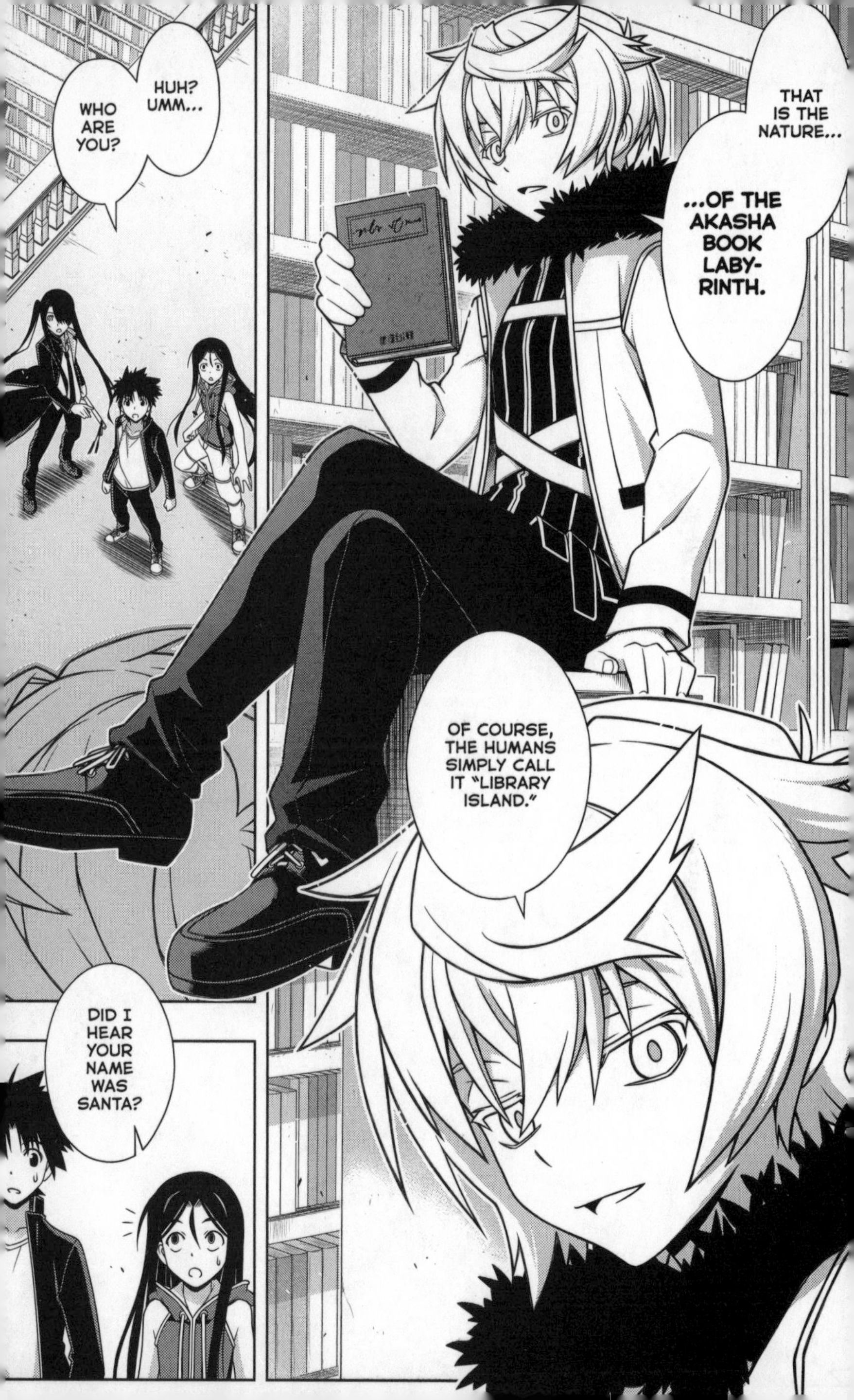
THAT IS THE NATURE...
...OF THE AKASHA BOOK LABY-RINTH.
OF COURSE, THE HUMANS SIMPLY CALL IT "LIBRARY ISLAND."
HUH? UMM...
WHO ARE YOU?
DID I HEAR YOUR NAME WAS SANTA?

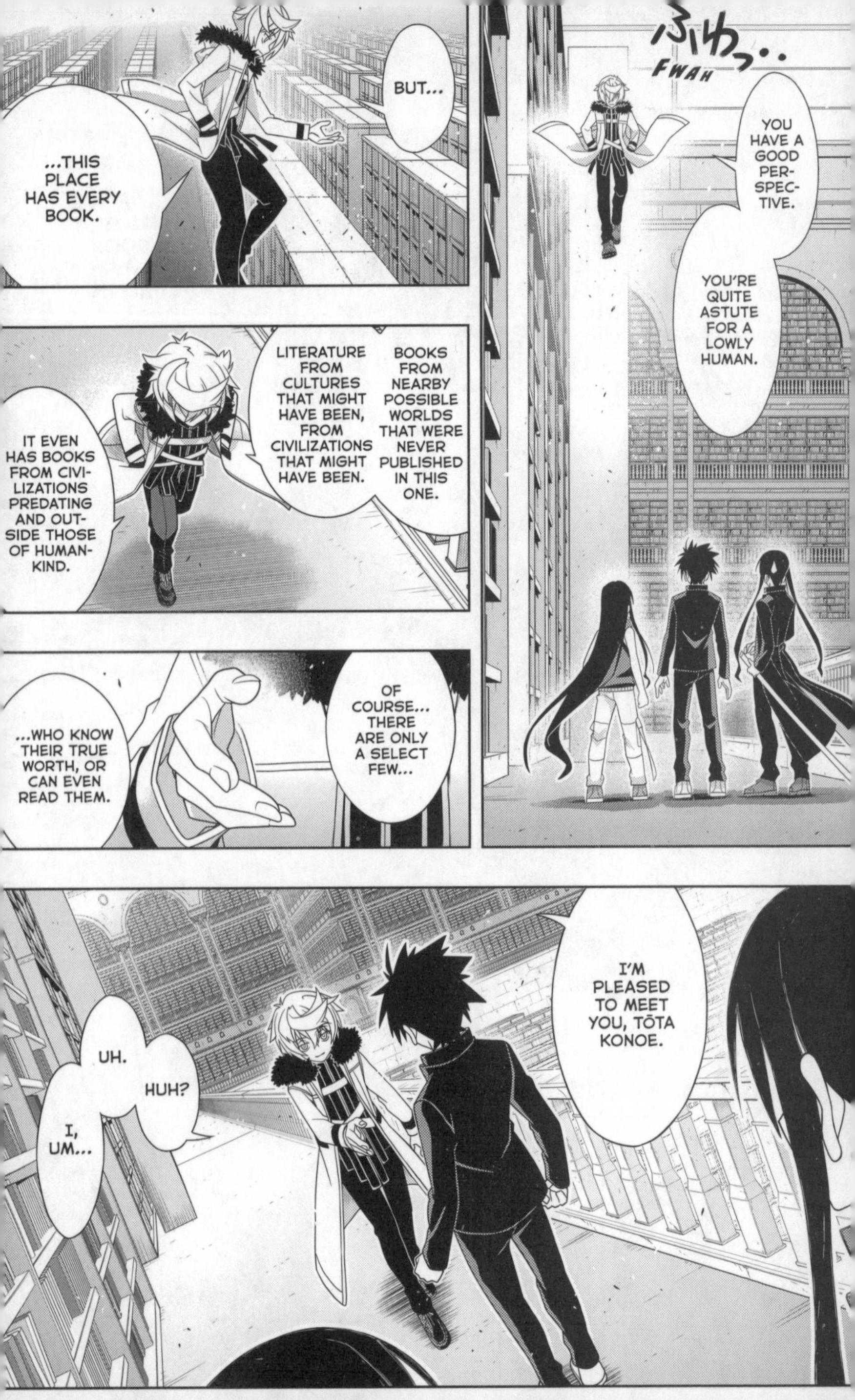
ふわっ..
FWAH
YOU HAVE A GOOD PER-SPEC-TIVE.
YOU'RE QUITE ASTUTE FOR A LOWLY HUMAN.
BUT...
...THIS PLACE HAS EVERY BOOK.
BOOKS FROM NEARBY POSSIBLE WORLDS THAT WERE NEVER PUBLISHED IN THIS ONE.
LITERATURE FROM CULTURES THAT MIGHT HAVE BEEN, FROM CIVILIZATIONS THAT MIGHT HAVE BEEN.
IT EVEN HAS BOOKS FROM CIVI-LIZATIONS PREDATING AND OUT-SIDE THOSE OF HUMAN-KIND.
OF COURSE... THERE ARE ONLY A SELECT FEW...
...WHO KNOW THEIR TRUE WORTH, OR CAN EVEN READ THEM.
I'M PLEASED TO MEET YOU, TŌTA KONOE.
UH.
HUH?
I, UM...

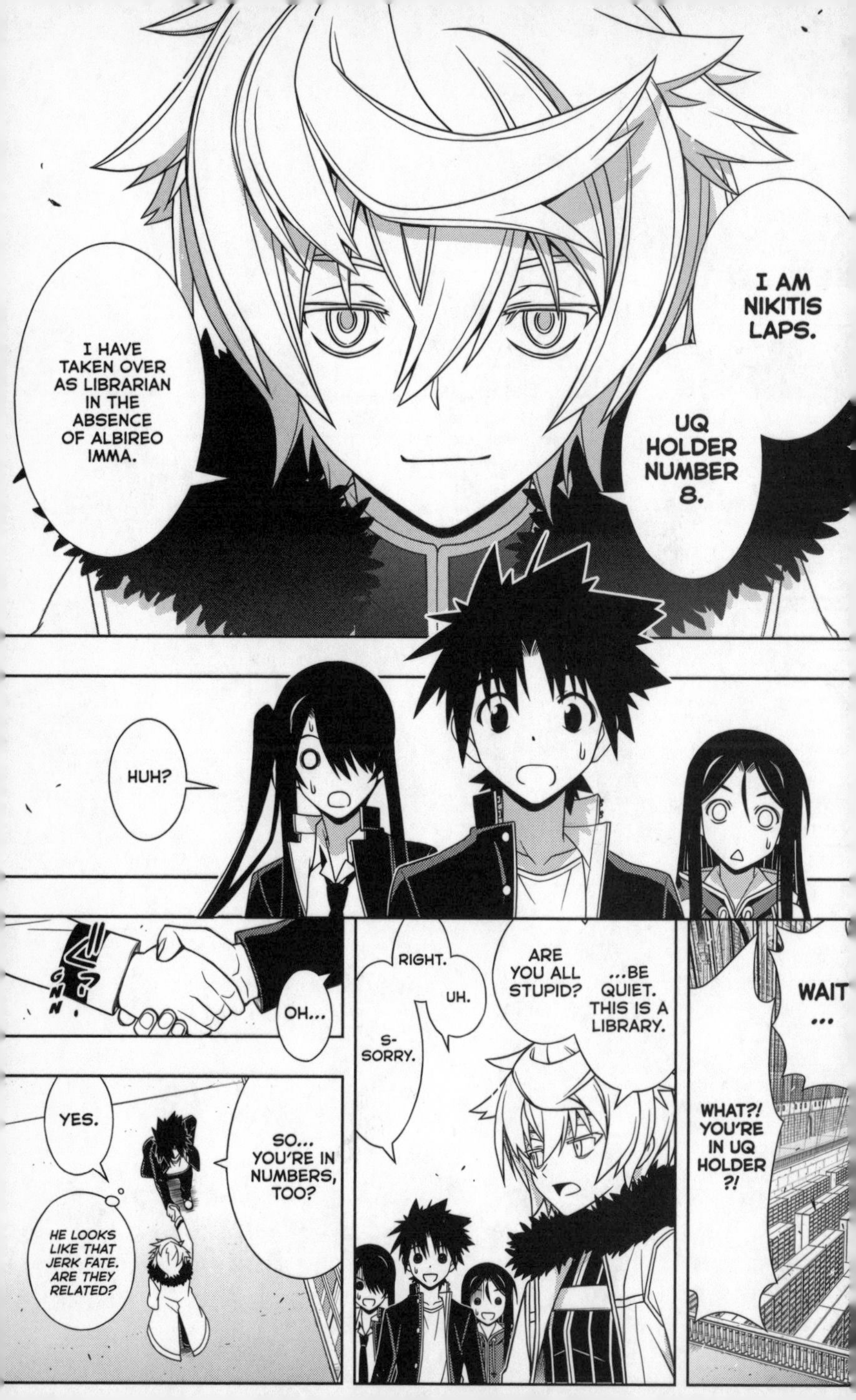
I AM NIKITIS LAPS.
UQ HOLDER NUMBER 8.
I HAVE TAKEN OVER AS LIBRARIAN IN THE ABSENCE OF ALBIREO IMMA.
HUH?
WAIT ...
WHAT?! YOU'RE IN UQ HOLDER ?!
...BE QUIET. THIS IS A LIBRARY.
ARE YOU ALL STUPID?
RIGHT.
UH.
S- SORRY.
GNN
OH...
SO... YOU'RE IN NUMBERS, TOO?
YES.
HE LOOKS LIKE THAT JERK FATE. ARE THEY RELATED?

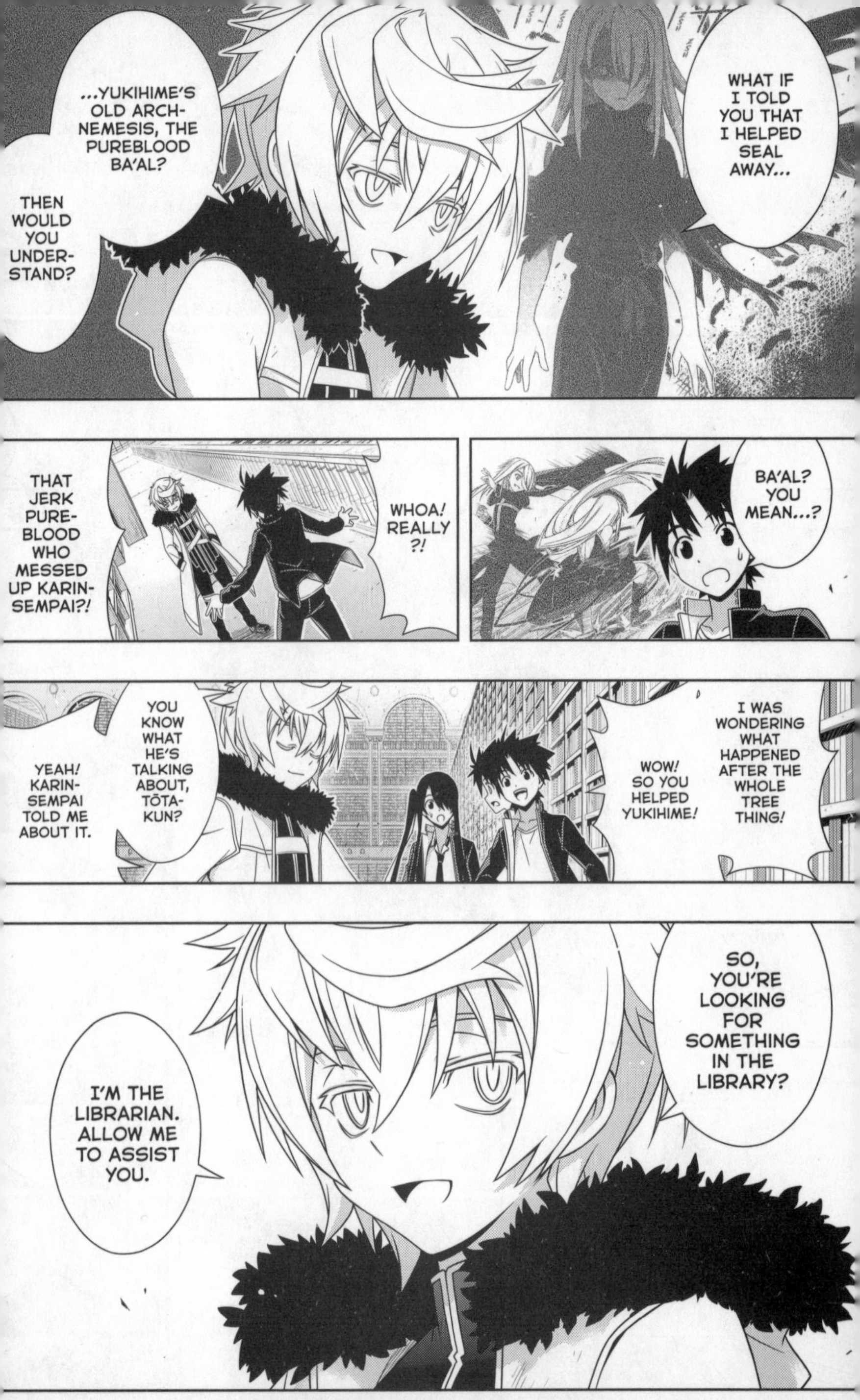
WHAT IF I TOLD YOU THAT I HELPED SEAL AWAY...
...YUKIHIME'S OLD ARCH-NEMESIS, THE PUREBLOOD BA'AL?
THEN WOULD YOU UNDERSTAND?
BA'AL? YOU MEAN...?
WHOA! REALLY?!
THAT JERK PUREBLOOD WHO MESSED UP KARIN-SEMPAI?!
I WAS WONDERING WHAT HAPPENED AFTER THE WHOLE TREE THING!
WOW! SO YOU HELPED YUKIHIME!
YOU KNOW WHAT HE'S TALKING ABOUT, TŌTA-KUN?
YEAH! KARIN-SEMPAI TOLD ME ABOUT IT.
SO, YOU'RE LOOKING FOR SOMETHING IN THE LIBRARY?
I'M THE LIBRARIAN. ALLOW ME TO ASSIST YOU.

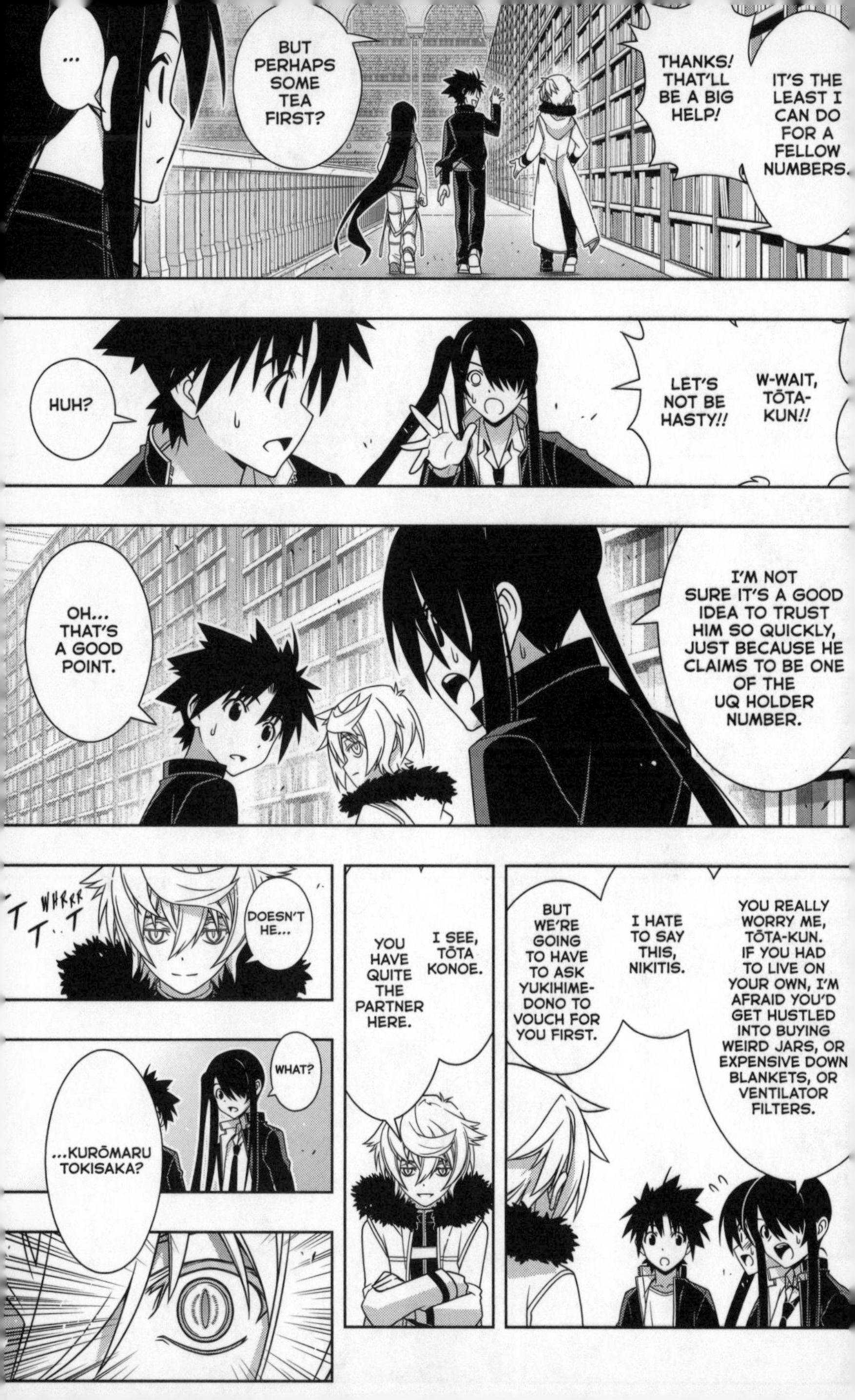
IT'S THE LEAST I CAN DO FOR A FELLOW NUMBERS.
THANKS! THAT'LL BE A BIG HELP!
BUT PERHAPS SOME TEA FIRST?
...
W-WAIT, TŌTA-KUN!!
LET'S NOT BE HASTY!!
HUH?
I'M NOT SURE IT'S A GOOD IDEA TO TRUST HIM SO QUICKLY, JUST BECAUSE HE CLAIMS TO BE ONE OF THE UQ HOLDER NUMBER.
OH... THAT'S A GOOD POINT.
YOU REALLY WORRY ME, TŌTA-KUN. IF YOU HAD TO LIVE ON YOUR OWN, I'M AFRAID YOU'D GET HUSTLED INTO BUYING WEIRD JARS, OR EXPENSIVE DOWN BLANKETS, OR VENTILATOR FILTERS.
I HATE TO SAY THIS, NIKITIS.
BUT WE'RE GOING TO HAVE TO ASK YUKIHIME-DONO TO VOUCH FOR YOU FIRST.
I SEE, TŌTA KONOE.
YOU HAVE QUITE THE PARTNER HERE.
DOESN'T HE...
WHRRR
T T T T
WHAT?
...KURŌMARU TOKISAKA?

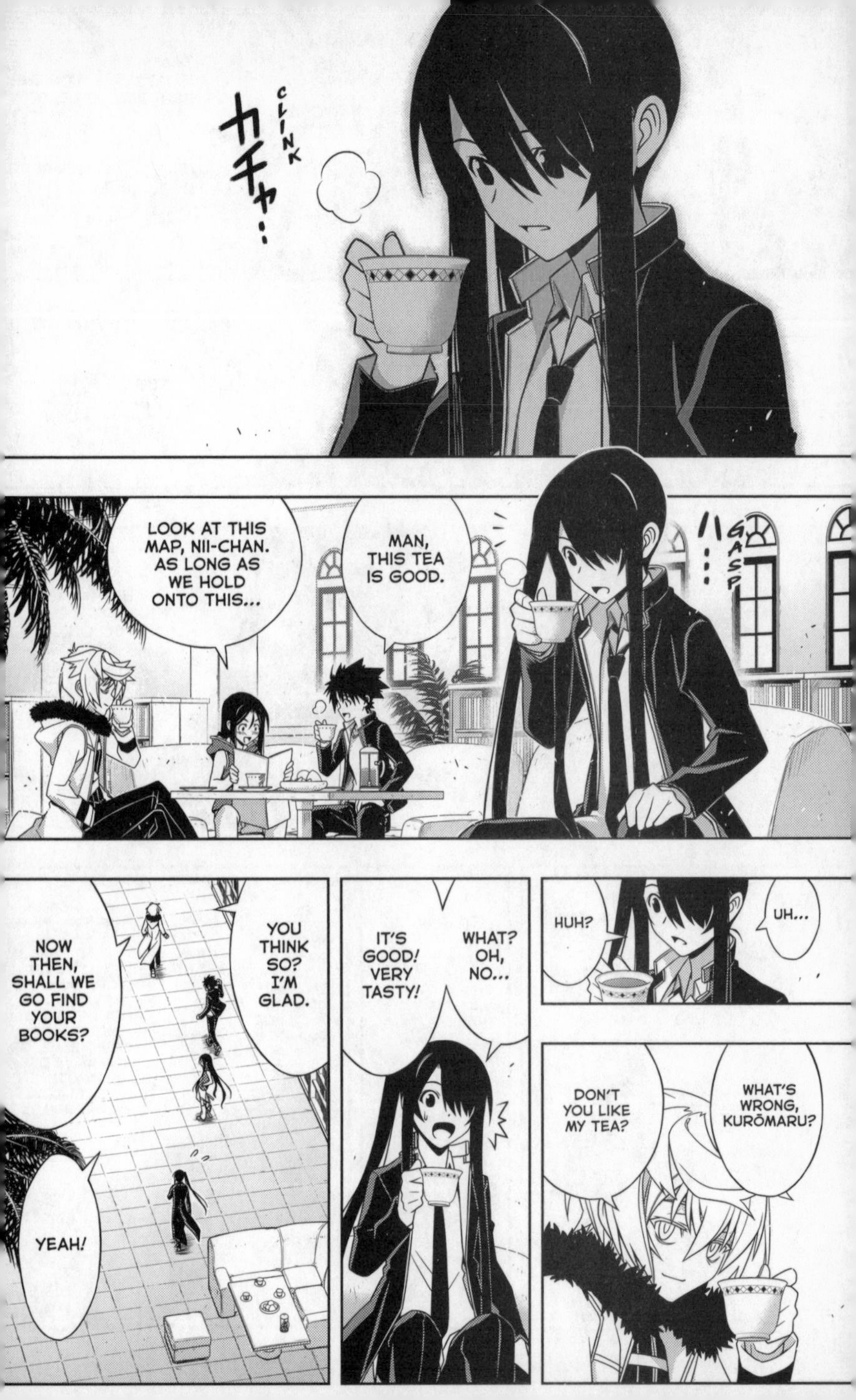
カチャ…
CLINK
ハッ…
GASP
MAN, THIS TEA IS GOOD.
LOOK AT THIS MAP, NII-CHAN. AS LONG AS WE HOLD ONTO THIS...
UH...
HUH?
WHAT'S WRONG, KURŌMARU?
DON'T YOU LIKE MY TEA?
WHAT? OH, NO...
IT'S GOOD! VERY TASTY!
YOU THINK SO? I'M GLAD.
NOW THEN, SHALL WE GO FIND YOUR BOOKS?
YEAH!

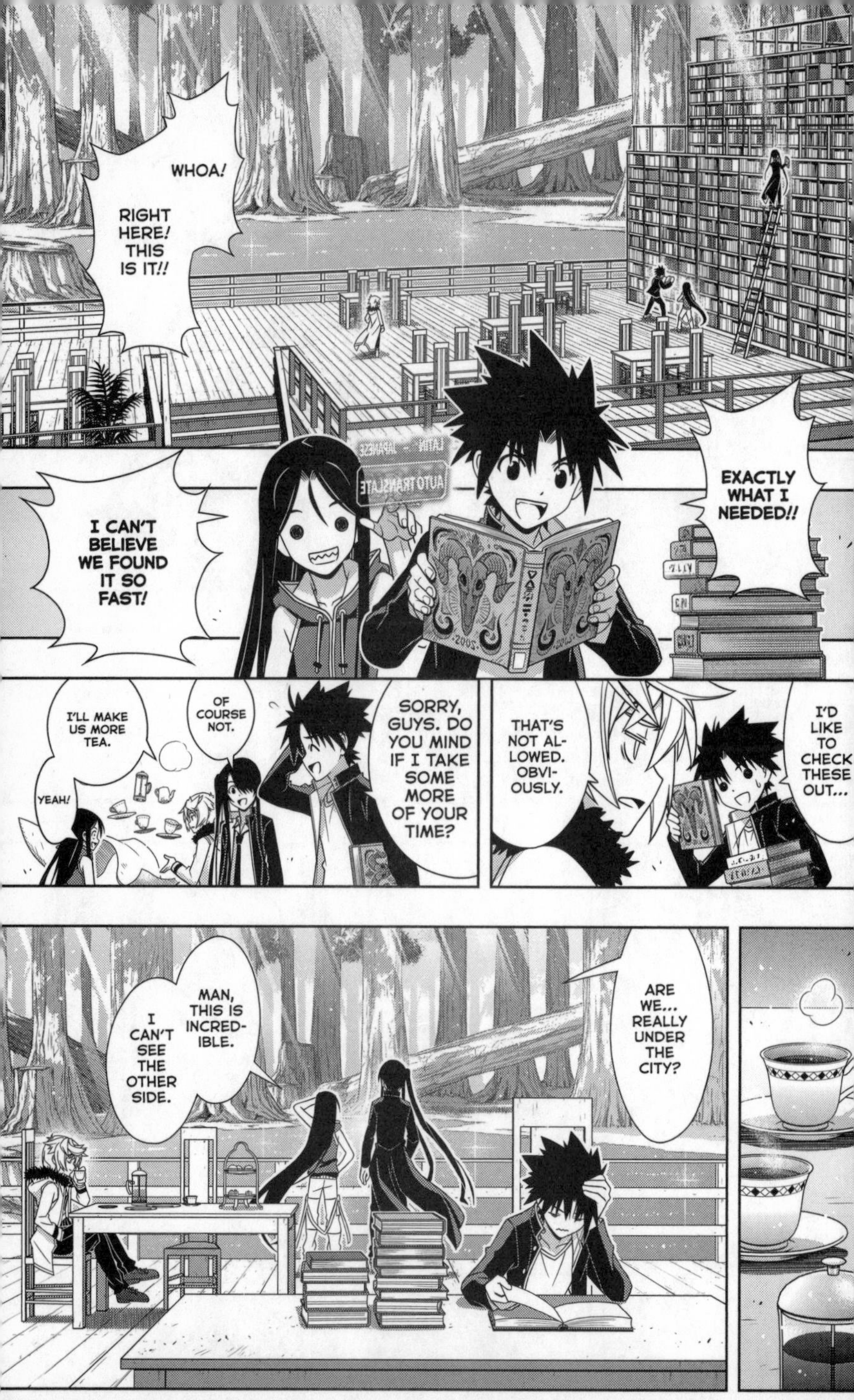
WHOA!
RIGHT HERE! THIS IS IT!!
EXACTLY WHAT I NEEDED!!
I CAN'T BELIEVE WE FOUND IT SO FAST!
I'D LIKE TO CHECK THESE OUT...
THAT'S NOT AL-LOWED. OBVI-OUSLY.
SORRY, GUYS. DO YOU MIND IF I TAKE SOME MORE OF YOUR TIME?
OF COURSE NOT.
I'LL MAKE US MORE TEA.
YEAH!
ARE WE... REALLY UNDER THE CITY?
MAN, THIS IS INCRED-IBLE.
I CAN'T SEE THE OTHER SIDE.

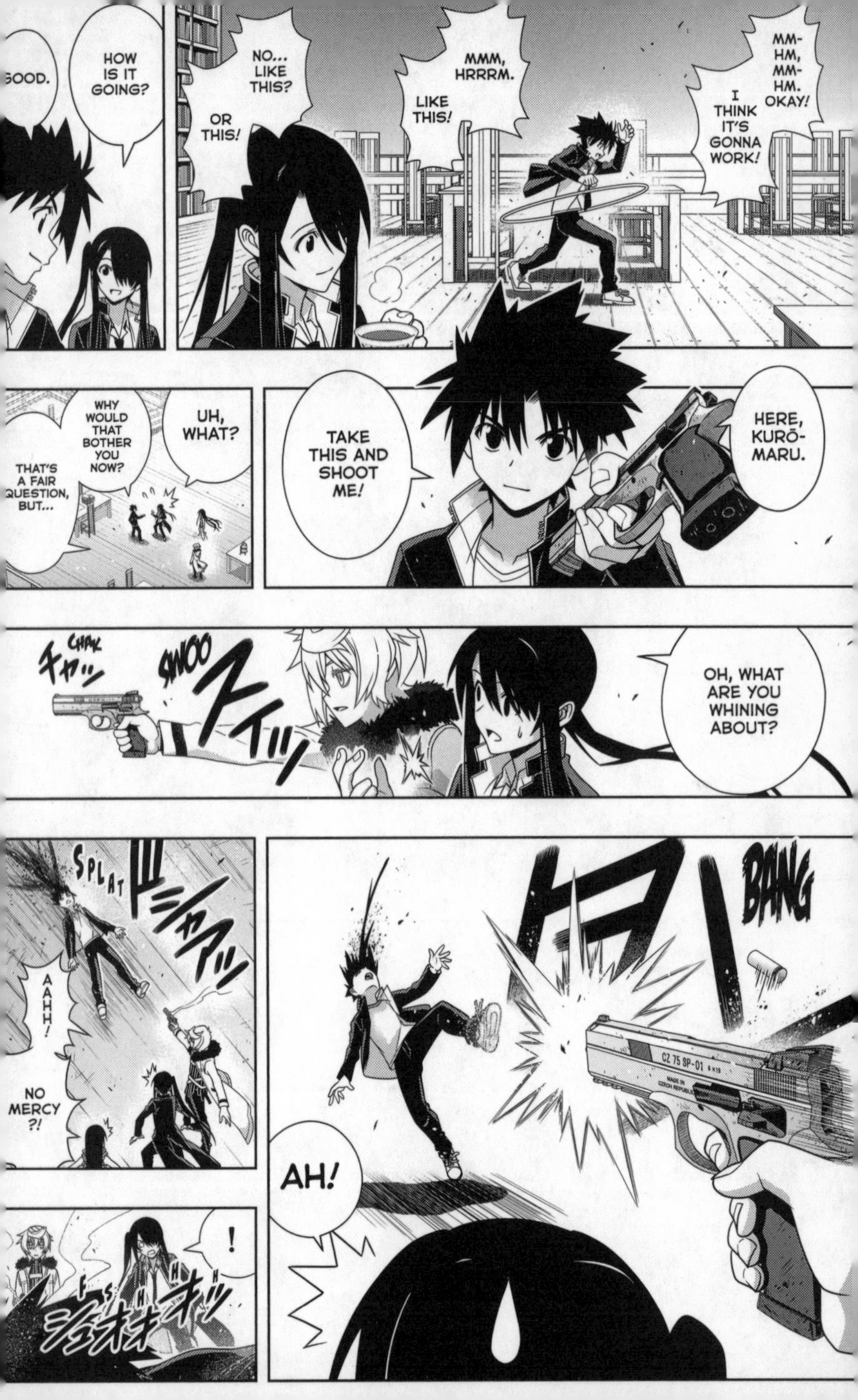
MM-HM, MM-HM. OKAY!
I THINK IT'S GONNA WORK!
MMM, HRRRM.
LIKE THIS!
NO... LIKE THIS?
OR THIS!
HOW IS IT GOING?
GOOD.
HERE, KURŌ-MARU.
TAKE THIS AND SHOOT ME!
UH, WHAT?
WHY WOULD THAT BOTHER YOU NOW?
THAT'S A FAIR QUESTION, BUT...
OH, WHAT ARE YOU WHINING ABOUT?
SWOO
CHAK
BANG
CZ 75 SP-01
AH!
SPLAT
AAHH!
NO MERCY?!
!
FSHHH

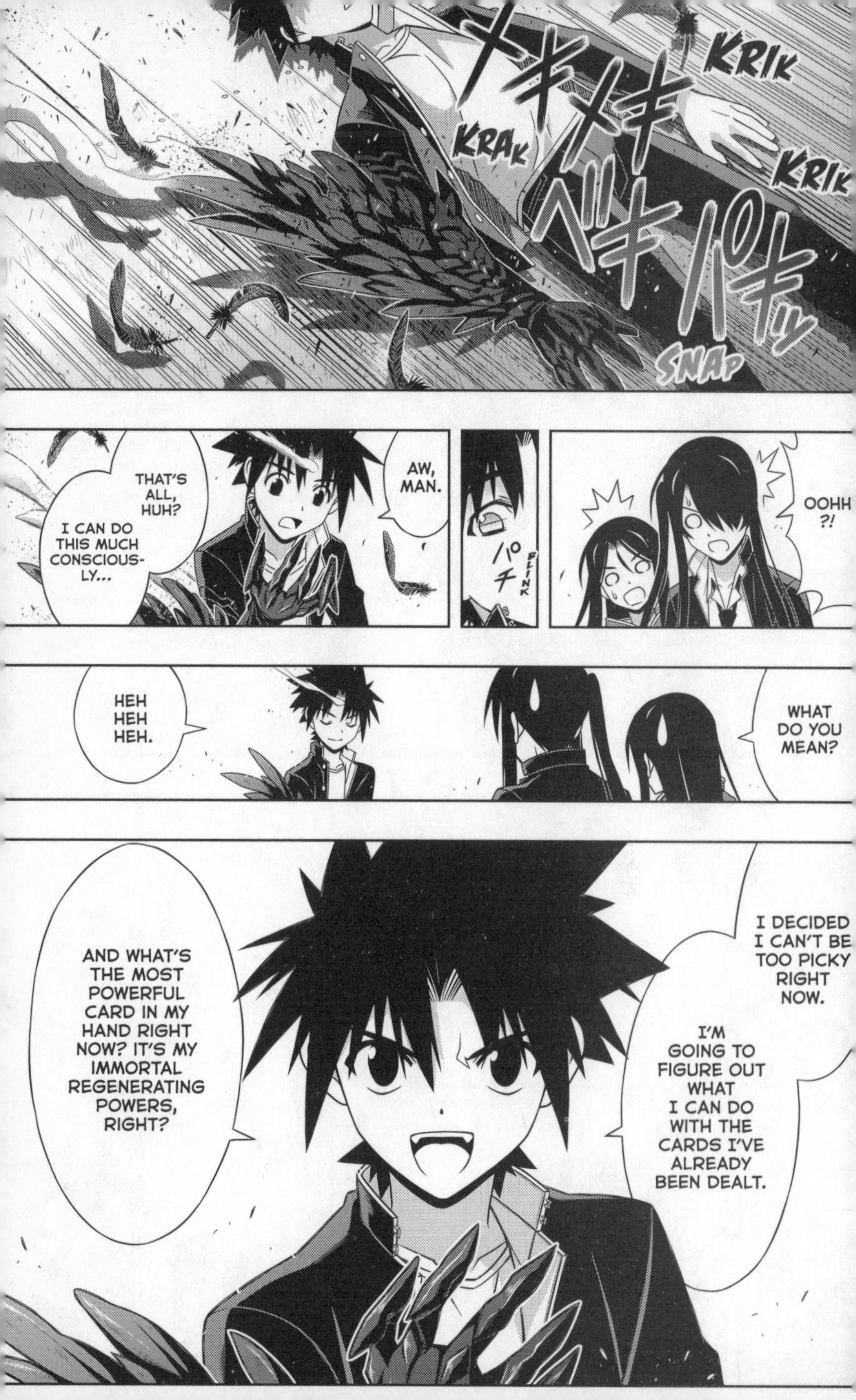

メキメキ
KRIK
KRIK
KRAK
ベキ パキッ
SNAP
OOHH ?!
パチ
BLINK
AW, MAN.
THAT'S ALL, HUH? I CAN DO THIS MUCH CONSCIOUSLY...
WHAT DO YOU MEAN?
HEH HEH HEH.
I DECIDED I CAN'T BE TOO PICKY RIGHT NOW.
I'M GOING TO FIGURE OUT WHAT I CAN DO WITH THE CARDS I'VE ALREADY BEEN DEALT.
AND WHAT'S THE MOST POWERFUL CARD IN MY HAND RIGHT NOW? IT'S MY IMMORTAL REGENERATING POWERS, RIGHT?

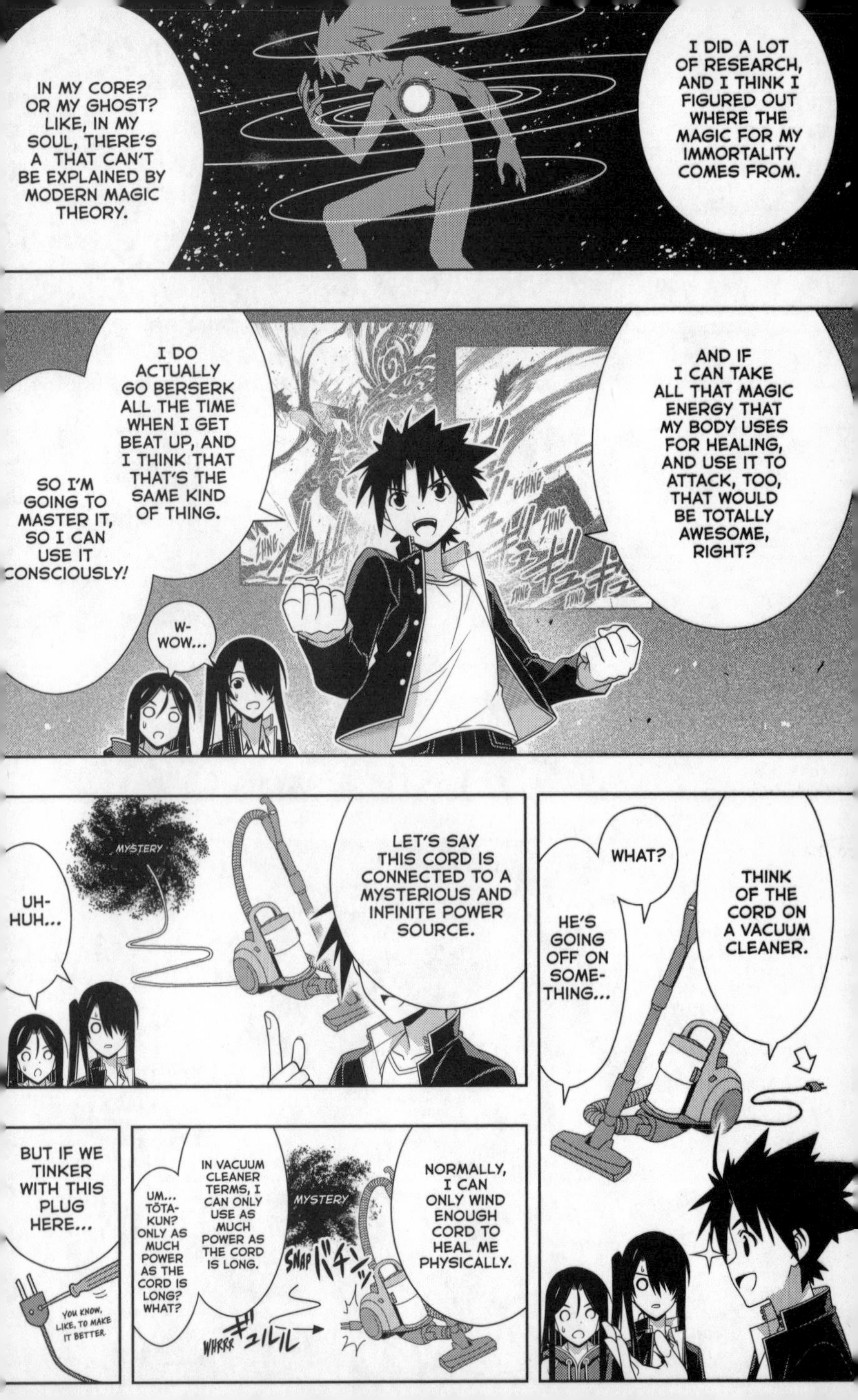
I DID A LOT OF RESEARCH, AND I THINK I FIGURED OUT WHERE THE MAGIC FOR MY IMMORTALITY COMES FROM.
IN MY CORE? OR MY GHOST? LIKE, IN MY SOUL, THERE'S A THAT CAN'T BE EXPLAINED BY MODERN MAGIC THEORY.
AND IF I CAN TAKE ALL THAT MAGIC ENERGY THAT MY BODY USES FOR HEALING, AND USE IT TO ATTACK, TOO, THAT WOULD BE TOTALLY AWESOME, RIGHT?
I DO ACTUALLY GO BERSERK ALL THE TIME WHEN I GET BEAT UP, AND I THINK THAT THAT'S THE SAME KIND OF THING.
SO I'M GOING TO MASTER IT, SO I CAN USE IT CONSCIOUSLY!
W- WOW...
THINK OF THE CORD ON A VACUUM CLEANER.
WHAT?
HE'S GOING OFF ON SOME-THING...
LET'S SAY THIS CORD IS CONNECTED TO A MYSTERIOUS AND INFINITE POWER SOURCE.
MYSTERY
UH- HUH...
NORMALLY, I CAN ONLY WIND ENOUGH CORD TO HEAL ME PHYSICALLY.
MYSTERY
SNAP
IN VACUUM CLEANER TERMS, I CAN ONLY USE AS MUCH POWER AS THE CORD IS LONG.
UM... TŌTA-KUN? ONLY AS MUCH POWER AS THE CORD IS LONG? WHAT?
WHRRR
BUT IF WE TINKER WITH THIS PLUG HERE...
YOU KNOW, LIKE, TO MAKE IT BETTER

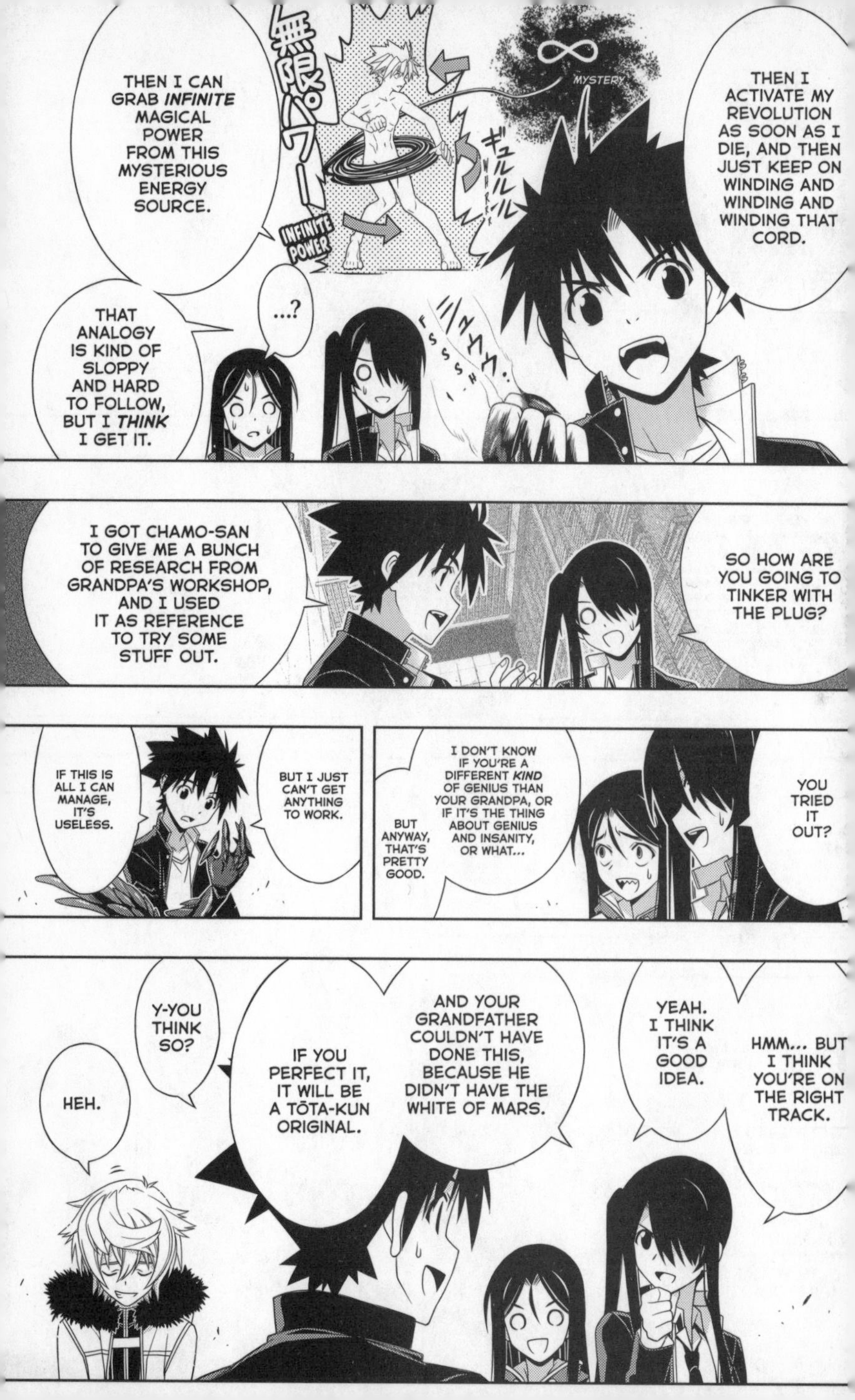

THEN I ACTIVATE MY REVOLUTION AS SOON AS I DIE, AND THEN JUST KEEP ON WINDING AND WINDING AND WINDING THAT CORD.
MYSTERY
WHRRR
無限パワー
INFINITE POWER
THEN I CAN GRAB *INFINITE* MAGICAL POWER FROM THIS MYSTERIOUS ENERGY SOURCE.
...?
FSSSH
THAT ANALOGY IS KIND OF SLOPPY AND HARD TO FOLLOW, BUT I *THINK* I GET IT.
SO HOW ARE YOU GOING TO TINKER WITH THE PLUG?
I GOT CHAMO-SAN TO GIVE ME A BUNCH OF RESEARCH FROM GRANDPA'S WORKSHOP, AND I USED IT AS REFERENCE TO TRY SOME STUFF OUT.
YOU TRIED IT OUT?
I DON'T KNOW IF YOU'RE A DIFFERENT *KIND* OF GENIUS THAN YOUR GRANDPA, OR IF IT'S THE THING ABOUT GENIUS AND INSANITY, OR WHAT...
BUT ANYWAY, THAT'S PRETTY GOOD.
BUT I JUST CAN'T GET ANYTHING TO WORK.
IF THIS IS ALL I CAN MANAGE, IT'S USELESS.
HMM... BUT I THINK YOU'RE ON THE RIGHT TRACK.
YEAH. I THINK IT'S A GOOD IDEA.
AND YOUR GRANDFATHER COULDN'T HAVE DONE THIS, BECAUSE HE DIDN'T HAVE THE WHITE OF MARS.
IF YOU PERFECT IT, IT WILL BE A TŌTA-KUN ORIGINAL.
Y-YOU THINK SO?
HEH.

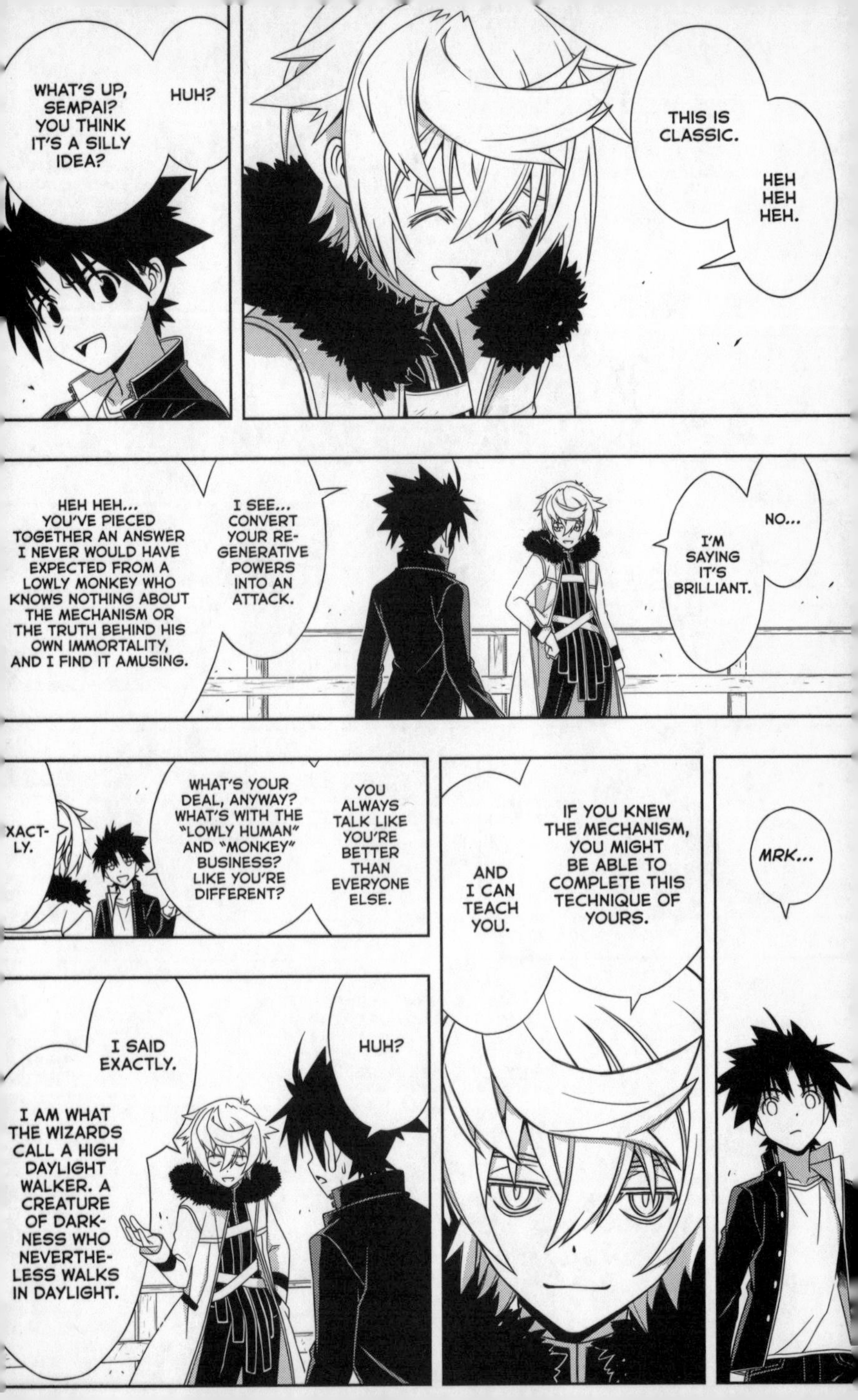
THIS IS CLASSIC.
HEH HEH HEH.
HUH?
WHAT'S UP, SEMPAI? YOU THINK IT'S A SILLY IDEA?
NO...
I'M SAYING IT'S BRILLIANT.
I SEE... CONVERT YOUR RE-GENERATIVE POWERS INTO AN ATTACK.
HEH HEH... YOU'VE PIECED TOGETHER AN ANSWER I NEVER WOULD HAVE EXPECTED FROM A LOWLY MONKEY WHO KNOWS NOTHING ABOUT THE MECHANISM OR THE TRUTH BEHIND HIS OWN IMMORTALITY, AND I FIND IT AMUSING.
MRK...
IF YOU KNEW THE MECHANISM, YOU MIGHT BE ABLE TO COMPLETE THIS TECHNIQUE OF YOURS.
AND I CAN TEACH YOU.
YOU ALWAYS TALK LIKE YOU'RE BETTER THAN EVERYONE ELSE.
WHAT'S YOUR DEAL, ANYWAY? WHAT'S WITH THE "LOWLY HUMAN" AND "MONKEY" BUSINESS? LIKE YOU'RE DIFFERENT?
XACT-LY.
HUH?
I SAID EXACTLY.
I AM WHAT THE WIZARDS CALL A HIGH DAYLIGHT WALKER. A CREATURE OF DARK-NESS WHO NEVERTHE-LESS WALKS IN DAYLIGHT.

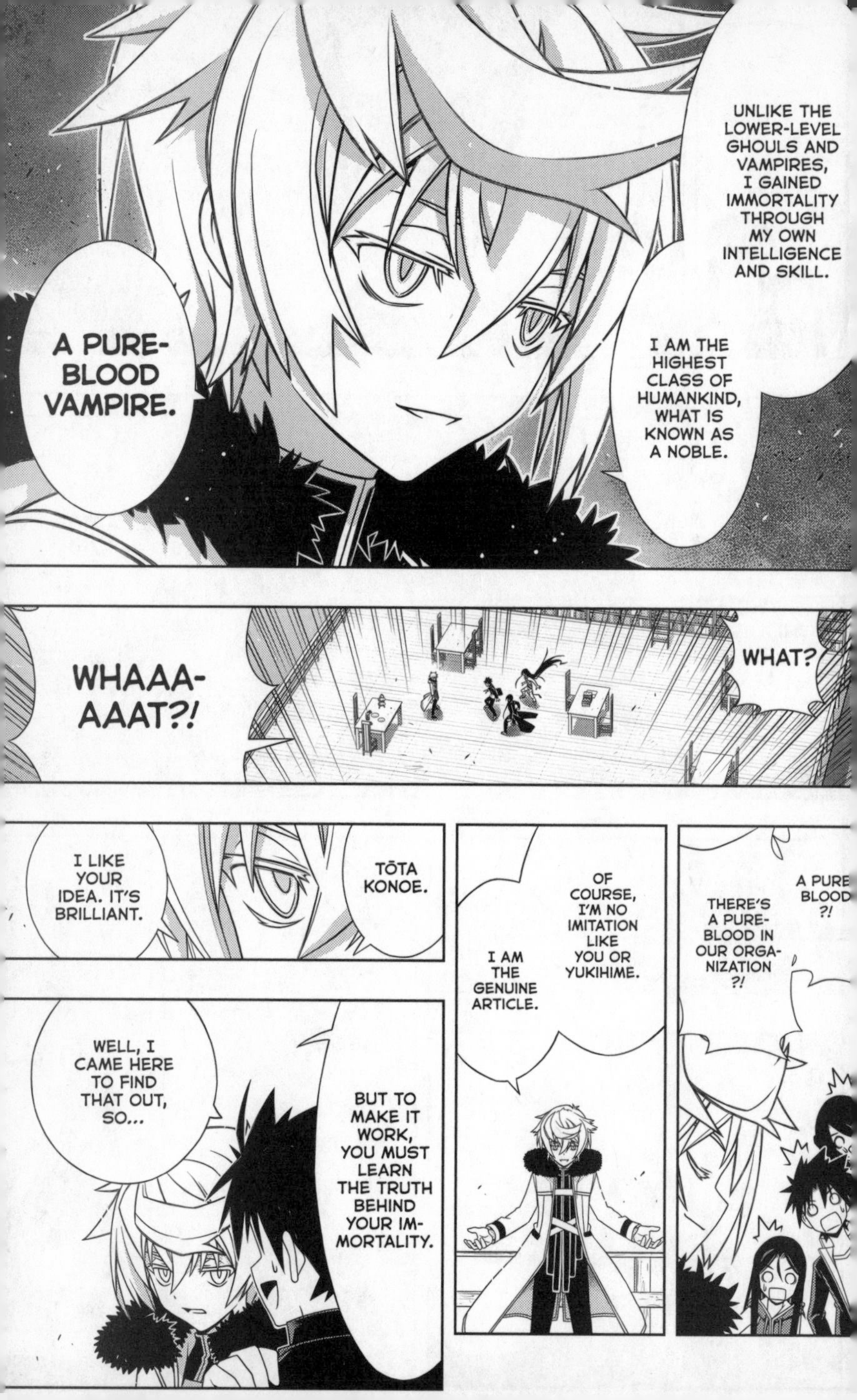
UNLIKE THE LOWER-LEVEL GHOULS AND VAMPIRES, I GAINED IMMORTALITY THROUGH MY OWN INTELLIGENCE AND SKILL.
I AM THE HIGHEST CLASS OF HUMANKIND, WHAT IS KNOWN AS A NOBLE.
A PURE-BLOOD VAMPIRE.
WHAT?
WHAAA-AAAT?!
A PURE BLOOD ?!
THERE'S A PURE-BLOOD IN OUR ORGANIZATION ?!
OF COURSE, I'M NO IMITATION LIKE YOU OR YUKIHIME.
I AM THE GENUINE ARTICLE.
TŌTA KONOE.
I LIKE YOUR IDEA. IT'S BRILLIANT.
BUT TO MAKE IT WORK, YOU MUST LEARN THE TRUTH BEHIND YOUR IMMORTALITY.
WELL, I CAME HERE TO FIND THAT OUT, SO...

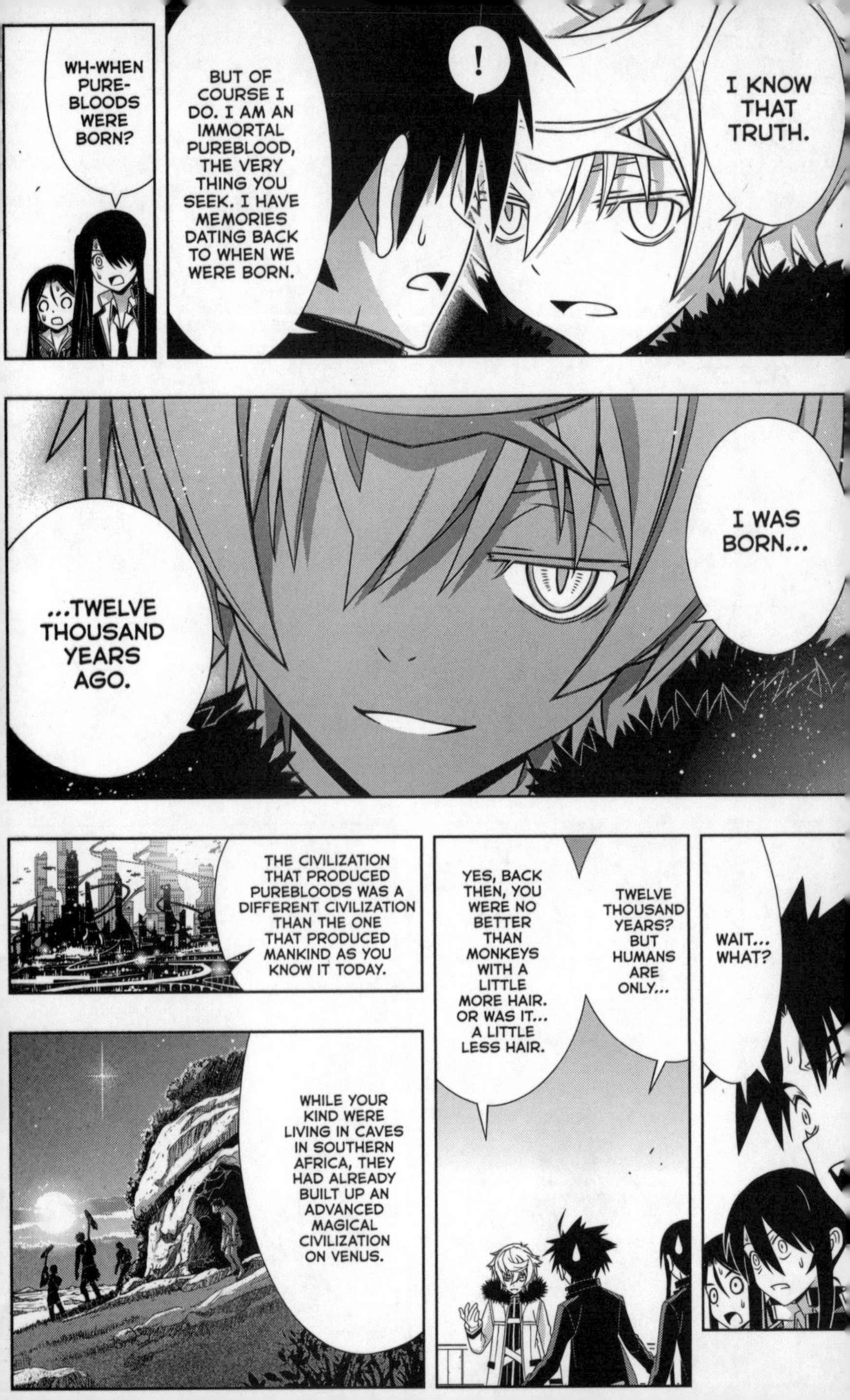
I KNOW THAT TRUTH.
!
BUT OF COURSE I DO. I AM AN IMMORTAL PUREBLOOD, THE VERY THING YOU SEEK. I HAVE MEMORIES DATING BACK TO WHEN WE WERE BORN.
WH-WHEN PURE-BLOODS WERE BORN?
I WAS BORN...
...TWELVE THOUSAND YEARS AGO.
WAIT... WHAT?
TWELVE THOUSAND YEARS? BUT HUMANS ARE ONLY...
YES, BACK THEN, YOU WERE NO BETTER THAN MONKEYS WITH A LITTLE MORE HAIR. OR WAS IT... A LITTLE LESS HAIR.
THE CIVILIZATION THAT PRODUCED PUREBLOODS WAS A DIFFERENT CIVILIZATION THAN THE ONE THAT PRODUCED MANKIND AS YOU KNOW IT TODAY.
WHILE YOUR KIND WERE LIVING IN CAVES IN SOUTHERN AFRICA, THEY HAD ALREADY BUILT UP AN ADVANCED MAGICAL CIVILIZATION ON VENUS.

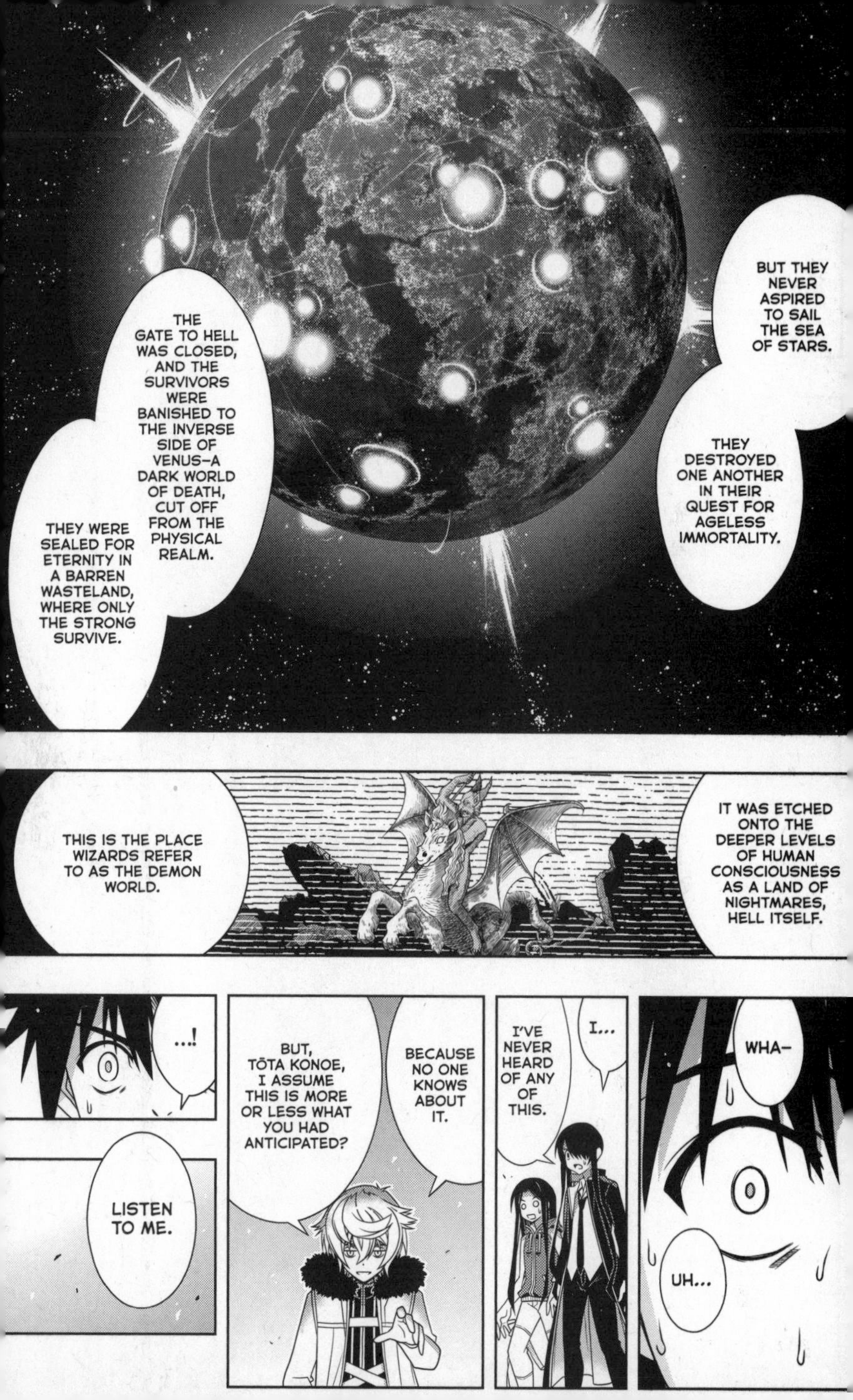
BUT THEY NEVER ASPIRED TO SAIL THE SEA OF STARS.
THEY DESTROYED ONE ANOTHER IN THEIR QUEST FOR AGELESS IMMORTALITY.
THE GATE TO HELL WAS CLOSED, AND THE SURVIVORS WERE BANISHED TO THE INVERSE SIDE OF VENUS—A DARK WORLD OF DEATH, CUT OFF FROM THE PHYSICAL REALM.
THEY WERE SEALED FOR ETERNITY IN A BARREN WASTELAND, WHERE ONLY THE STRONG SURVIVE.
IT WAS ETCHED ONTO THE DEEPER LEVELS OF HUMAN CONSCIOUSNESS AS A LAND OF NIGHTMARES, HELL ITSELF.
THIS IS THE PLACE WIZARDS REFER TO AS THE DEMON WORLD.
WHA—
UH...
I...
I'VE NEVER HEARD OF ANY OF THIS.
BECAUSE NO ONE KNOWS ABOUT IT.
BUT, TŌTA KONOE, I ASSUME THIS IS MORE OR LESS WHAT YOU HAD ANTICIPATED?
...!
LISTEN TO ME.

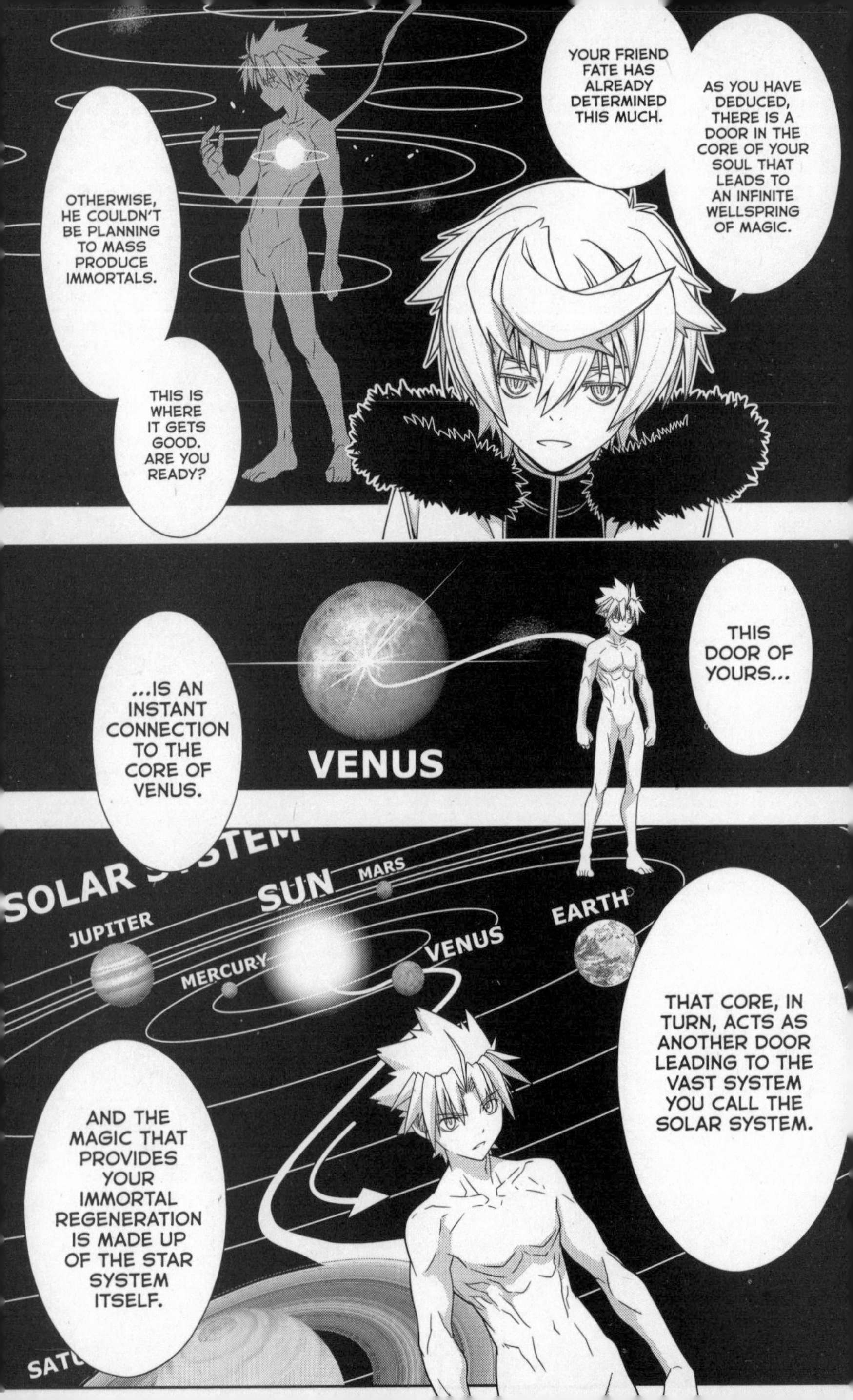
AS YOU HAVE DEDUCED, THERE IS A DOOR IN THE CORE OF YOUR SOUL THAT LEADS TO AN INFINITE WELLSPRING OF MAGIC.
YOUR FRIEND FATE HAS ALREADY DETERMINED THIS MUCH.
OTHERWISE, HE COULDN'T BE PLANNING TO MASS PRODUCE IMMORTALS.
THIS IS WHERE IT GETS GOOD. ARE YOU READY?
THIS DOOR OF YOURS...
VENUS
...IS AN INSTANT CONNECTION TO THE CORE OF VENUS.
THAT CORE, IN TURN, ACTS AS ANOTHER DOOR LEADING TO THE VAST SYSTEM YOU CALL THE SOLAR SYSTEM.
EARTH
MARS
SUN
VENUS
MERCURY
JUPITER
AND THE MAGIC THAT PROVIDES YOUR IMMORTAL REGENERATION IS MADE UP OF THE STAR SYSTEM ITSELF.

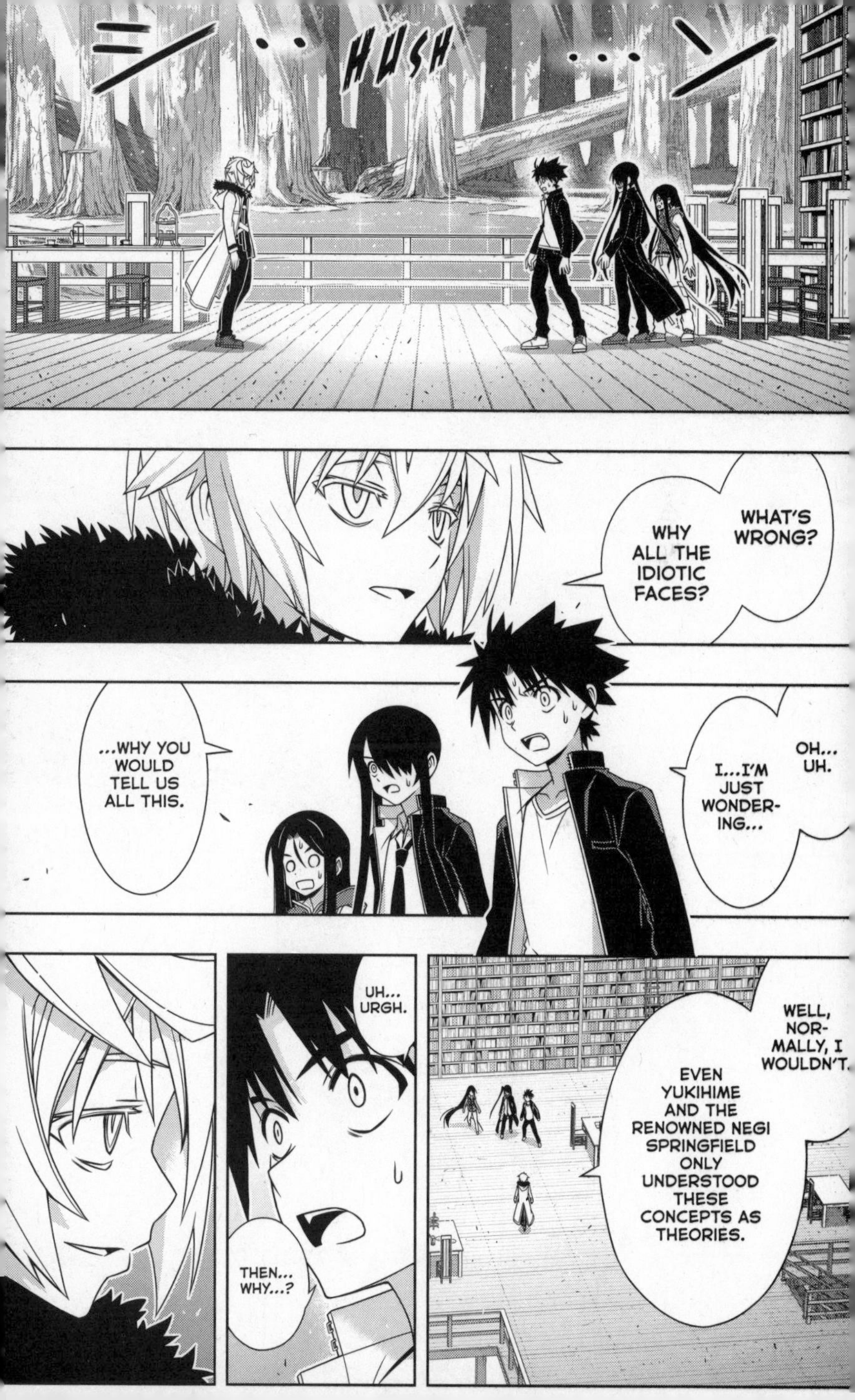

...
HUSH
...
WHAT'S WRONG?
WHY ALL THE IDIOTIC FACES?
OH... UH.
I...I'M JUST WONDER-ING...
...WHY YOU WOULD TELL US ALL THIS.
WELL, NOR-MALLY, I WOULDN'T.
EVEN YUKIHIME AND THE RENOWNED NEGI SPRINGFIELD ONLY UNDERSTOOD THESE CONCEPTS AS THEORIES.
UH... URGH.
THEN... WHY...?

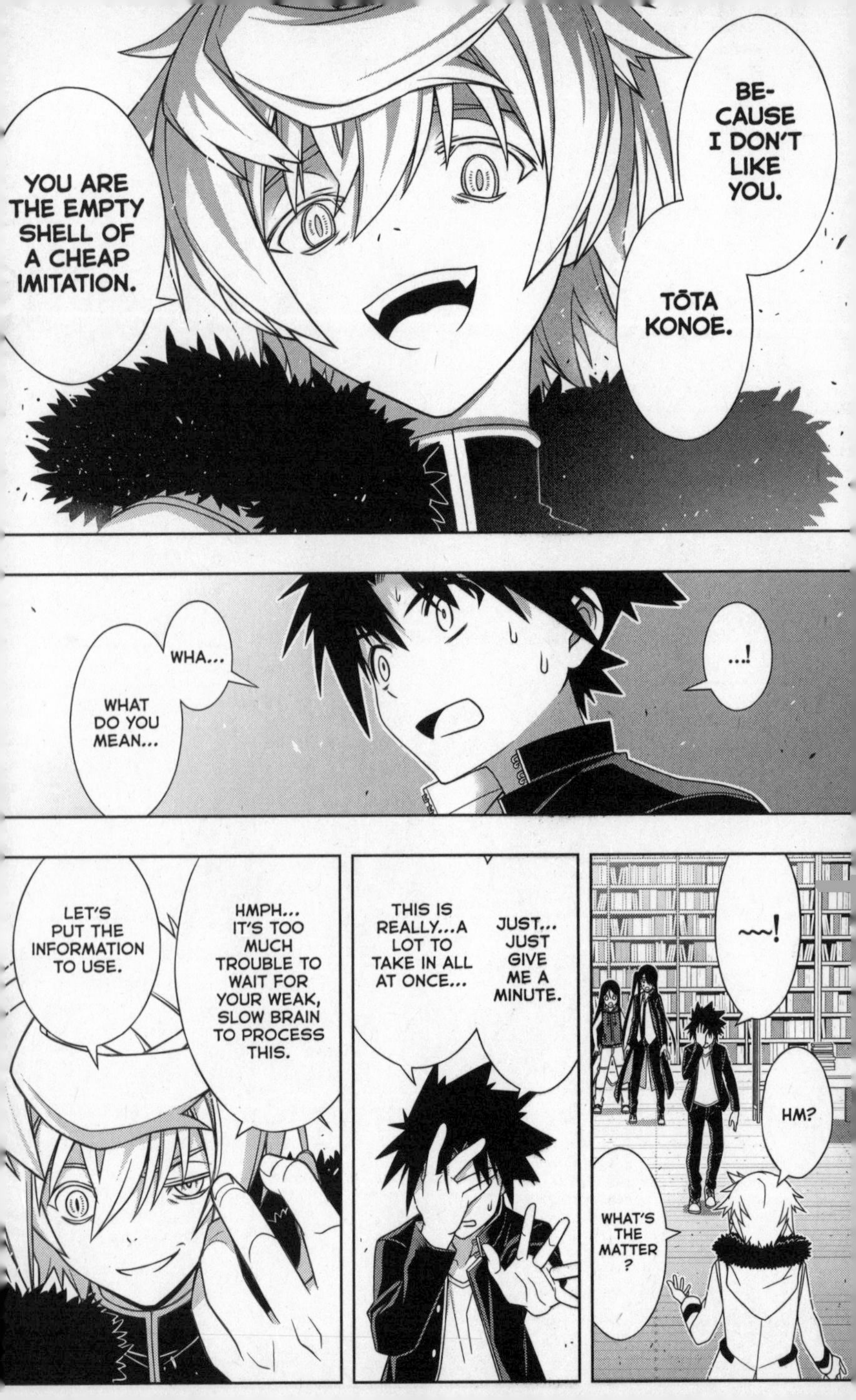
BE-CAUSE I DON'T LIKE YOU.
TŌTA KONOE.
YOU ARE THE EMPTY SHELL OF A CHEAP IMITATION.
...!
WHA...
WHAT DO YOU MEAN...
~~~!
HM?
WHAT'S THE MATTER?
JUST... JUST GIVE ME A MINUTE.
THIS IS REALLY...A LOT TO TAKE IN ALL AT ONCE...
HMPH... IT'S TOO MUCH TROUBLE TO WAIT FOR YOUR WEAK, SLOW BRAIN TO PROCESS THIS.
LET'S PUT THE INFORMATION TO USE.
~~~

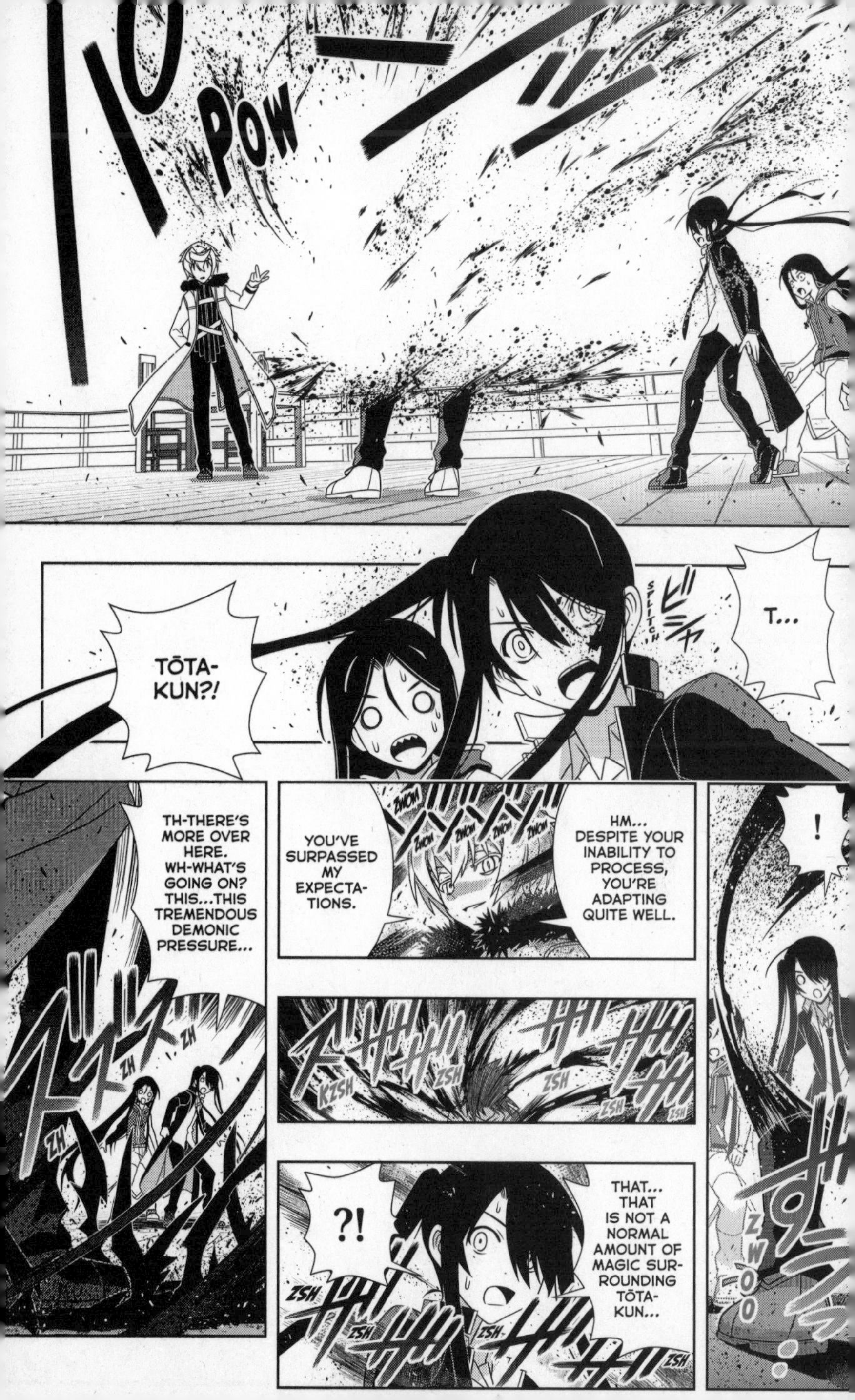
POW
SPLITCH
T...
TŌTA-KUN?!
!
ZWOO
HM... DESPITE YOUR INABILITY TO PROCESS, YOU'RE ADAPTING QUITE WELL.
YOU'VE SURPASSED MY EXPECTATIONS.
ZWOM
KZSH
ZSH
THAT... THAT IS NOT A NORMAL AMOUNT OF MAGIC SURROUNDING TŌTA-KUN...
?!
ZSH
TH-THERE'S MORE OVER HERE. WH-WHAT'S GOING ON? THIS...THIS TREMENDOUS DEMONIC PRESSURE...
ZH

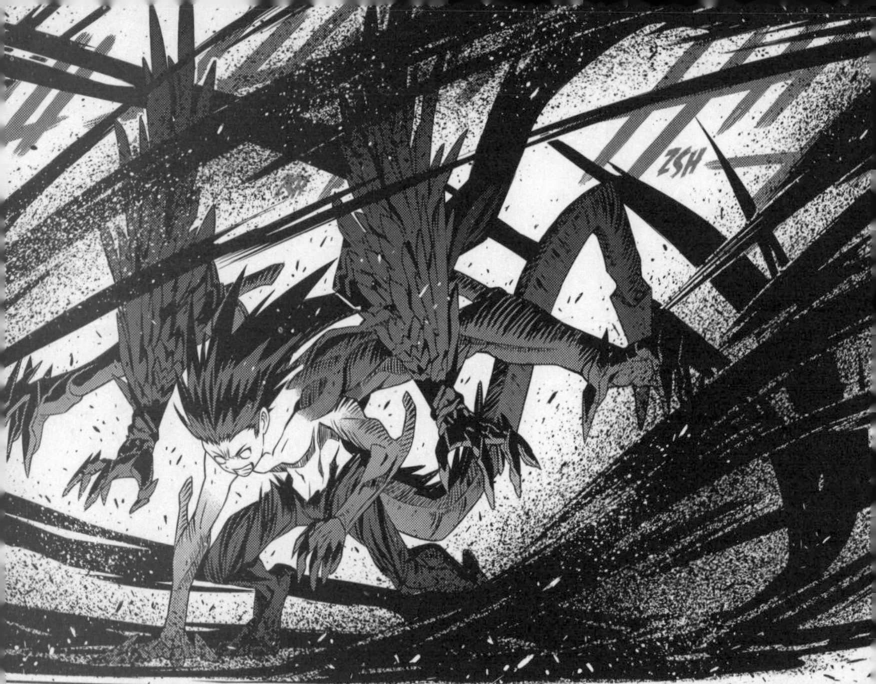
ZSH

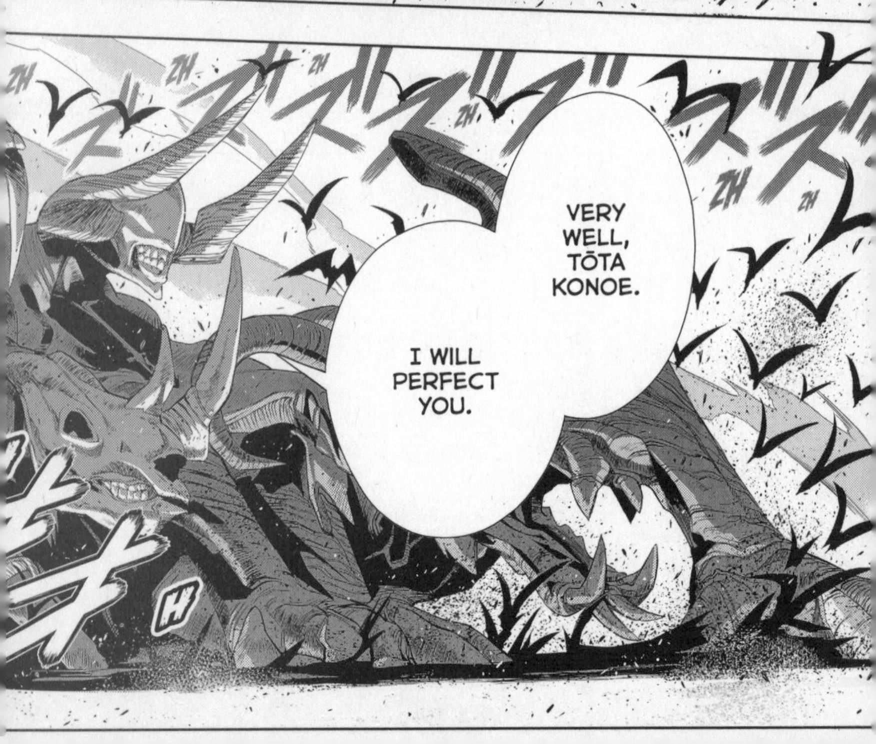
ZH
ZH
VERY WELL, TŌTA KONOE.
I WILL PERFECT YOU.
ZH
ZH
ZH

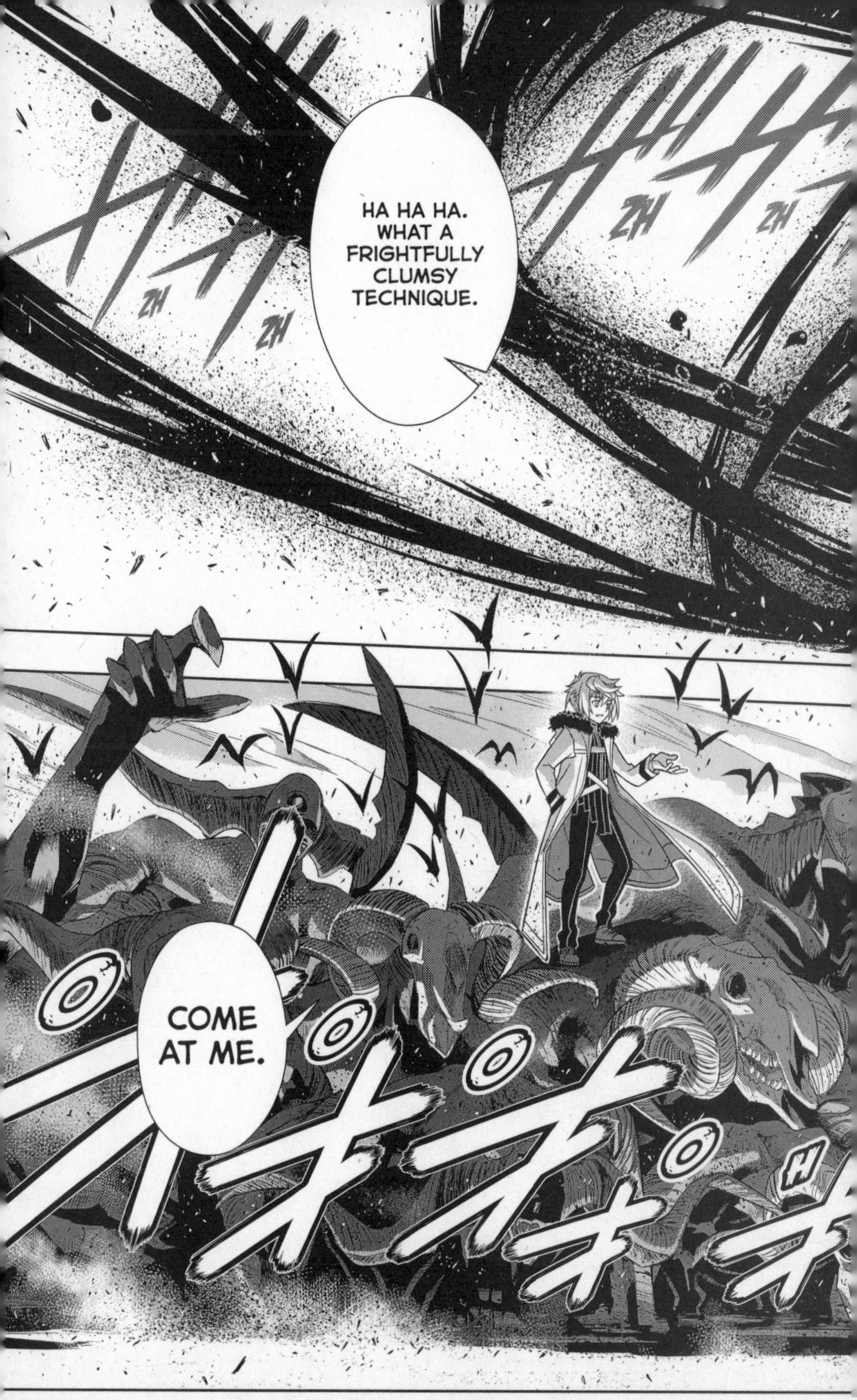
ZH
ZH
ZH
ZH
HA HA HA. WHAT A FRIGHTFULLY CLUMSY TECHNIQUE.
COME AT ME.
H

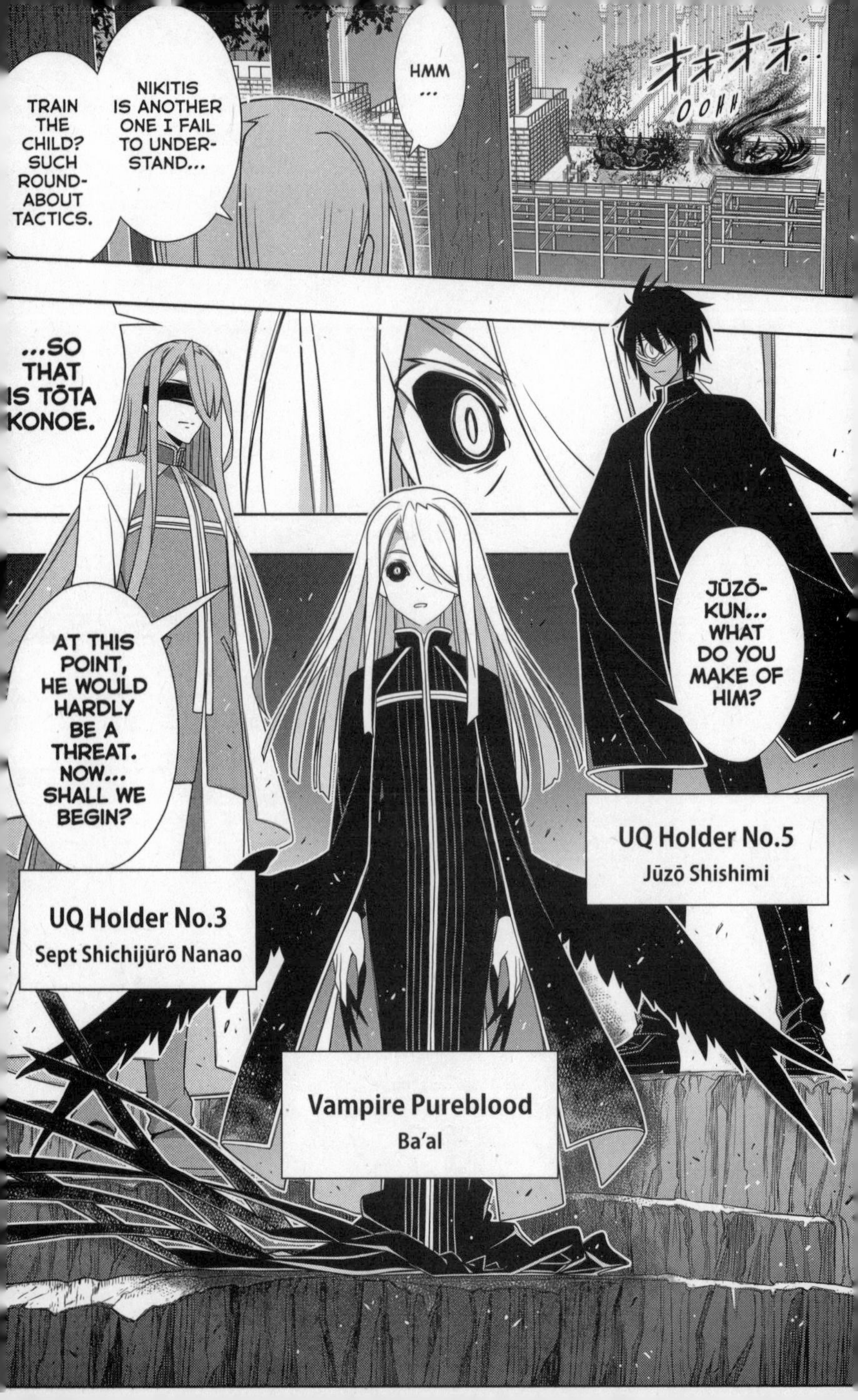

OOHH
HMM...
NIKITIS IS ANOTHER ONE I FAIL TO UNDER-STAND...
TRAIN THE CHILD? SUCH ROUND-ABOUT TACTICS.
...SO THAT IS TŌTA KONOE.
JŪZŌ-KUN... WHAT DO YOU MAKE OF HIM?
AT THIS POINT, HE WOULD HARDLY BE A THREAT. NOW... SHALL WE BEGIN?
UQ Holder No.5
Jūzō Shishimi
Vampire Pureblood
Ba'al
UQ Holder No.3
Sept Shichijūrō Nanao

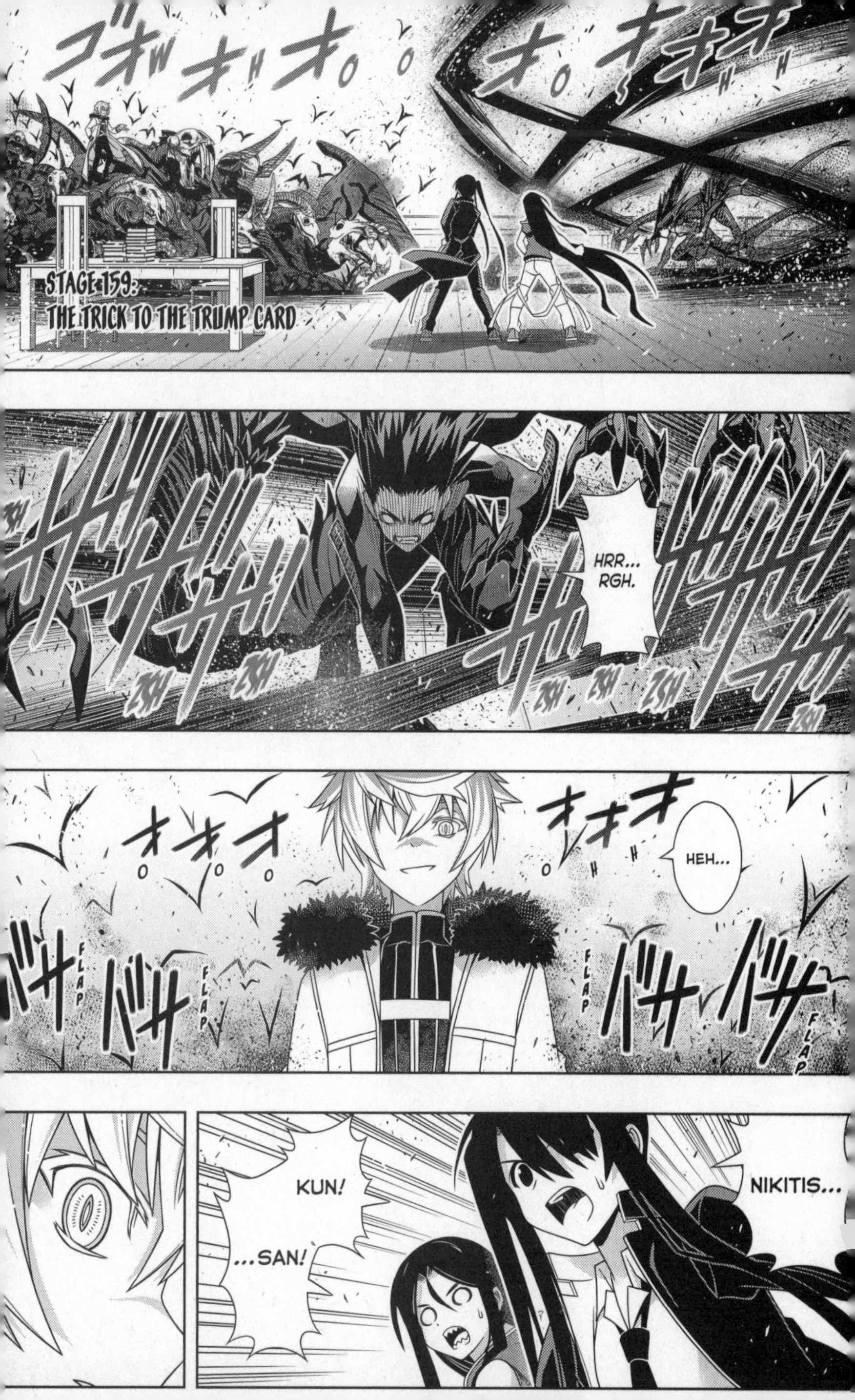
STAGE 159:
THE TRICK TO THE TRUMP CARD
ZSH
HRR... RGH.
HEH...
FLAP
NIKITIS...
KUN!
...SAN!

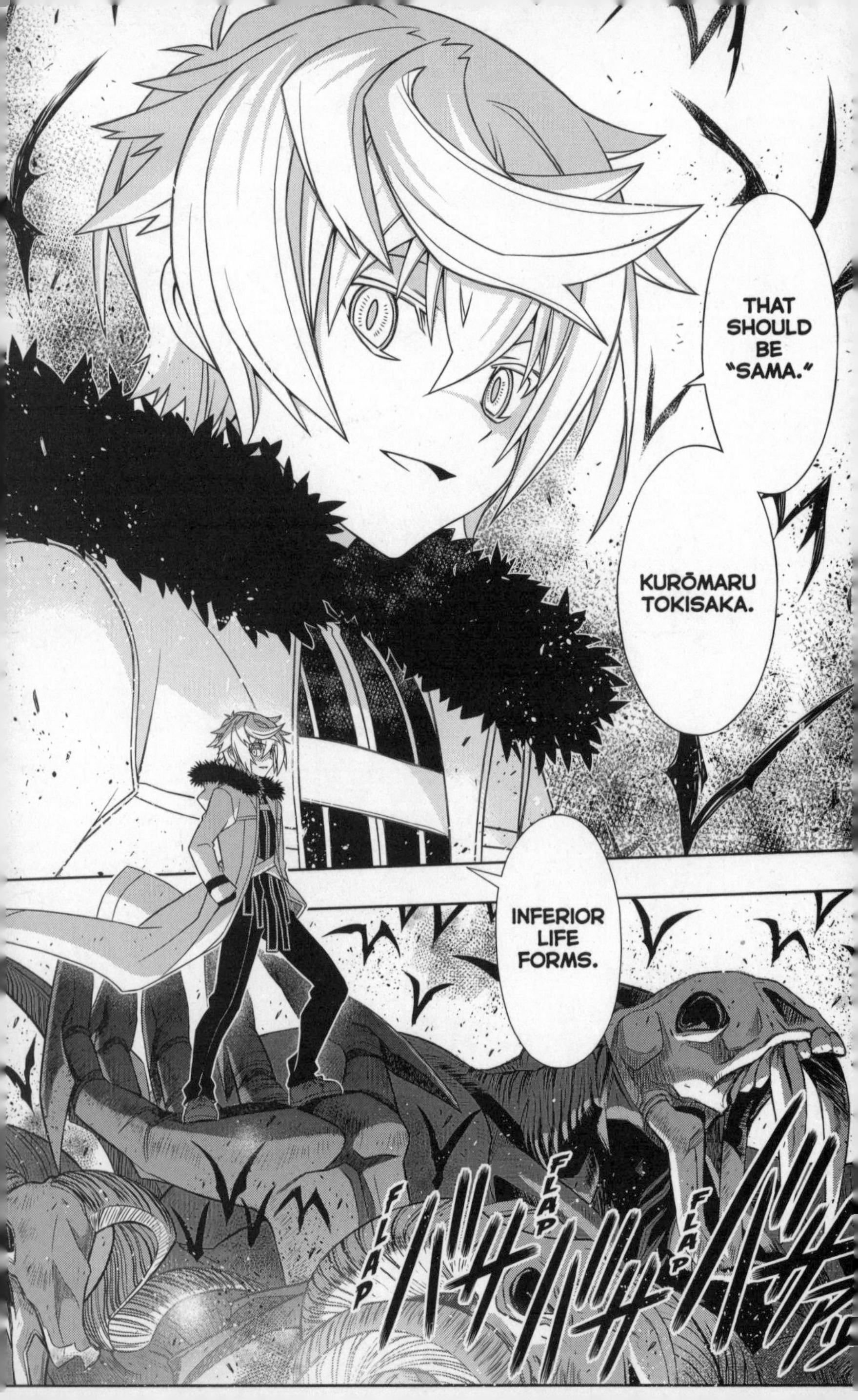
THAT SHOULD BE "SAMA."
KURŌMARU TOKISAKA.
INFERIOR LIFE FORMS.
FLAP
FLAP
FLAP

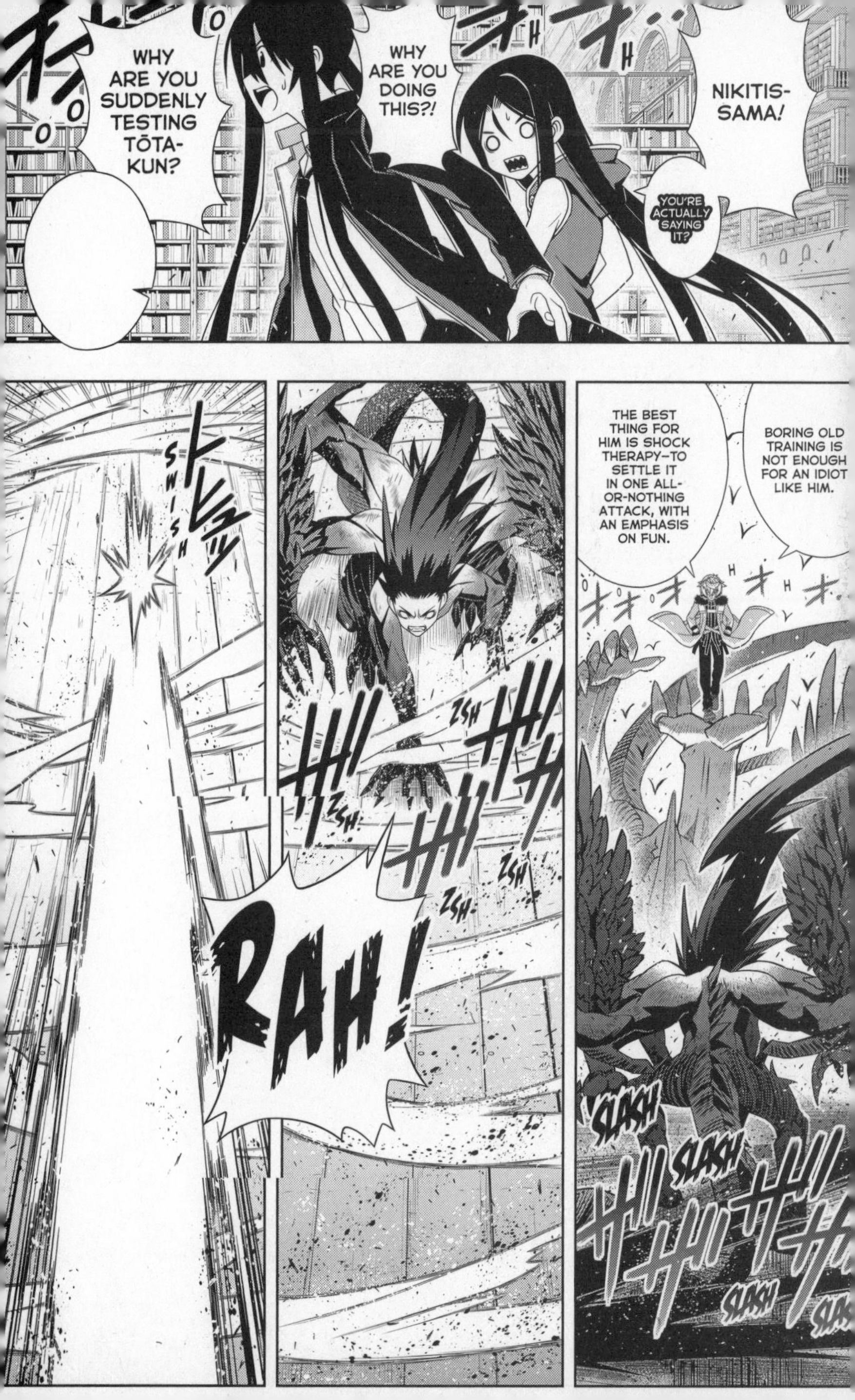

H
H
NIKITIS-SAMA!
YOU'RE ACTUALLY SAYING IT?
WHY ARE YOU DOING THIS?!
O
WHY ARE YOU SUDDENLY TESTING TŌTA-KUN?
O
O
BORING OLD TRAINING IS NOT ENOUGH FOR AN IDIOT LIKE HIM.
THE BEST THING FOR HIM IS SHOCK THERAPY—TO SETTLE IT IN ONE ALL-OR-NOTHING ATTACK, WITH AN EMPHASIS ON FUN.
H
H
O
O
SLASH
SLASH
SLASH
SLASH
ZSH
ZSH
ZSH
ZSH
RAH!
SWISH

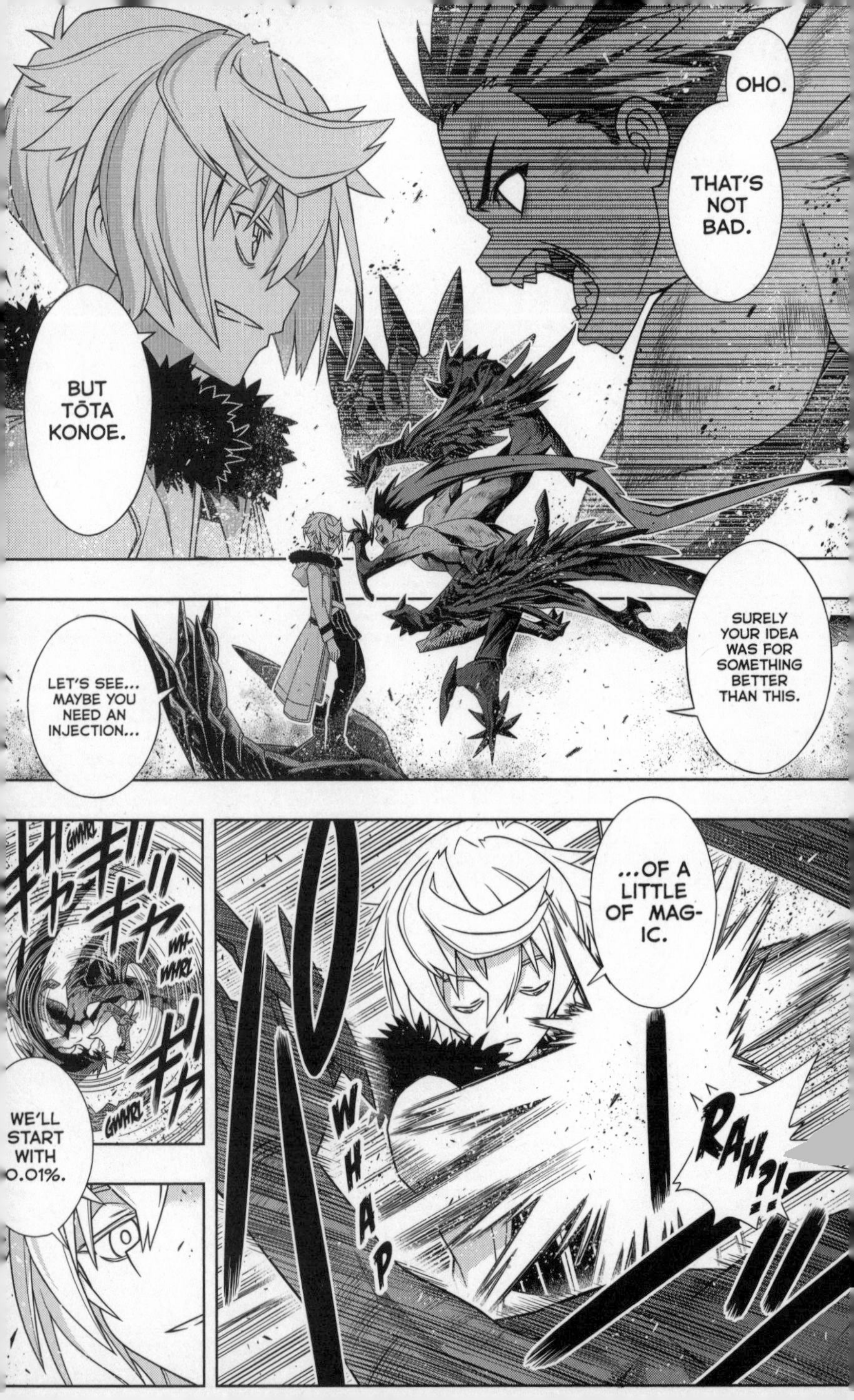
OHO.
THAT'S NOT BAD.
BUT TŌTA KONOE.
SURELY YOUR IDEA WAS FOR SOMETHING BETTER THAN THIS.
LET'S SEE... MAYBE YOU NEED AN INJECTION...
...OF A LITTLE OF MAG-IC.
WHAP
RAH?!!
GWHRL
WHWHRL
GWHRL
WE'LL START WITH 0.01%.

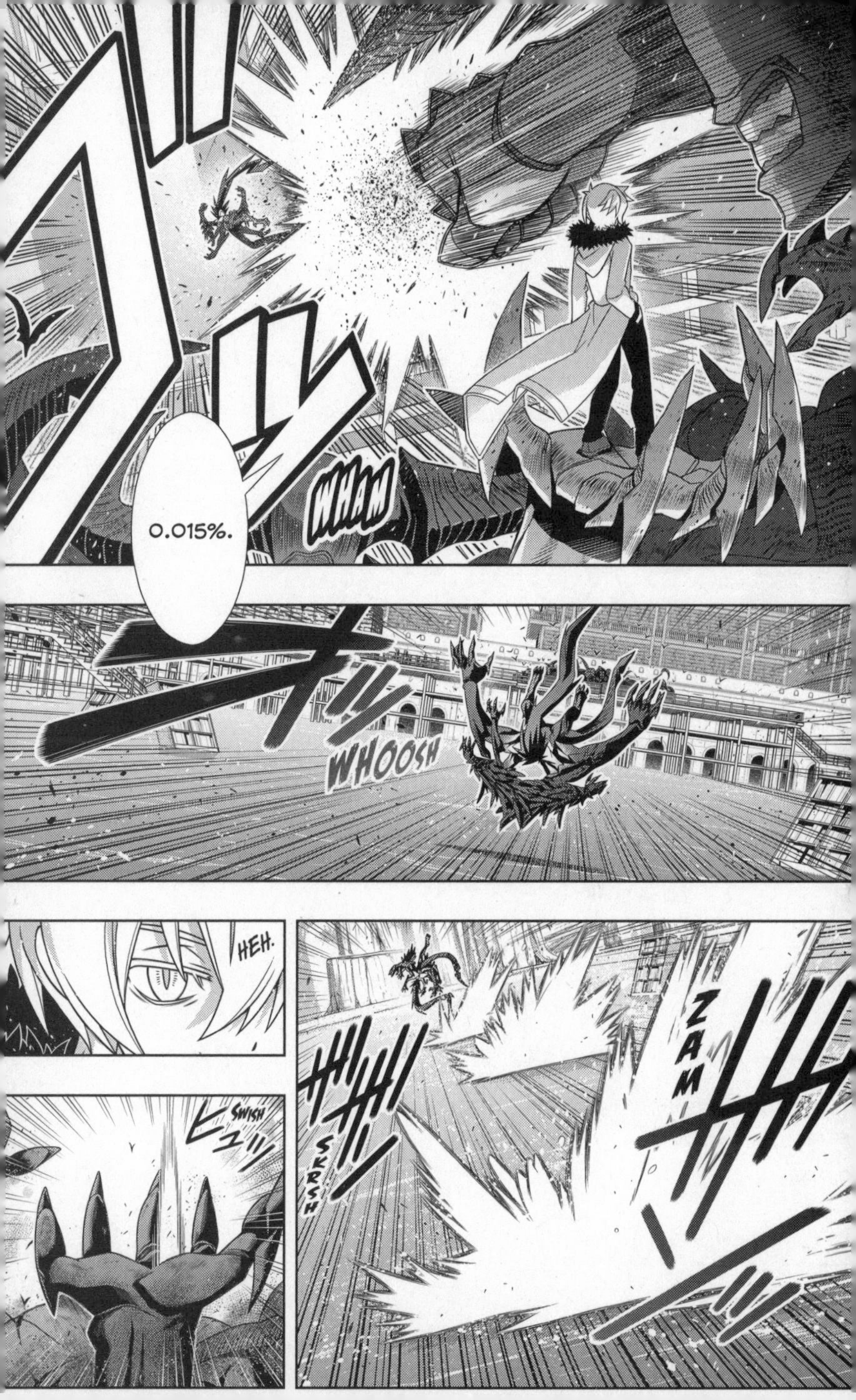
0.015%.
WHAM
WHOOSH
ZAM
SKRSH
HEH.
SWISH

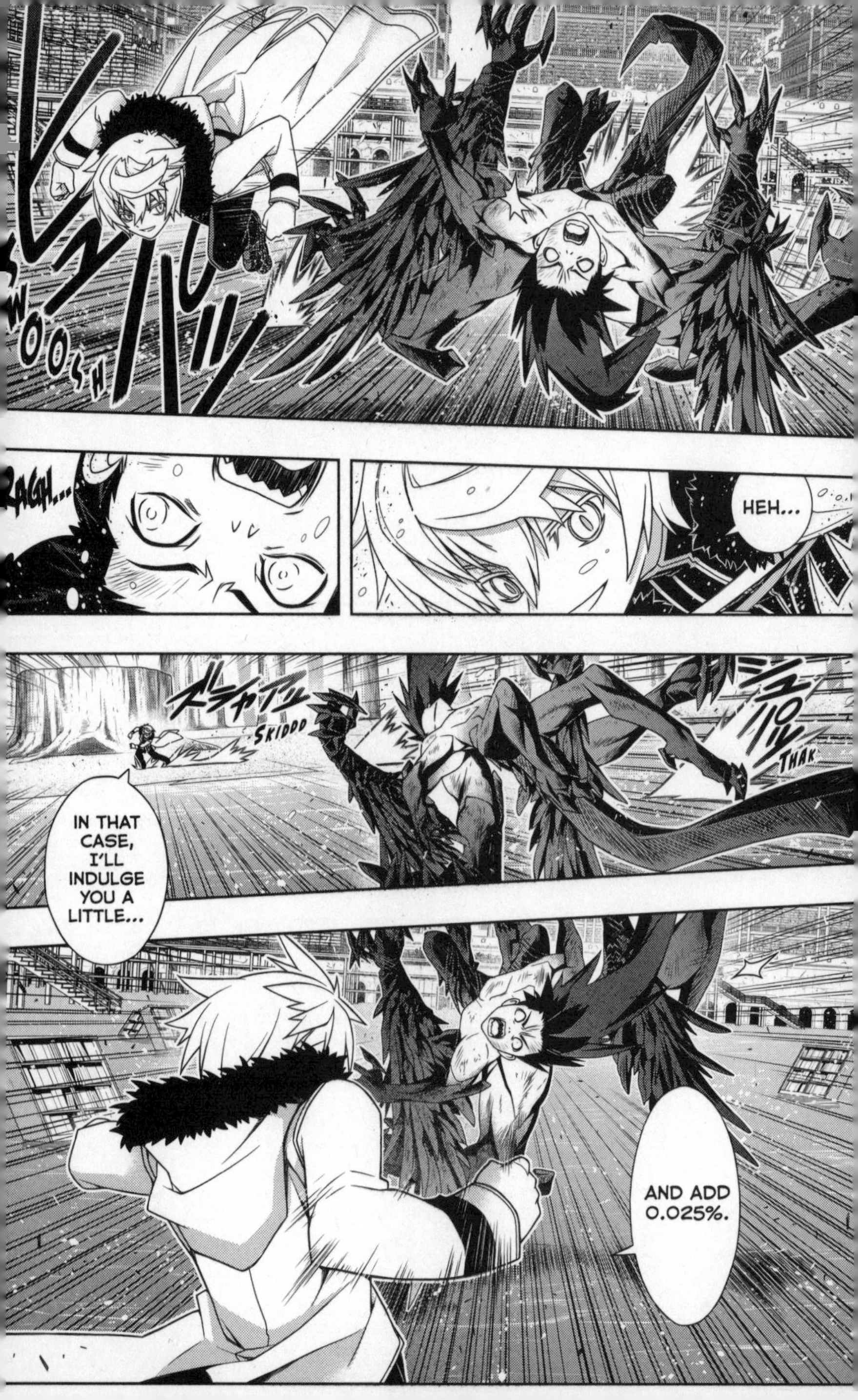
WOOSH
HEH...
RAGH...
THAK
SKIDDD
IN THAT CASE, I'LL INDULGE YOU A LITTLE...
AND ADD 0.025%.

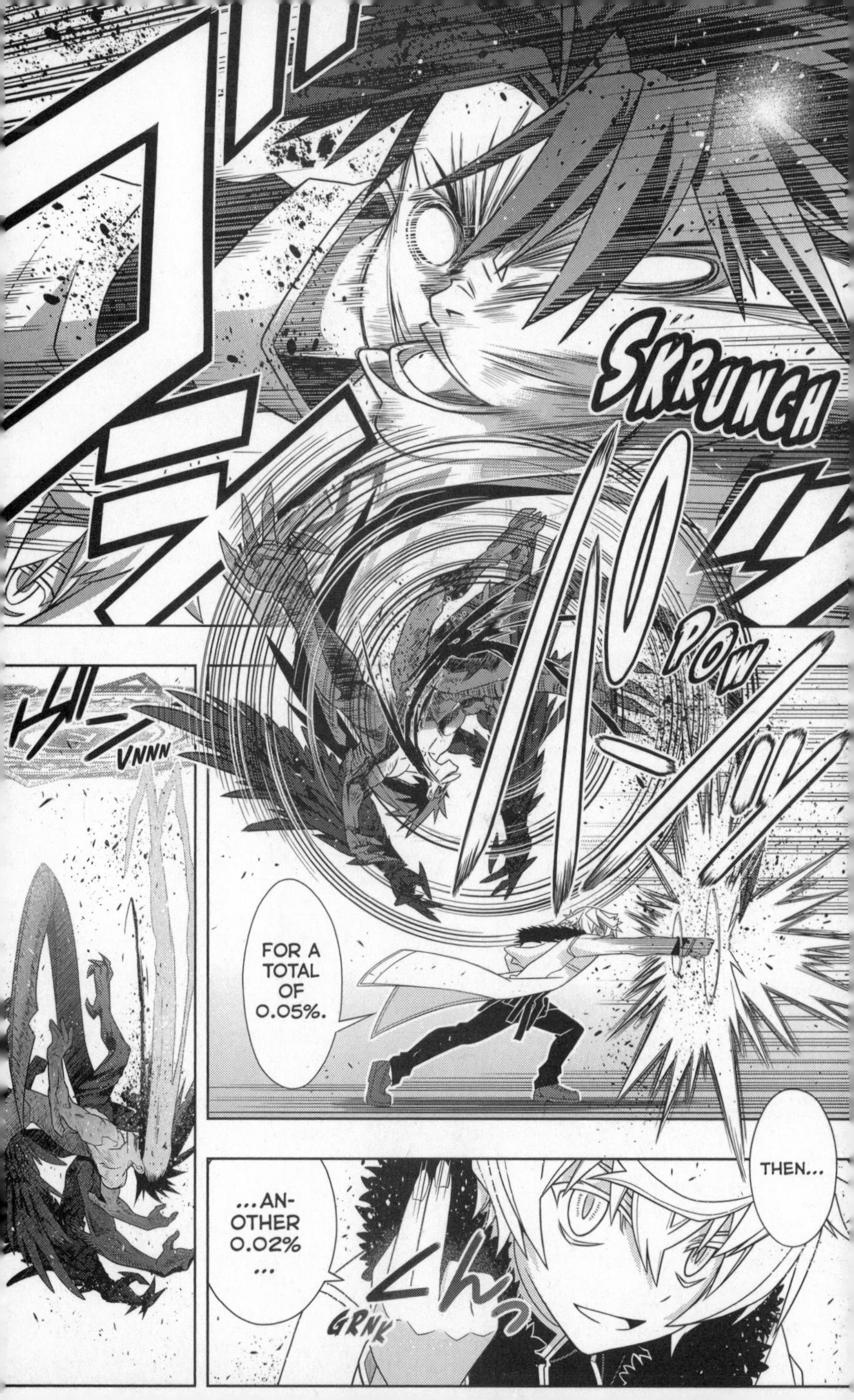
SKRUNCH
POW
FOR A TOTAL OF 0.05%.
THEN...
...AN-OTHER 0.02%...
GRNK
VNNN

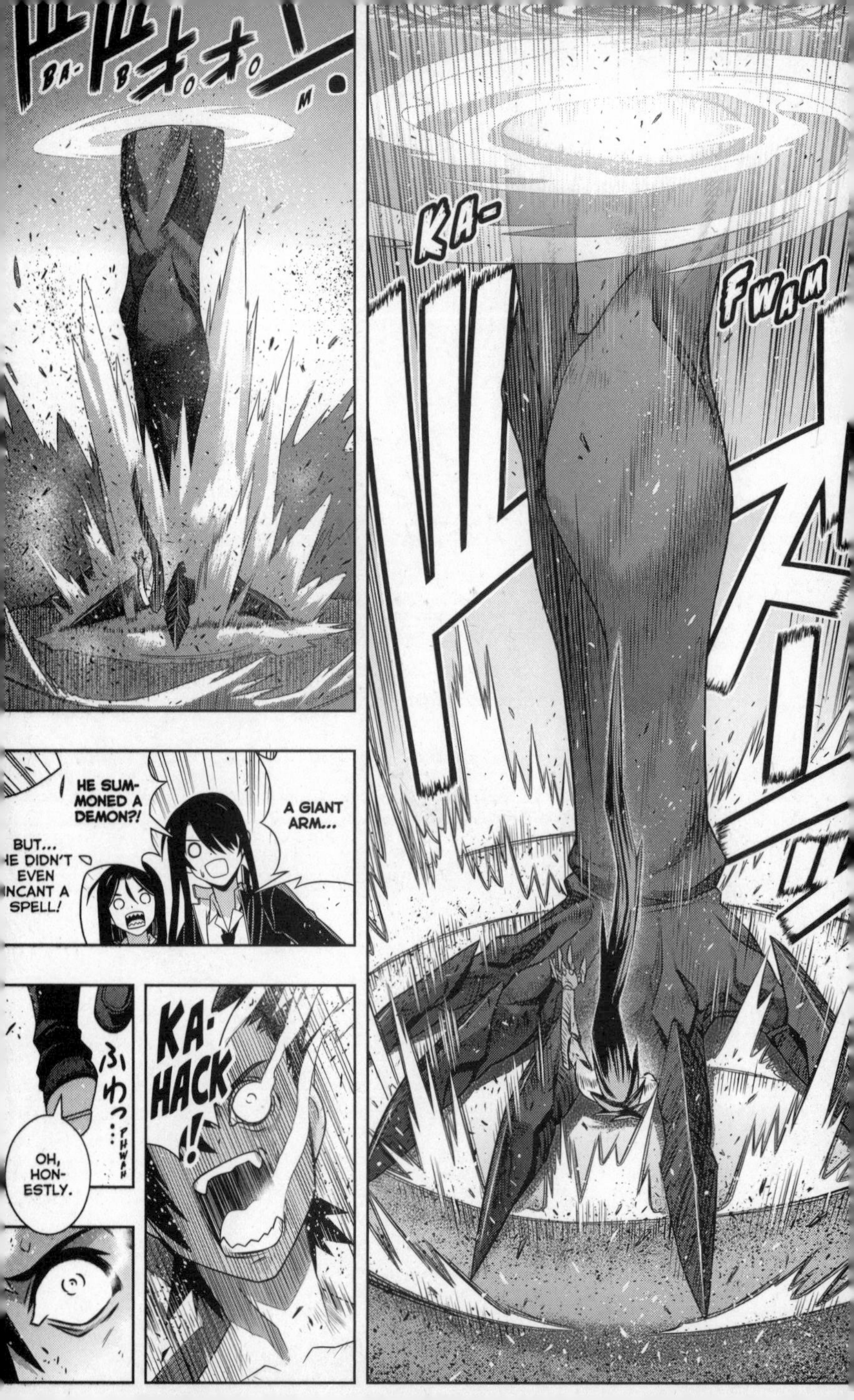
KA-
FWAM
BA-BOOM
A GIANT ARM...
HE SUMMONED A DEMON?!
BUT... HE DIDN'T EVEN INCANT A SPELL!
KA-HACK!!
ふわっ…
PHWAH
OH, HONESTLY.

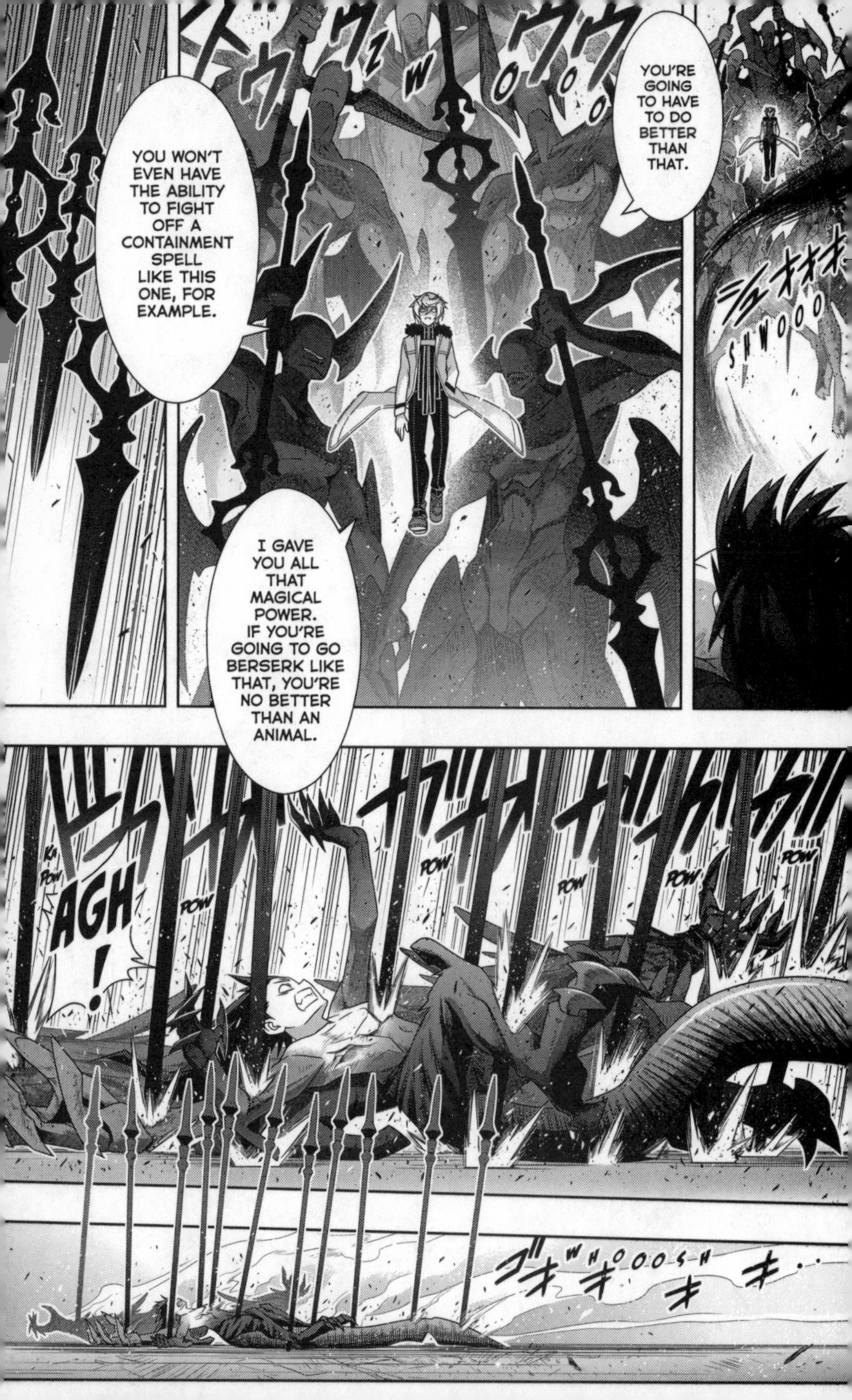
SHWOOO
WOOOO
YOU'RE GOING TO HAVE TO DO BETTER THAN THAT.
I GAVE YOU ALL THAT MAGICAL POWER. IF YOU'RE GOING TO GO BERSERK LIKE THAT, YOU'RE NO BETTER THAN AN ANIMAL.
YOU WON'T EVEN HAVE THE ABILITY TO FIGHT OFF A CONTAINMENT SPELL LIKE THIS ONE, FOR EXAMPLE.
POW
POW
POW
POW
POW
KA POW
AGH!
WHOOOSH...

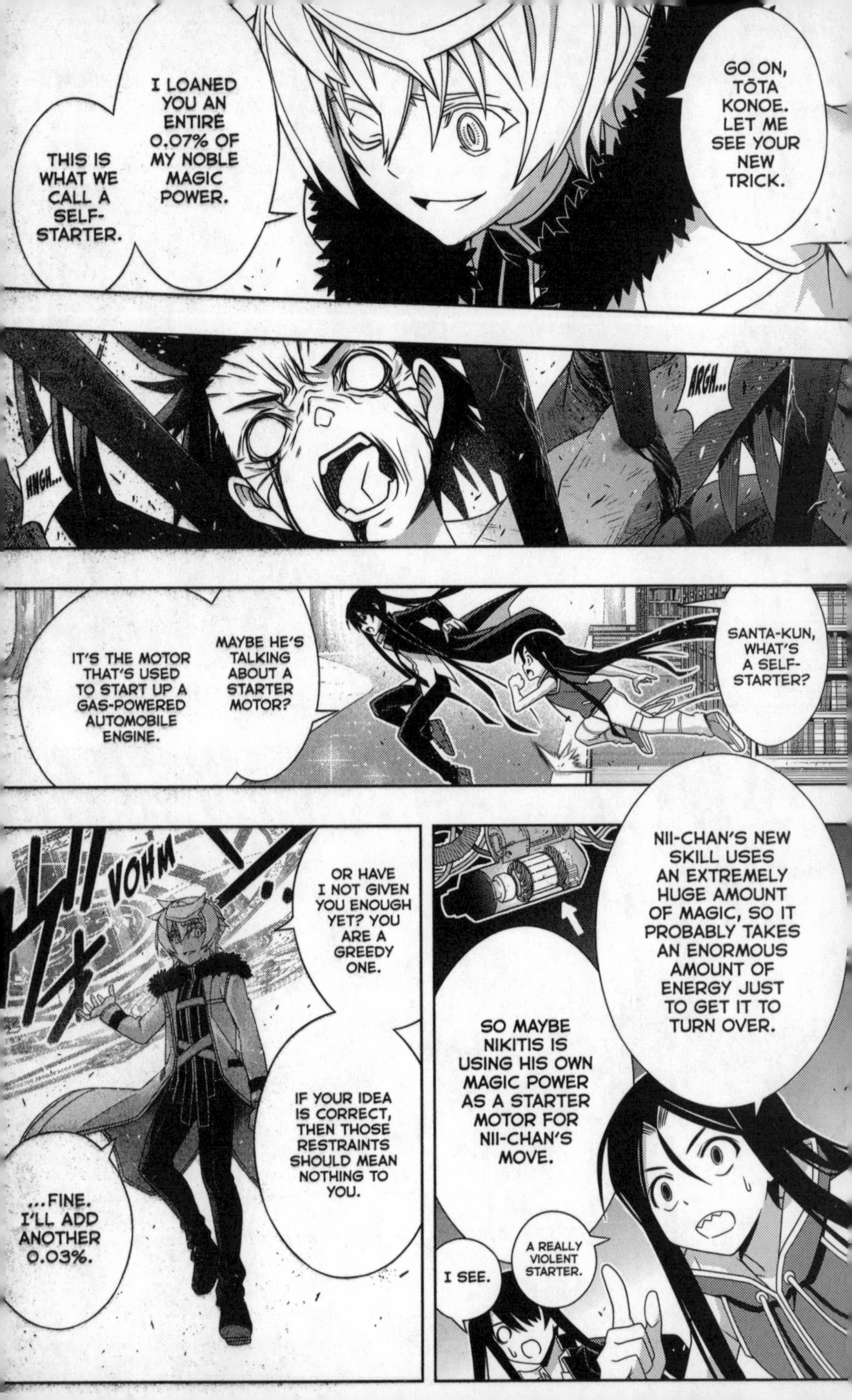
GO ON, TŌTA KONOE. LET ME SEE YOUR NEW TRICK.
I LOANED YOU AN ENTIRE 0.07% OF MY NOBLE MAGIC POWER.
THIS IS WHAT WE CALL A SELF-STARTER.
ARGH...
HNGH...
SANTA-KUN, WHAT'S A SELF-STARTER?
MAYBE HE'S TALKING ABOUT A STARTER MOTOR?
IT'S THE MOTOR THAT'S USED TO START UP A GAS-POWERED AUTOMOBILE ENGINE.
NII-CHAN'S NEW SKILL USES AN EXTREMELY HUGE AMOUNT OF MAGIC, SO IT PROBABLY TAKES AN ENORMOUS AMOUNT OF ENERGY JUST TO GET IT TO TURN OVER.
SO MAYBE NIKITIS IS USING HIS OWN MAGIC POWER AS A STARTER MOTOR FOR NII-CHAN'S MOVE.
A REALLY VIOLENT STARTER.
I SEE.
VOHM
OR HAVE I NOT GIVEN YOU ENOUGH YET? YOU ARE A GREEDY ONE.
IF YOUR IDEA IS CORRECT, THEN THOSE RESTRAINTS SHOULD MEAN NOTHING TO YOU.
...FINE. I'LL ADD ANOTHER 0.03%.

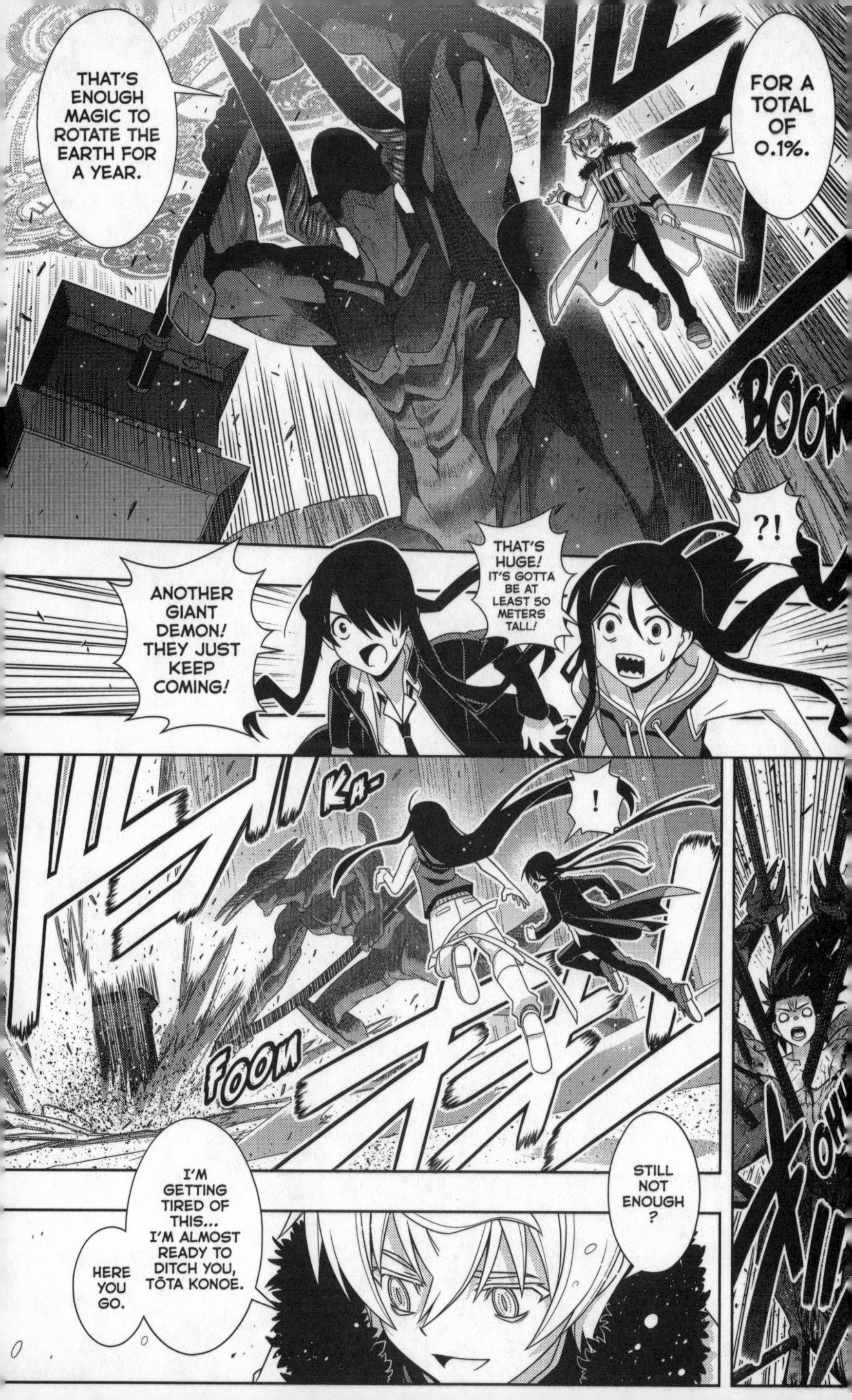
FOR A TOTAL OF 0.1%.
THAT'S ENOUGH MAGIC TO ROTATE THE EARTH FOR A YEAR.
BOOM
?!
THAT'S HUGE! IT'S GOTTA BE AT LEAST 50 METERS TALL!
ANOTHER GIANT DEMON! THEY JUST KEEP COMING!
KA-
!
FOOM
STILL NOT ENOUGH?
I'M GETTING TIRED OF THIS... I'M ALMOST READY TO DITCH YOU, TŌTA KONOE.
HERE YOU GO.

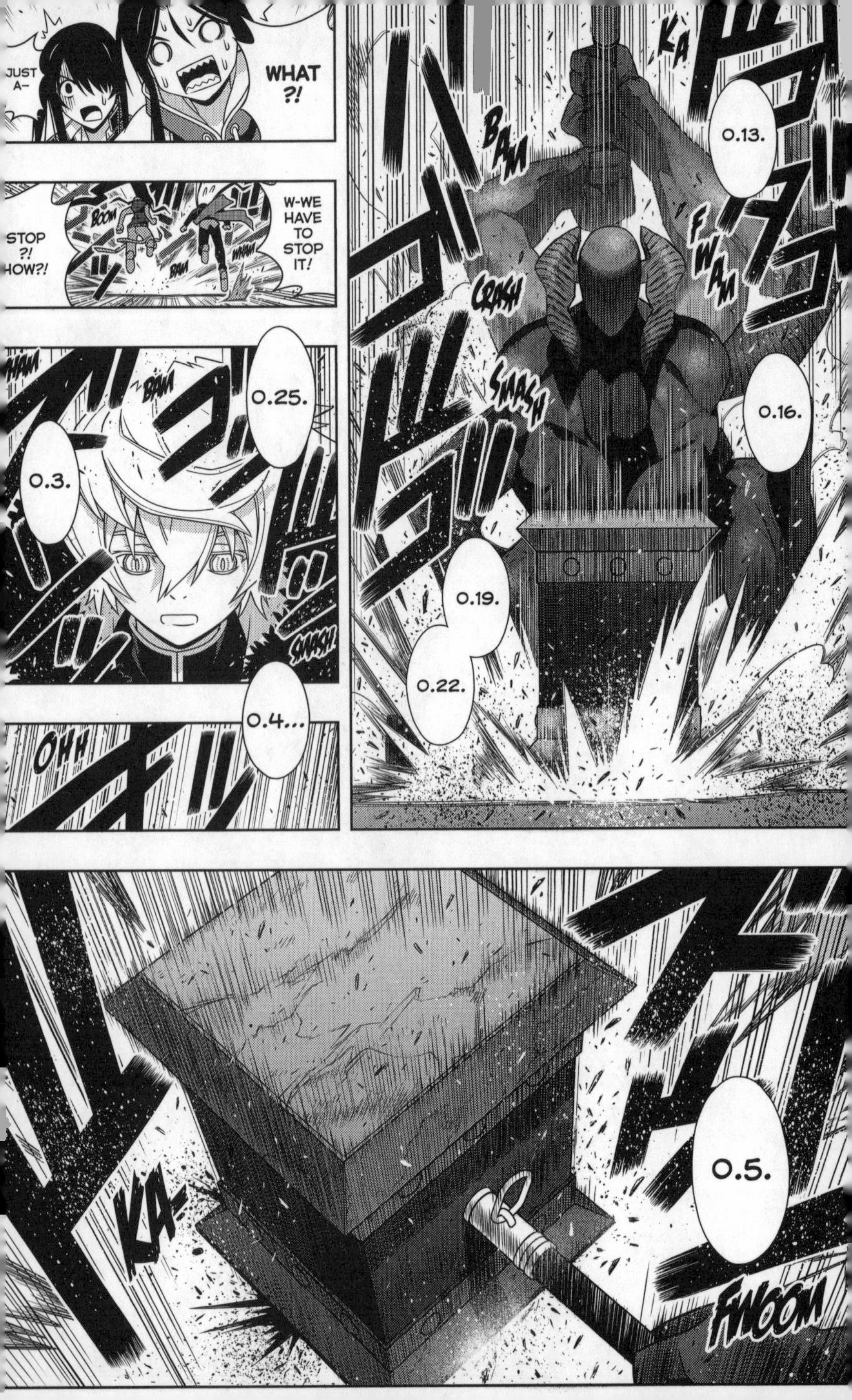

KA
0.13.
BAM
FWAM
CRASH
SMASH
0.16.
0.19.
0.22.
WHAT?!
JUST A-
W-WE HAVE TO STOP IT!
STOP?! HOW?!
BOOM
BAM
0.25.
BAM
0.3.
SMASH
0.4...
OHH
0.5.
FWOOM
KA-

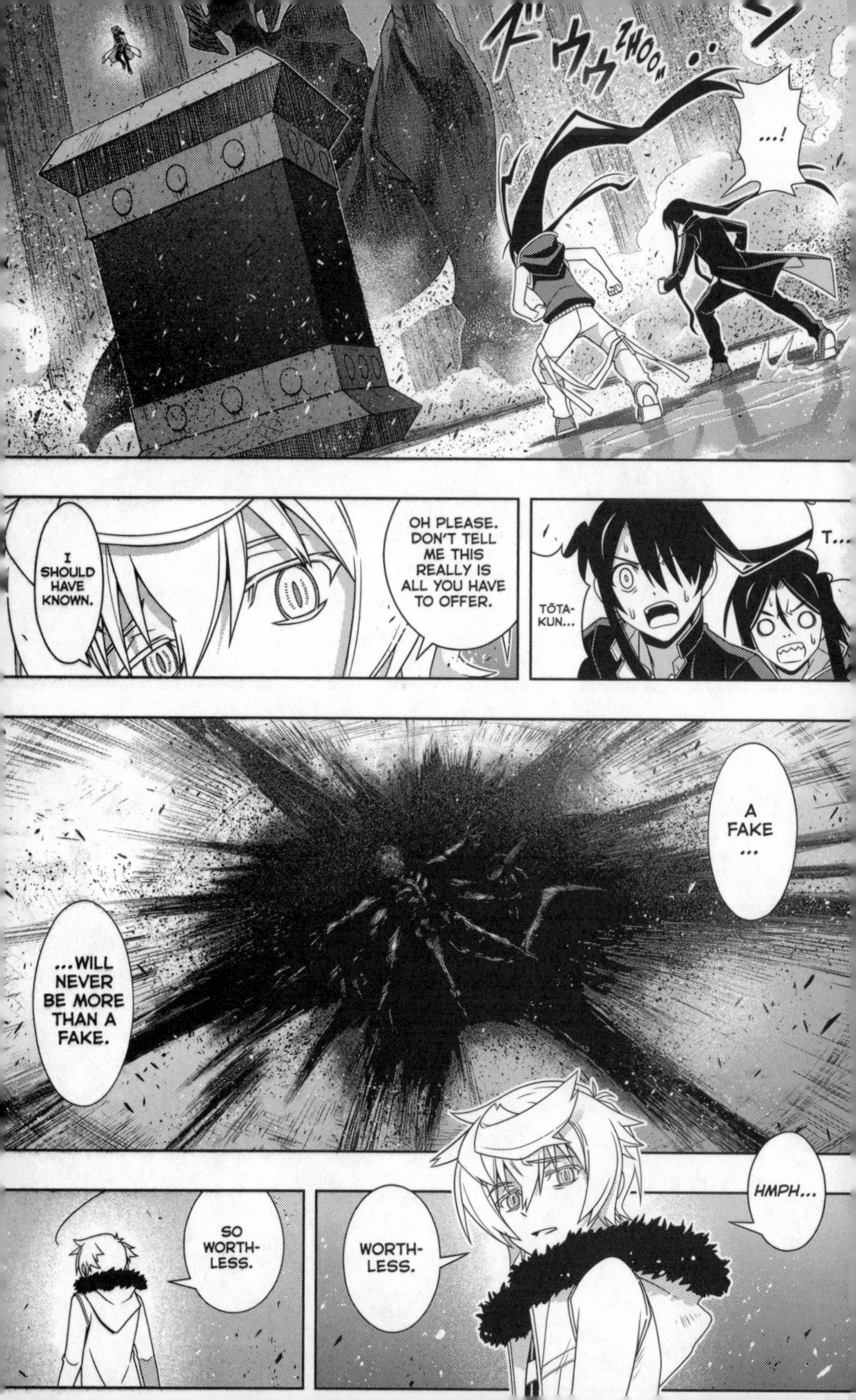
ズゥゥ ZHOOM
...!
T...
TŌTA-KUN...
OH PLEASE. DON'T TELL ME THIS REALLY IS ALL YOU HAVE TO OFFER.
I SHOULD HAVE KNOWN.
A FAKE ...
...WILL NEVER BE MORE THAN A FAKE.
HMPH...
WORTH-LESS.
SO WORTH-LESS.

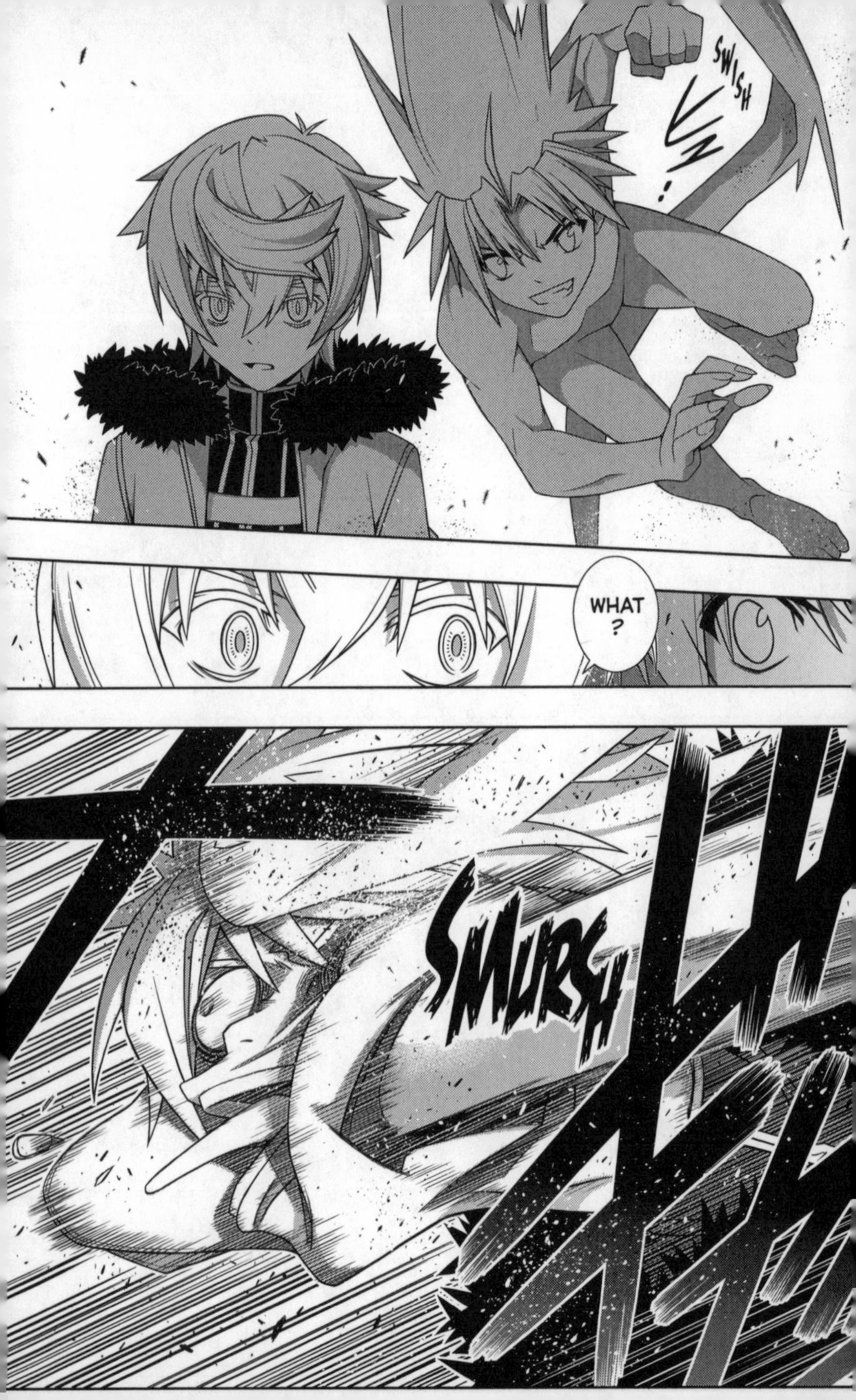
SWISH
WHAT?
SMURSH

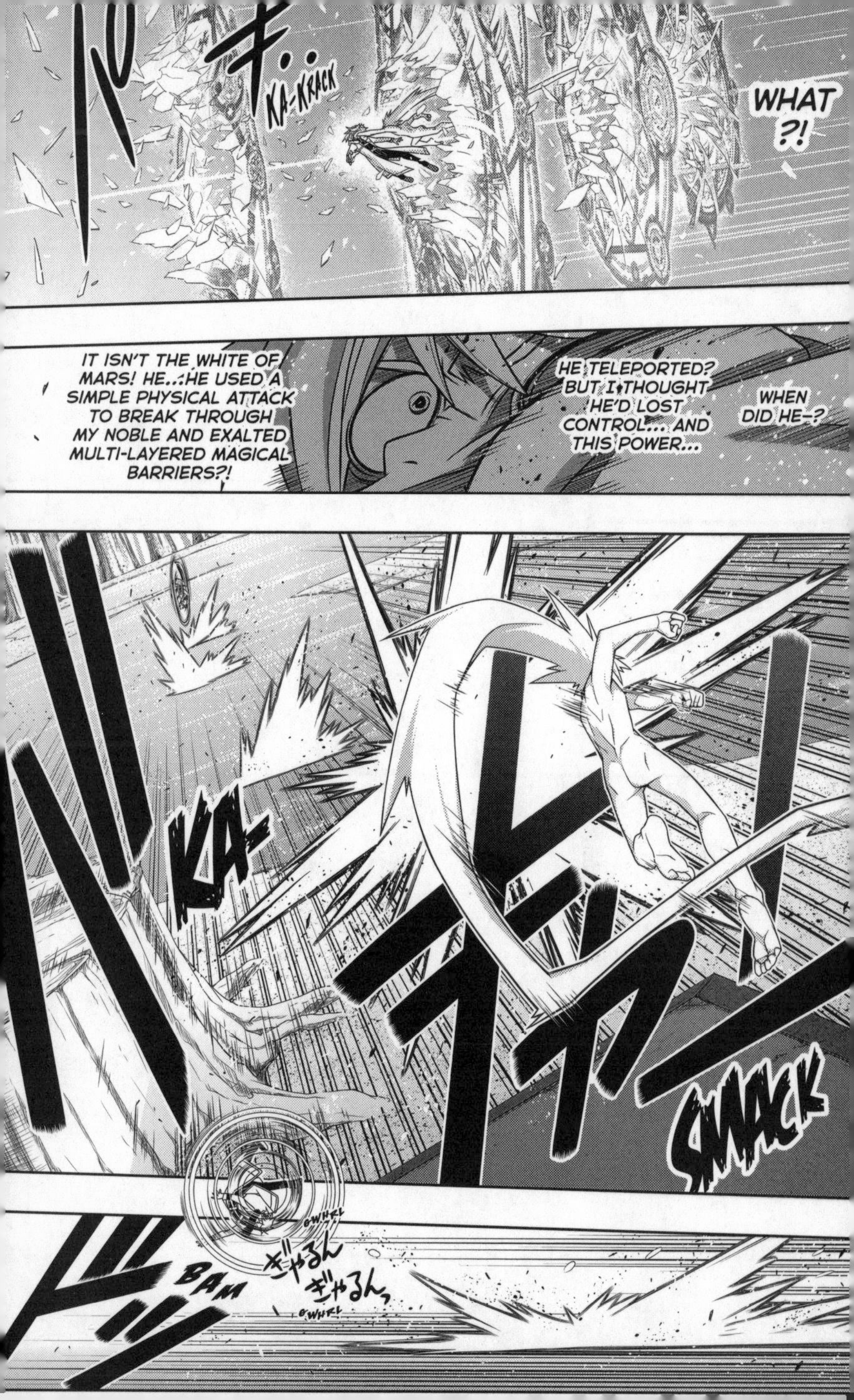
WHAT ?!
KA-KRACK
WHEN DID HE–?
HE TELEPORTED? BUT I THOUGHT HE'D LOST CONTROL... AND THIS POWER...
IT ISN'T THE WHITE OF MARS! HE... HE USED A SIMPLE PHYSICAL ATTACK TO BREAK THROUGH MY NOBLE AND EXALTED MULTI-LAYERED MAGICAL BARRIERS?!
KA-
SMACK
WHRL
ぎゃるん
ぎゃるんっ
WHRL
BAM

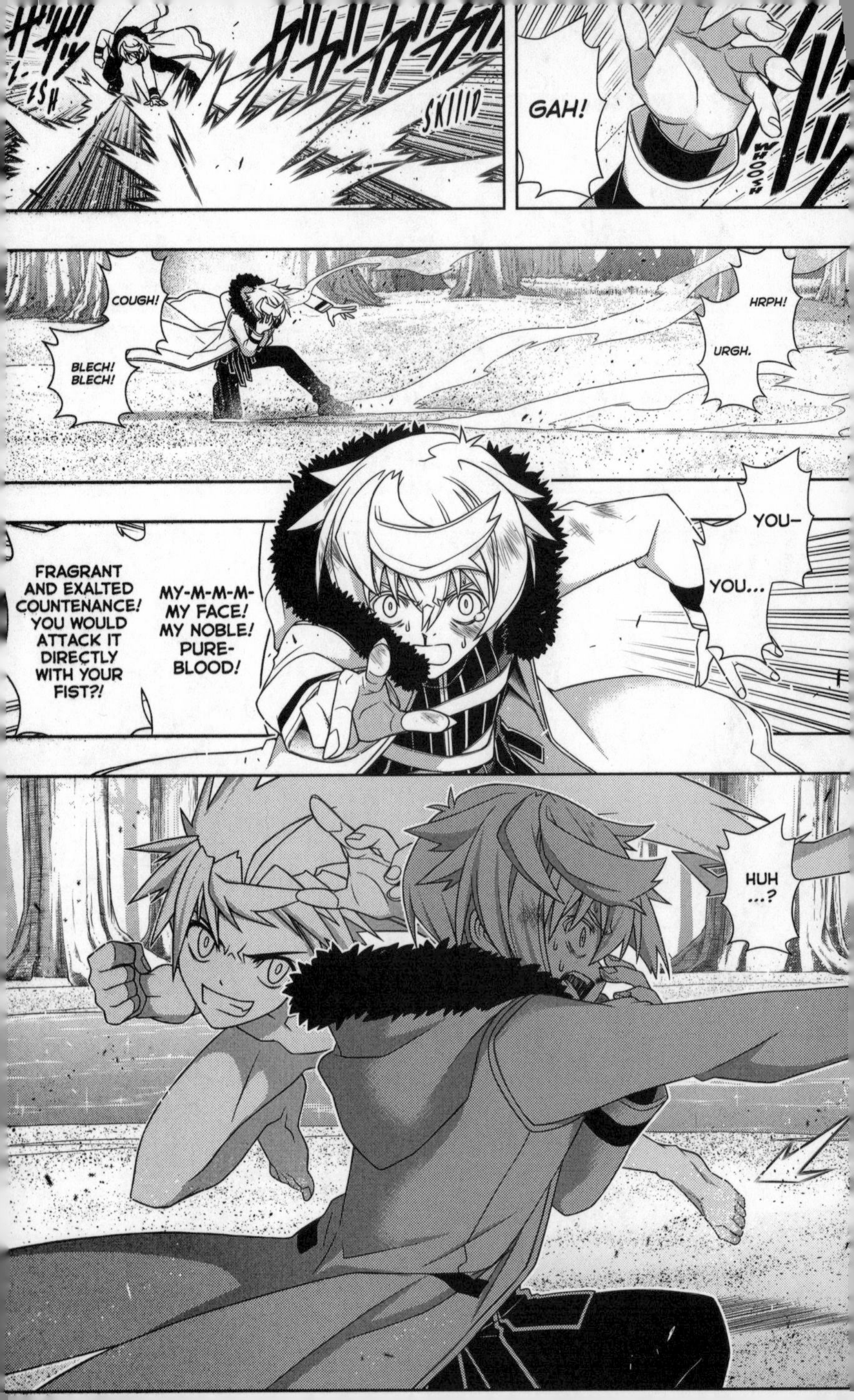
GAH!
WHOOSH
Z-ZSH
SKIIIID
HRPH!
URGH.
COUGH!
BLECH! BLECH!
YOU—
YOU...
MY-M-M-M-MY FACE! MY NOBLE! PURE-BLOOD!
FRAGRANT AND EXALTED COUNTENANCE! YOU WOULD ATTACK IT DIRECTLY WITH YOUR FIST?!
HUH ...?

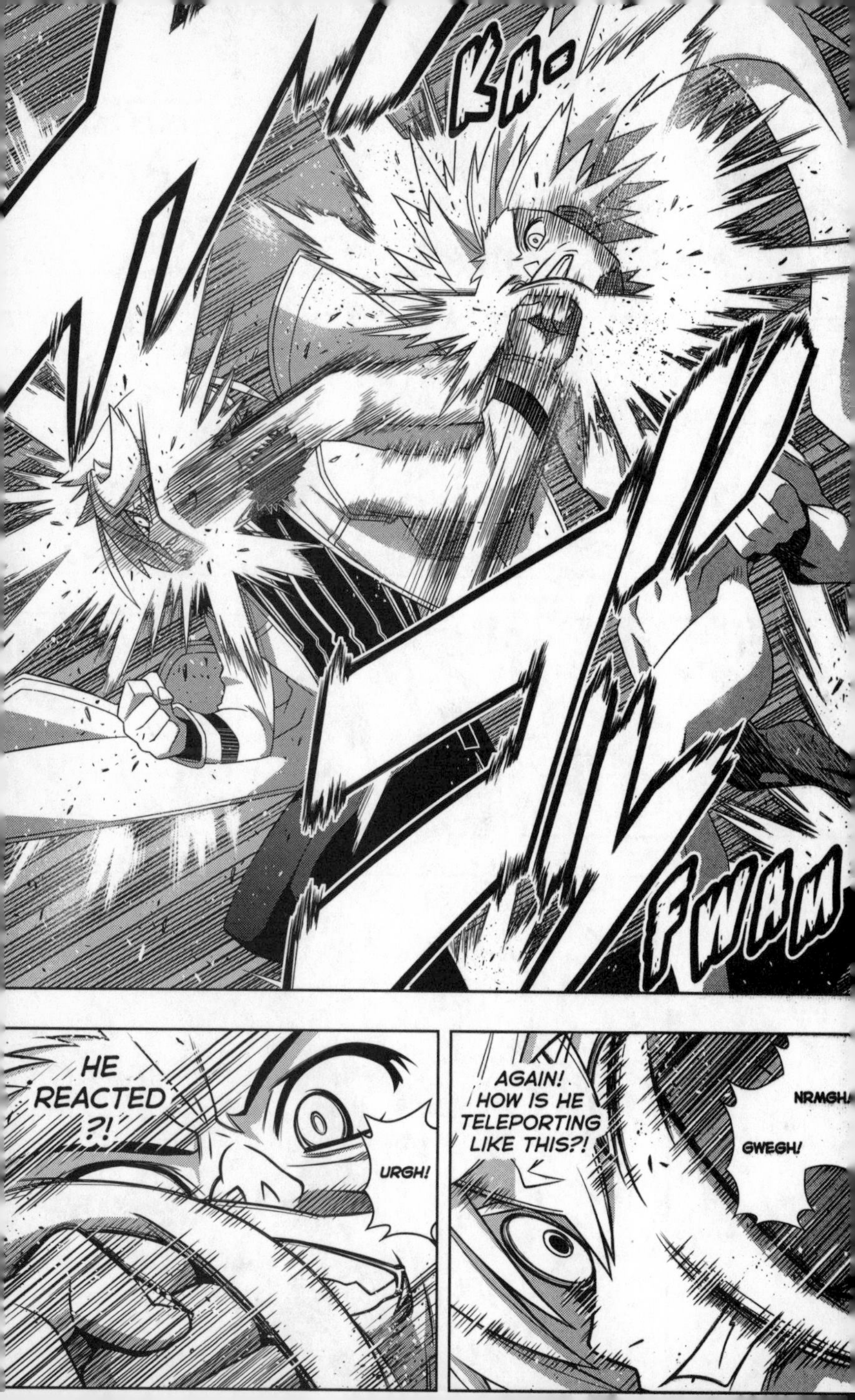
KA-
FWAM
AGAIN! HOW IS HE TELEPORTING LIKE THIS?!
NRMGHA
GWEGH!
HE REACTED ?!
URGH!

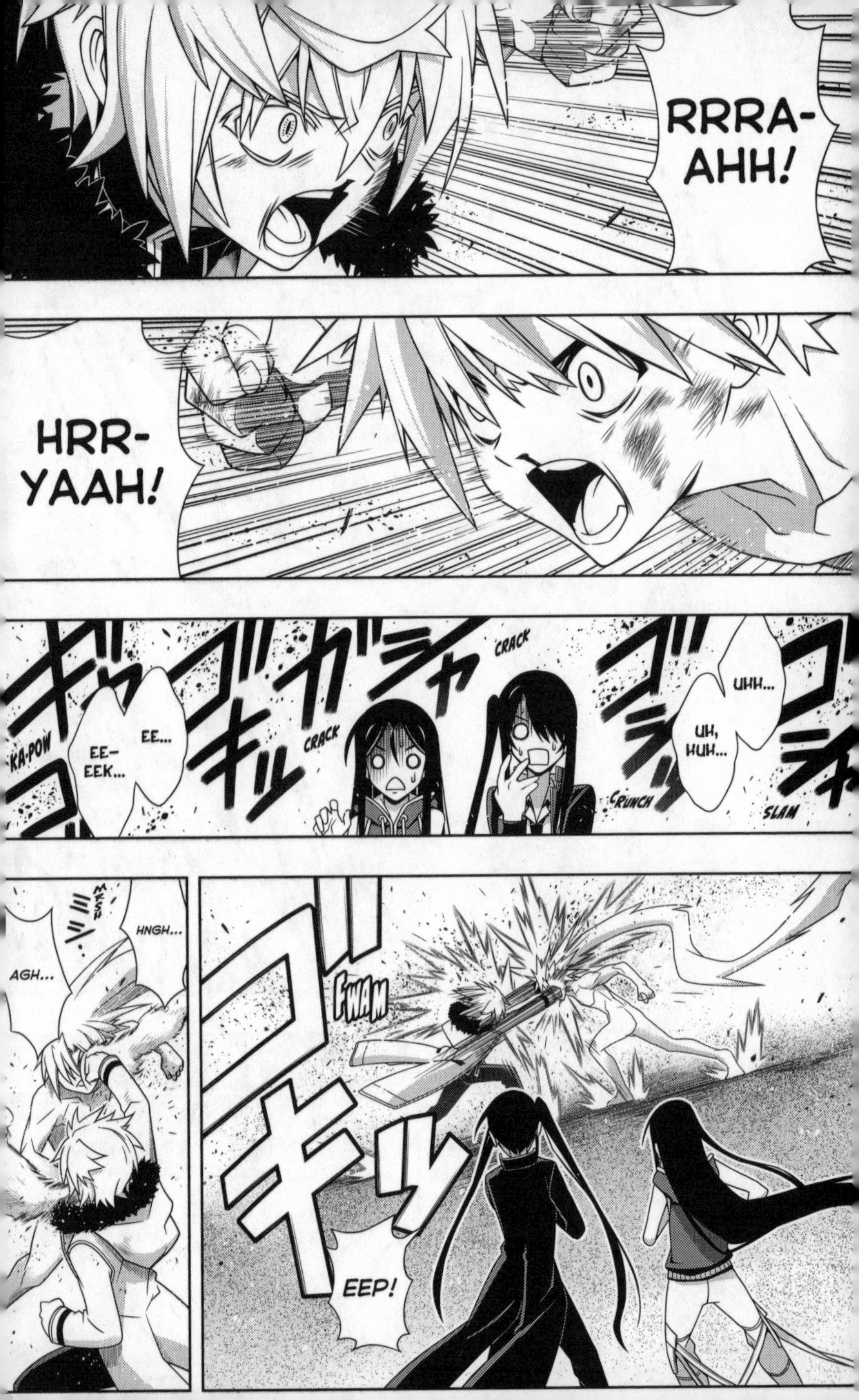
RRRA-AHH!
HRR-YAAH!
SLAM
UHH...
UH, HUH...
CRUNCH
CRACK
CRACK
EE...
EE-EEK...
KA-POW
FWAM
EEP!
MKSH
HNGH...
AGH...

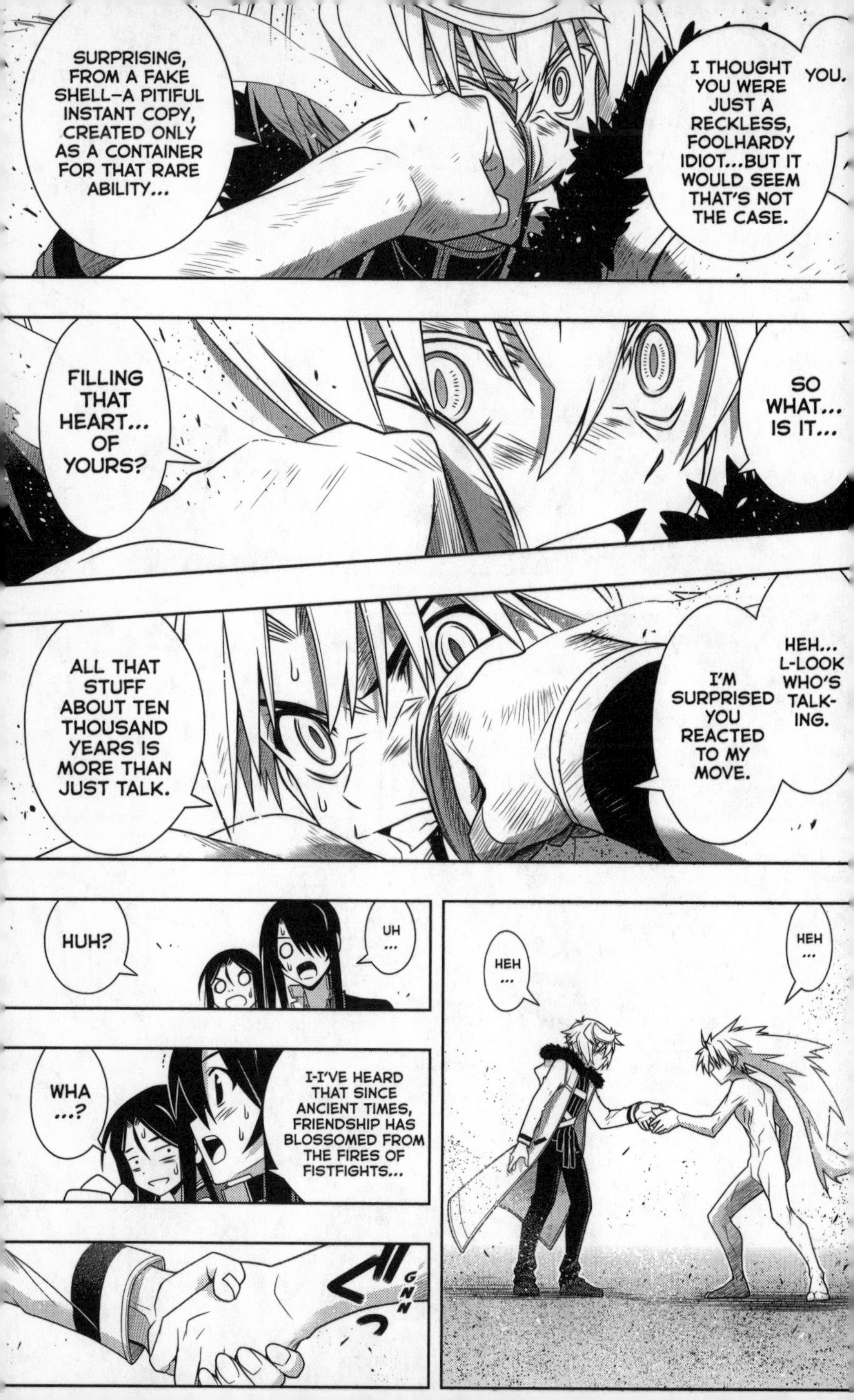
YOU.
I THOUGHT YOU WERE JUST A RECKLESS, FOOLHARDY IDIOT...BUT IT WOULD SEEM THAT'S NOT THE CASE.
SURPRISING, FROM A FAKE SHELL—A PITIFUL INSTANT COPY, CREATED ONLY AS A CONTAINER FOR THAT RARE ABILITY...
SO WHAT... IS IT...
FILLING THAT HEART... OF YOURS?
HEH... L-LOOK WHO'S TALKING.
I'M SURPRISED YOU REACTED TO MY MOVE.
ALL THAT STUFF ABOUT TEN THOUSAND YEARS IS MORE THAN JUST TALK.
HEH ...
HEH ...
UH ...
HUH?
I-I'VE HEARD THAT SINCE ANCIENT TIMES, FRIENDSHIP HAS BLOSSOMED FROM THE FIRES OF FISTFIGHTS...
WHA ...?
GNN

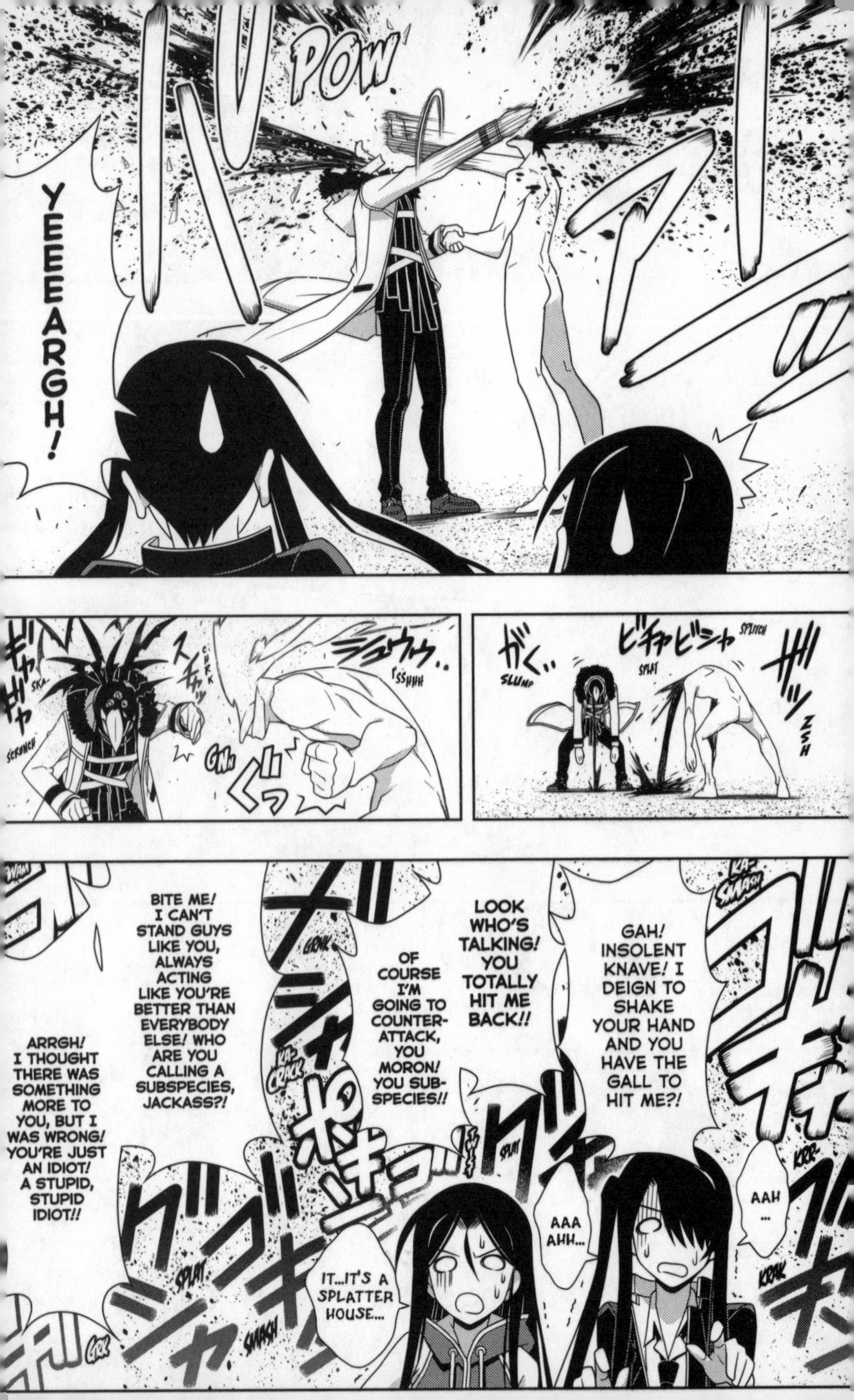
POW
YEEEARGH!
SLUMP
SPLITCH
SPLAT
ZSH
SKA
SCRUNCH
CHRK
FSSHHH
GNH
KA-SMASH
GAH! INSOLENT KNAVE! I DEIGN TO SHAKE YOUR HAND AND YOU HAVE THE GALL TO HIT ME?!
LOOK WHO'S TALKING! YOU TOTALLY HIT ME BACK!!
OF COURSE I'M GOING TO COUNTER-ATTACK, YOU MORON! YOU SUB-SPECIES!!
GRNK
BITE ME! I CAN'T STAND GUYS LIKE YOU, ALWAYS ACTING LIKE YOU'RE BETTER THAN EVERYBODY ELSE! WHO ARE YOU CALLING A SUBSPECIES, JACKASS?!
WAM
ARRGH! I THOUGHT THERE WAS SOMETHING MORE TO YOU, BUT I WAS WRONG! YOU'RE JUST AN IDIOT! A STUPID, STUPID IDIOT!!
KA-CRACK
SPLAT
KRR-
AAH...
KRAK
AAA AHH...
IT...IT'S A SPLATTER HOUSE...
SPLAT
SMASH
GRK

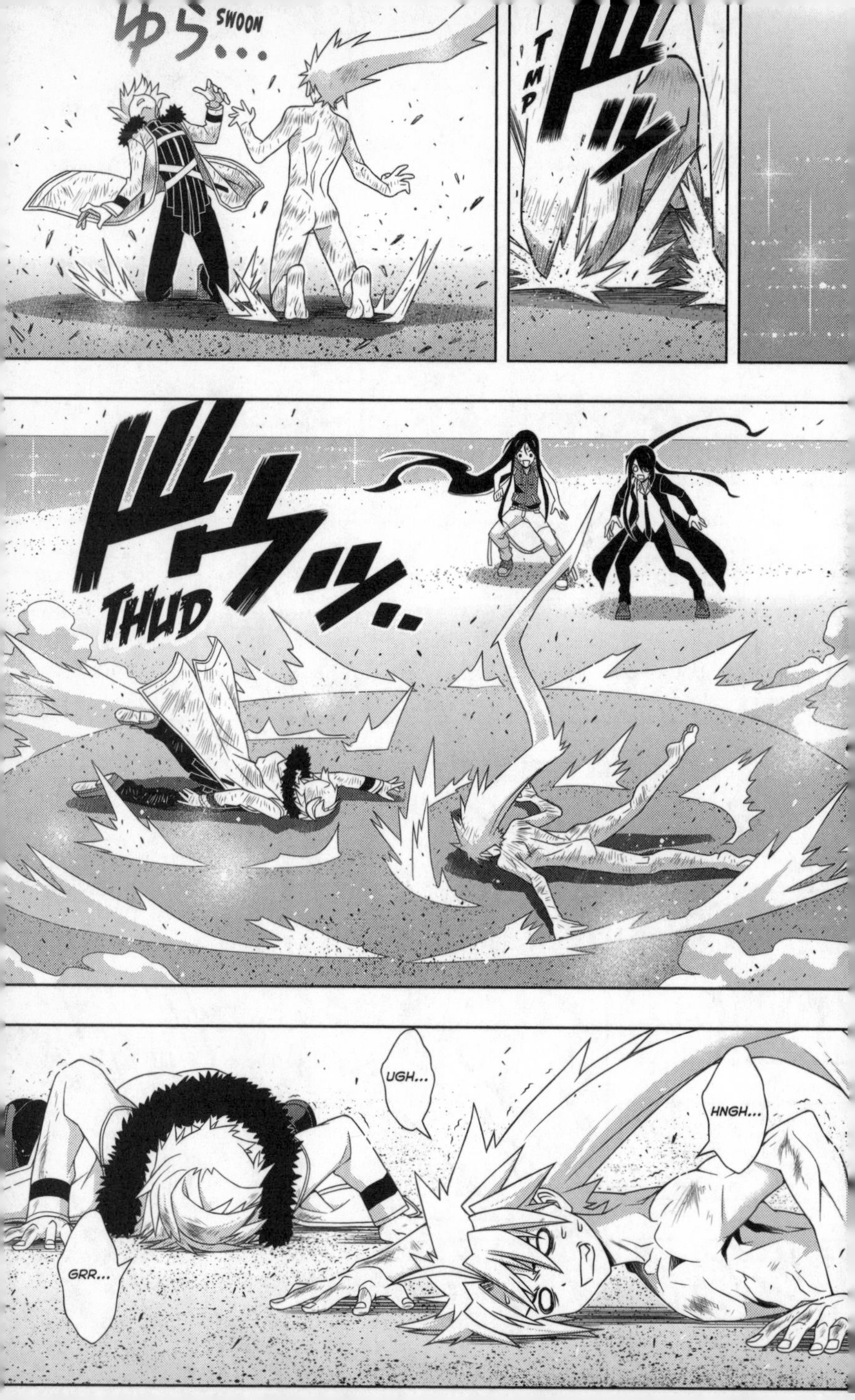
ドッ
TMP
ゆら…
SWOON
ドサッ..
THUD
HNGH...
UGH...
GRR...

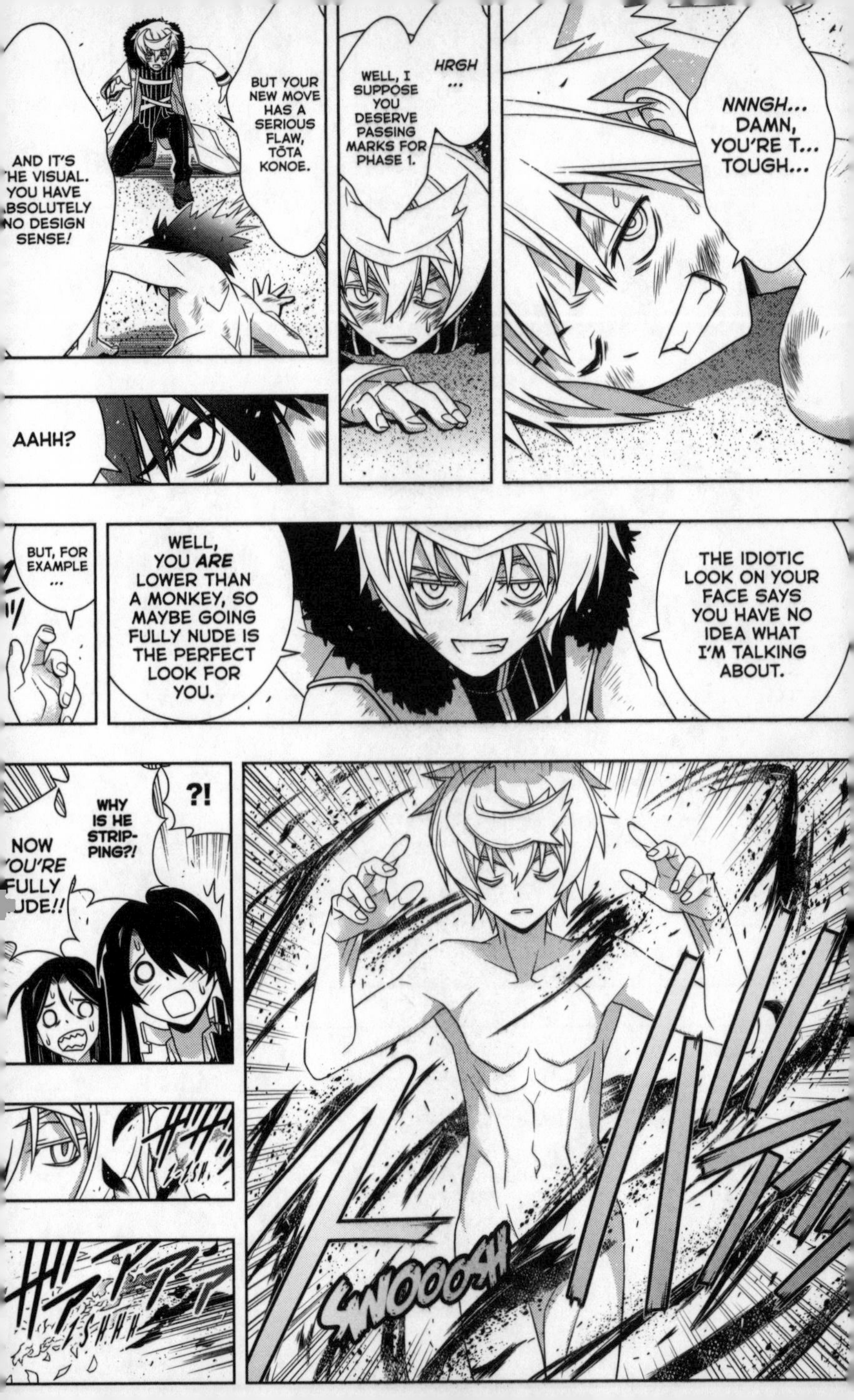
NNNGH... DAMN, YOU'RE T... TOUGH...
HRGH ...
WELL, I SUPPOSE YOU DESERVE PASSING MARKS FOR PHASE 1.
BUT YOUR NEW MOVE HAS A SERIOUS FLAW, TŌTA KONOE.
AND IT'S 'HE VISUAL. YOU HAVE BSOLUTELY NO DESIGN SENSE!
AAHH?
THE IDIOTIC LOOK ON YOUR FACE SAYS YOU HAVE NO IDEA WHAT I'M TALKING ABOUT.
WELL, YOU *ARE* LOWER THAN A MONKEY, SO MAYBE GOING FULLY NUDE IS THE PERFECT LOOK FOR YOU.
BUT, FOR EXAMPLE ...
SWOOOSH
?!
WHY IS HE STRIP-PING?!
NOW 'OU'RE FULLY JDE!!

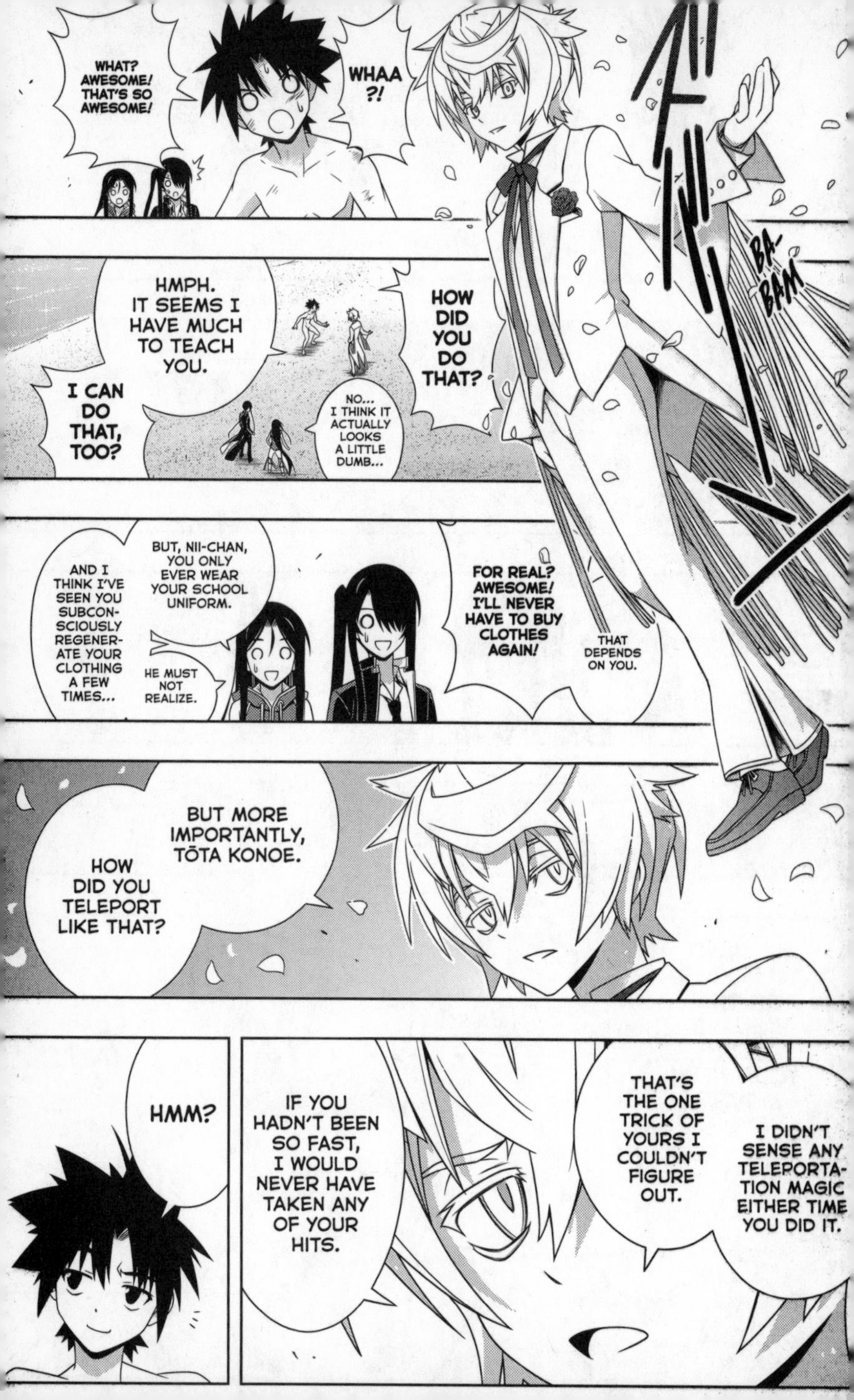
BA-BAM
WHAA?!
WHAT? AWESOME! THAT'S SO AWESOME!
HOW DID YOU DO THAT?
NO... I THINK IT ACTUALLY LOOKS A LITTLE DUMB...
HMPH. IT SEEMS I HAVE MUCH TO TEACH YOU.
I CAN DO THAT, TOO?
FOR REAL? AWESOME! I'LL NEVER HAVE TO BUY CLOTHES AGAIN!
THAT DEPENDS ON YOU.
BUT, NII-CHAN, YOU ONLY EVER WEAR YOUR SCHOOL UNIFORM.
HE MUST NOT REALIZE.
AND I THINK I'VE SEEN YOU SUBCONSCIOUSLY REGENERATE YOUR CLOTHING A FEW TIMES...
BUT MORE IMPORTANTLY, TŌTA KONOE.
HOW DID YOU TELEPORT LIKE THAT?
I DIDN'T SENSE ANY TELEPORTATION MAGIC EITHER TIME YOU DID IT.
THAT'S THE ONE TRICK OF YOURS I COULDN'T FIGURE OUT.
IF YOU HADN'T BEEN SO FAST, I WOULD NEVER HAVE TAKEN ANY OF YOUR HITS.
HMM?

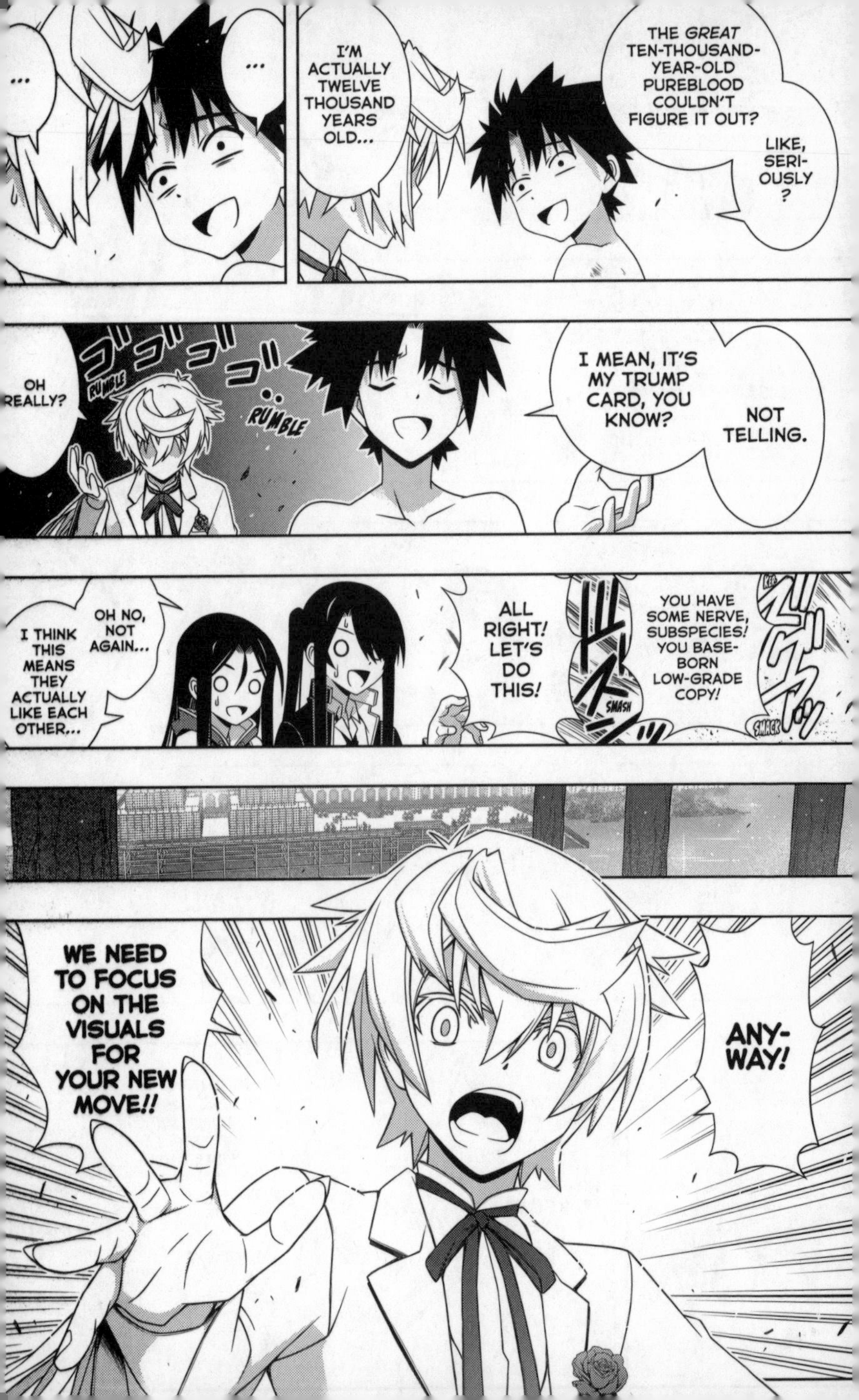

THE *GREAT* TEN-THOUSAND-YEAR-OLD PUREBLOOD COULDN'T FIGURE IT OUT?
LIKE, SERIOUSLY?
I'M ACTUALLY TWELVE THOUSAND YEARS OLD...
...
...
NOT TELLING.
I MEAN, IT'S MY TRUMP CARD, YOU KNOW?
RUMBLE
RUMBLE
OH REALLY?
SMACK
YOU HAVE SOME NERVE, SUBSPECIES! YOU BASE-BORN LOW-GRADE COPY!
SMASH
ALL RIGHT! LET'S DO THIS!
OH NO, NOT AGAIN...
I THINK THIS MEANS THEY ACTUALLY LIKE EACH OTHER...
ANY-WAY!
WE NEED TO FOCUS ON THE VISUALS FOR YOUR NEW MOVE!!

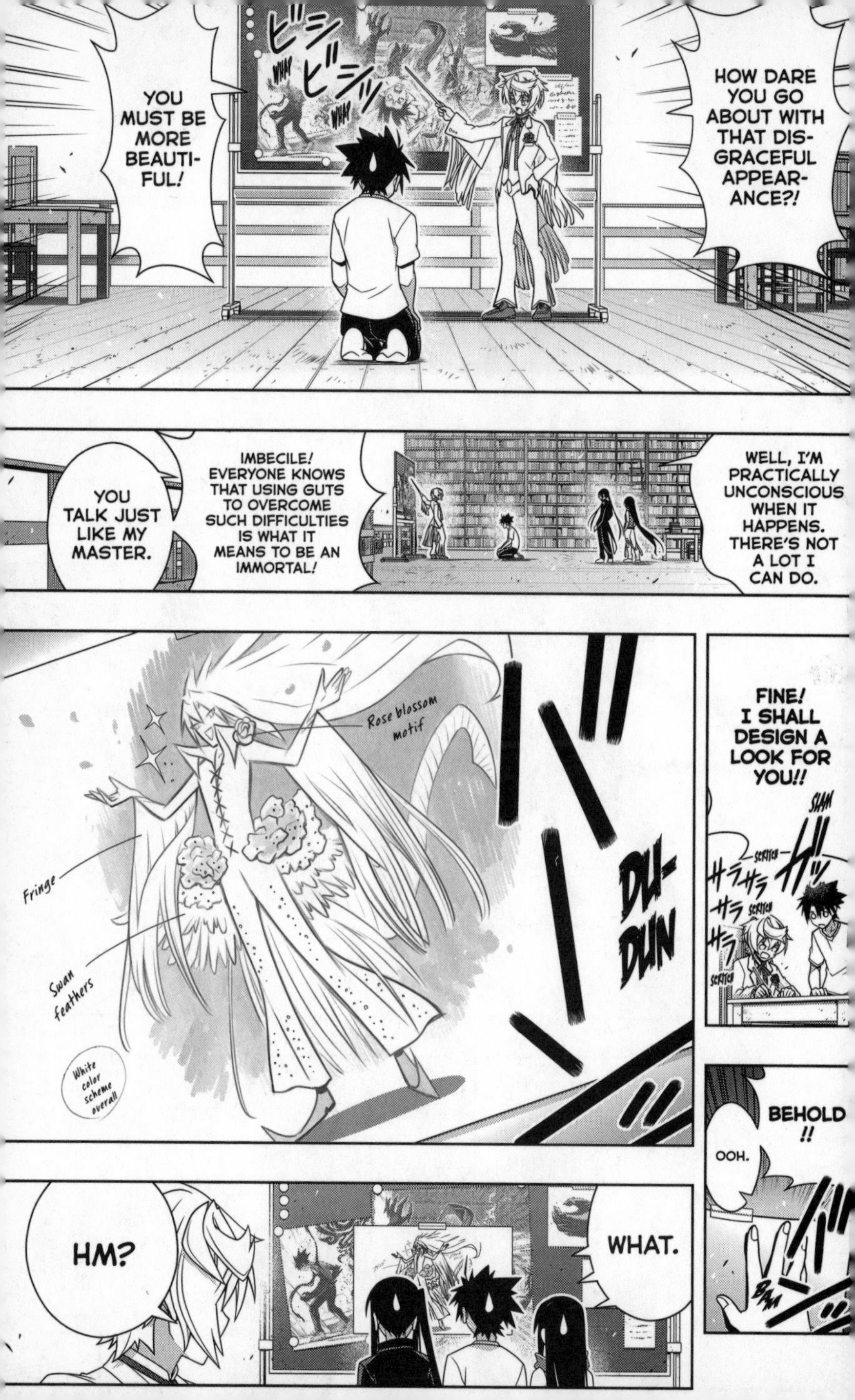
HOW DARE YOU GO ABOUT WITH THAT DIS-GRACEFUL APPEAR-ANCE?!
ビシ
WHAP
ビシッ
WHAP
YOU MUST BE MORE BEAUTI-FUL!
WELL, I'M PRACTICALLY UNCONSCIOUS WHEN IT HAPPENS. THERE'S NOT A LOT I CAN DO.
IMBECILE! EVERYONE KNOWS THAT USING GUTS TO OVERCOME SUCH DIFFICULTIES IS WHAT IT MEANS TO BE AN IMMORTAL!
YOU TALK JUST LIKE MY MASTER.
FINE! I SHALL DESIGN A LOOK FOR YOU!!
SLAM
SCRITCH
サラサラ
サラ
SCRITCH
サラ
SCRITCH
BEHOLD!!
OOH.
BAM
DU-DUN
Rose blossom motif
Fringe
Swan feathers
White color scheme overall
WHAT.
HM?

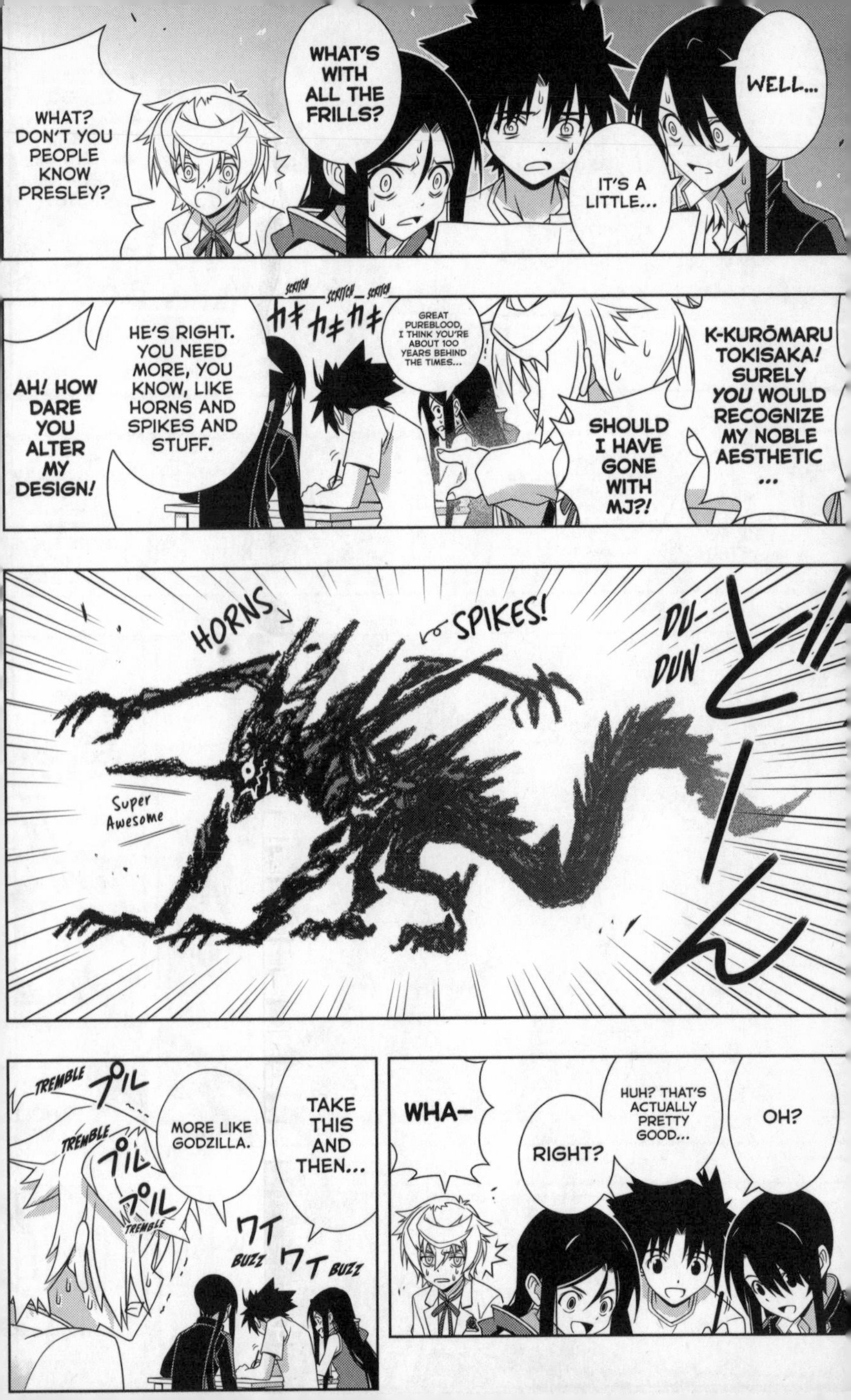
WELL...
IT'S A LITTLE...
WHAT'S WITH ALL THE FRILLS?
WHAT? DON'T YOU PEOPLE KNOW PRESLEY?
K-KURŌMARU TOKISAKA! SURELY *YOU* WOULD RECOGNIZE MY NOBLE AESTHETIC ...
SHOULD I HAVE GONE WITH MJ?!
GREAT PUREBLOOD, I THINK YOU'RE ABOUT 100 YEARS BEHIND THE TIMES...
カキ SCRITCH カキ SCRITCH カキ SCRITCH
HE'S RIGHT. YOU NEED MORE, YOU KNOW, LIKE HORNS AND SPIKES AND STUFF.
AH! HOW DARE YOU ALTER MY DESIGN!
どーん DU-DUN
SPIKES!
HORNS
Super Awesome
OH?
HUH? THAT'S ACTUALLY PRETTY GOOD...
RIGHT?
WHA-
TAKE THIS AND THEN...
MORE LIKE GODZILLA.
プル TREMBLE プル TREMBLE プル TREMBLE
ワイ BUZZ ワイ BUZZ

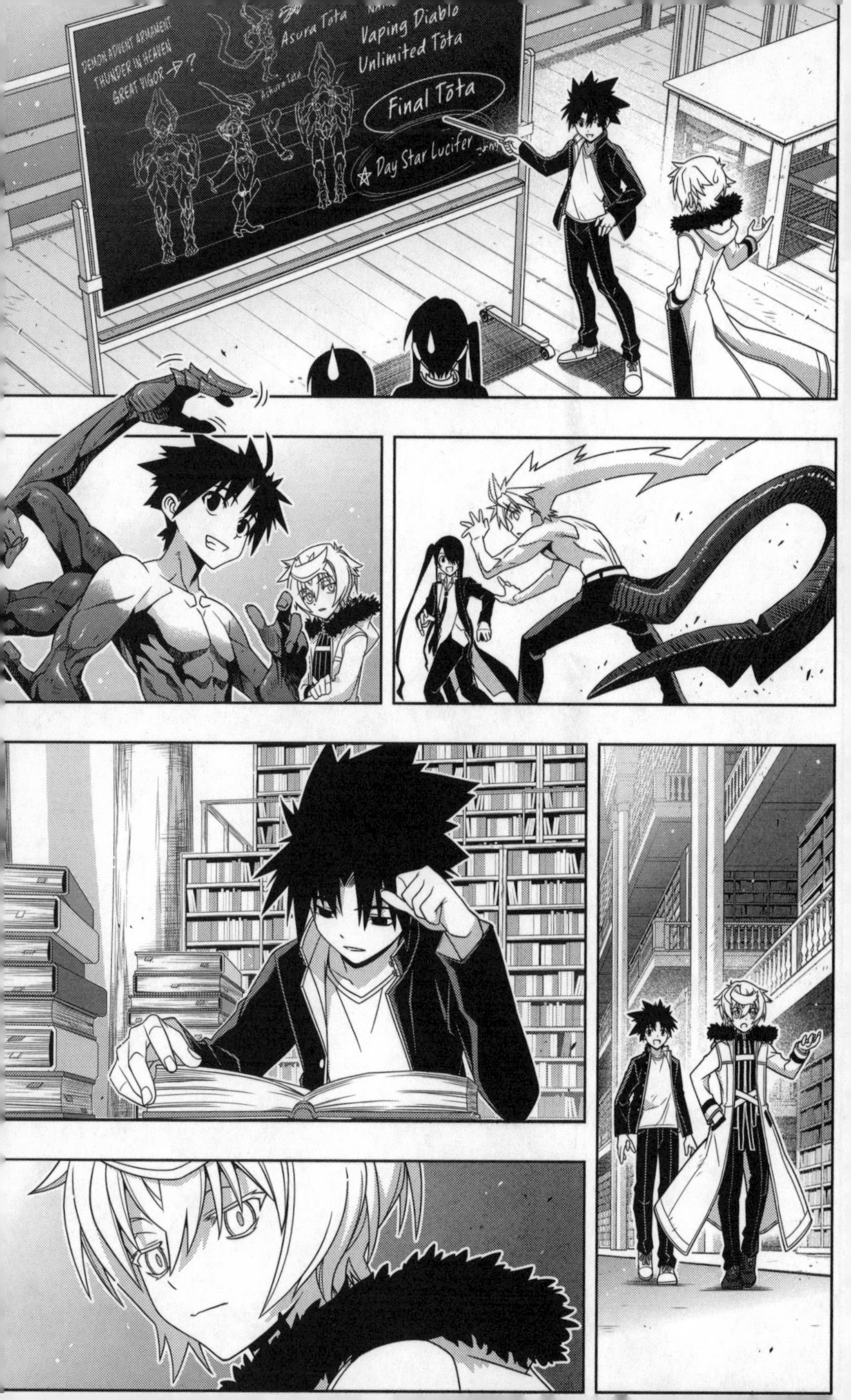
Vaping Diablo
Unlimited Tōta
Final Tōta
☆ Day Star Lucifer
Asura Tōta
Ashura Tōta
DEMON ADVENT ARMAMENT
THUNDER IN HEAVEN
GREAT VIGOR → ?

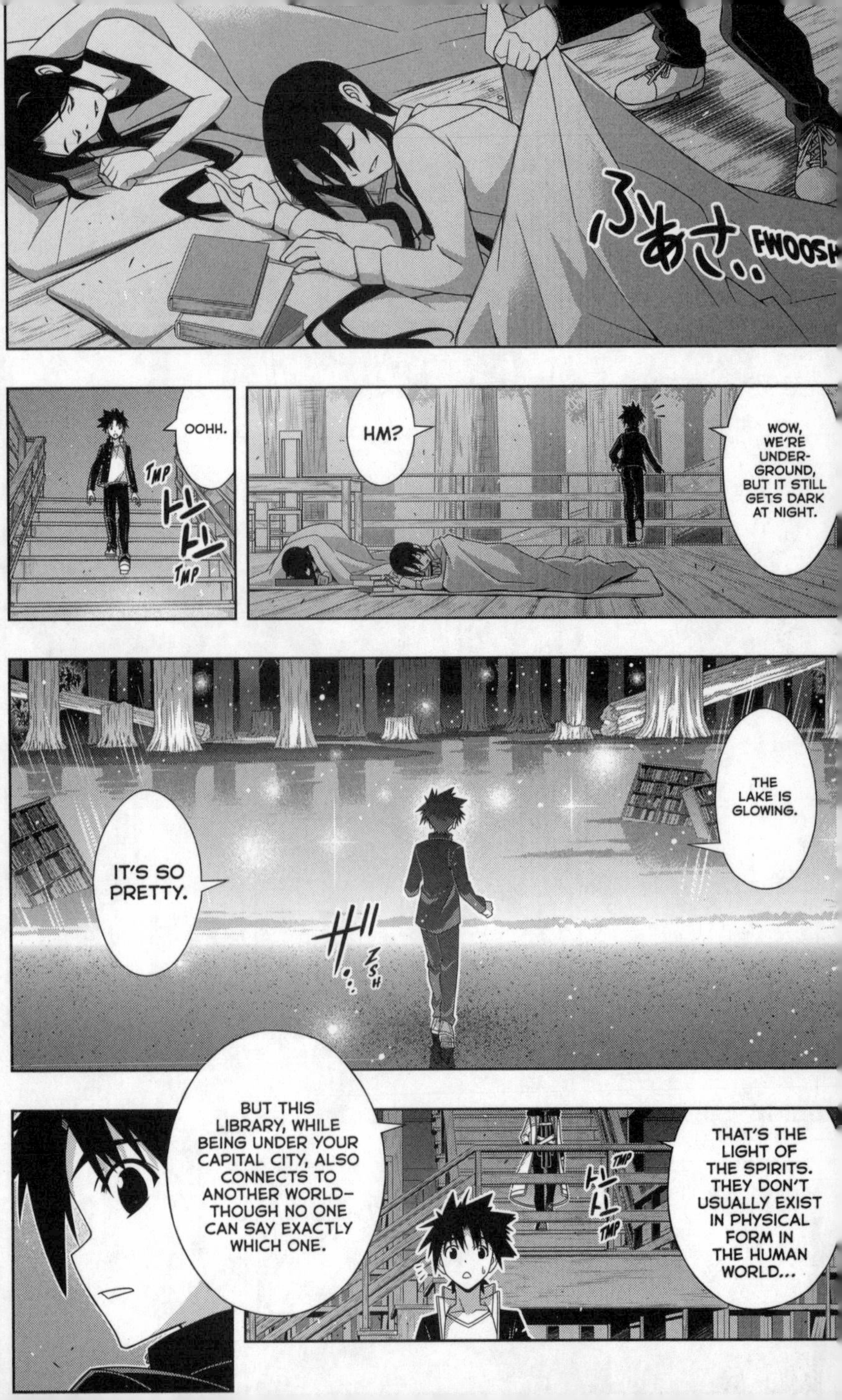
ふあさ..
FWOOSH
WOW, WE'RE UNDER-GROUND, BUT IT STILL GETS DARK AT NIGHT.
HM?
OOHH.
TMP
トン トン
TMP
THE LAKE IS GLOWING.
IT'S SO PRETTY.
ZSH
THAT'S THE LIGHT OF THE SPIRITS. THEY DON'T USUALLY EXIST IN PHYSICAL FORM IN THE HUMAN WORLD...
TMP
トン トン
TMP
BUT THIS LIBRARY, WHILE BEING UNDER YOUR CAPITAL CITY, ALSO CONNECTS TO ANOTHER WORLD—THOUGH NO ONE CAN SAY EXACTLY WHICH ONE.

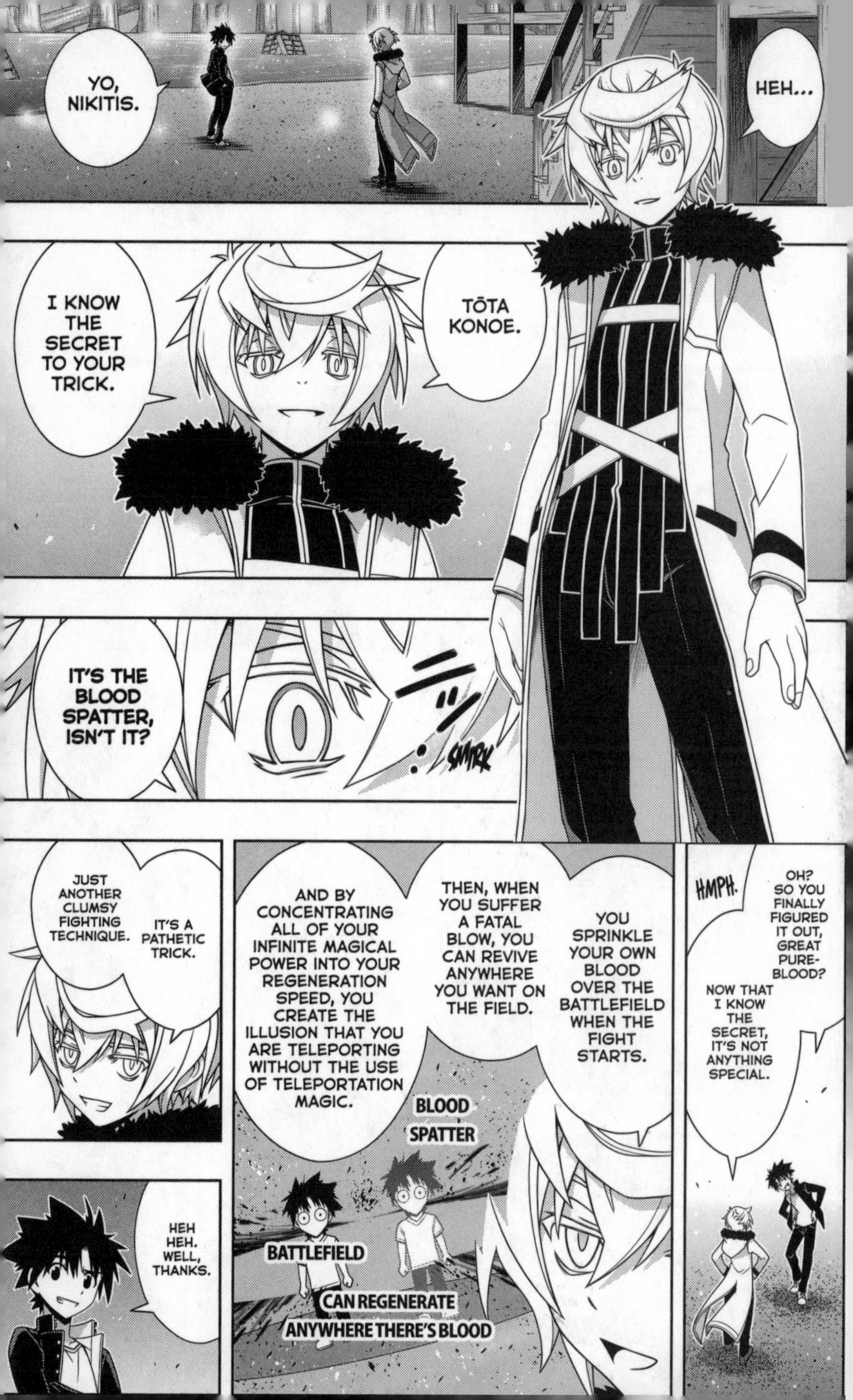

YO, NIKITIS.
HEH...
TŌTA KONOE.
I KNOW THE SECRET TO YOUR TRICK.
IT'S THE BLOOD SPATTER, ISN'T IT?
SMIRK
OH? SO YOU FINALLY FIGURED IT OUT, GREAT PURE-BLOOD?
HMPH.
NOW THAT I KNOW THE SECRET, IT'S NOT ANYTHING SPECIAL.
YOU SPRINKLE YOUR OWN BLOOD OVER THE BATTLEFIELD WHEN THE FIGHT STARTS.
THEN, WHEN YOU SUFFER A FATAL BLOW, YOU CAN REVIVE ANYWHERE YOU WANT ON THE FIELD.
AND BY CONCENTRATING ALL OF YOUR INFINITE MAGICAL POWER INTO YOUR REGENERATION SPEED, YOU CREATE THE ILLUSION THAT YOU ARE TELEPORTING WITHOUT THE USE OF TELEPORTATION MAGIC.
BLOOD SPATTER
BATTLEFIELD
CAN REGENERATE ANYWHERE THERE'S BLOOD
IT'S A PATHETIC TRICK.
JUST ANOTHER CLUMSY FIGHTING TECHNIQUE.
HEH HEH. WELL, THANKS.

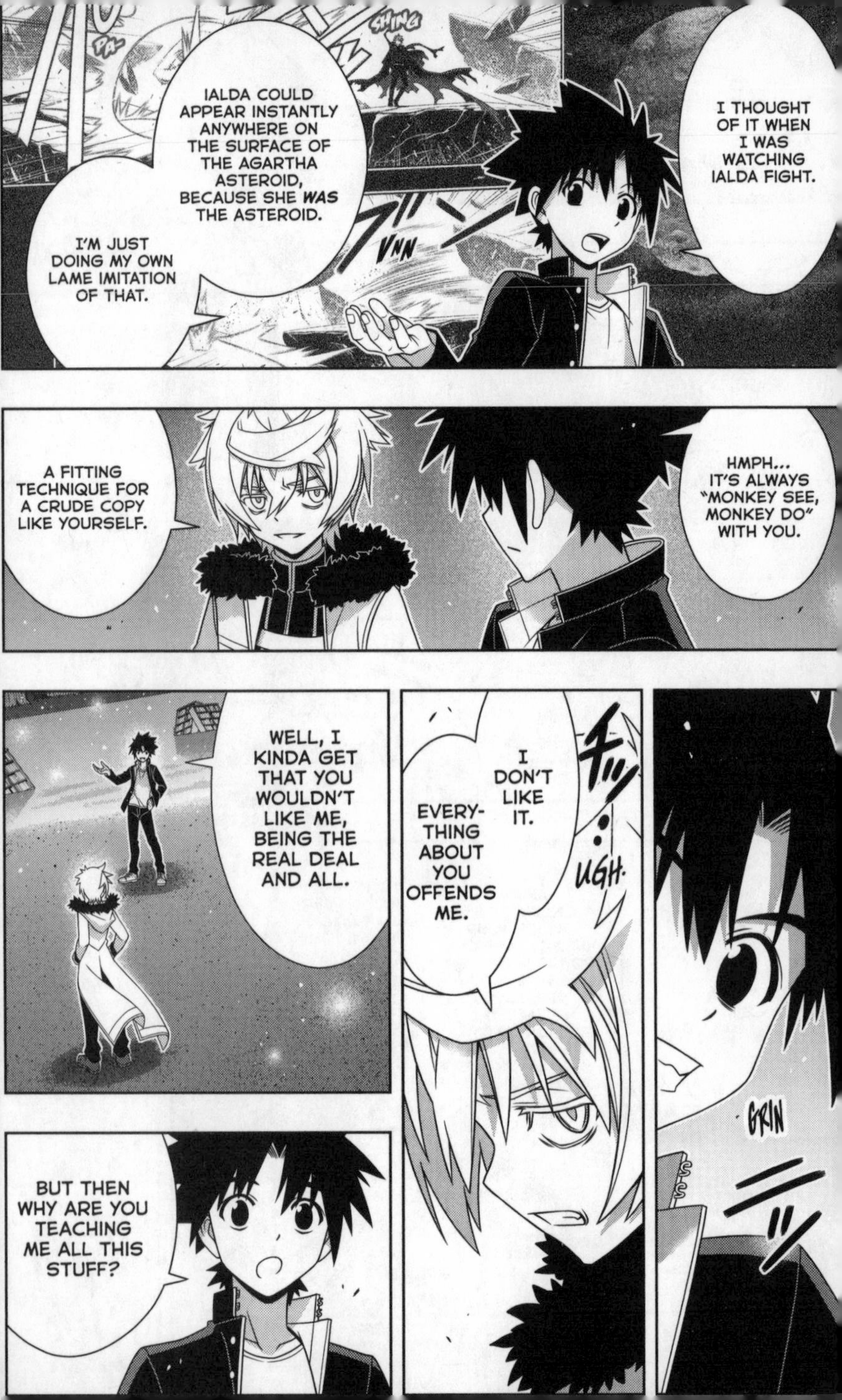
I THOUGHT OF IT WHEN I WAS WATCHING IALDA FIGHT.
SHING
IALDA COULD APPEAR INSTANTLY ANYWHERE ON THE SURFACE OF THE AGARTHA ASTEROID, BECAUSE SHE WAS THE ASTEROID.
VNN
I'M JUST DOING MY OWN LAME IMITATION OF THAT.
HMPH... IT'S ALWAYS "MONKEY SEE, MONKEY DO" WITH YOU.
A FITTING TECHNIQUE FOR A CRUDE COPY LIKE YOURSELF.
GRIN
I DON'T LIKE IT.
EVERYTHING ABOUT YOU OFFENDS ME.
UGH.
WELL, I KINDA GET THAT YOU WOULDN'T LIKE ME, BEING THE REAL DEAL AND ALL.
BUT THEN WHY ARE YOU TEACHING ME ALL THIS STUFF?

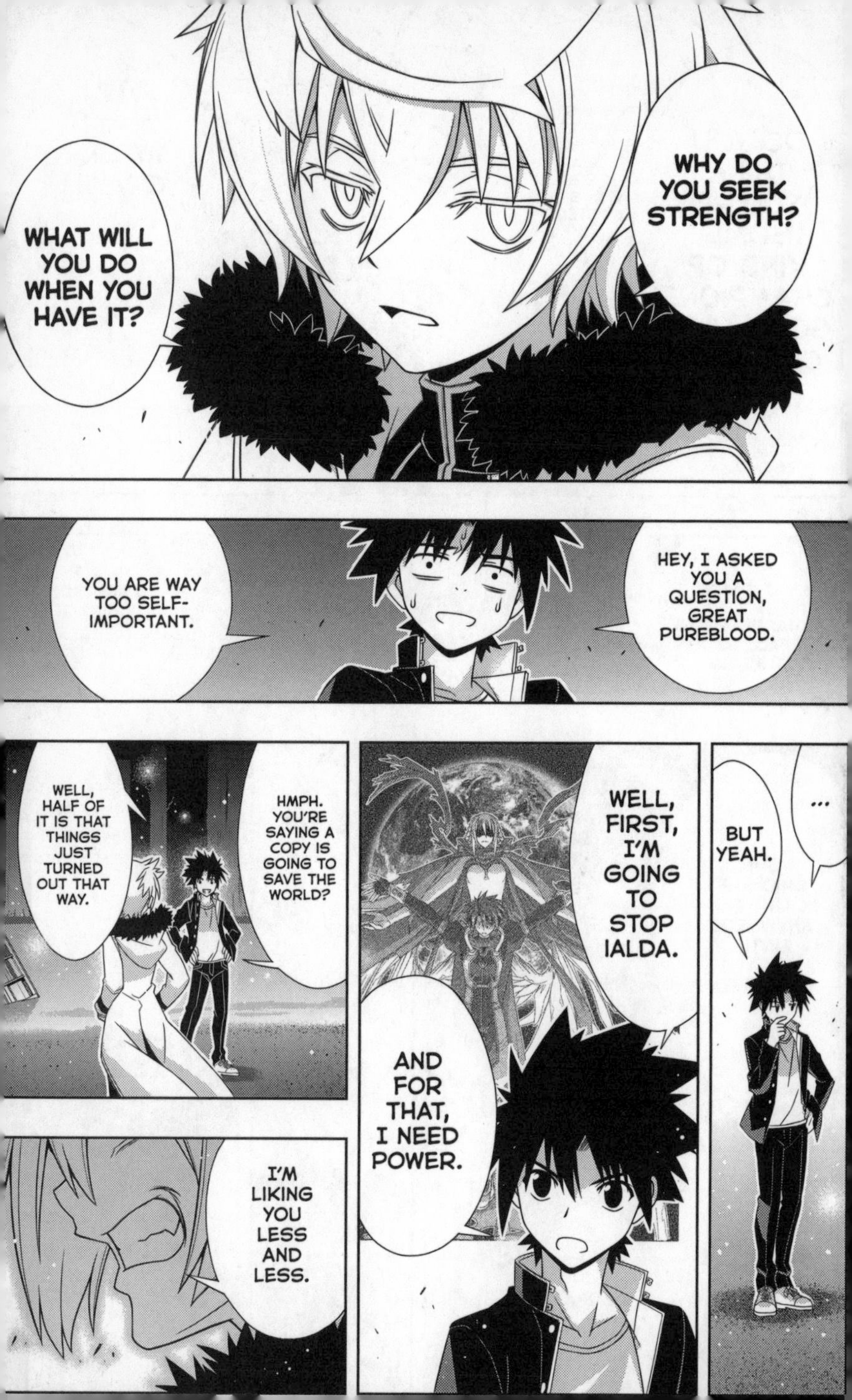
WHY DO YOU SEEK STRENGTH?
WHAT WILL YOU DO WHEN YOU HAVE IT?
HEY, I ASKED YOU A QUESTION, GREAT PUREBLOOD.
YOU ARE WAY TOO SELF-IMPORTANT.
...
BUT YEAH.
WELL, FIRST, I'M GOING TO STOP IALDA.
AND FOR THAT, I NEED POWER.
HMPH. YOU'RE SAYING A COPY IS GOING TO SAVE THE WORLD?
WELL, HALF OF IT IS THAT THINGS JUST TURNED OUT THAT WAY.
I'M LIKING YOU LESS AND LESS.

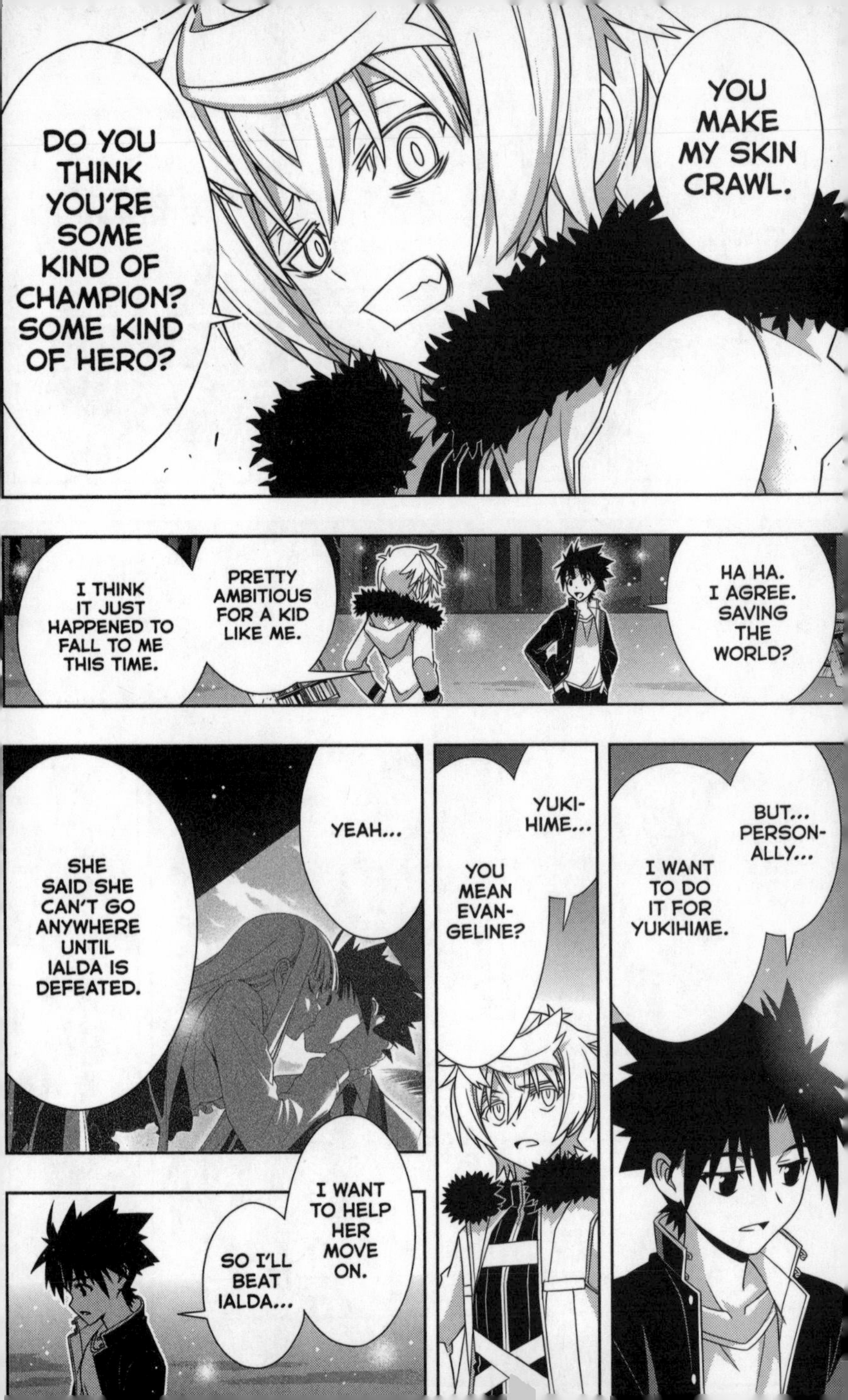
YOU MAKE MY SKIN CRAWL.
DO YOU THINK YOU'RE SOME KIND OF CHAMPION? SOME KIND OF HERO?
HA HA. I AGREE. SAVING THE WORLD?
PRETTY AMBITIOUS FOR A KID LIKE ME.
I THINK IT JUST HAPPENED TO FALL TO ME THIS TIME.
BUT... PERSONALLY...
I WANT TO DO IT FOR YUKIHIME.
YUKI-HIME...
YOU MEAN EVAN-GELINE?
YEAH...
SHE SAID SHE CAN'T GO ANYWHERE UNTIL IALDA IS DEFEATED.
I WANT TO HELP HER MOVE ON.
SO I'LL BEAT IALDA...

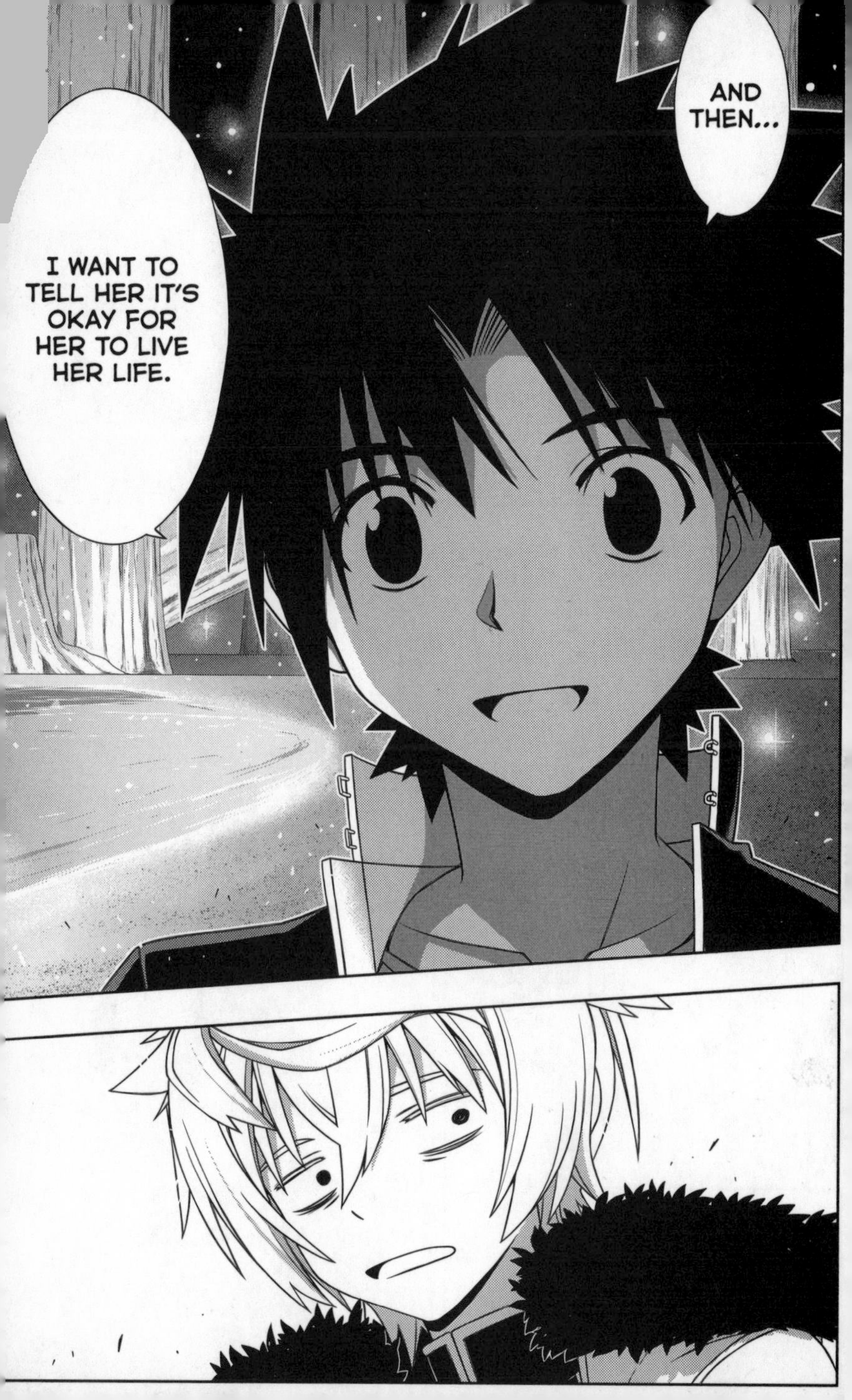
AND THEN...
I WANT TO TELL HER IT'S OKAY FOR HER TO LIVE HER LIFE.

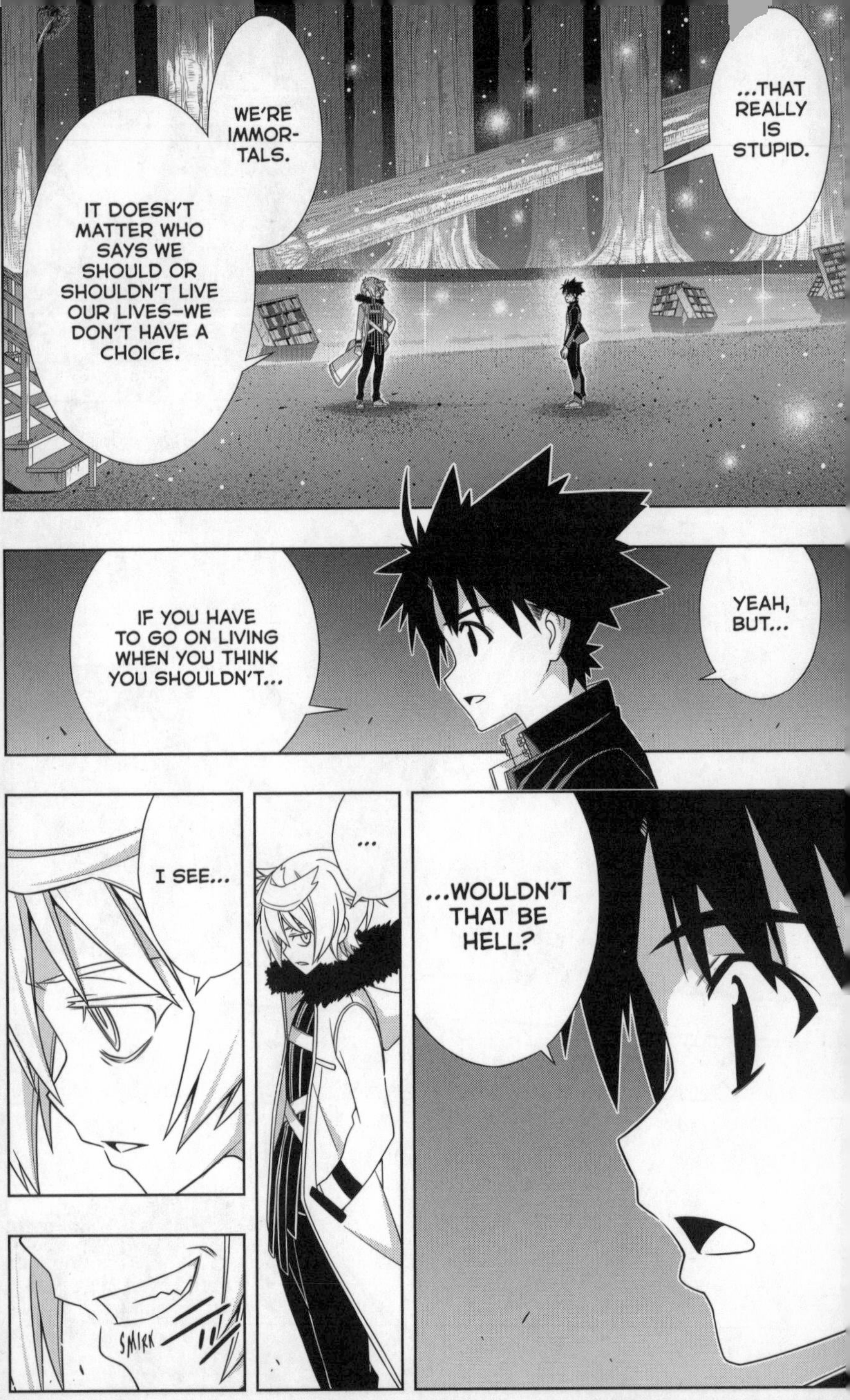
...THAT REALLY IS STUPID.
WE'RE IMMORTALS.
IT DOESN'T MATTER WHO SAYS WE SHOULD OR SHOULDN'T LIVE OUR LIVES—WE DON'T HAVE A CHOICE.
YEAH, BUT...
IF YOU HAVE TO GO ON LIVING WHEN YOU THINK YOU SHOULDN'T...
...WOULDN'T THAT BE HELL?
...
I SEE...
SMIRK

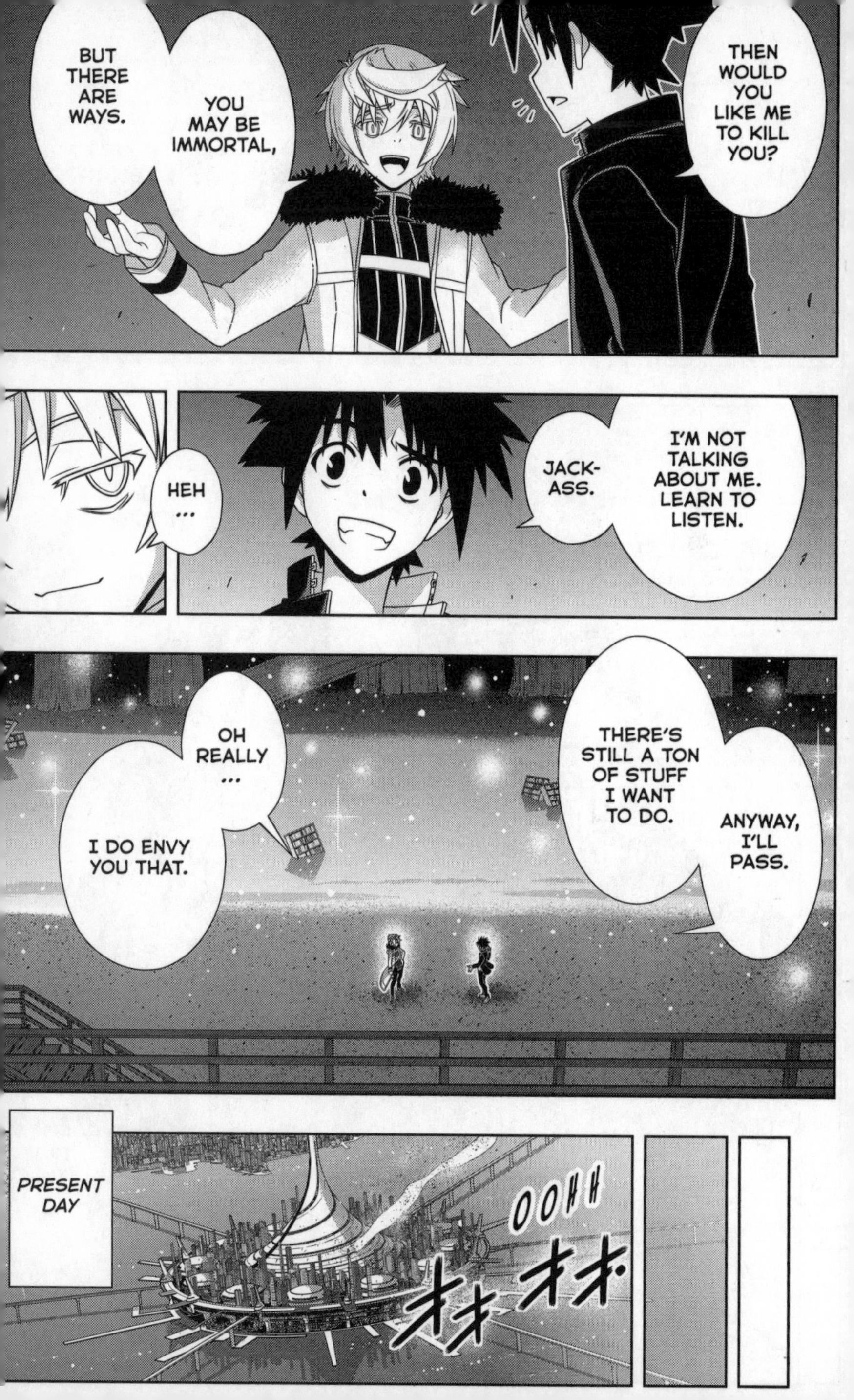
THEN WOULD YOU LIKE ME TO KILL YOU?
YOU MAY BE IMMORTAL,
BUT THERE ARE WAYS.
I'M NOT TALKING ABOUT ME. LEARN TO LISTEN.
JACK-ASS.
HEH ...
ANYWAY, I'LL PASS.
THERE'S STILL A TON OF STUFF I WANT TO DO.
OH REALLY ...
I DO ENVY YOU THAT.
PRESENT DAY
OOHH
オォオオ

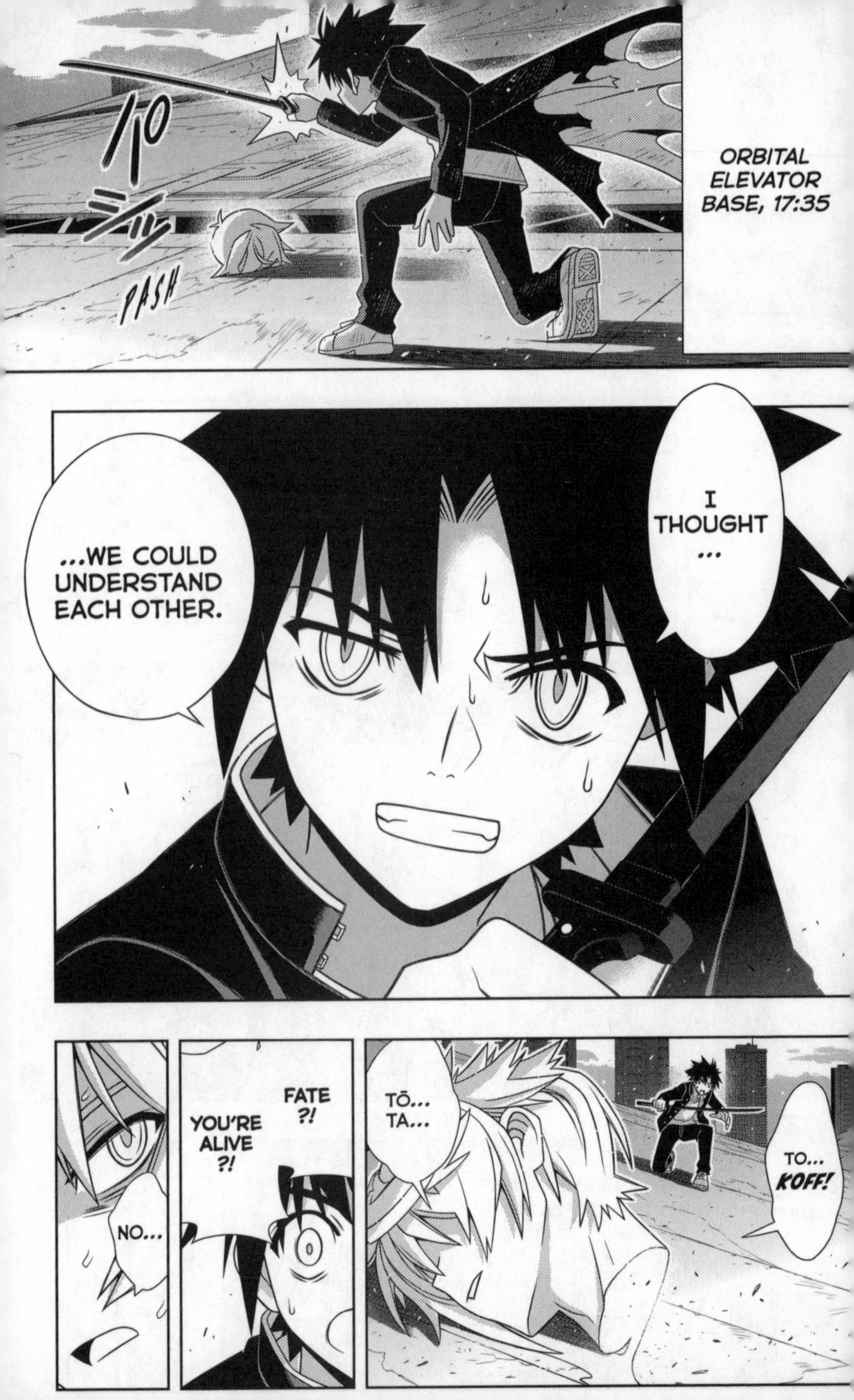
ORBITAL ELEVATOR BASE, 17:35
PASH
I THOUGHT...
...WE COULD UNDERSTAND EACH OTHER.
TO... KOFF!
TŌ... TA...
FATE?!
YOU'RE ALIVE?!
NO...

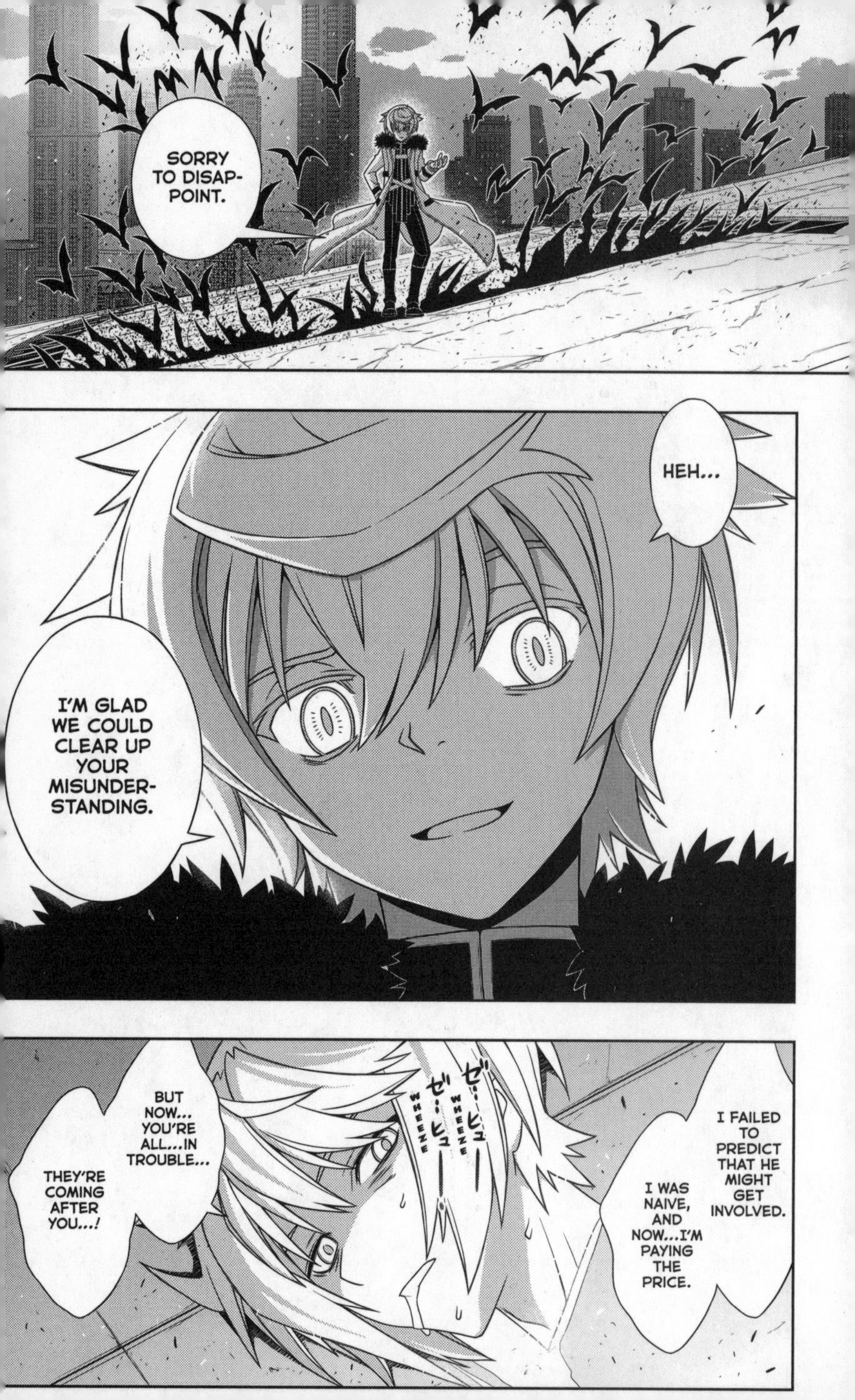
SORRY TO DISAP-POINT.
HEH...
I'M GLAD WE COULD CLEAR UP YOUR MISUNDER-STANDING.
I FAILED TO PREDICT THAT HE MIGHT GET INVOLVED.
I WAS NAIVE, AND NOW...I'M PAYING THE PRICE.
WHEEZE
WHEEZE
BUT NOW... YOU'RE ALL...IN TROUBLE...
THEY'RE COMING AFTER YOU...!

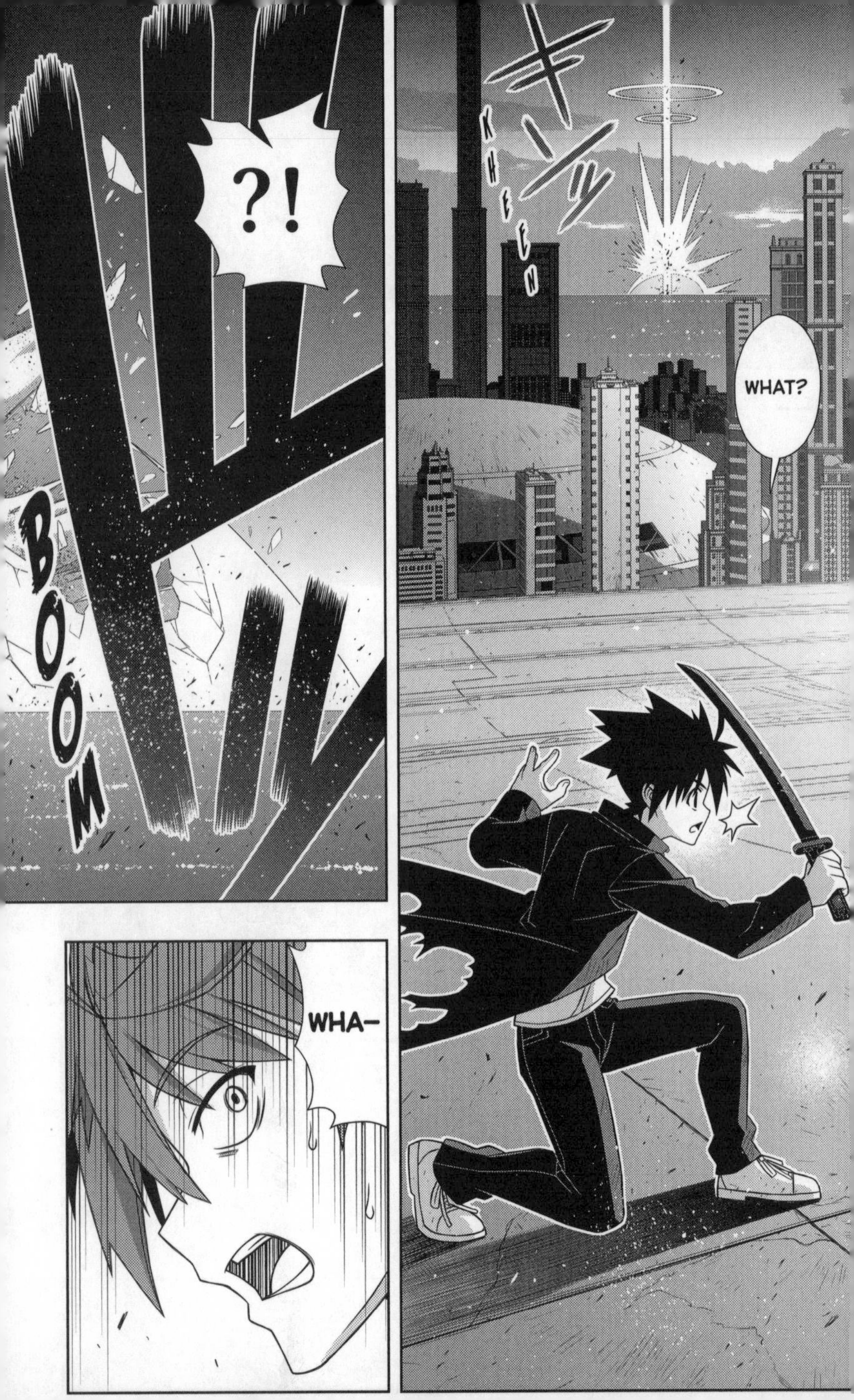
KHEEN
WHAT?
?!
BOOM
WHA-

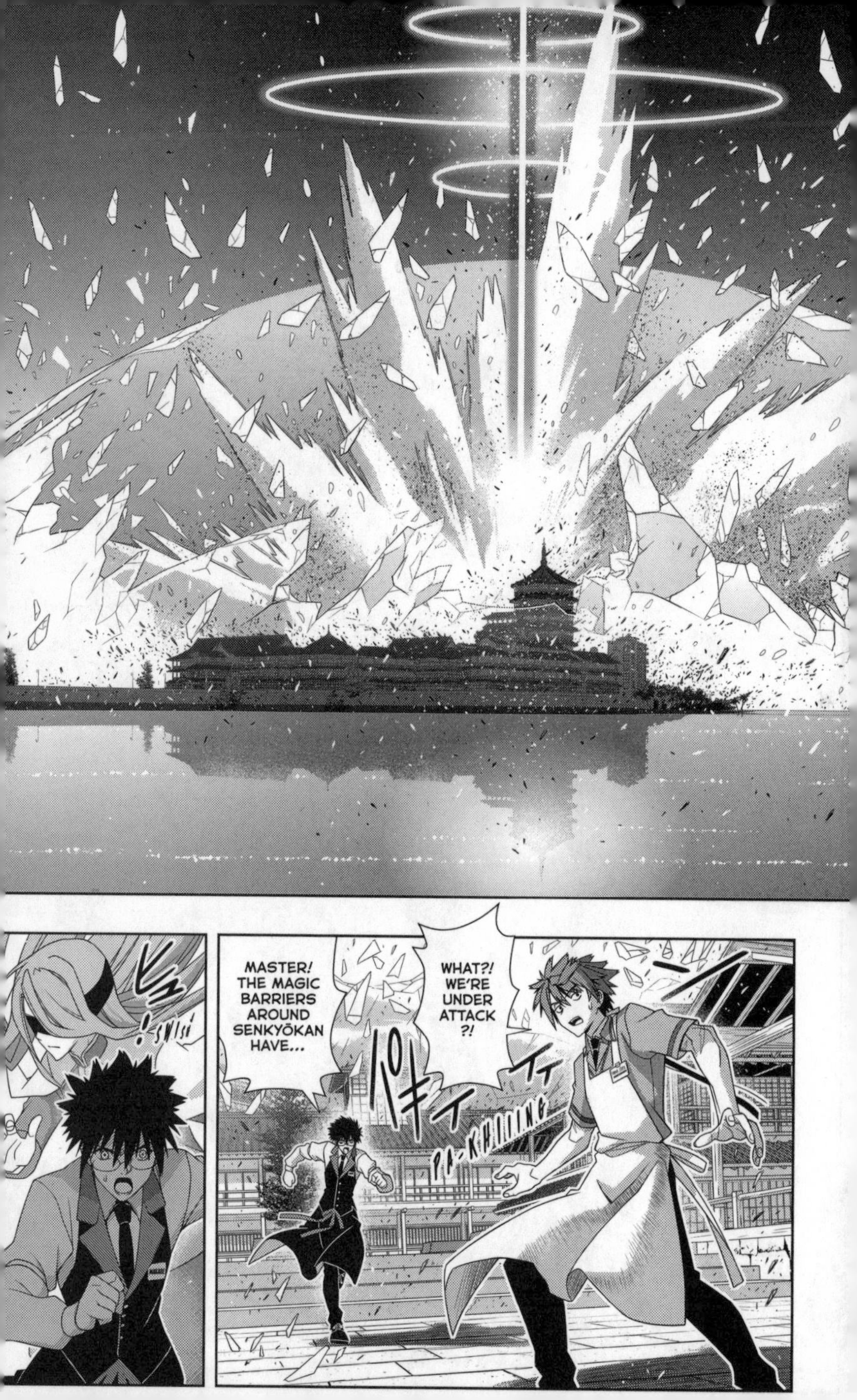
WHAT?! WE'RE UNDER ATTACK?!
MASTER! THE MAGIC BARRIERS AROUND SENKYŌKAN HAVE...
PA-KHIIIING
SWISH

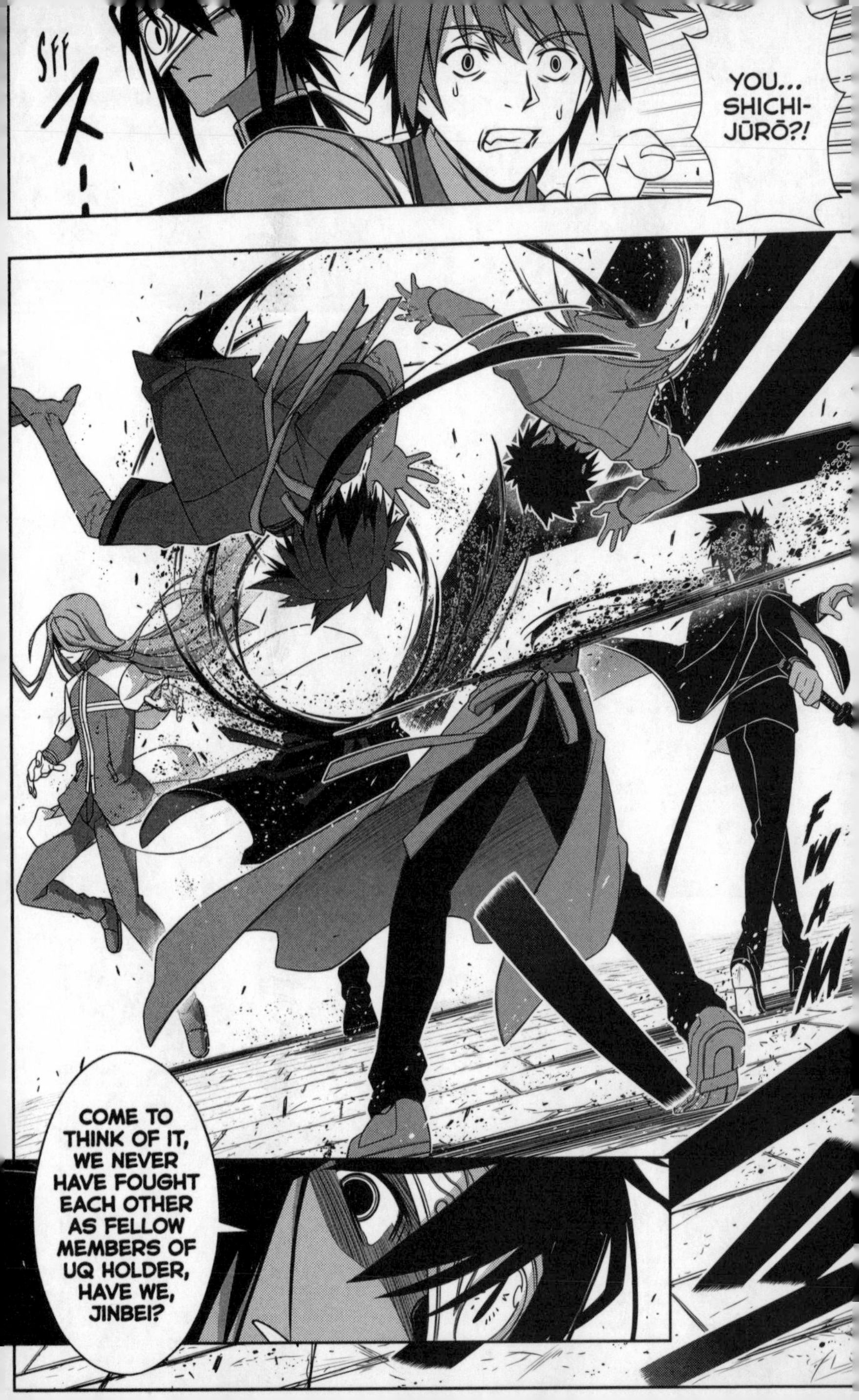
YOU... SHICHI-JŪRŌ?!
SFF
FWAM
COME TO THINK OF IT, WE NEVER HAVE FOUGHT EACH OTHER AS FELLOW MEMBERS OF UQ HOLDER, HAVE WE, JINBEI?

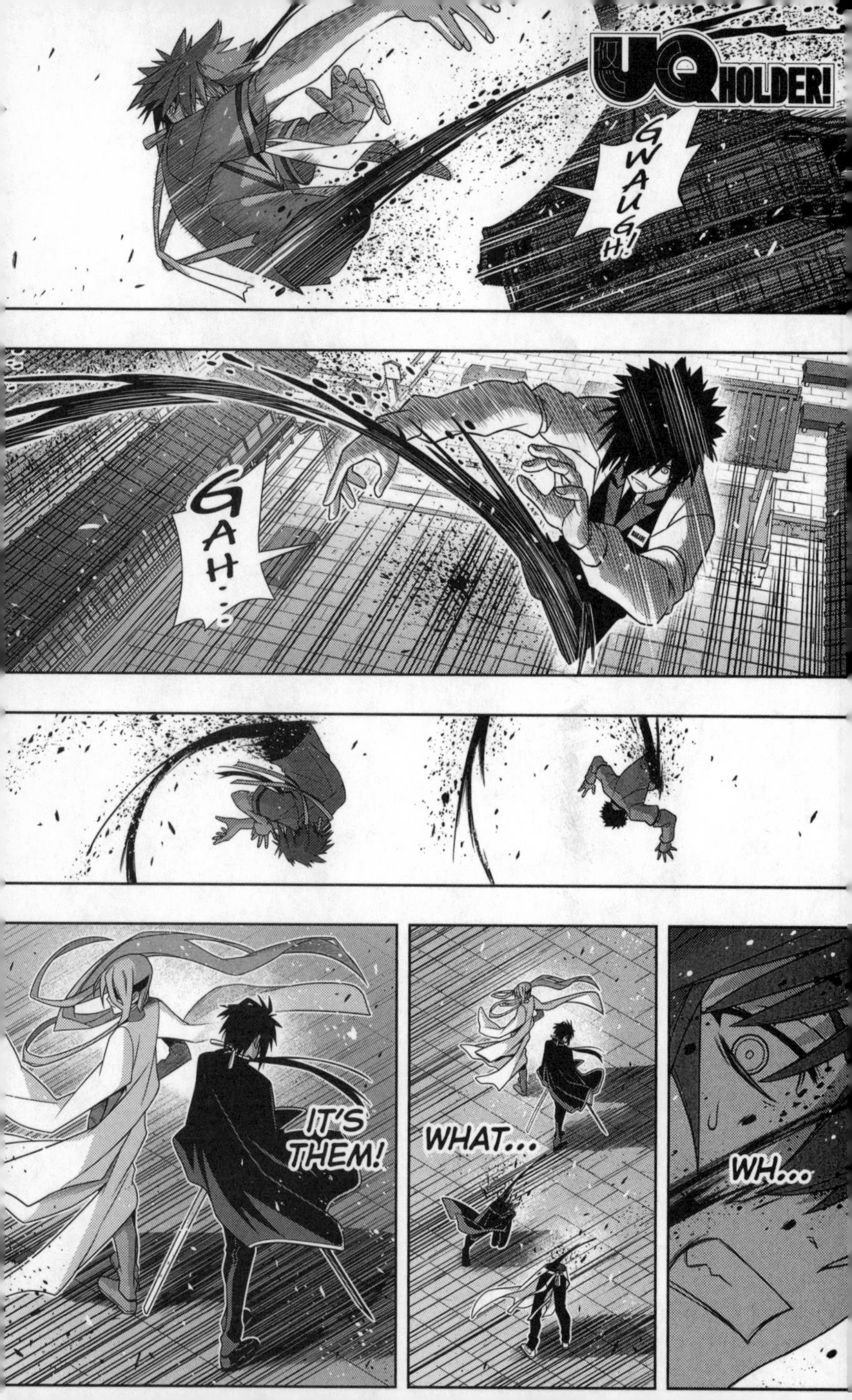
UQ HOLDER!
GWAUGH!
GAH...
WH...
WHAT...
IT'S THEM!

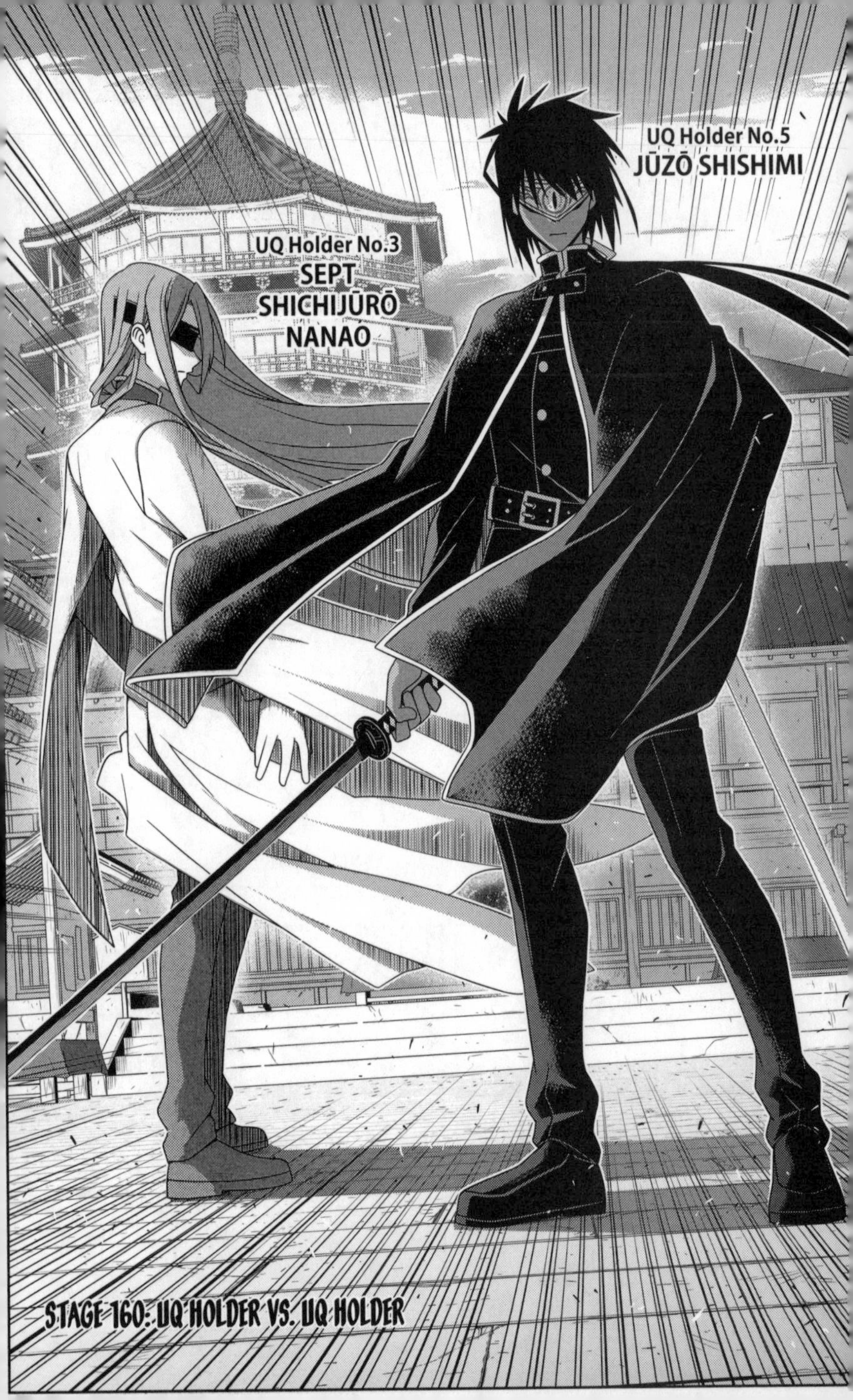
UQ Holder No.5
JŪZŌ SHISHIMI
UQ Holder No.3
SEPT
SHICHIJŪRŌ
NANAO
STAGE 160: UQ HOLDER VS. UQ HOLDER

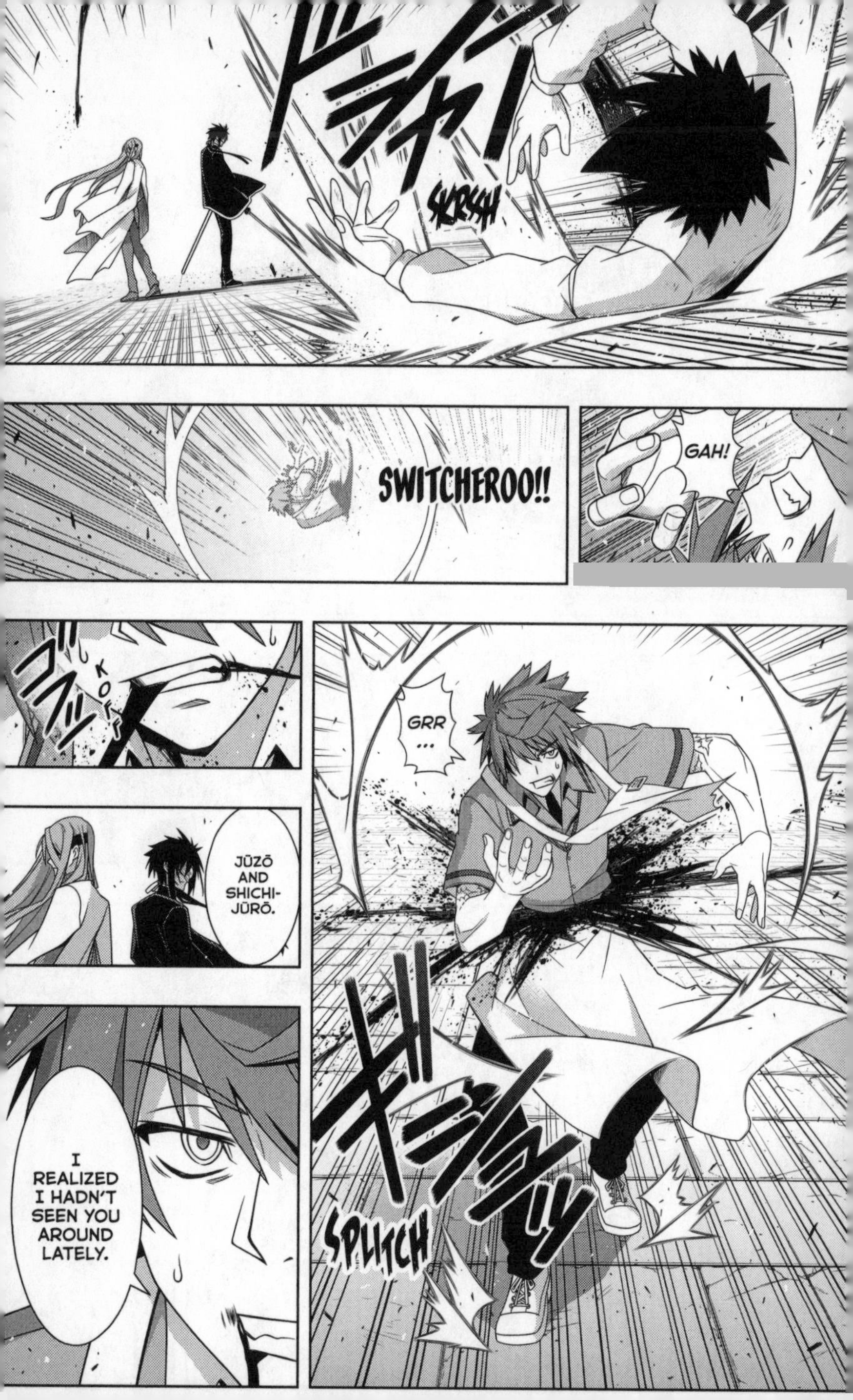
SKRSSH
GAH!
SWITCHEROO!!
GRR ...
SPLITCH
KOFF
JŪZŌ AND SHICHI-JŪRŌ.
I REALIZED I HADN'T SEEN YOU AROUND LATELY.

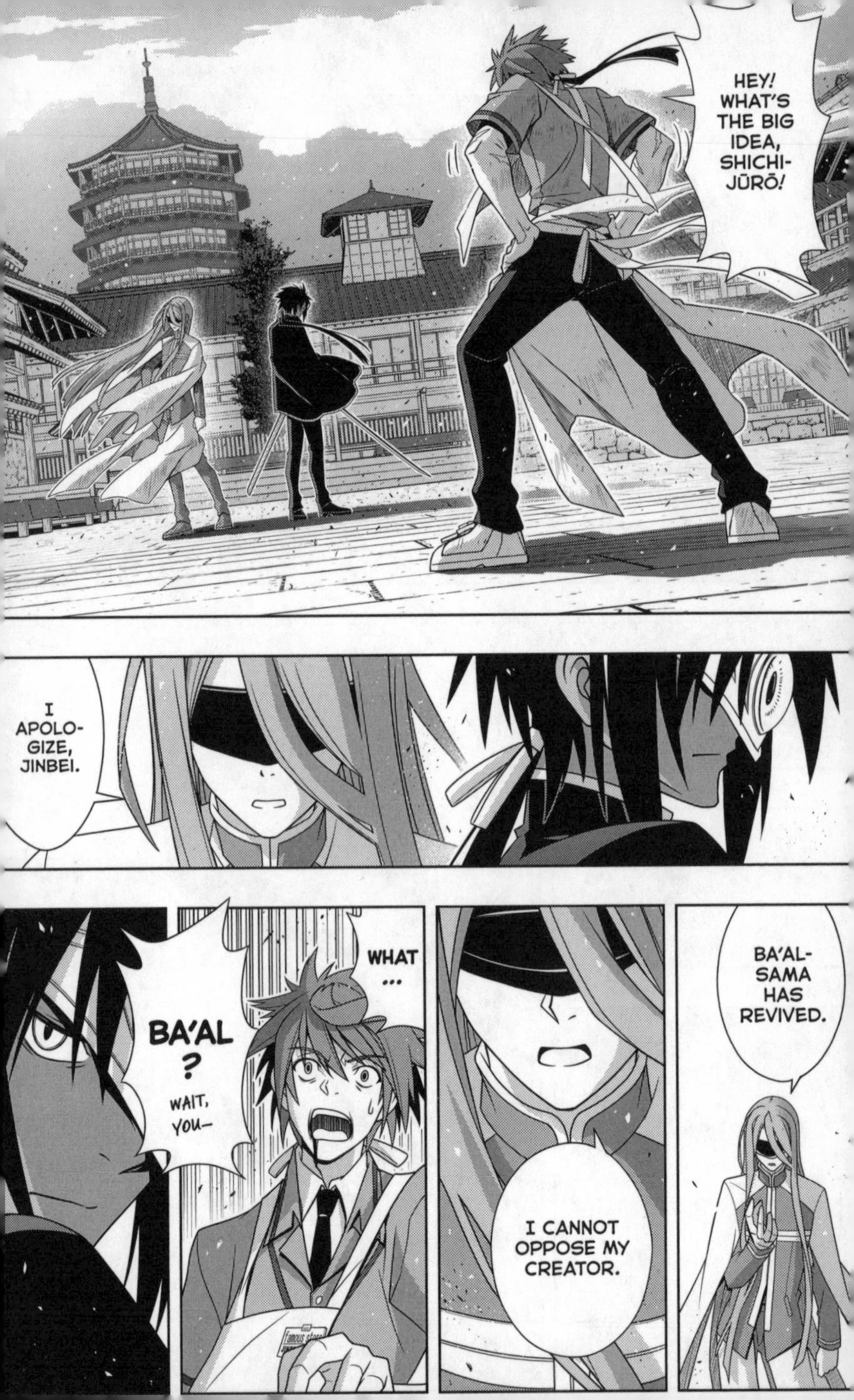
HEY! WHAT'S THE BIG IDEA, SHICHI-JŪRŌ!
I APOLO-GIZE, JINBEI.
BA'AL-SAMA HAS REVIVED.
I CANNOT OPPOSE MY CREATOR.
WHAT ...
BA'AL?
WAIT, YOU—

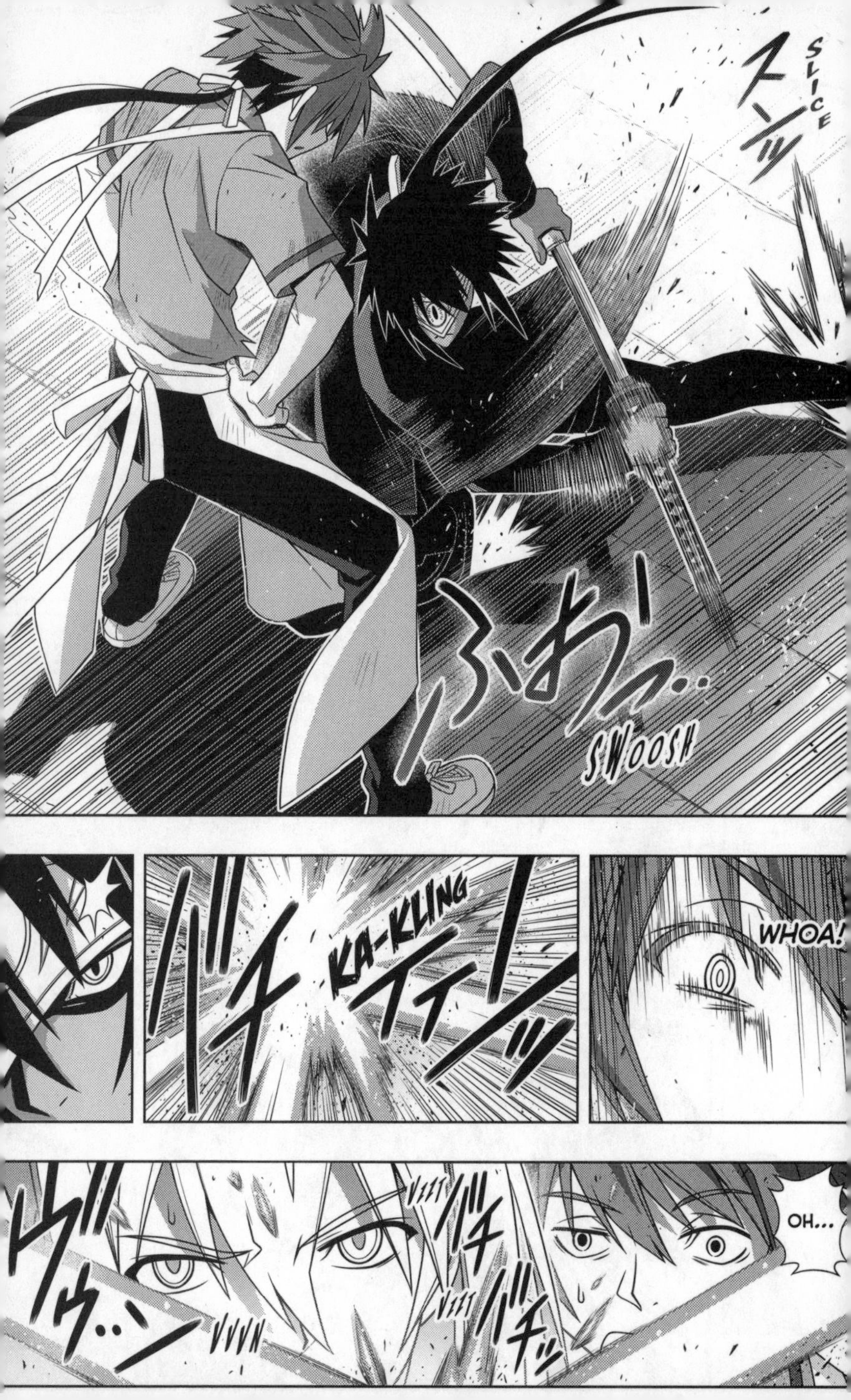
SLICE
SWOOSH
WHOA!
KA-KLING
OH...
VZZT
VZZT
VVVN

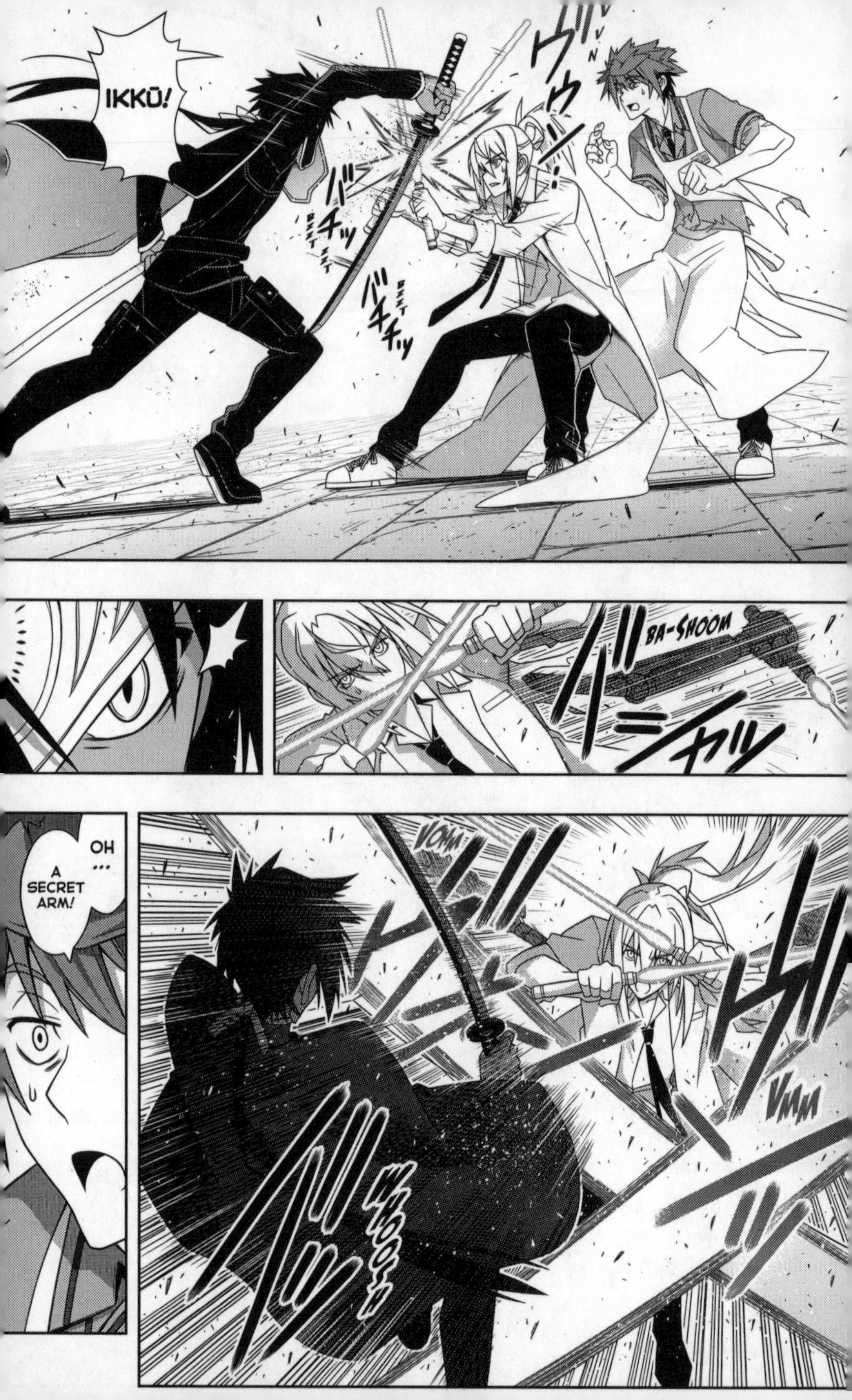

VVVN
IKKŪ!
BZZT BZZT
BZZT
BA-SHOOM
...
VOMM
VMMM
OH ...
A SECRET ARM!

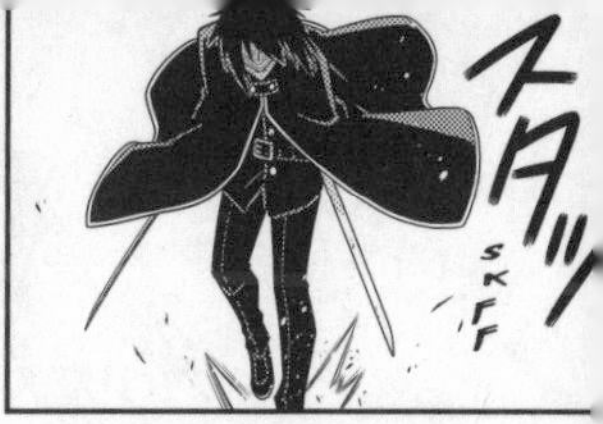
SKFF
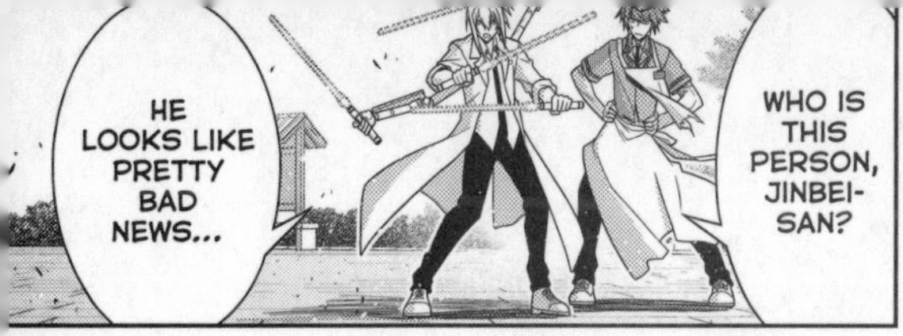
WHO IS THIS PERSON, JINBEI-SAN?
HE LOOKS LIKE PRETTY BAD NEWS...
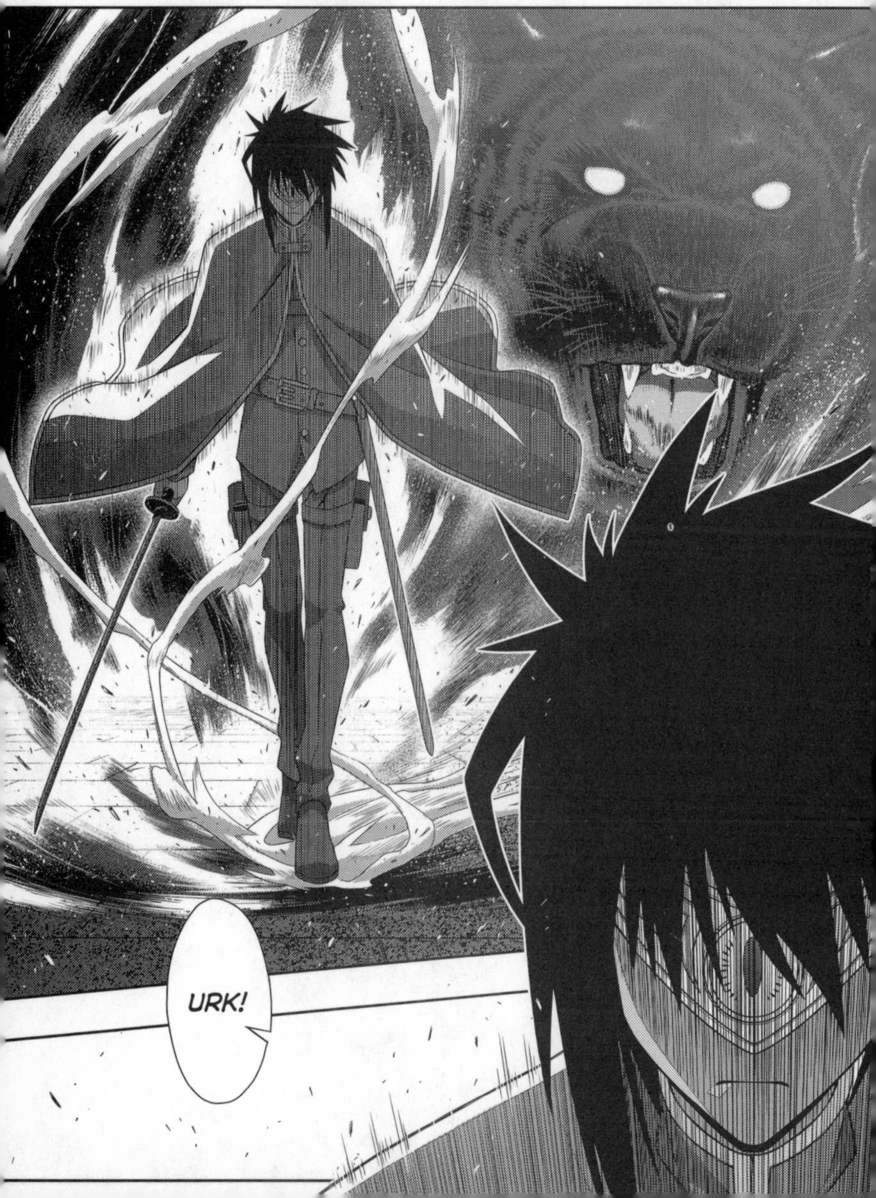
URK!

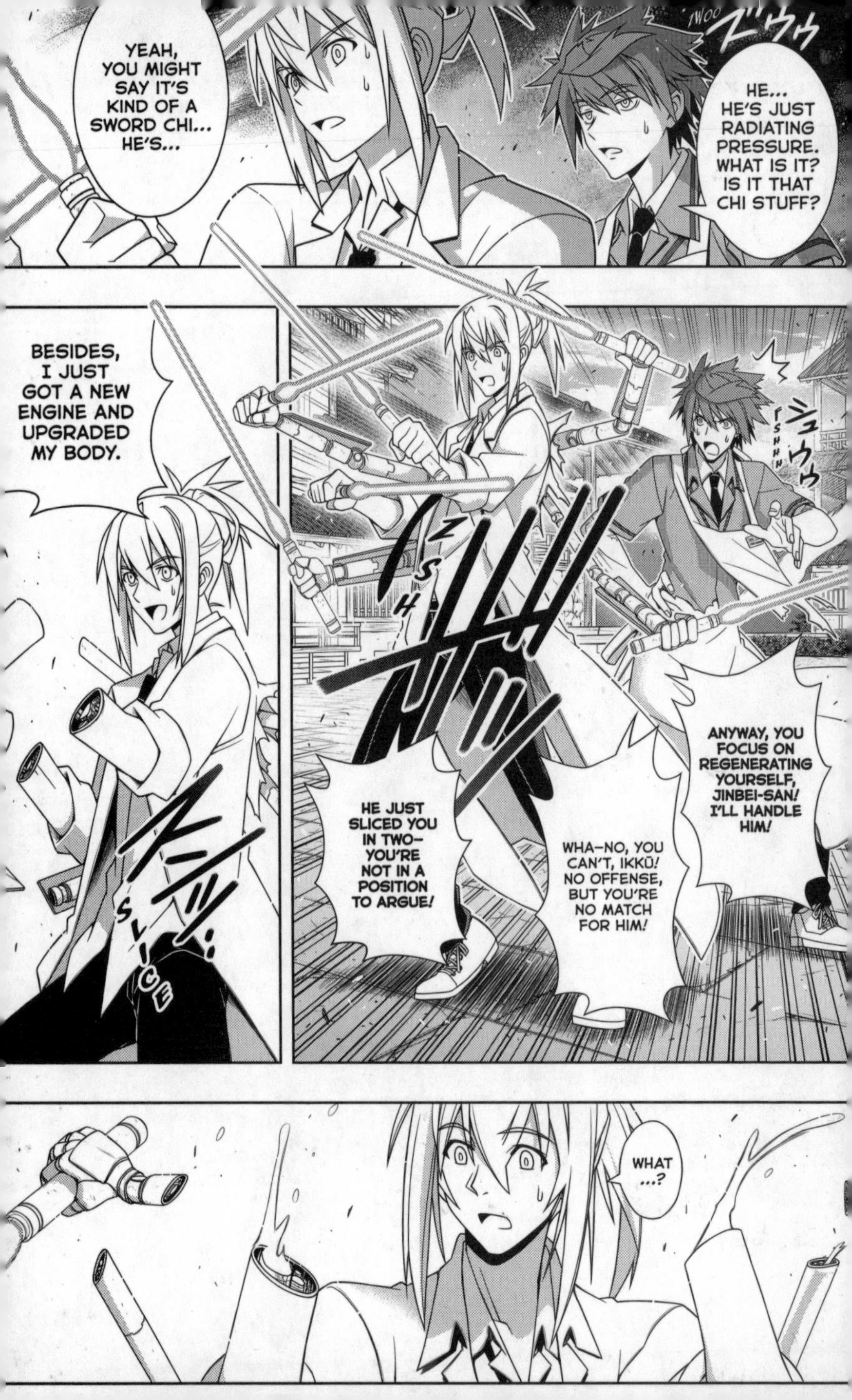
IWOO
HE... HE'S JUST RADIATING PRESSURE. WHAT IS IT? IS IT THAT CHI STUFF?
YEAH, YOU MIGHT SAY IT'S KIND OF A SWORD CHI... HE'S...
FSHHH
ZSHH
ANYWAY, YOU FOCUS ON REGENERATING YOURSELF, JINBEI-SAN! I'LL HANDLE HIM!
WHA-NO, YOU CAN'T, IKKŪ! NO OFFENSE, BUT YOU'RE NO MATCH FOR HIM!
HE JUST SLICED YOU IN TWO–YOU'RE NOT IN A POSITION TO ARGUE!
BESIDES, I JUST GOT A NEW ENGINE AND UPGRADED MY BODY.
SLICE
WHAT ...?

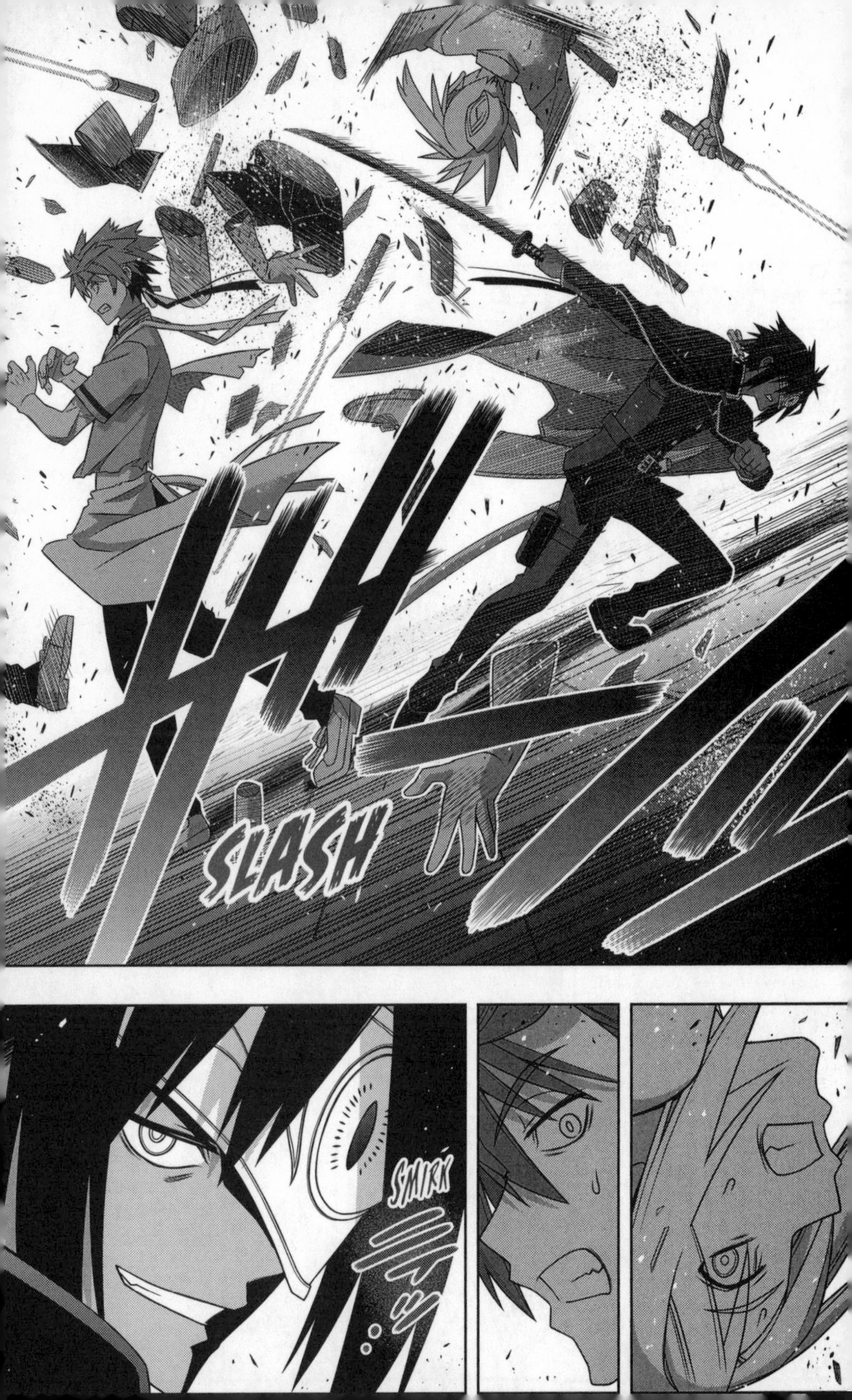
SLASH
SMIRK

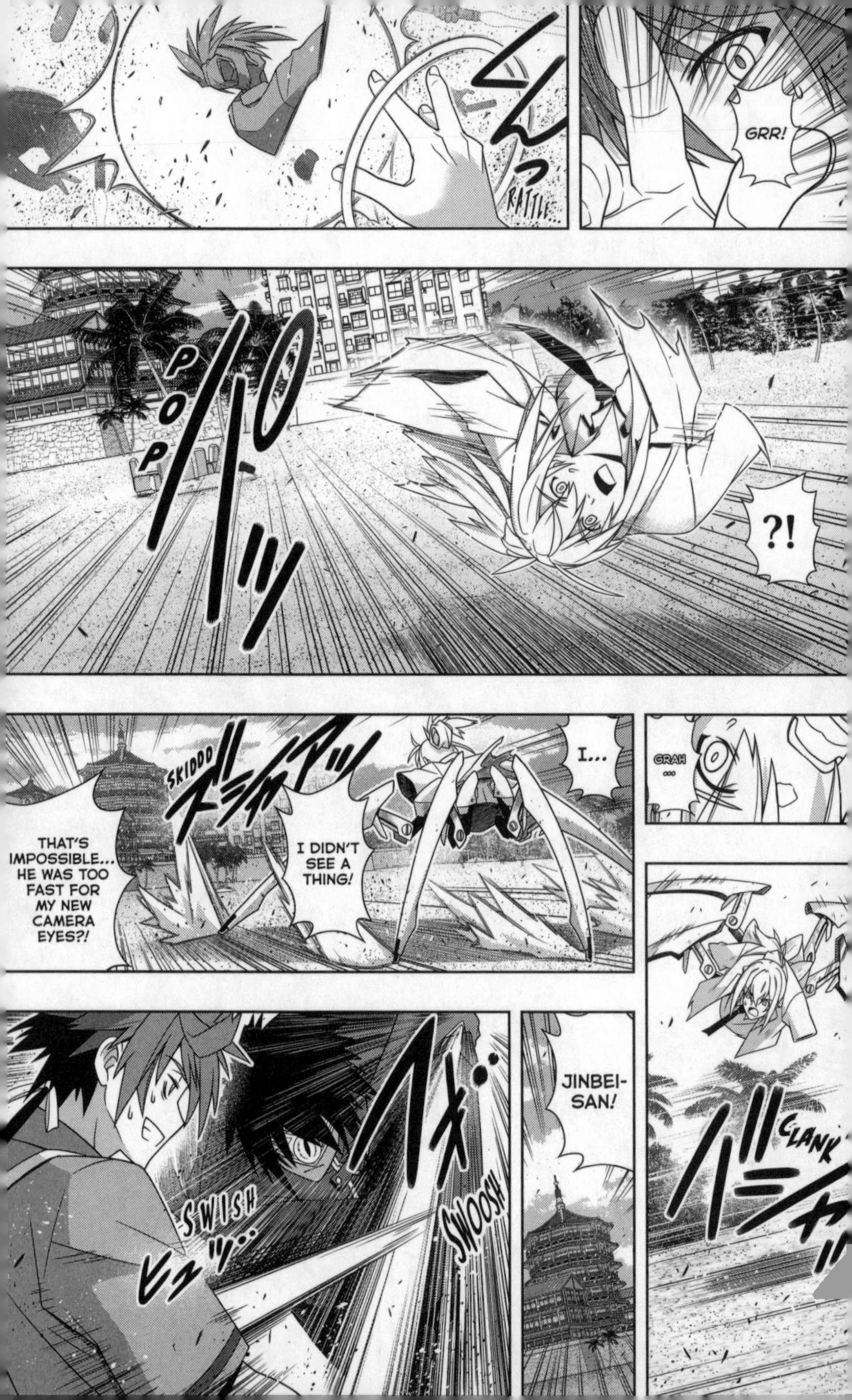
GRR!
RATTLE...
?!
POP
GRAH ...
I...
I DIDN'T SEE A THING!
SKIDOO
THAT'S IMPOSSIBLE... HE WAS TOO FAST FOR MY NEW CAMERA EYES?!
CLANK
JINBEI-SAN!
SWOOSH
SWISH

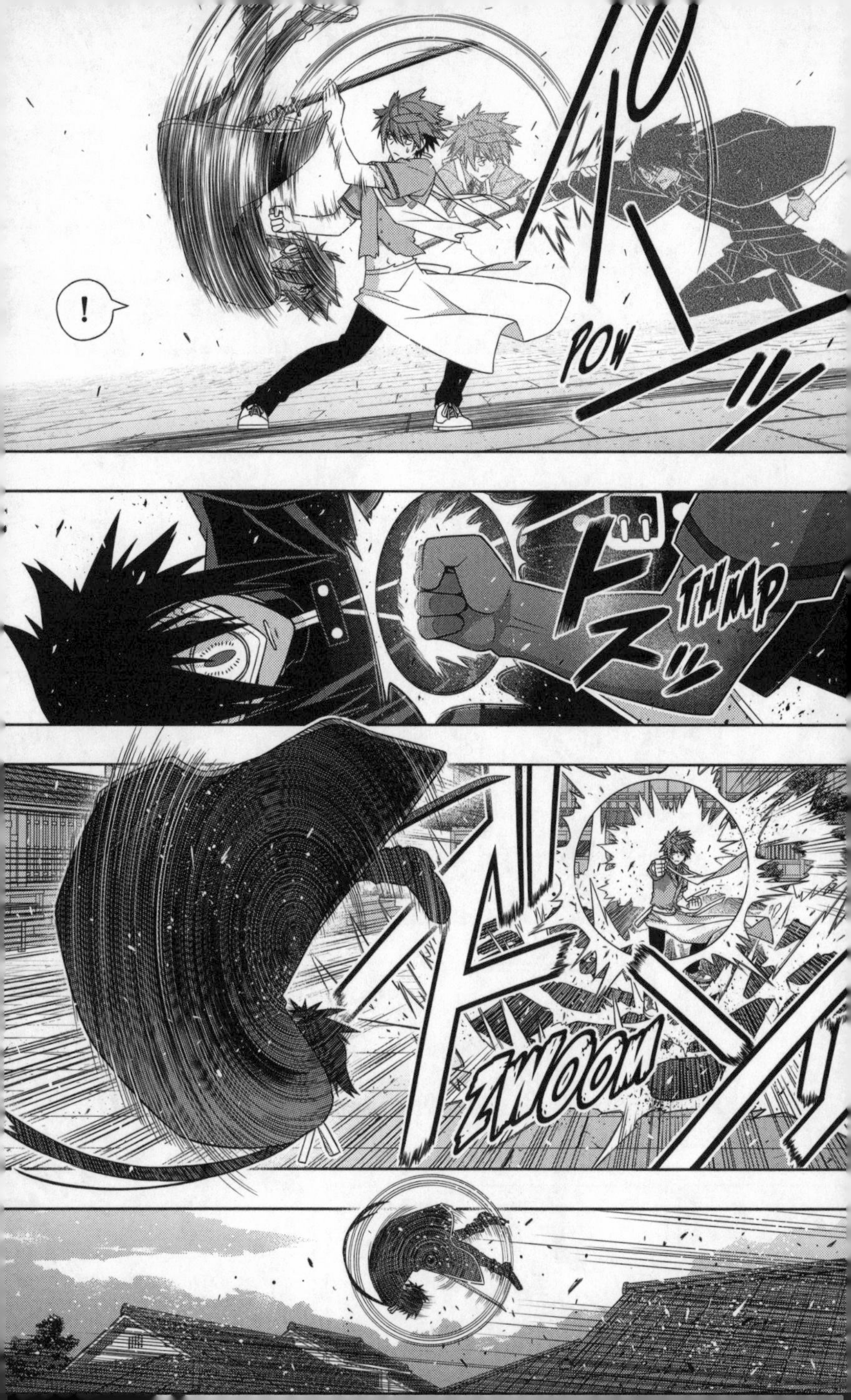
POW
!
THMP
ドスッ
ZWOOM

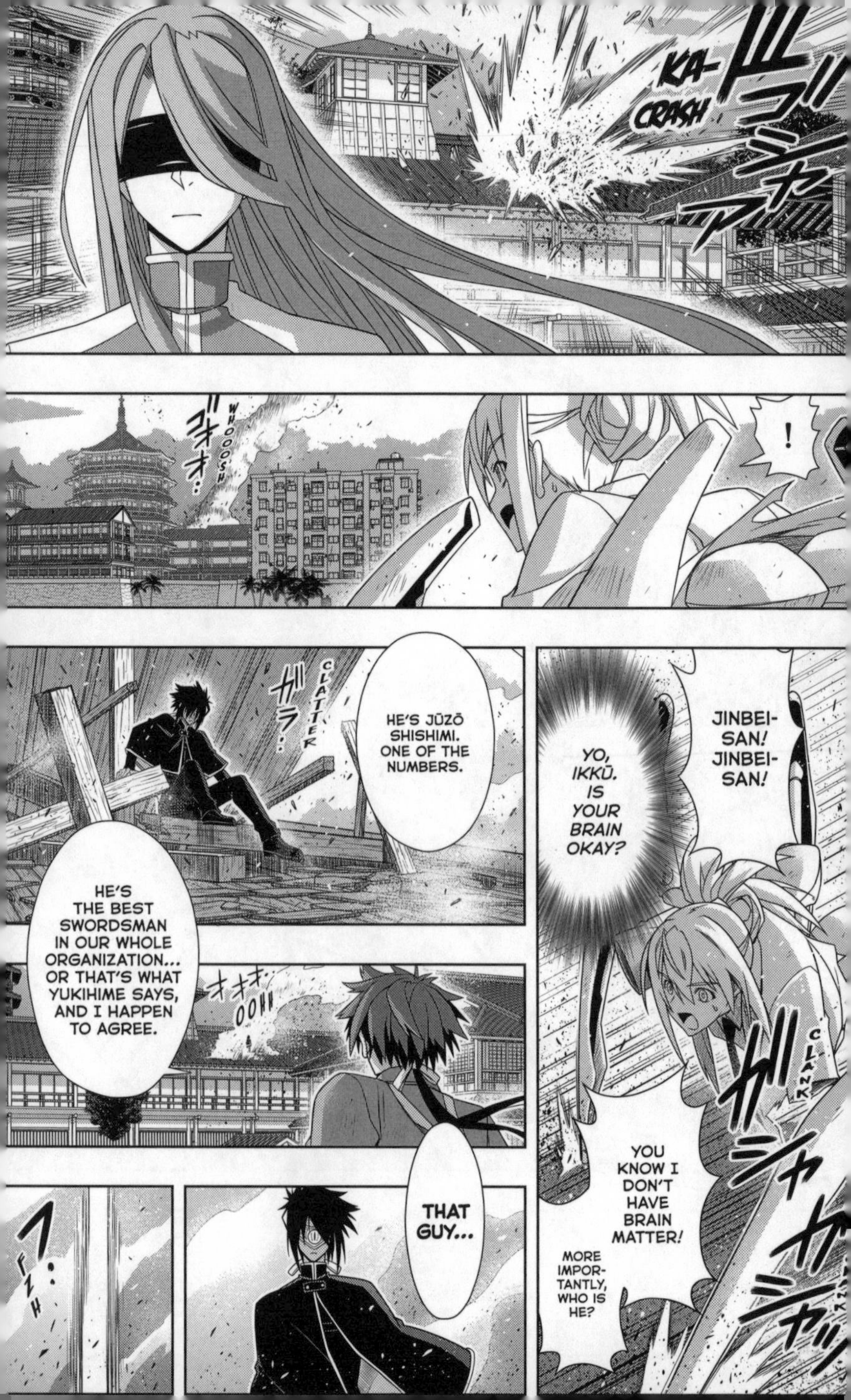
KA-CRASH
!
WHOOOSH
JINBEI-SAN! JINBEI-SAN!
YO, IKKŪ. IS YOUR BRAIN OKAY?
CLANK
YOU KNOW I DON'T HAVE BRAIN MATTER!
MORE IMPORTANTLY, WHO IS HE?
CLANK
CLATTER
HE'S JŪZŌ SHISHIMI. ONE OF THE NUMBERS.
HE'S THE BEST SWORDSMAN IN OUR WHOLE ORGANIZATION... OR THAT'S WHAT YUKIHIME SAYS, AND I HAPPEN TO AGREE.
OOHH
THAT GUY...
FZH

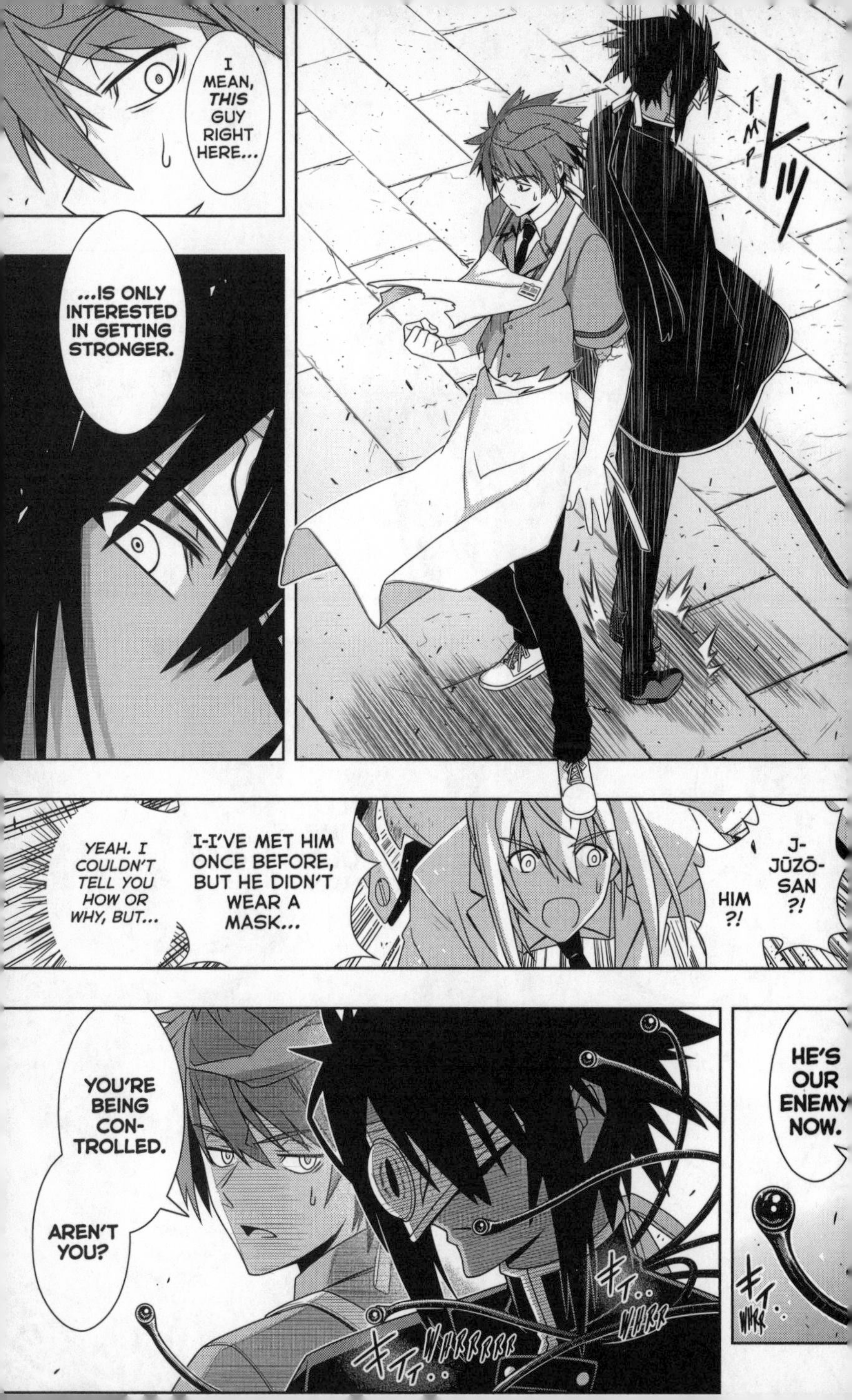
TMP
I MEAN, *THIS* GUY RIGHT HERE...
...IS ONLY INTERESTED IN GETTING STRONGER.
J-JŪZŌ-SAN?!
HIM?!
I-I'VE MET HIM ONCE BEFORE, BUT HE DIDN'T WEAR A MASK...
YEAH. I COULDN'T TELL YOU HOW OR WHY, BUT...
HE'S OUR ENEMY NOW.
YOU'RE BEING CON-TROLLED.
AREN'T YOU?

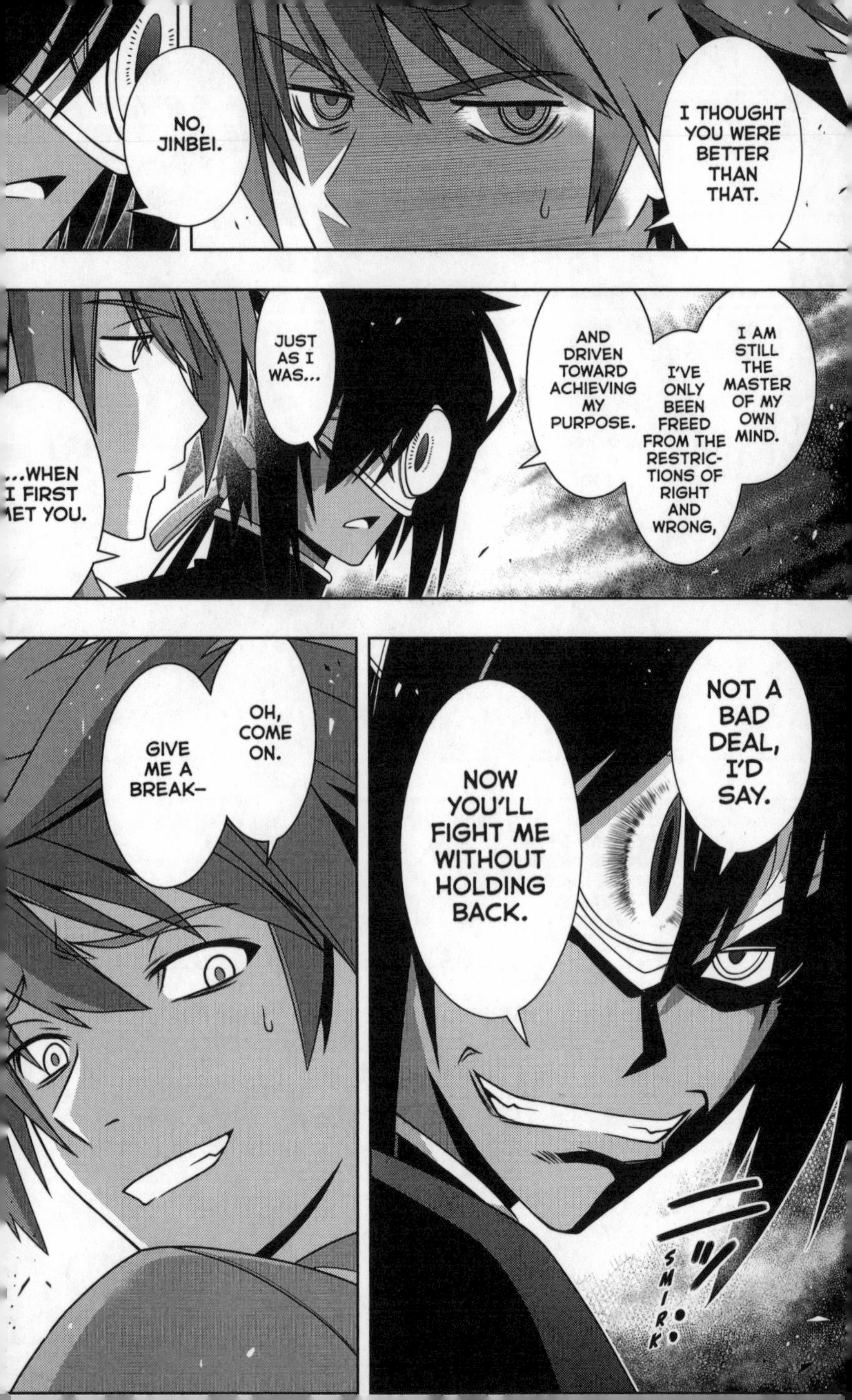
I THOUGHT YOU WERE BETTER THAN THAT.
NO, JINBEI.
I AM STILL THE MASTER OF MY OWN MIND.
I'VE ONLY BEEN FREED FROM THE RESTRICTIONS OF RIGHT AND WRONG,
AND DRIVEN TOWARD ACHIEVING MY PURPOSE.
JUST AS I WAS...
...WHEN I FIRST MET YOU.
NOT A BAD DEAL, I'D SAY.
NOW YOU'LL FIGHT ME WITHOUT HOLDING BACK.
SMIRK
OH, COME ON.
GIVE ME A BREAK–

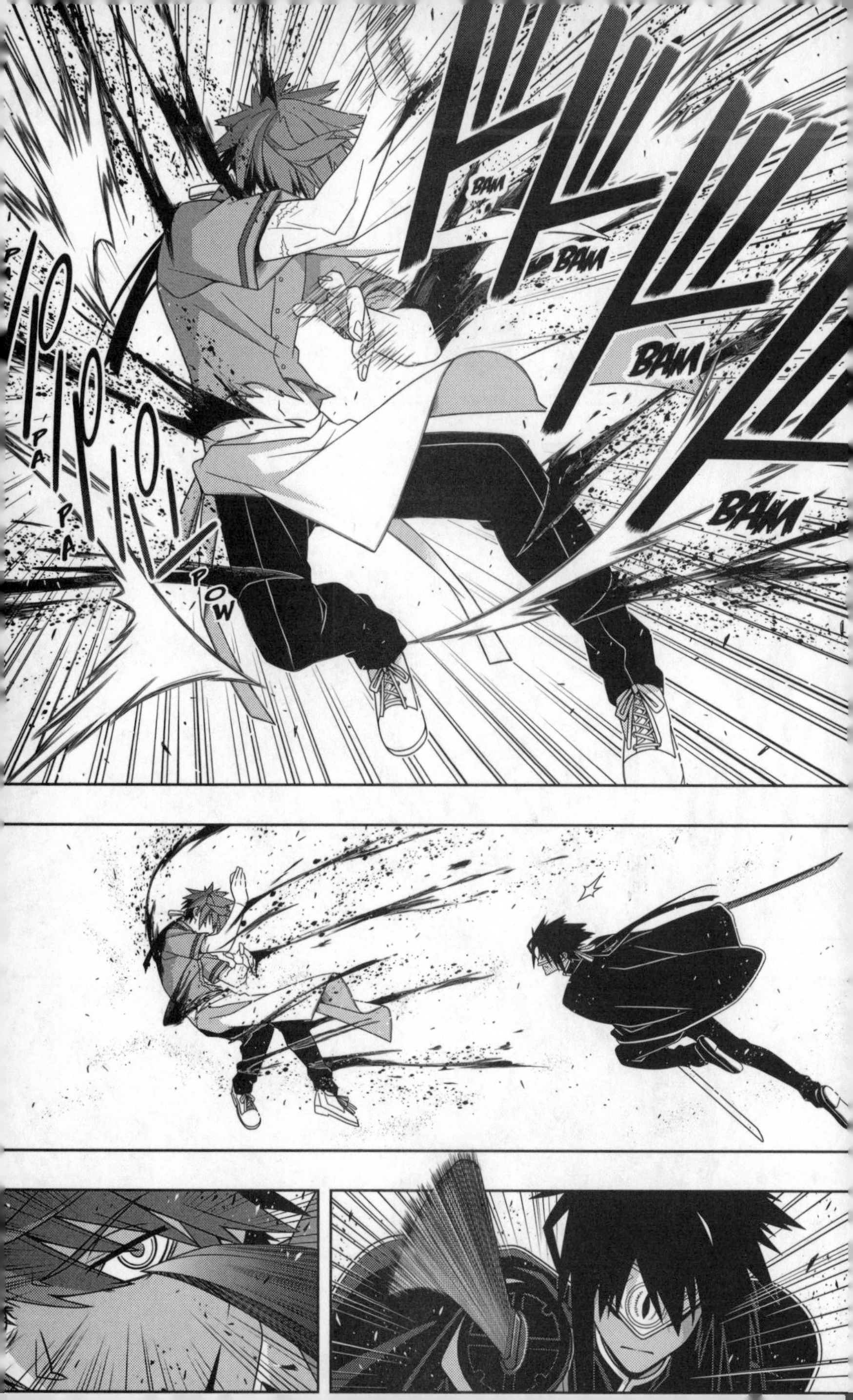
BAM
BAM
BAM
BAM
PA
PA
PA
POW

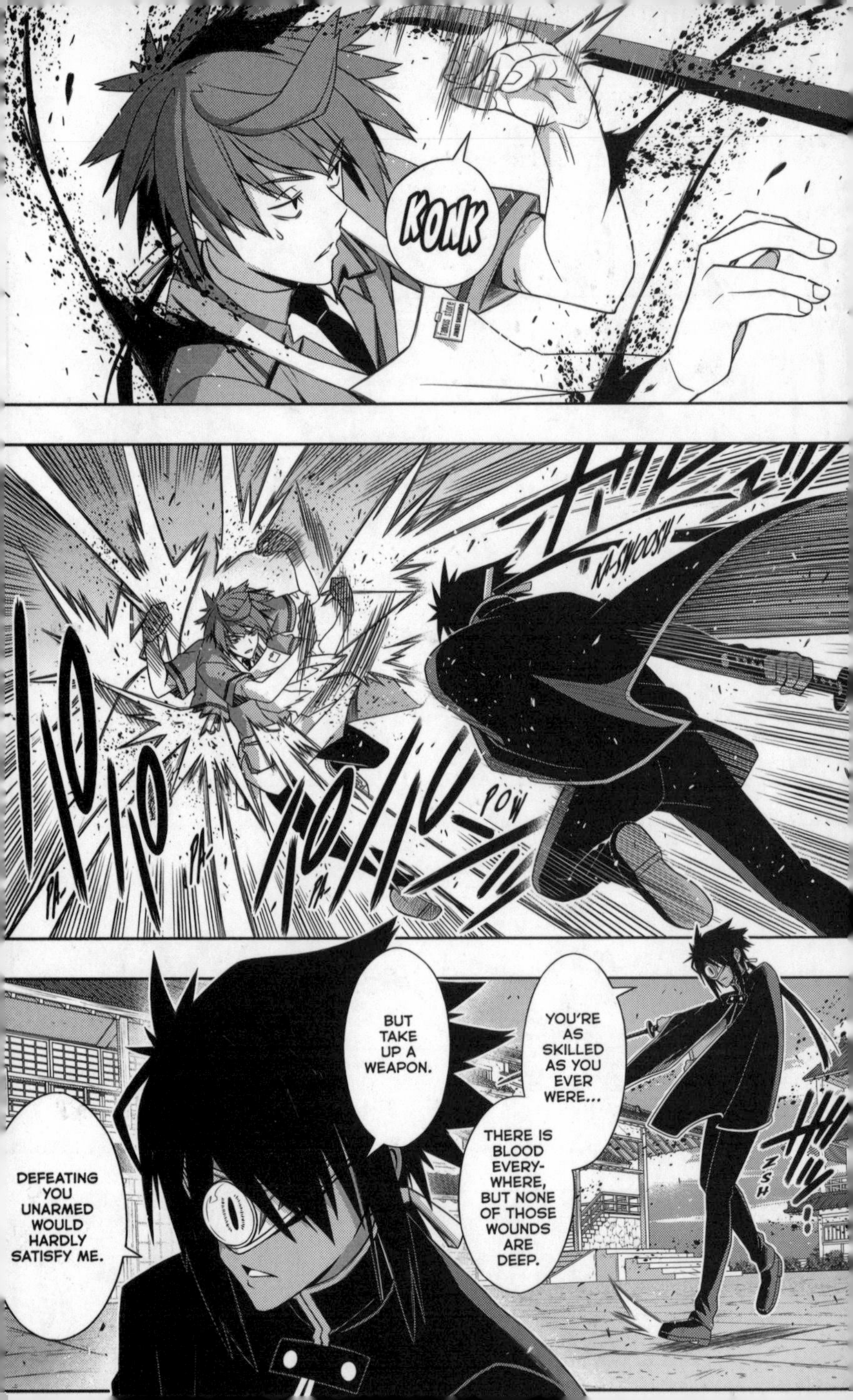
KONK
KA-SWOOSH
POW
PA
PA
PA
ZSH
YOU'RE AS SKILLED AS YOU EVER WERE...
THERE IS BLOOD EVERY-WHERE, BUT NONE OF THOSE WOUNDS ARE DEEP.
BUT TAKE UP A WEAPON.
DEFEATING YOU UNARMED WOULD HARDLY SATISFY ME.

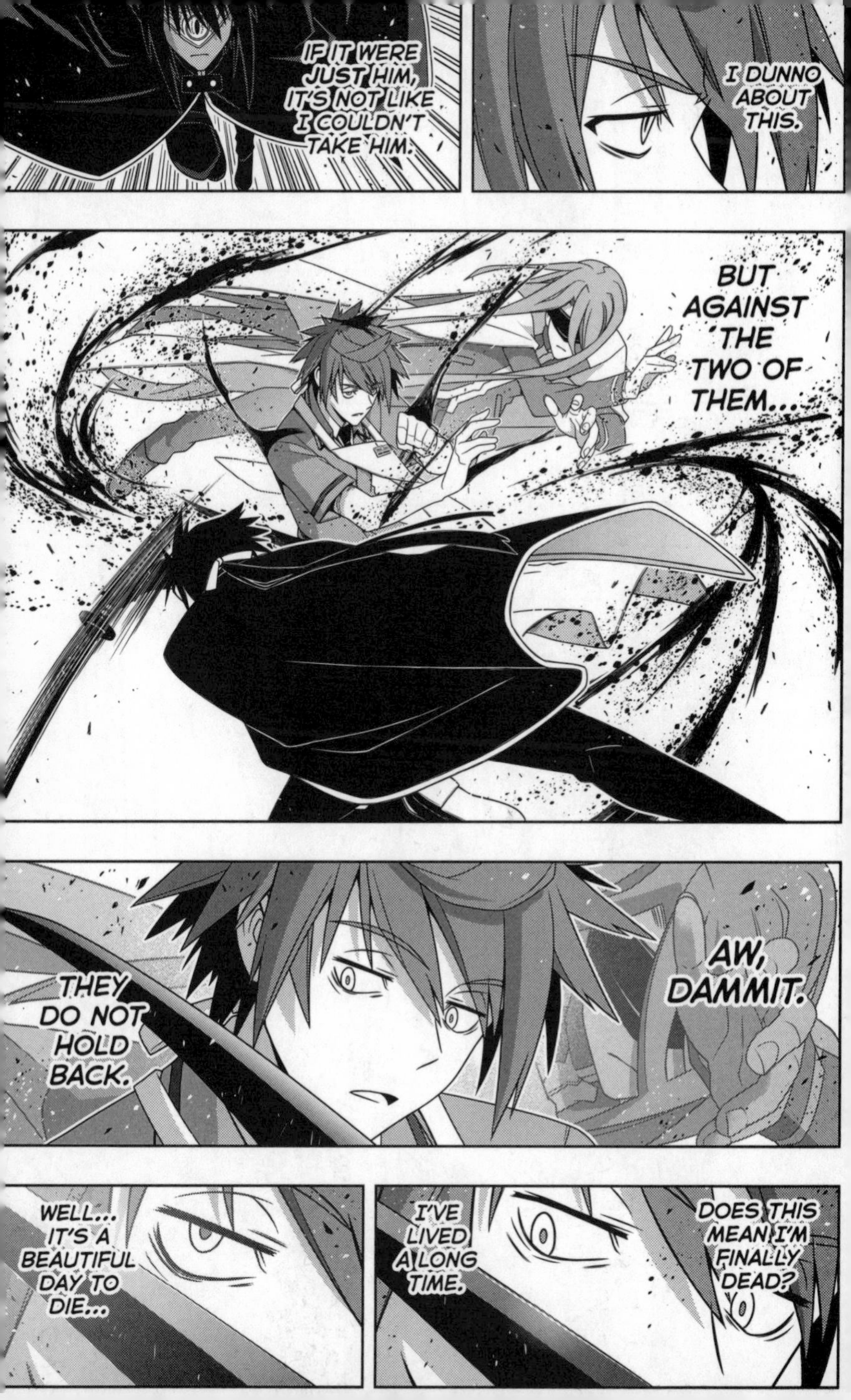
I DUNNO ABOUT THIS.
IF IT WERE JUST HIM, IT'S NOT LIKE I COULDN'T TAKE HIM.
BUT AGAINST THE TWO OF THEM...
AW, DAMMIT.
THEY DO NOT HOLD BACK.
DOES THIS MEAN I'M FINALLY DEAD?
I'VE LIVED A LONG TIME.
WELL... IT'S A BEAUTIFUL DAY TO DIE...

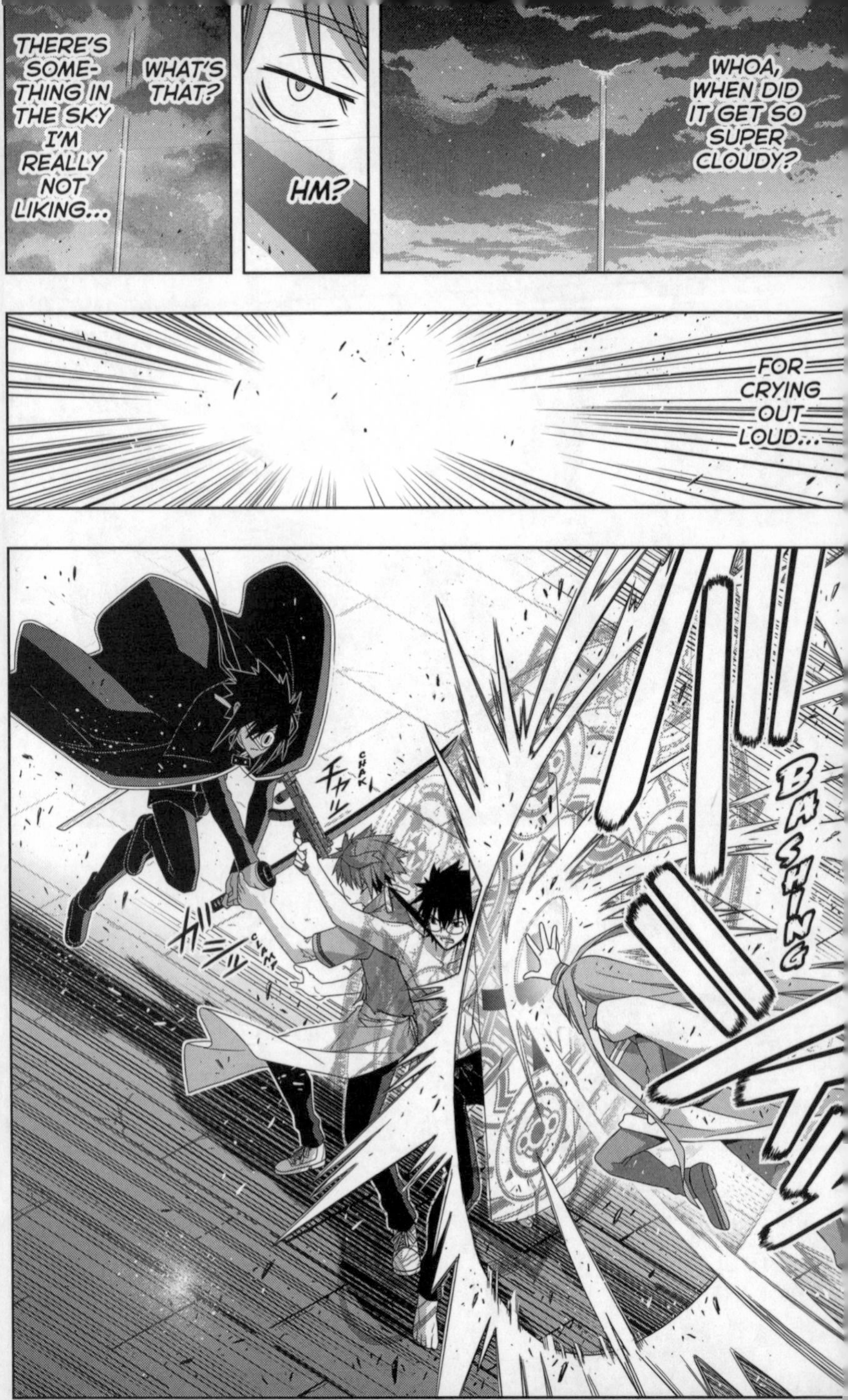
WHOA, WHEN DID IT GET SO SUPER CLOUDY?
HM?
WHAT'S THAT?
THERE'S SOME-THING IN THE SKY I'M REALLY NOT LIKING...
FOR CRYING OUT LOUD...
BASHING
チャカッ
CHAK!
ガシッ

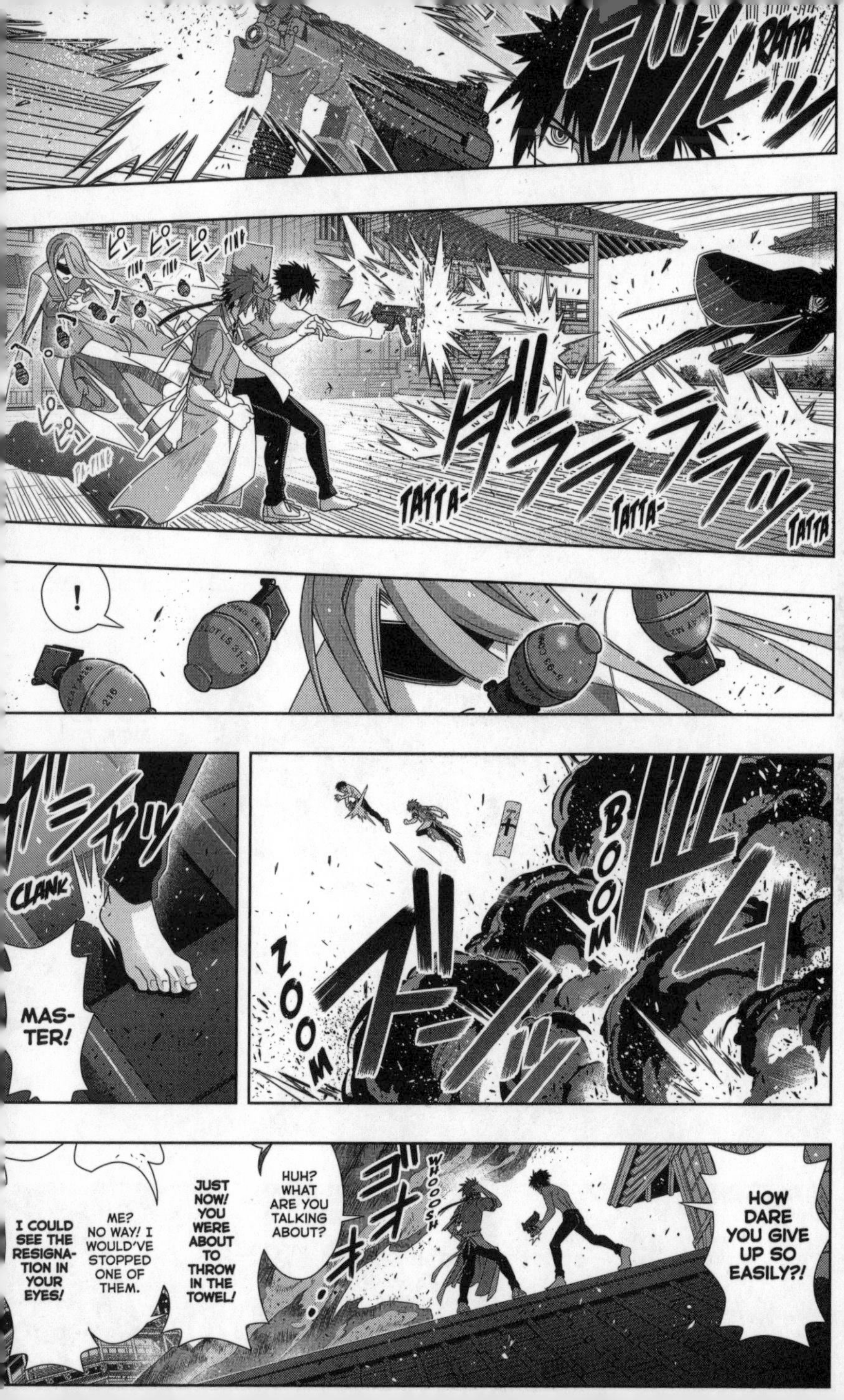
RATTA
PING
PING
PING
PA-PING
TATTA
TATTA-
TATTA-
!
BOOM
ZOOM
CLANK
MAS-TER!
HOW DARE YOU GIVE UP SO EASILY?!
WHOOOSH
HUH? WHAT ARE YOU TALKING ABOUT?
JUST NOW! YOU WERE ABOUT TO THROW IN THE TOWEL!
ME? NO WAY! I WOULD'VE STOPPED ONE OF THEM.
I COULD SEE THE RESIGNATION IN YOUR EYES!

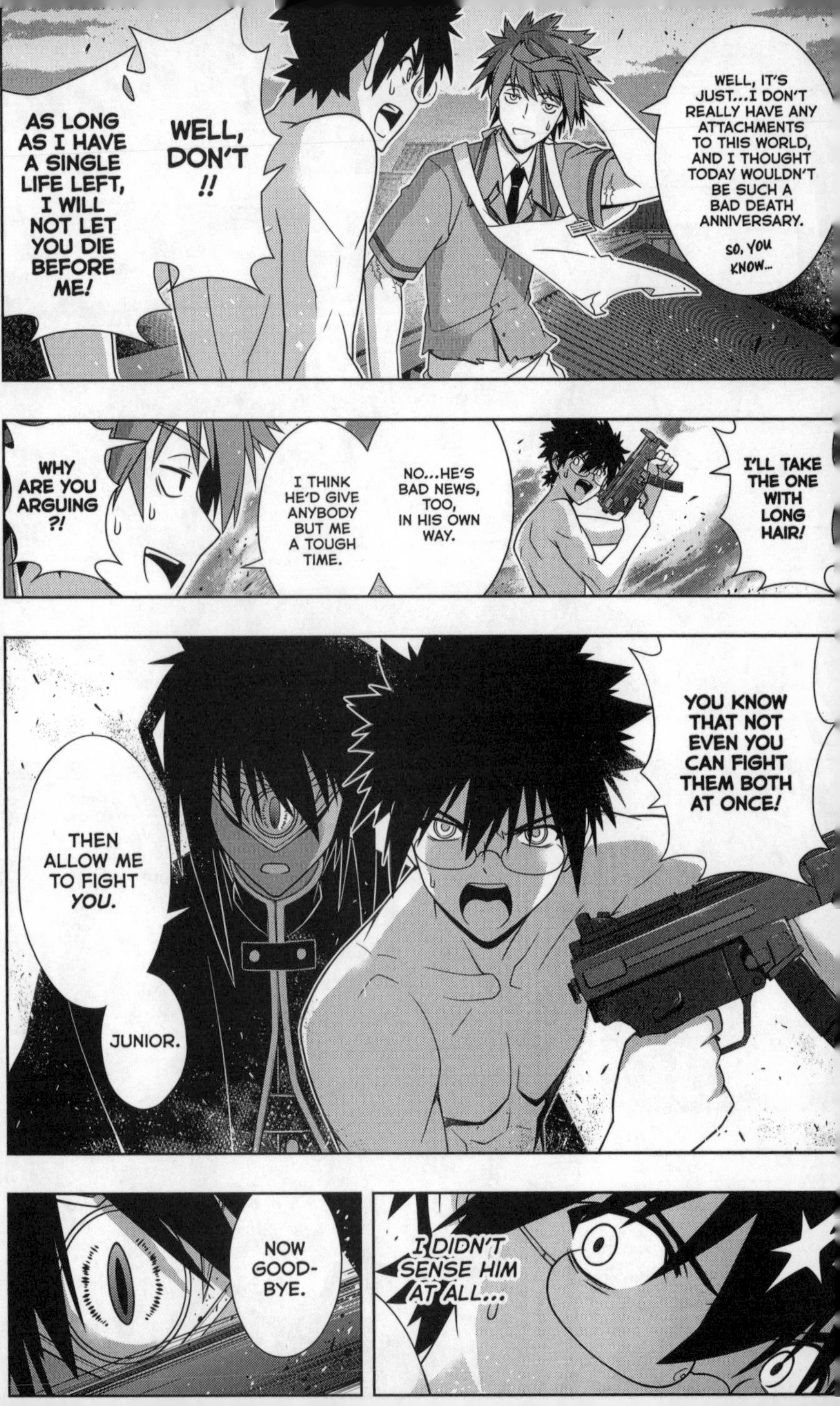
WELL, IT'S JUST...I DON'T REALLY HAVE ANY ATTACHMENTS TO THIS WORLD, AND I THOUGHT TODAY WOULDN'T BE SUCH A BAD DEATH ANNIVERSARY.
SO, YOU KNOW...
WELL, DON'T !!
AS LONG AS I HAVE A SINGLE LIFE LEFT, I WILL NOT LET YOU DIE BEFORE ME!
I'LL TAKE THE ONE WITH LONG HAIR!
NO...HE'S BAD NEWS, TOO, IN HIS OWN WAY.
I THINK HE'D GIVE ANYBODY BUT ME A TOUGH TIME.
WHY ARE YOU ARGUING ?!
YOU KNOW THAT NOT EVEN YOU CAN FIGHT THEM BOTH AT ONCE!
THEN ALLOW ME TO FIGHT *YOU*.
JUNIOR.
I DIDN'T SENSE HIM AT ALL...
NOW GOOD-BYE.

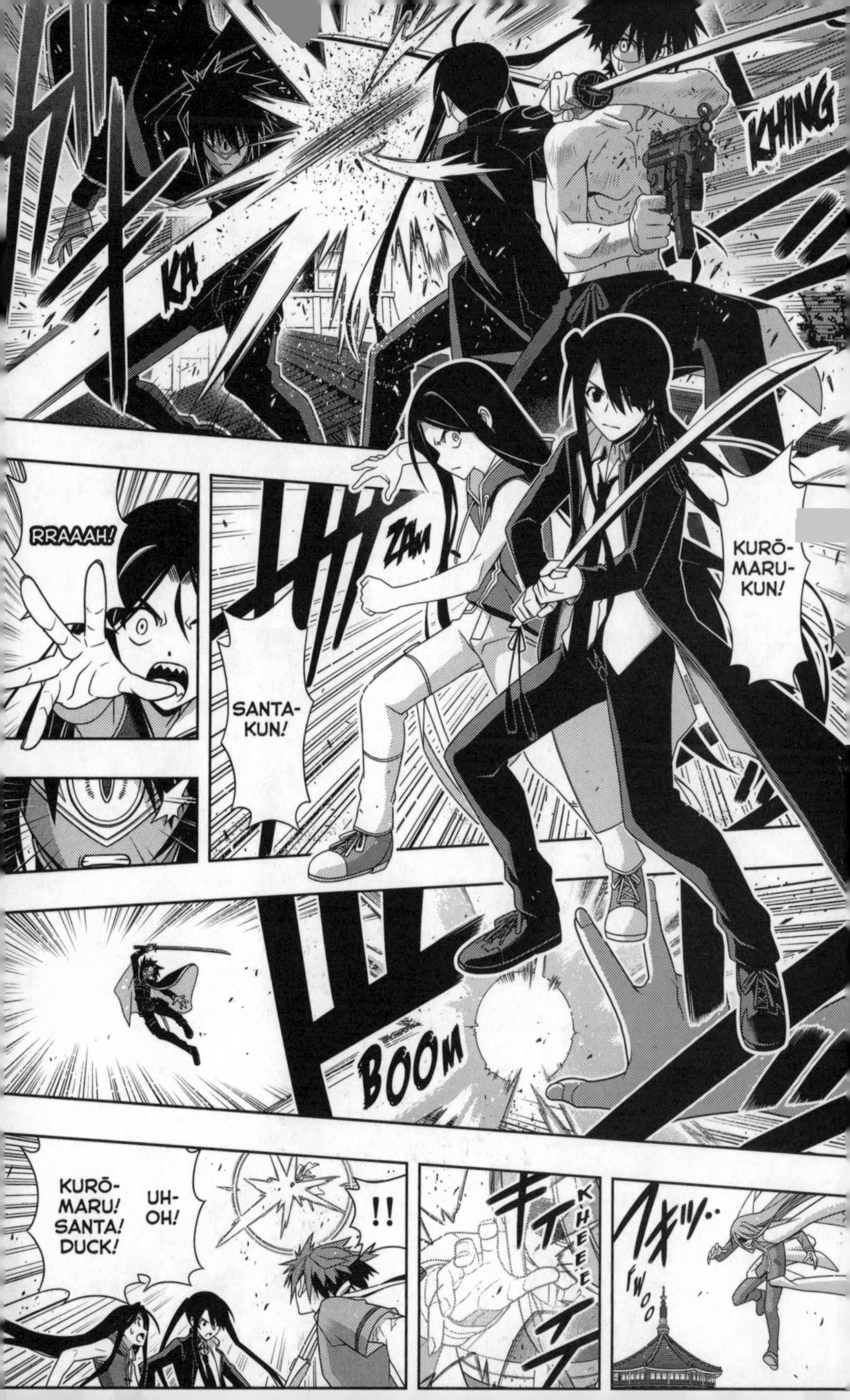
KHING
KA
KURŌ-MARU-KUN!
ZAM
SANTA-KUN!
RRAAAH!
BOOM
FWOO
KHEEE
!!
UH-OH!
KURŌ-MARU! SANTA! DUCK!

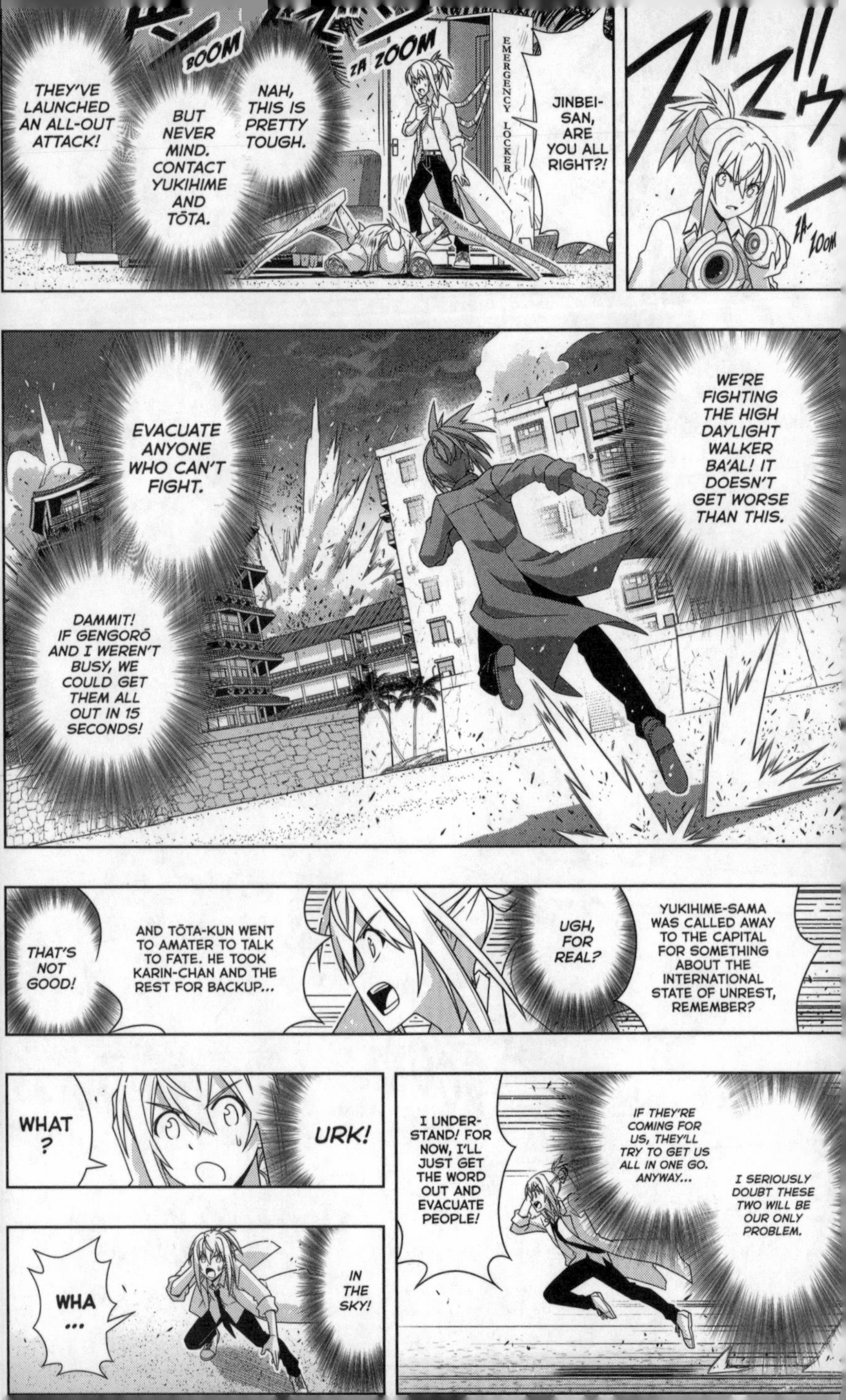
ZA-ZOOM
BOOM
ZA ZOOM
EMERGENCY LOCKER
JINBEI-SAN, ARE YOU ALL RIGHT?!
NAH, THIS IS PRETTY TOUGH.
BUT NEVER MIND. CONTACT YUKIHIME AND TŌTA.
THEY'VE LAUNCHED AN ALL-OUT ATTACK!
WE'RE FIGHTING THE HIGH DAYLIGHT WALKER BA'AL! IT DOESN'T GET WORSE THAN THIS.
EVACUATE ANYONE WHO CAN'T FIGHT.
DAMMIT! IF GENGORŌ AND I WEREN'T BUSY, WE COULD GET THEM ALL OUT IN 15 SECONDS!
YUKIHIME-SAMA WAS CALLED AWAY TO THE CAPITAL FOR SOMETHING ABOUT THE INTERNATIONAL STATE OF UNREST, REMEMBER?
UGH, FOR REAL?
AND TŌTA-KUN WENT TO AMATER TO TALK TO FATE. HE TOOK KARIN-CHAN AND THE REST FOR BACKUP...
THAT'S NOT GOOD!
IF THEY'RE COMING FOR US, THEY'LL TRY TO GET US ALL IN ONE GO. ANYWAY...
I SERIOUSLY DOUBT THESE TWO WILL BE OUR ONLY PROBLEM.
I UNDERSTAND! FOR NOW, I'LL JUST GET THE WORD OUT AND EVACUATE PEOPLE!
URK!
WHAT?
IN THE SKY!
WHA...

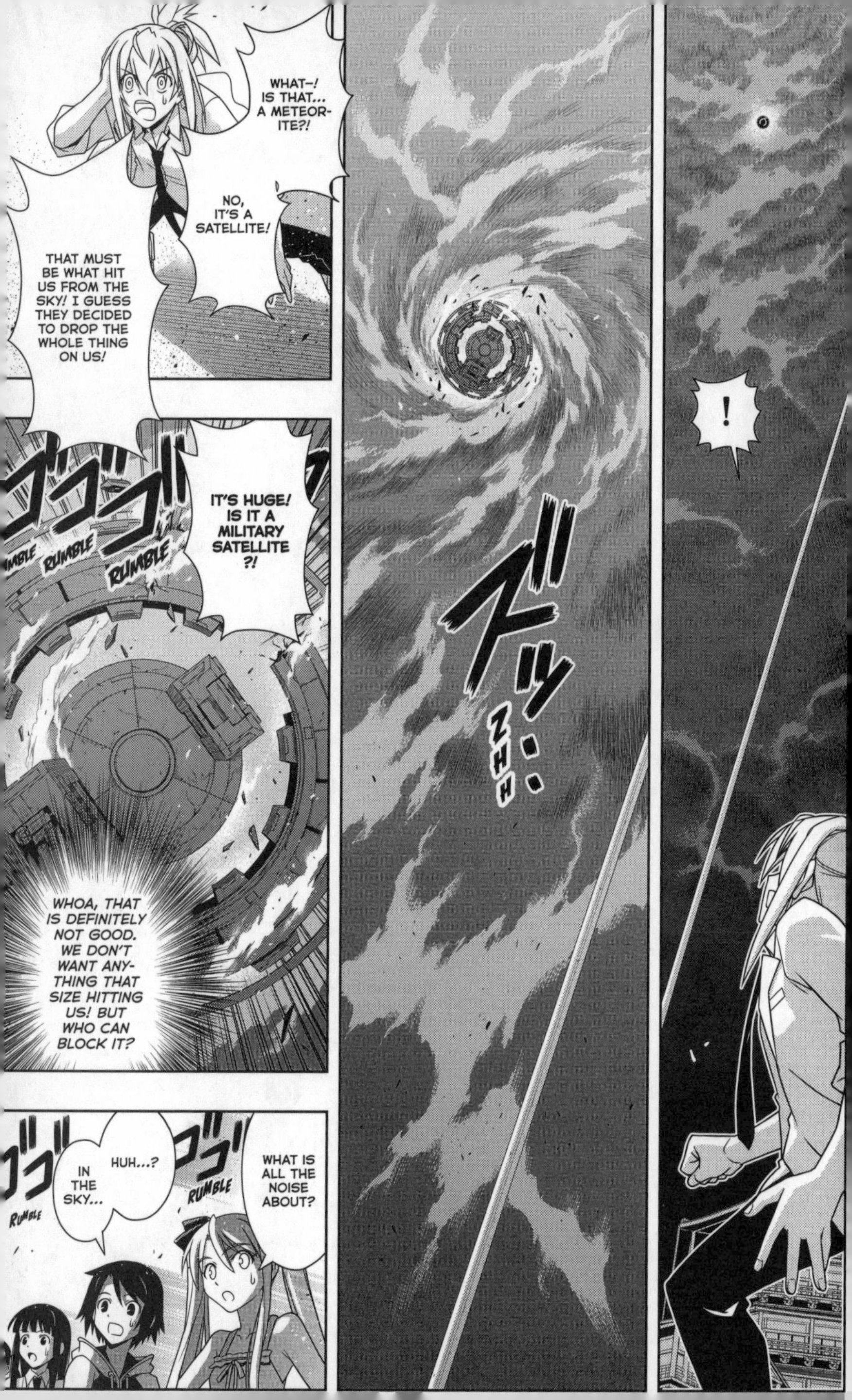
!
ZHH
WHAT–! IS THAT... A METEORITE?!
NO, IT'S A SATELLITE!
THAT MUST BE WHAT HIT US FROM THE SKY! I GUESS THEY DECIDED TO DROP THE WHOLE THING ON US!
IT'S HUGE! IS IT A MILITARY SATELLITE ?!
RUMBLE
RUMBLE
WHOA, THAT IS DEFINITELY NOT GOOD. WE DON'T WANT ANY-THING THAT SIZE HITTING US! BUT WHO CAN BLOCK IT?
WHAT IS ALL THE NOISE ABOUT?
RUMBLE
HUH...?
IN THE SKY...
RUMBLE

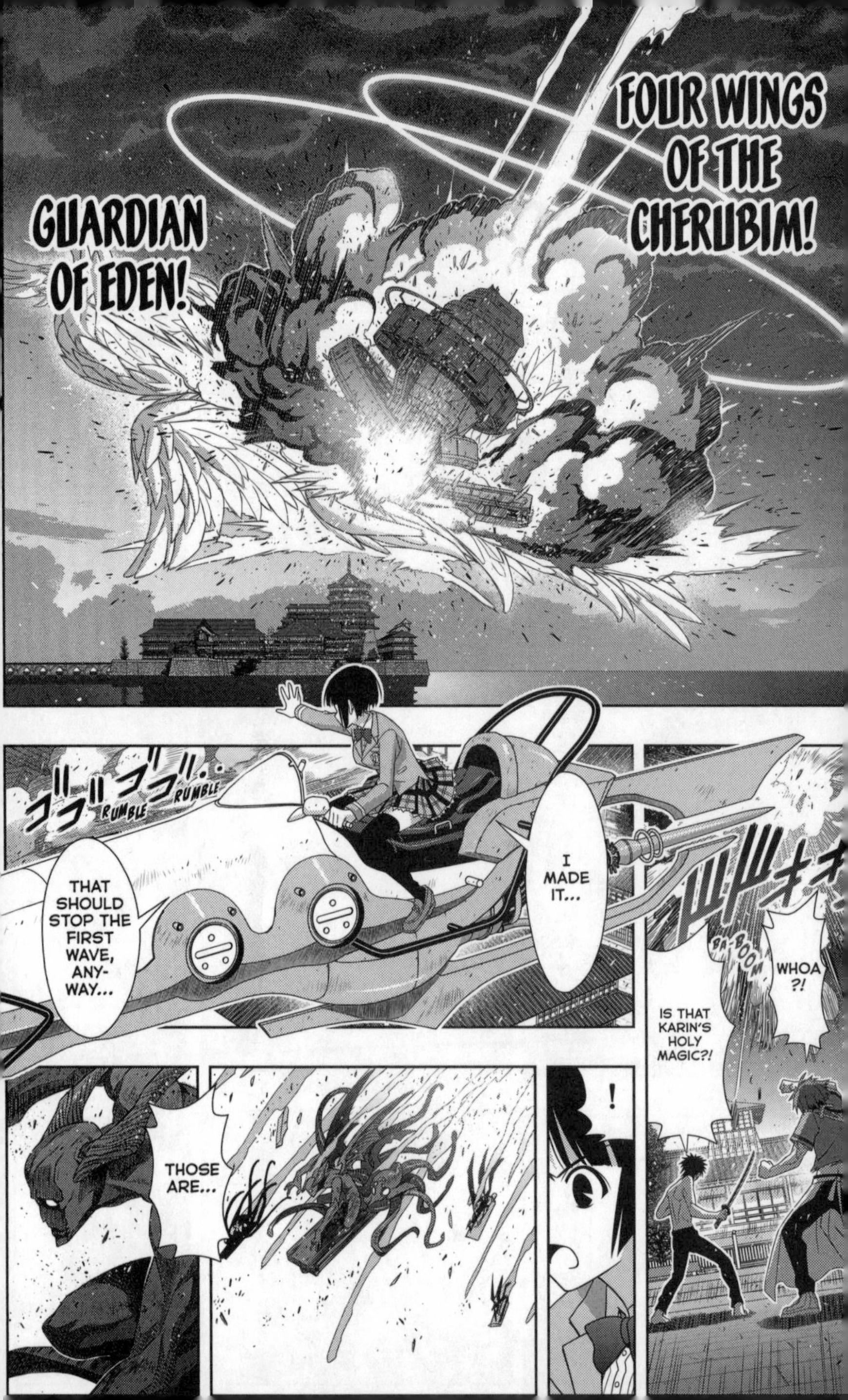
FOUR WINGS OF THE CHERUBIM!
GUARDIAN OF EDEN!
BA-BOOM
WHOA?!
IS THAT KARIN'S HOLY MAGIC?!
I MADE IT...
THAT SHOULD STOP THE FIRST WAVE, ANYWAY...
RUMBLE RUMBLE
!
THOSE ARE...

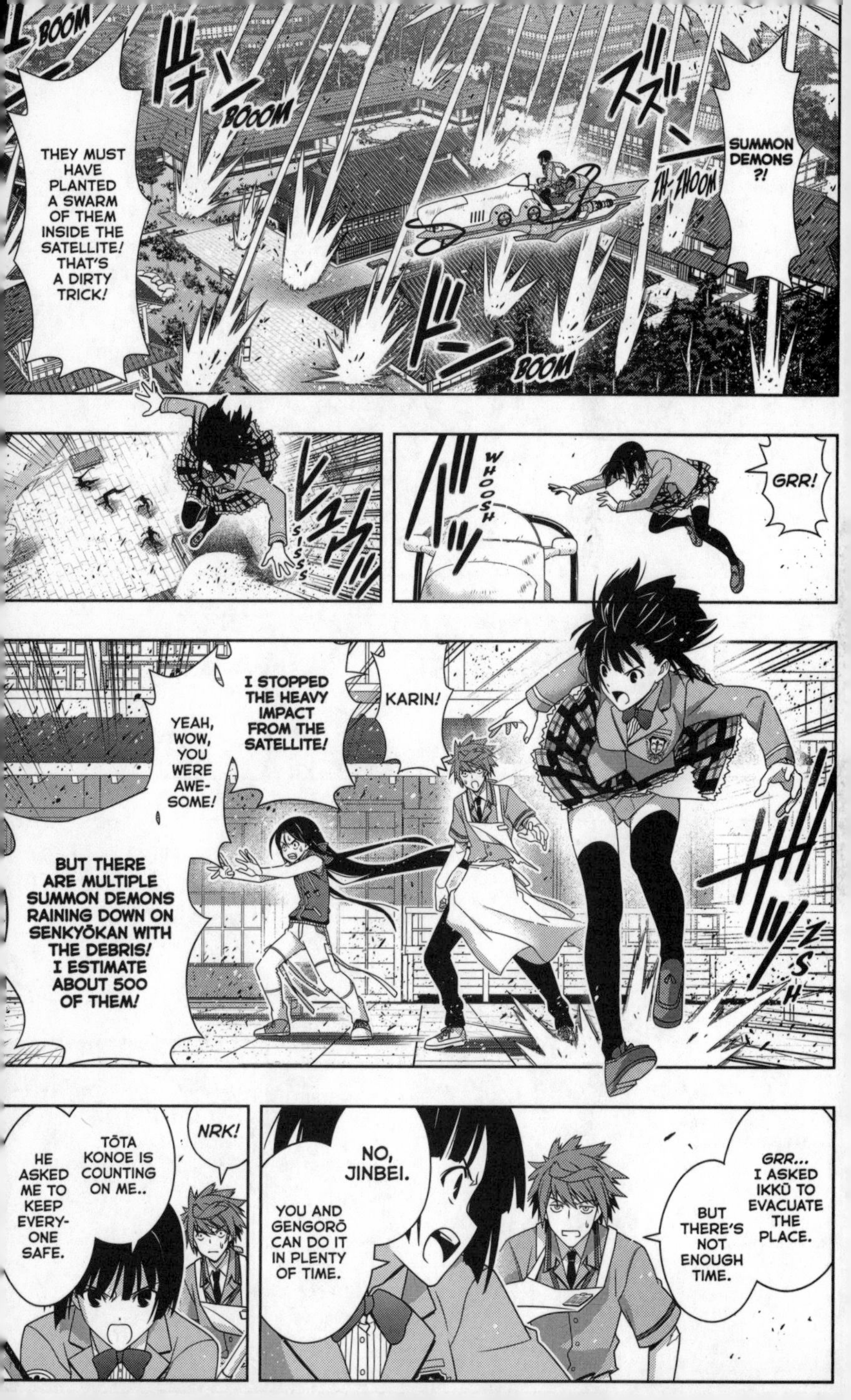
SUMMON DEMONS?!
ZH-ZHOOM
BOOOM
BOOM
THEY MUST HAVE PLANTED A SWARM OF THEM INSIDE THE SATELLITE! THAT'S A DIRTY TRICK!
BOOM
GRR!
WHOOSH
SISSS
ZSH
KARIN!
I STOPPED THE HEAVY IMPACT FROM THE SATELLITE!
YEAH, WOW, YOU WERE AWE-SOME!
BUT THERE ARE MULTIPLE SUMMON DEMONS RAINING DOWN ON SENKYŌKAN WITH THE DEBRIS! I ESTIMATE ABOUT 500 OF THEM!
GRR... I ASKED IKKŪ TO EVACUATE THE PLACE.
BUT THERE'S NOT ENOUGH TIME.
NO, JINBEI.
YOU AND GENGORŌ CAN DO IT IN PLENTY OF TIME.
NRK!
TŌTA KONOE IS COUNTING ON ME..
HE ASKED ME TO KEEP EVERY-ONE SAFE.

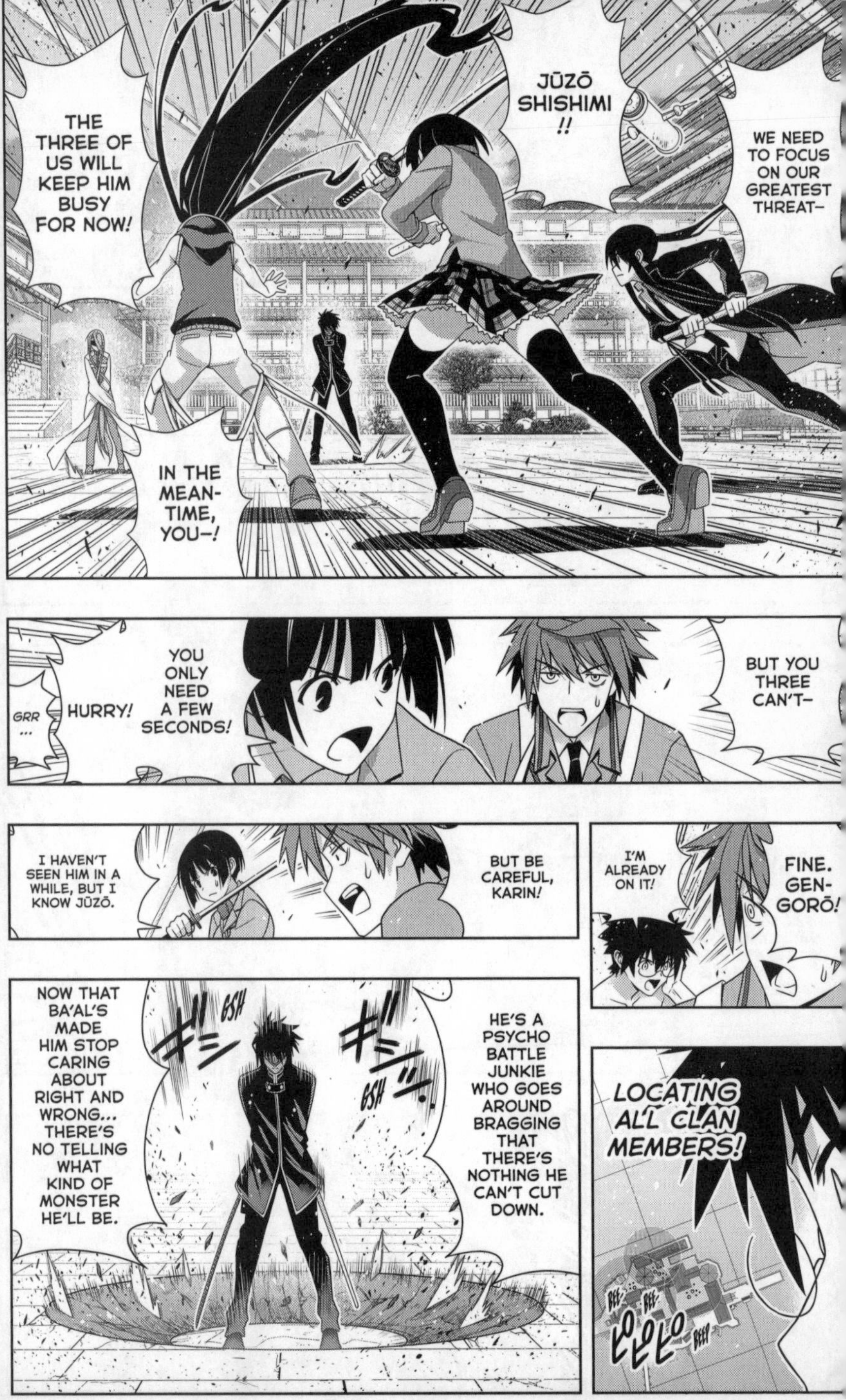
WE NEED TO FOCUS ON OUR GREATEST THREAT–
JŪZŌ SHISHIMI!!
THE THREE OF US WILL KEEP HIM BUSY FOR NOW!
IN THE MEAN-TIME, YOU–!
BUT YOU THREE CAN'T–
YOU ONLY NEED A FEW SECONDS!
HURRY!
GRR ...
FINE. GEN-GORŌ!
I'M ALREADY ON IT!
BUT BE CAREFUL, KARIN!
I HAVEN'T SEEN HIM IN A WHILE, BUT I KNOW JŪZŌ.
LOCATING ALL CLAN MEMBERS!
BEE- BEE- BEEP
HE'S A PSYCHO BATTLE JUNKIE WHO GOES AROUND BRAGGING THAT THERE'S NOTHING HE CAN'T CUT DOWN.
GSH
GSH
NOW THAT BA'AL'S MADE HIM STOP CARING ABOUT RIGHT AND WRONG... THERE'S NO TELLING WHAT KIND OF MONSTER HE'LL BE.

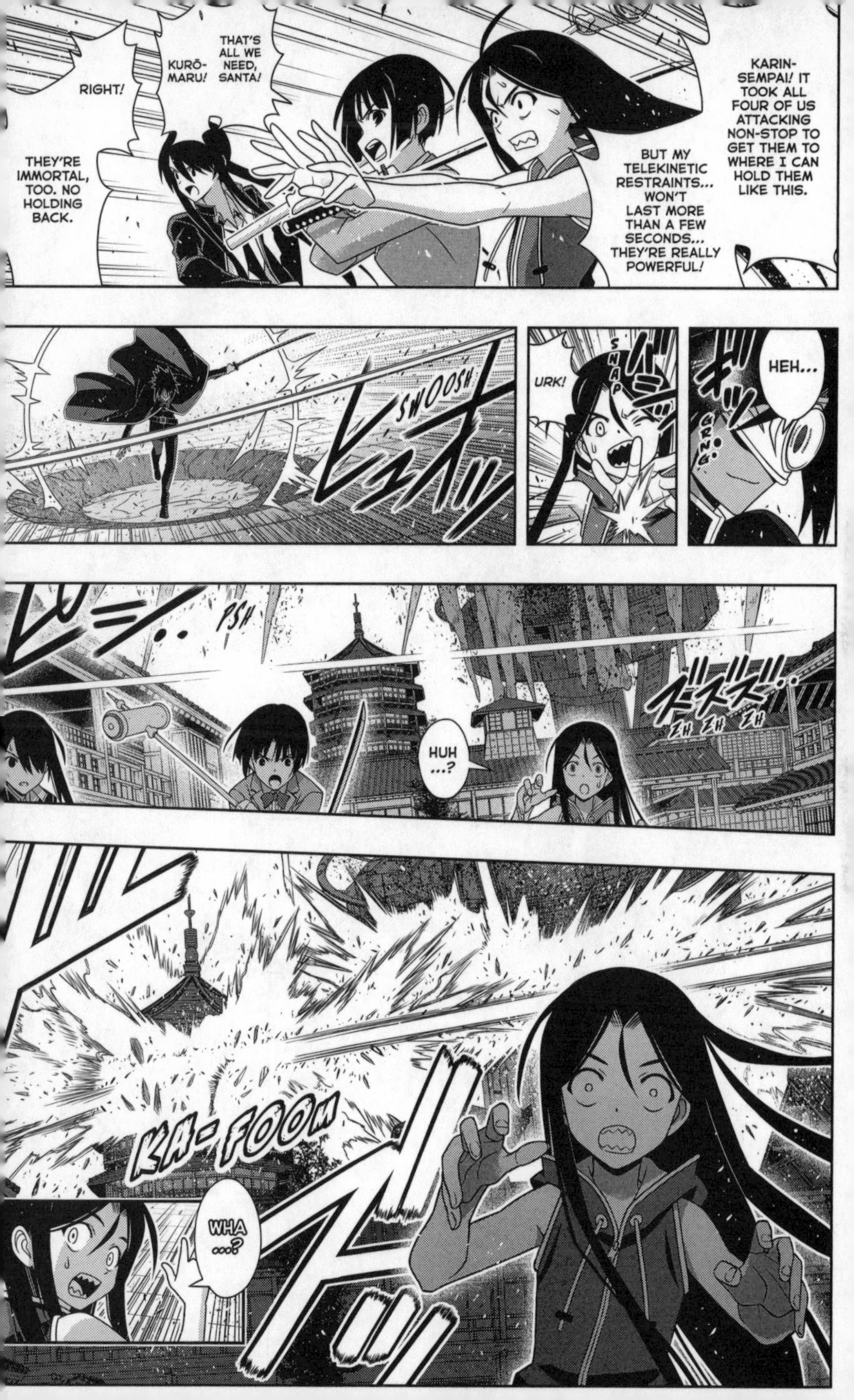
KARIN-SEMPAI! IT TOOK ALL FOUR OF US ATTACKING NON-STOP TO GET THEM TO WHERE I CAN HOLD THEM LIKE THIS.
BUT MY TELEKINETIC RESTRAINTS... WON'T LAST MORE THAN A FEW SECONDS... THEY'RE REALLY POWERFUL!
THAT'S ALL WE NEED, SANTA!
KURŌ-MARU!
RIGHT!
THEY'RE IMMORTAL, TOO. NO HOLDING BACK.
HEH...
GRNG
SNAP
URK!
SWOOSH
ZH ZH ZH
HUH ...?
PSH
KA-FOOM
WHA ...?

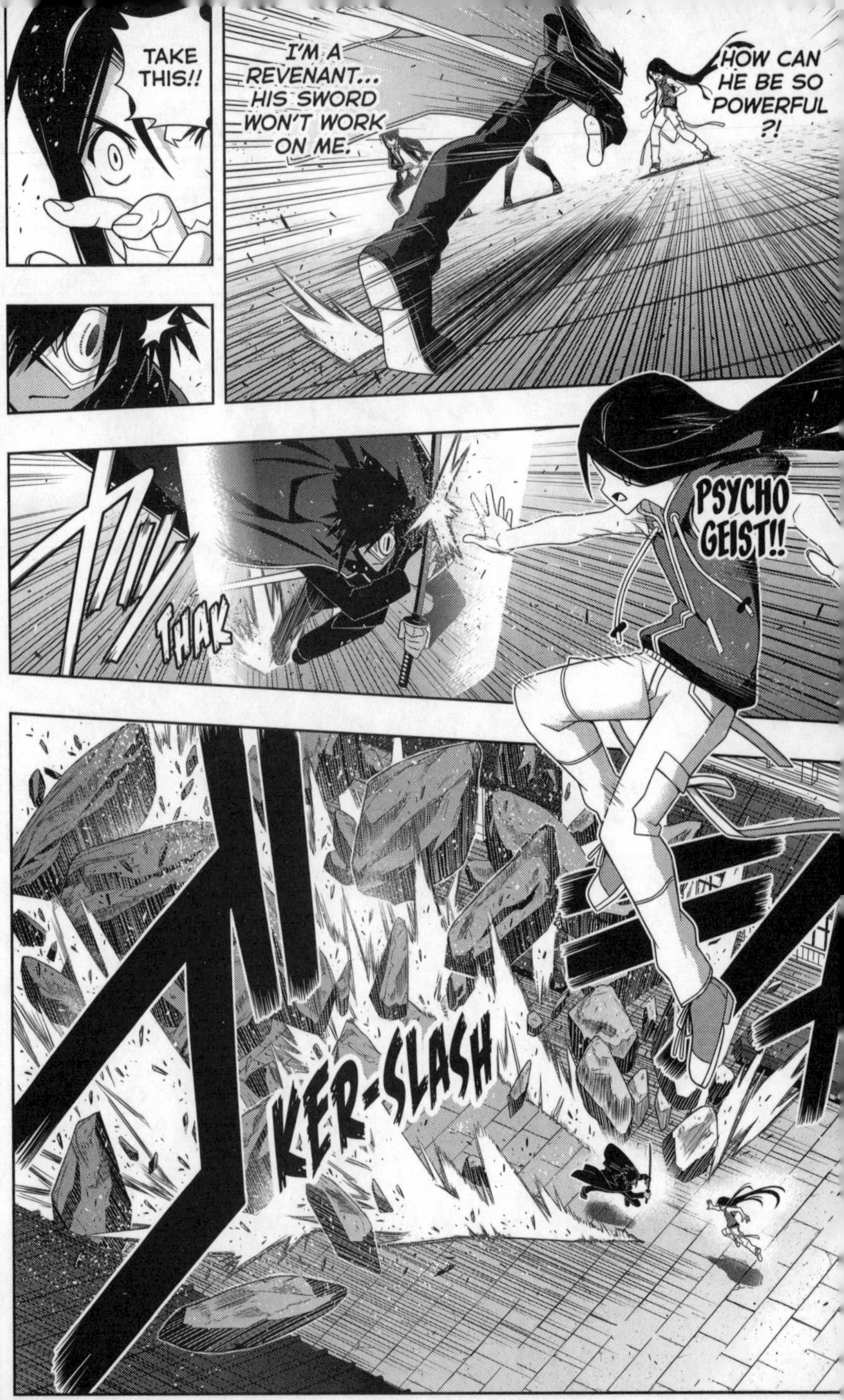
HOW CAN HE BE SO POWERFUL ?!
I'M A REVENANT... HIS SWORD WON'T WORK ON ME.
TAKE THIS!!
PSYCHO GEIST!!
THAK
KER-SLASH

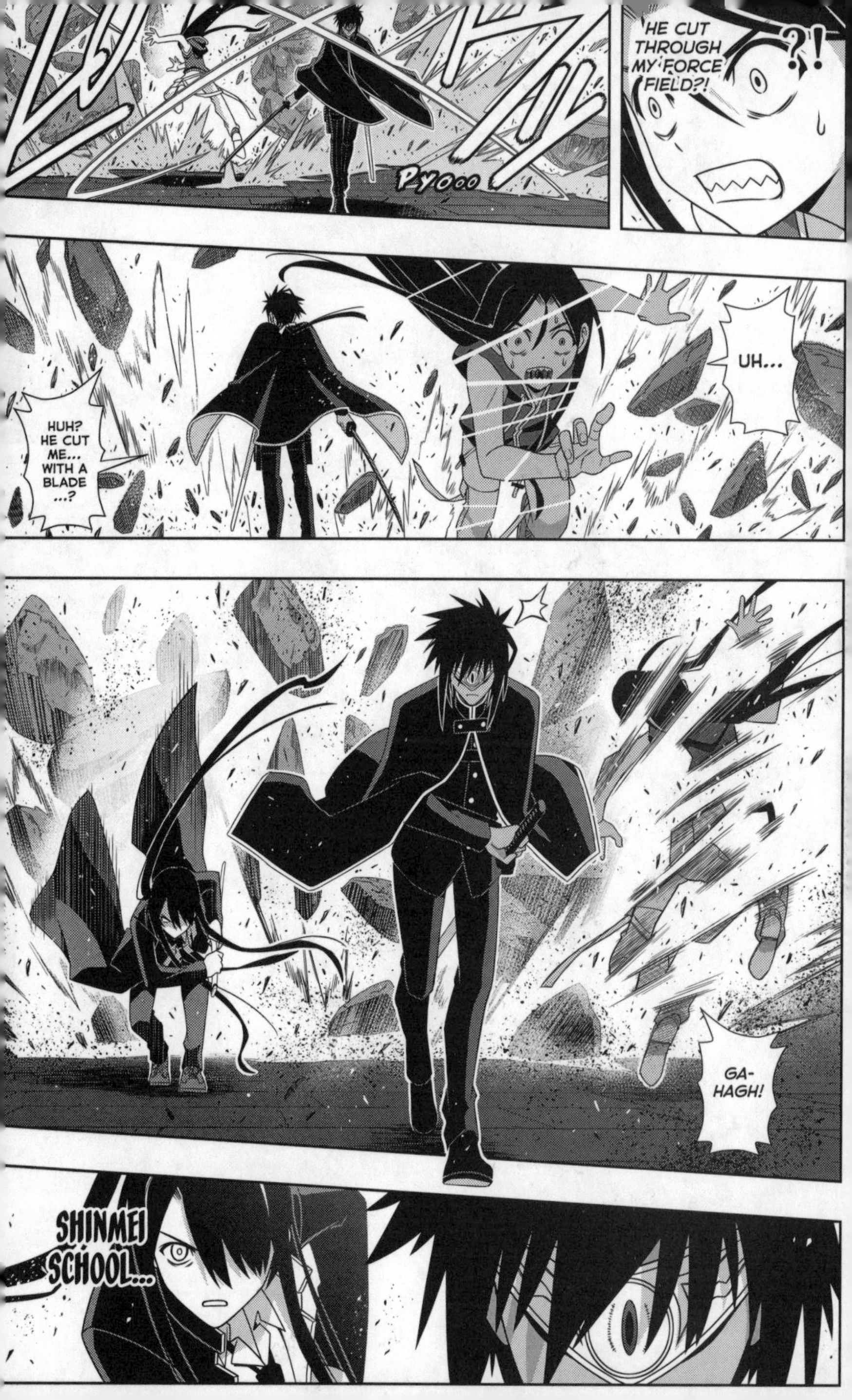
HE CUT THROUGH MY FORCE FIELD?!
?!
PYO...
UH...
HUH? HE CUT ME... WITH A BLADE ...?
GA-HAGH!
SHINMEI SCHOOL...

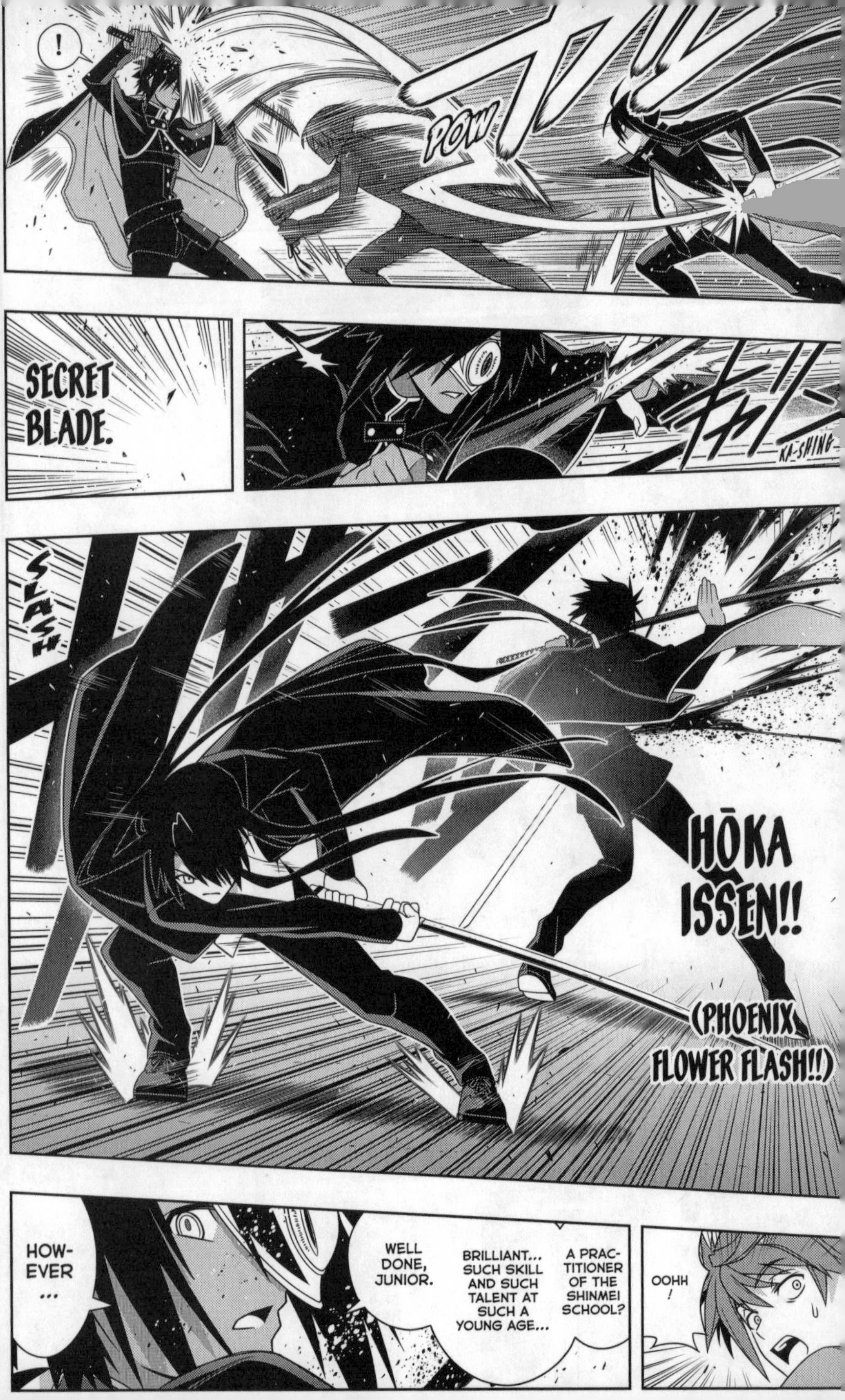
!
POW
KA-SHING
SECRET BLADE.
HŌKA ISSEN!!
(PHOENIX FLOWER FLASH!!)
SLASH
OOHH!
A PRAC-TITIONER OF THE SHINMEI SCHOOL?
BRILLIANT... SUCH SKILL AND SUCH TALENT AT SUCH A YOUNG AGE...
WELL DONE, JUNIOR.
HOW-EVER...

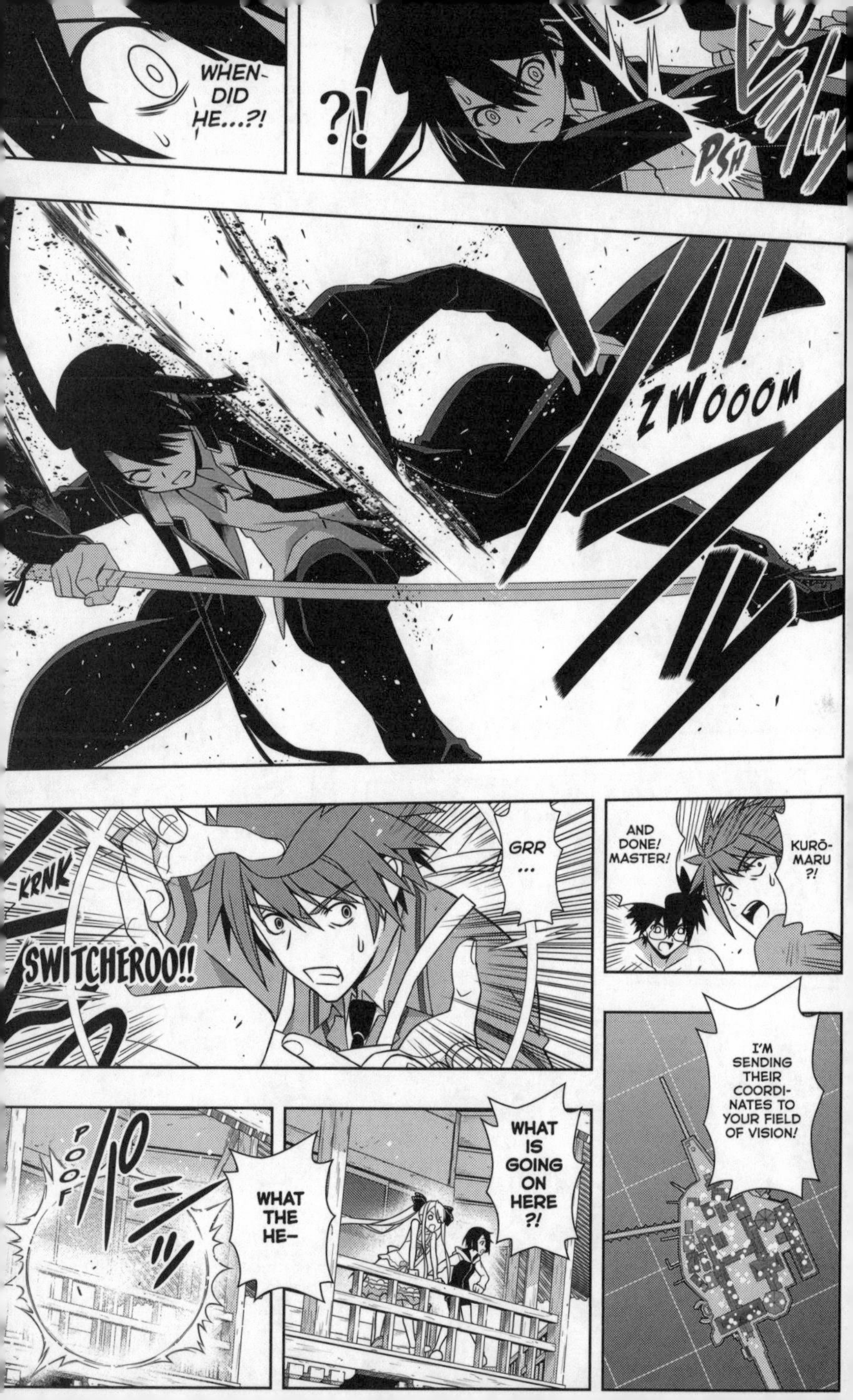
?!
PSH
WHEN-DID HE...?!
ZWOOOM
KURŌ-MARU ?!
AND DONE! MASTER!
GRR ...
KRNK
SWITCHEROO!!
I'M SENDING THEIR COORDI-NATES TO YOUR FIELD OF VISION!
WHAT IS GOING ON HERE ?!
WHAT THE HE-
POOF

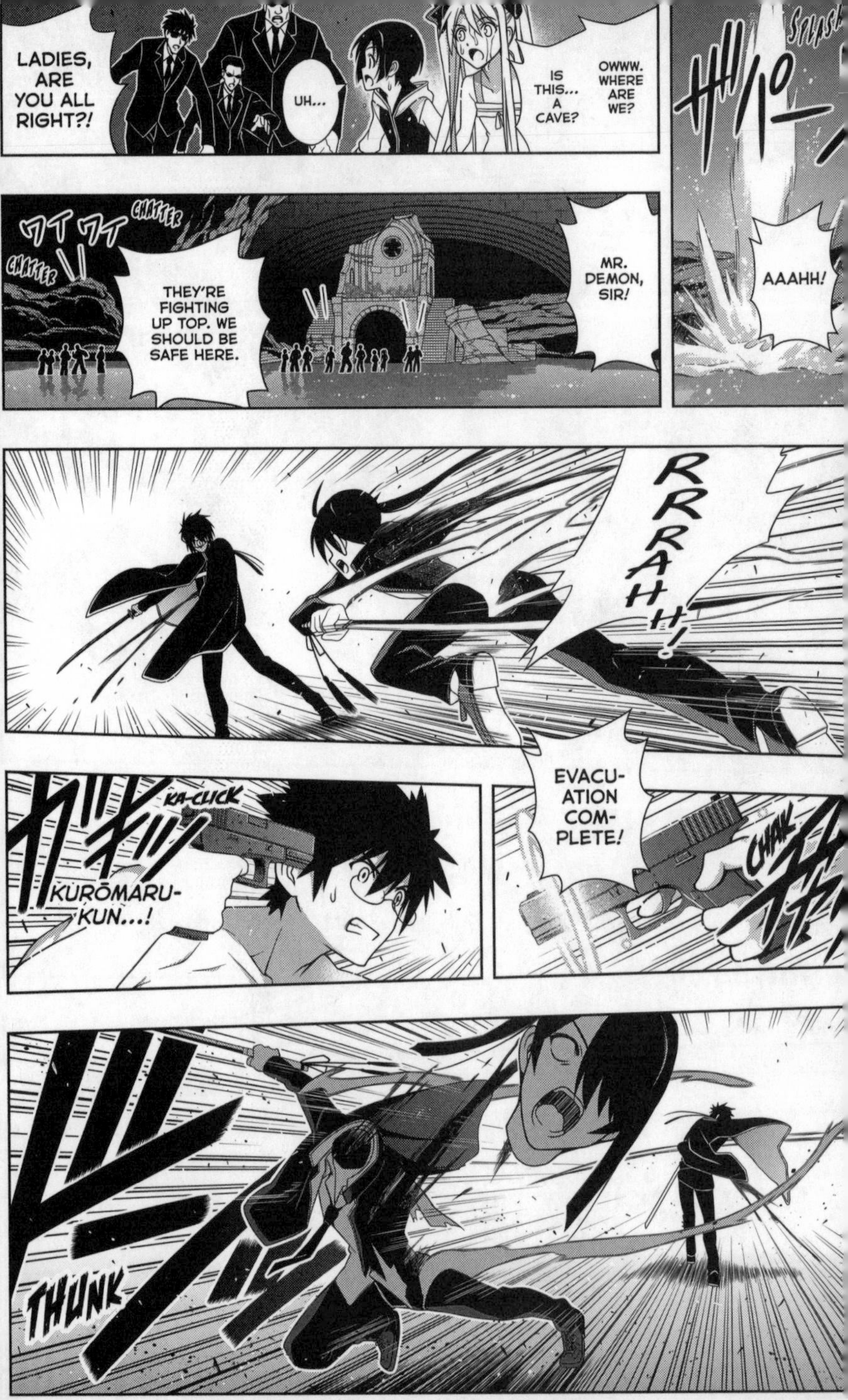
SPLASH
AAAHH!
OWWW. WHERE ARE WE?
IS THIS... A CAVE?
UH...
LADIES, ARE YOU ALL RIGHT?!
MR. DEMON, SIR!
THEY'RE FIGHTING UP TOP. WE SHOULD BE SAFE HERE.
CHATTER
ワイ ワイ
CHATTER
RRRAHH!
EVACU-ATION COM-PLETE!
CHAK
KA-CLICK
KURŌMARU-KUN...!
THUNK

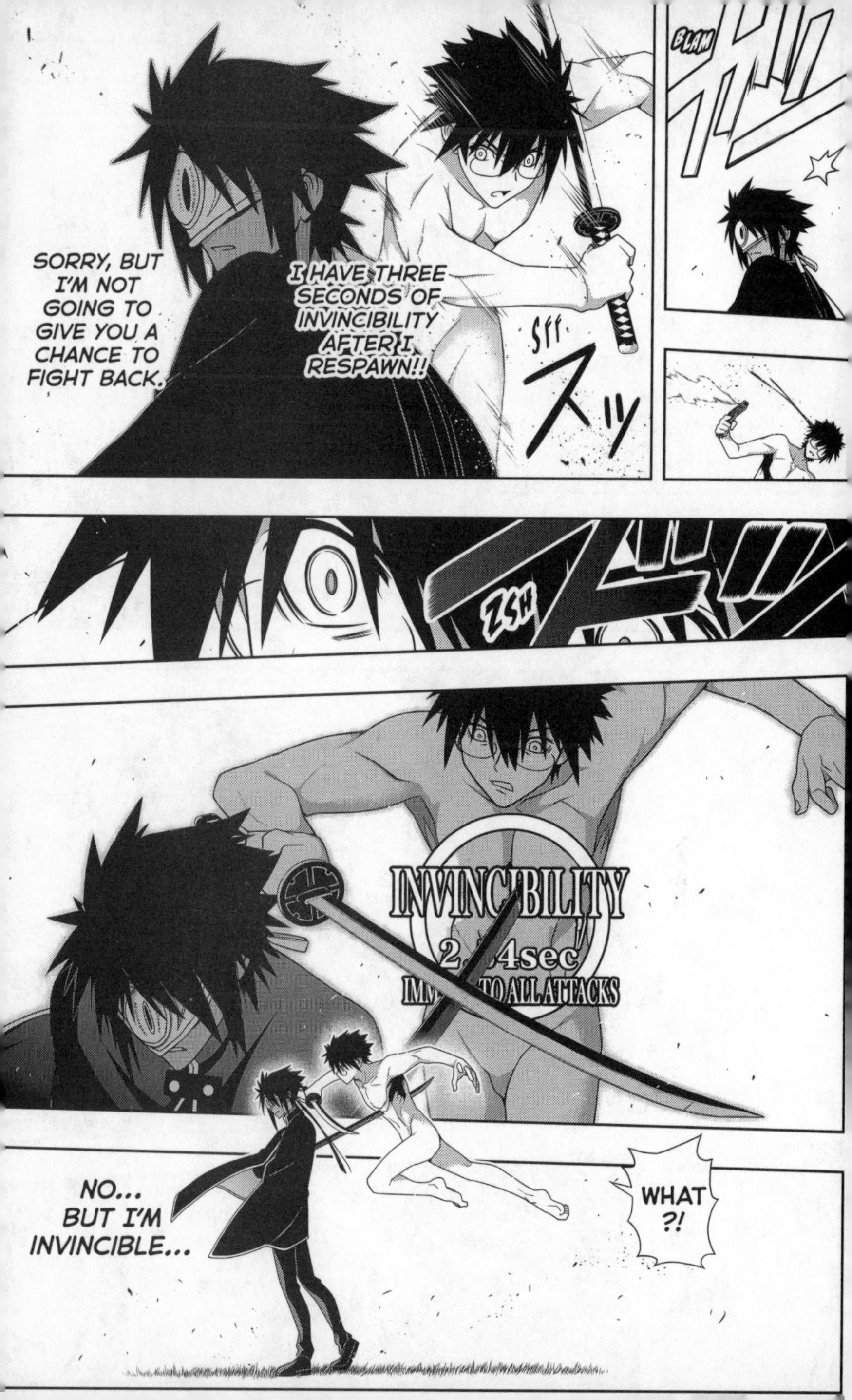
BLAM
I HAVE THREE SECONDS OF INVINCIBILITY AFTER I RESPAWN!!
SORRY, BUT I'M NOT GOING TO GIVE YOU A CHANCE TO FIGHT BACK.
SFF
ZSH
INVINCIBILITY
TO ALL ATTACKS
WHAT?!
NO... BUT I'M INVINCIBLE...

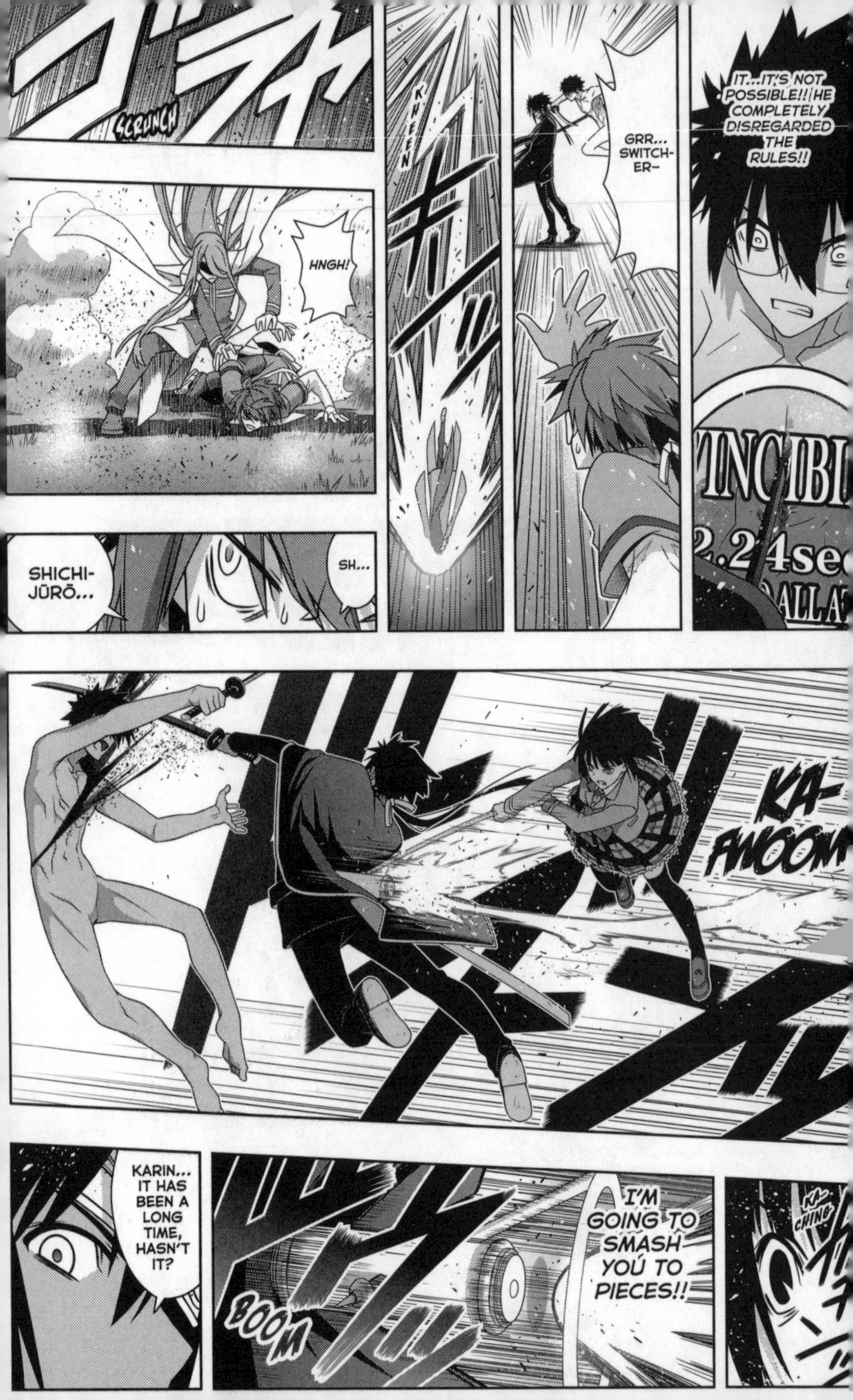
IT...IT'S NOT POSSIBLE!! HE COMPLETELY DISREGARDED THE RULES!!
GRR... SWITCHER–
KHEEN
SCRUNCH
HNGH!
SH...
SHICHIJŪRŌ...
KA-FWOOM
KA-CHING
I'M GOING TO SMASH YOU TO PIECES!!
BOOM
KARIN... IT HAS BEEN A LONG TIME, HASN'T IT?

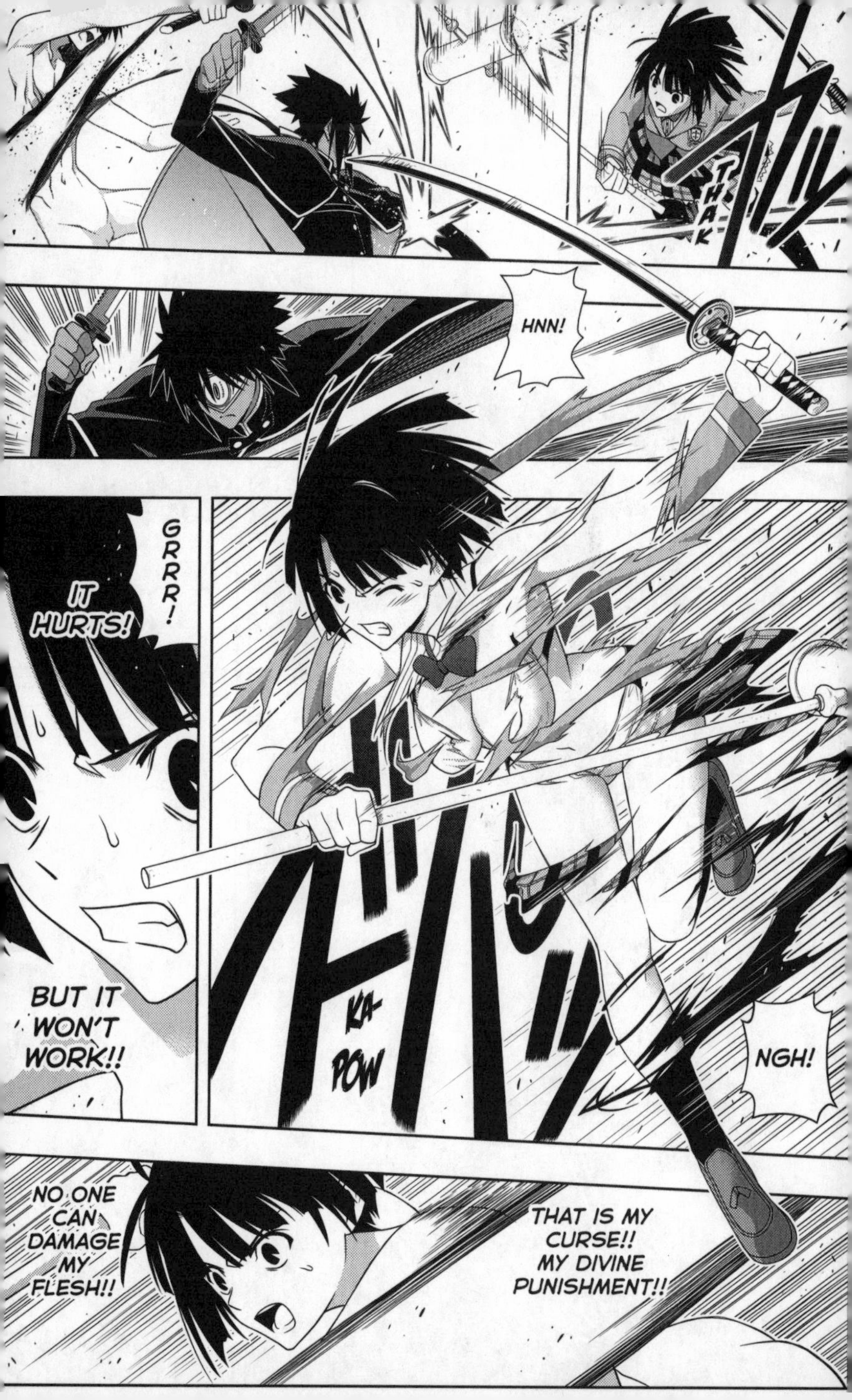
THAK
HNN!
NGH!
KA-POW
GRRR!
IT HURTS!
BUT IT WON'T WORK!!
NO ONE CAN DAMAGE MY FLESH!!
THAT IS MY CURSE!! MY DIVINE PUNISHMENT!!

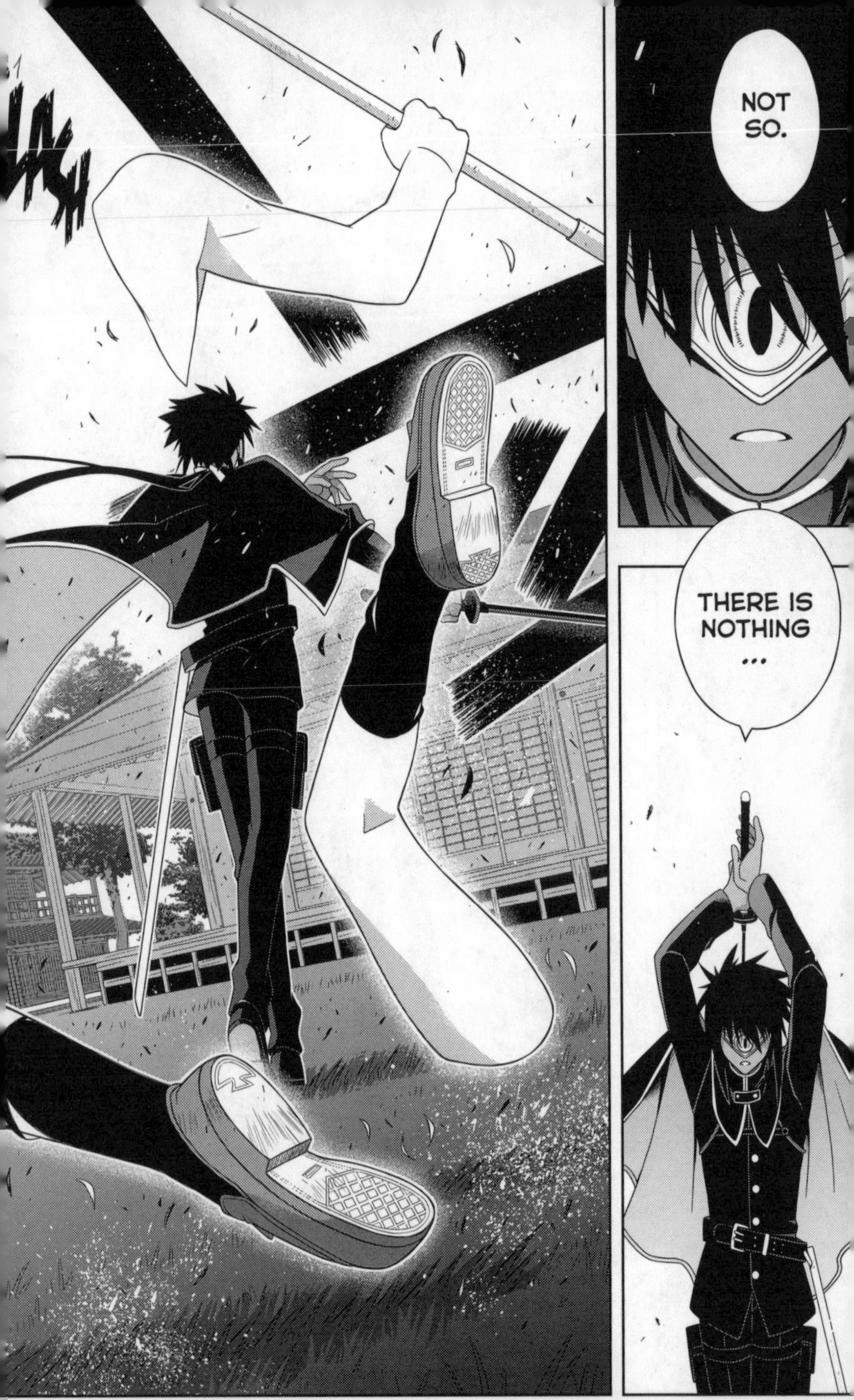
NOT SO.
THERE IS NOTHING ...
LASH

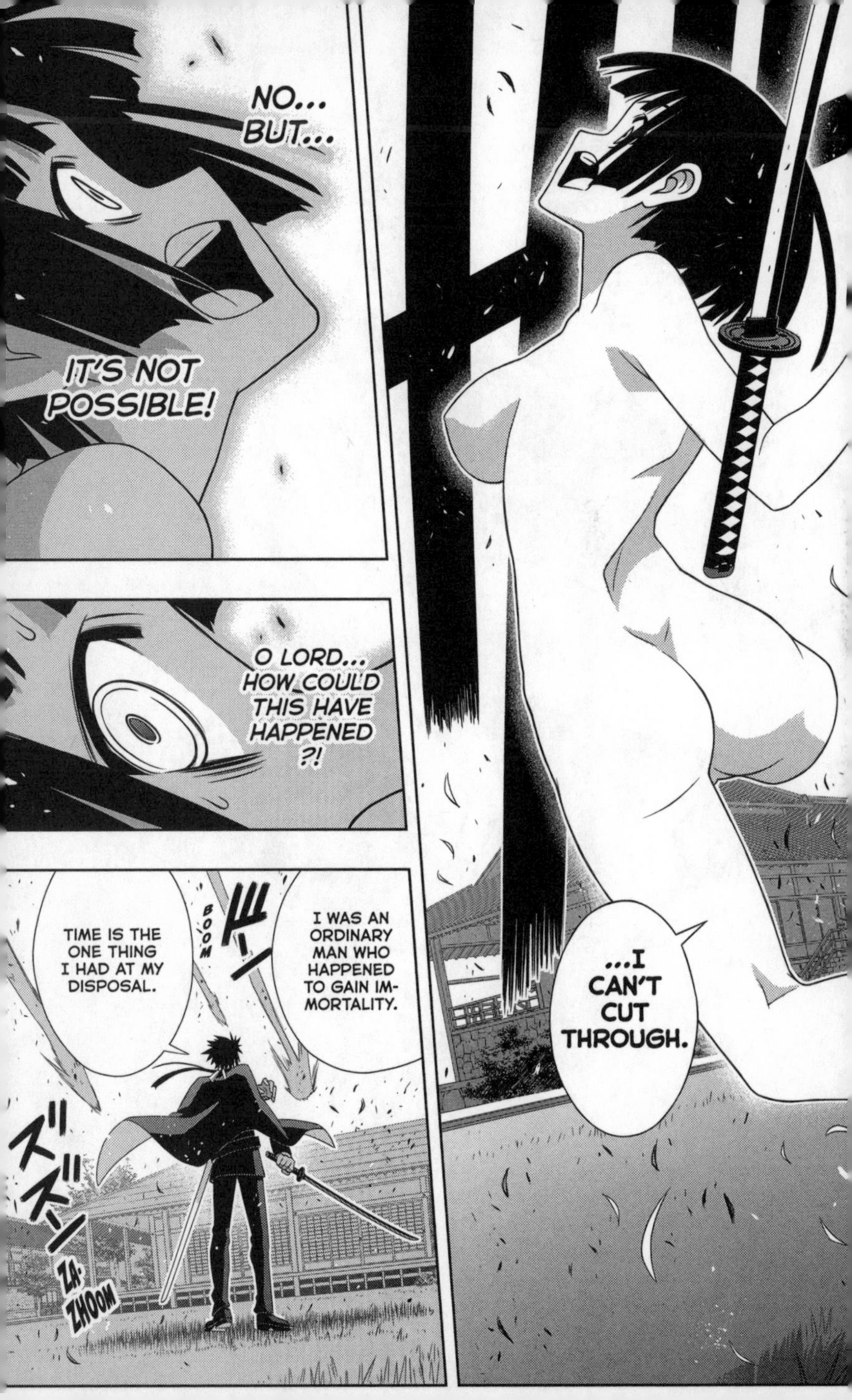
...I CAN'T CUT THROUGH.
NO... BUT...
IT'S NOT POSSIBLE!
O LORD... HOW COULD THIS HAVE HAPPENED ?!
I WAS AN ORDINARY MAN WHO HAPPENED TO GAIN IM-MORTALITY.
BOOM
TIME IS THE ONE THING I HAD AT MY DISPOSAL.
ZA-ZHOOM

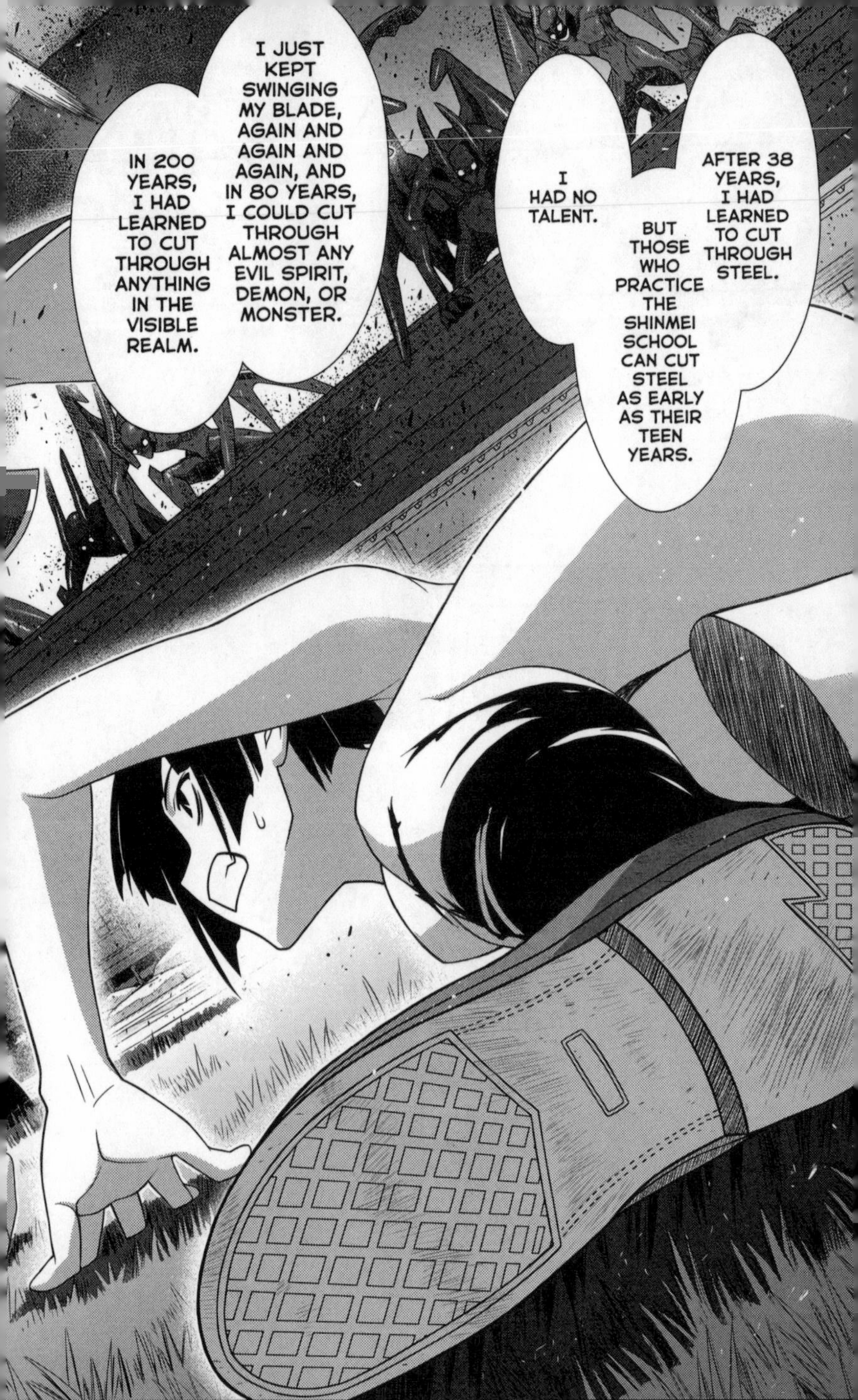
AFTER 38 YEARS, I HAD LEARNED TO CUT THROUGH STEEL.
I HAD NO TALENT.
BUT THOSE WHO PRACTICE THE SHINMEI SCHOOL CAN CUT STEEL AS EARLY AS THEIR TEEN YEARS.
I JUST KEPT SWINGING MY BLADE, AGAIN AND AGAIN AND AGAIN, AND IN 80 YEARS, I COULD CUT THROUGH ALMOST ANY EVIL SPIRIT, DEMON, OR MONSTER.
IN 200 YEARS, I HAD LEARNED TO CUT THROUGH ANYTHING IN THE VISIBLE REALM.

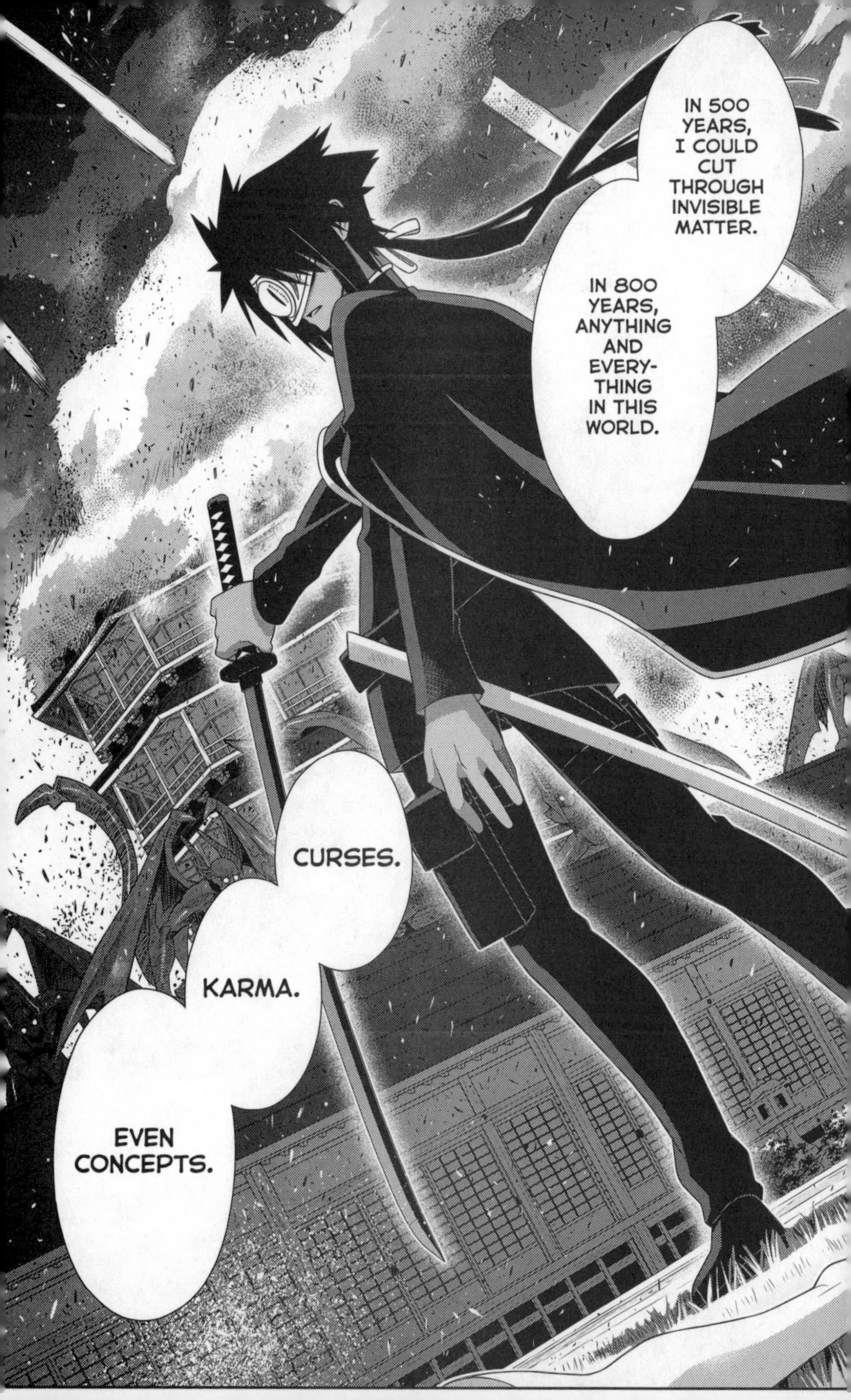
IN 500 YEARS, I COULD CUT THROUGH INVISIBLE MATTER.
IN 800 YEARS, ANYTHING AND EVERY-THING IN THIS WORLD.
CURSES.
KARMA.
EVEN CONCEPTS.

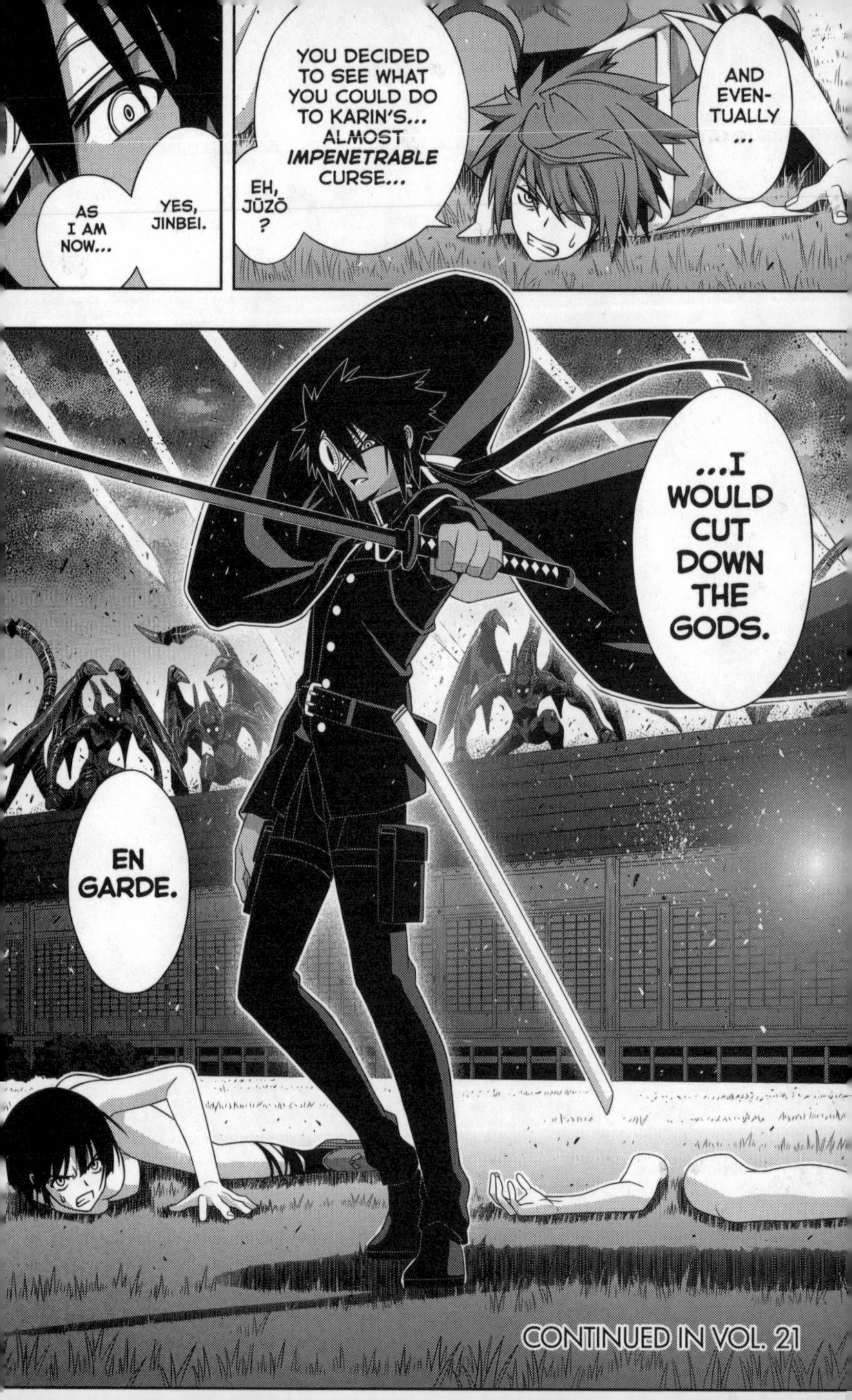
YOU DECIDED TO SEE WHAT YOU COULD DO TO KARIN'S... ALMOST *IMPENETRABLE* CURSE...
EH, JŪZŌ?
AND EVENTUALLY...
YES, JINBEI.
AS I AM NOW...
...I WOULD CUT DOWN THE GODS.
EN GARDE.

CONTINUED IN VOL. 21

UQ HOLDER!

STAFF

Ken Akamatsu

Takashi Takemoto

Kenichi Nakamura

Keiichi Yamashita

Yuri Sasaki

Madoka Akanuma

Thanks to Ran Ayanaga

**One of CLAMP's biggest hits returns
in this definitive, premium, hardcover
20th anniversary collector's edition!**

CLAMP

Chobits

20TH ANNIVERSARY EDITION

"A wonderfully
entertaining story
that would be a
great installment in
anybody's manga
collection."
— Anime News Network

"CLAMP is an all-
female manga-
creating team whose
feminine touch shows
in this entertaining,
sci-fi soap opera."
— Publishers Weekly

Chobits © CLAMP-ShigatsuTsuitachi CO.,LTD./Kodansha Ltd.

Poor college student Hideki is down on his luck. All he wants is a
good job, a girlfriend, and his very own "persocom"—the latest
and greatest in humanoid computer technology. Hideki's luck
changes one night when he finds Chi—a persocom thrown out
in a pile of trash. But Hideki soon discovers that there's much
more to his cute new persocom than meets the eye.

KC
KODANSHA
COMICS

The art-deco cyberpunk classic from the creators of *xxxHOLiC* and *Cardcaptor Sakura!*

"Starred Review.
This experimental
sci-fi work from
CLAMP reads like a
romantic version of
AKIRA."
—Publishers Weekly

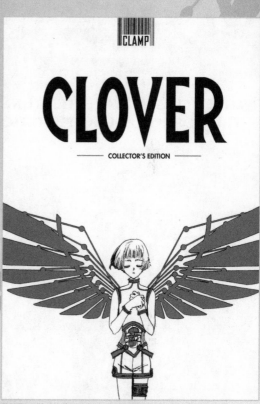

CLOVER © CLAMP ShigatsuTsuitachi CO.,LTD./Kodansha Ltd.

Su was born into a bleak future, where the government keeps tight control over children with magical powers—codenamed "Clovers." With Su being the only "four-leaf" Clover in the world, she has been kept isolated nearly her whole life. Can ex-military agent Kazuhiko deliver her to the happiness she seeks? Experience the complete series in this hardcover edition, which also includes over twenty pages of ravishing color art!

MAGIC KNIGHT RAYEARTH

25TH ANNIVERSARY EDITION

CLAMP

A BELOVED CLASSIC MAKES ITS STUNNING RETURN IN THIS GORGEOUS, LIMITED EDITION BOX SET!

his tale of three Tokyo teenagers who cross through a magical
ortal and become the champions of another world is a modern
manga classic. The box set includes three volumes of manga
overing the entire first series of *Magic Knight Rayearth*, plus the
eries's super-rare full-color art book companion, all printed at a
arger size than ever before on premium paper, featuring a newly-
evised translation and lettering, and exquisite foil-stamped covers.
A strictly limited edition, this will be gone in a flash!

Magic Knight Rayearth 25th Anniversary Manga Box Set 1 © CLAMP ShigatsuTsuitachi CO.,LTD./Kodansha Ltd.

Young characters and steampunk setting, like *Howl's Moving Castle* and *Battle Angel Alita*

Beyond the Clouds © 2018 Nicke / Ki-oon

A boy with a talent for machines and a mysterious girl whose wings he's fixed will take you beyond the clouds! In the tradition of the high-flying, resonant adventure stories of Studio Ghibli comes a gorgeous tale about the longing of young hearts for adventure and friendship!

The boys are back, in 400-page hardcovers that are as pretty and badass as they are!

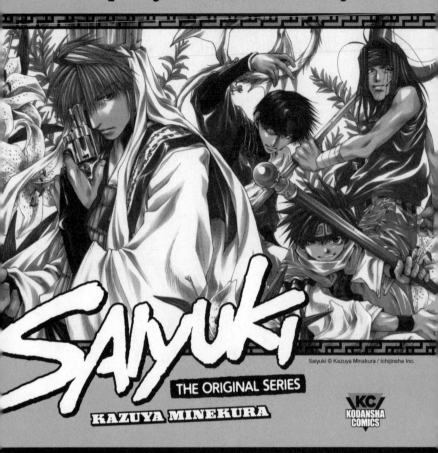

Saiyuki © Kazuya Minakura / Ichijinsha Inc.

SAIYUKI
THE ORIGINAL SERIES
KAZUYA MINEKURA

KC KODANSHA COMICS

"AN EDGY COMIC LOOK AT AN ANCIENT CHINESE TALE." —YALSA

Genjo Sanzo is a Buddhist priest in the city of Togenkyo, which is being ravaged by yokai spirits that have fallen out of balance with the natural order. His superiors send him on a journey far to the west to discover why this is happening and how to stop it. His companions are three yokai with human souls. But this is no day trip — the four will encounter many discoveries and horrors on the way.

FEATURES NEW TRANSLATION, COLOR PAGES, AND BEAUTIFUL WRAPAROUND COVER ART!

THE SWEET SCENT OF LOVE IS IN THE AIR! FOR FANS OF OFFBEAT ROMANCES LIKE *WOTAKOI*

Sweat and Soap © Kintetsu Yamada / Kodansha Ltd.

In an office romance, there's a fine line between sexy and awkward... and that line is where Asako — a woman who sweats copiously — meets Koutarou — a perfume developer who can't get enough of Asako's, er, scent. Don't miss a romcom manga like no other!

UQ HOLDER! 20 is a work of fiction. Names, characters, places, and incidents are the products of the author's imagination or are used fictitiously. Any resemblance to actual events, locales, or persons, living or dead, is entirely coincidental.

A Kodansha Comics Trade Paperback Original
UQ HOLDER! 20 copyright © 2019 Ken Akamatsu
English translation copyright © 2020 Ken Akamatsu

All rights reserved.

Published in the United States by Kodansha Comics, an imprint of Kodansha USA Publishing, LLC, New York.

Publication rights for this English edition arranged through Kodansha Ltd., Tokyo.

First published in Japan in 2019 by Kodansha Ltd., Tokyo.

ISBN 978-1-63236-978-9

Printed in the United States of America.

www.kodanshacomics.com

9 8 7 6 5 4 3 2 1
Translation: Alethea Nibley & Athena Nibley
Lettering: James Dashiell
Editing: Jennifer Sherman
Kodansha Comics edition cover design by Phil Balsman

Publisher: Kiichiro Sugawara

Director of publishing services: Ben Applegate
Associate director of operations: Stephen Pakula
Publishing services managing editor: Noelle Webster
Assistant production manager: Emi Lotto, Angela Zurlo